I0837000

A. Lincoln

HISTORY

OF

THE ADMINISTRATION

OF

PRESIDENT LINCOLN:

INCLUDING HIS

SPEECHES, LETTERS, ADDRESSES, PROCLAMATIONS, AND MESSAGES.

WITH A PRELIMINARY SKETCH OF HIS LIFE.

BY

HENRY J. RAYMOND.

NEW YORK:
J. C. DERBY & N. C. MILLER,
NO. 5 SPRUCE STREET.
1864.

C. A. ALVORD, STEREOTYPER AND PRINTER.

PREFACE.

THIS volume does not profess to be, in any exact and important sense, a History of the Administration of President LINCOLN. Such a work would require access to sources of information which cannot, from the nature of the case, be open to the public for many years to come.

Its object is merely to collect and collate the speeches, messages, proclamations, and other documents in which the President has embodied, from time to time, his sentiments on the affairs of the country, and set forth the motives which have prompted the successive acts of his Administration. In the narrative which accompanies these papers the writer has sought only to record the circumstances essential to an appreciation of the papers themselves, and not by any means to give a complete history of the events by which this momentous period in the career of our country has been marked.

If the public shall find in this work any important aid in forming a judgment of the policy by which President LINCOLN is seeking to carry the Nation through the crisis of a civil war, its purpose will have been accomplished.

H. J. R.

NEW YORK, *May* 5, 1864.

CONTENTS.

LIFE OF ABRAHAM LINCOLN.

Abraham Lincoln was born on the 12th of February, 1809, in Hardin county, Kentucky. His early life, like that of most of the great men whom our country has produced, was spent in poverty and in toil. At seven years of age he was sent to school to a Mr. Hazel, carrying with him an old copy of Dilworth's Spelling Book, one of the three books that formed the family library. His father keenly felt the disadvantages arising from his own lack of education, and determined, in spite of difficulties almost inconceivable, to give his son better facilities for study than he had himself enjoyed. His mother was a Christian woman, and desired earnestly that he should learn to read the Bible.

Thomas Lincoln, his father, finding a life in a Slave State a most unsatisfactory one for himself, and presenting only the prospect of a hopeless struggle in the future for his children, determined upon removal, and when Abraham was in the eighth year of his age, the plan was carried into execution. The old home was sold, their small stock of valuables placed upon a raft, and the little family took its way to a new home in the wilds of Indiana, where free labor would have no competition with slave labor, and the poor white man might hope that in time his children could take an honorable position, won by industry and careful economy. The place of their destination was Spencer county, Indiana. For the last few miles they were obliged to cut their road as they went on. "With the resolution of veteran pioneers they toiled, sometimes being able to pick their way for a long distance without chopping, and then coming to a standstill in consequence of dense forests. Suffice it to say, that they were obliged to cut a road so much of the way that several days were employed in going eighteen miles. It was a difficult, wearisome, trying journey, and Mr. Lincoln often said, that he never passed through a harder experience than he did in going from Thompson's Ferry to Spencer county, Indiana."

Thus, before he was eight years old, Abraham Lincoln began the serious business of life. Their cabin was built of logs, and even the aid of such a mere child was of account in the wilderness where they now found themselves, after seven days of weary travel. Their neighbors, none of whom lived nearer than two or three miles, welcomed the strangers, and lent a hand towards building the rude dwelling in which the future President lay down, after fatiguing but healthful toil, to dream the dreams of childhood, undisturbed by thoughts of the future.

In this log-house, consisting of a room below and a room above, furnished by Thomas Lincoln and his son's own hands, Abraham passed the next twelve years of his life. So long as his mother lived, she assisted him in learning to read, and before her death, which occurred when he was ten years of age, she had the satisfaction of seeing him read that Book which he has never since neglected.

After a while he learned to write. This was an accomplishment which some of the friendly neighbors thought unnecessary, but his father quietly persisted, and the boy was set down as a prodigy when he wrote to an old friend of his mother's, a travelling preacher, and begged him to come and preach a sermon over his mother's grave. Three months after, Parson Elkins came, and friends assembled, a year after her death, to pay a last tribute of respect to one universally beloved and respected. Her son's share in securing the presence of the clergyman was not unmentioned, and Abraham soon found himself called upon to write letters for his neighbors.

His father married a second time a Mrs. Sally Johnston, who proved an excellent mother to her step-son, and who now survives to take her share of the credit to which she is entitled for her faithful care. In the course of a year or two a Mr. Crawford, one of the settlers, opened a school in his own cabin, and Abraham's father embraced the opportunity to send him, in order that he might add some knowledge of arithmetic to his reading and writing. With buckskin clothes, a raccoon skin cap, and an old arithmetic which had been somewhere found for him, he commenced his studies in the "higher branches." His progress was rapid, and his perseverance and faithfulness won the interest and esteem of his teacher.

In that thinly settled country a book was a great rarity, but whenever Mr. Lincoln heard of one he endeavored to procure it for Abraham's perusal. In this way he became acquainted with Bunyan's Pilgrim's Progress, Esop's Fables, a Life of Henry Clay, and Weems's Life of Washington. The "hatchet" story of Washington, which has done more to make boys truthful than a hundred solemn exhortations, made a strong impression upon Abraham, and was one of those unseen, gentle influences, which helped to form his character for integrity and honesty. Its effect may be traced in the following story, which bids fair to become as never-failing an accompaniment to a Life of Lincoln as the hatchet case to that of Washington.

Mr. Crawford had lent him a copy of Ramsay's Life of Washington. During a severe storm Abraham improved his leisure by reading his book. One night he laid it down carefully, as he thought, and the next morning he found it soaked through! The wind had changed, the storm had beaten in through a crack in the logs, and the appearance of the book was ruined. How could he face the owner under such circumstances? He had no money to offer as a return, but he took the book, went directly to Mr. Crawford, showed him the irreparable injury, and frankly and honestly offered to work for him until he should be satisfied. Mr. Crawford accepted the offer and gave Abraham the book for his own, in return for three days' steady labor in "pulling fodder." His manliness and straightforwardness won the esteem of the Crawfords, and indeed of all the neighborhood.

At nineteen years of age he made a trip to New-Orleans, in company with a son of the owner of a flatboat, who intrusted a valuable cargo to their care. On the way they were attacked by seven negroes, and their lives and property were in great danger, but owing to their good use of the muscular force they had acquired as backwoodsmen, they succeeded in driving off the invaders, and pushing their boat out into the stream in safety. The result of the voyage was satisfactory to the owner, and Abraham Lincoln gained, in addition to his ten dollars a month, a reputation as a youth of promising business talent.

In 1830 Thomas Lincoln decided to make another change, and the log cabin which had been so long their home was deserted for a new one near Decatur, Illinois. This time the journey occupied fifteen days. Abraham was now twenty-one, but he did not begin his independent life until he had aided his father in settling his family, breaking the ground for corn, and *making a rail fence* around the farm. These rails have passed into song and story. "During the sitting of the Republican State Convention at Decatur, a banner, attached to two of these rails, and bearing an appropriate inscription, was brought into the assemblage, and formally presented to that body, amid a scene of unparalleled enthusiasm. After that they were in demand in every State of the Union in which free labor is honored, where they were borne in processions of the people, and hailed by hundreds of thousands of freemen, as a symbol of triumph, and as a glorious vindication of freedom and of the rights and dignity of free labor. These, however, were far from being the first or only rails made by Lincoln. He was a practised hand at the business. Mr. Lincoln has now a cane made from one of the rails split by his own hands in boyhood." After the first winter in Illinois, which was one of uncommon severity, and required more than his father's care to keep the family in food, which was mostly obtained by hunting, Abraham Lincoln began life for himself. Sometimes he hired himself out as a farm-hand, sometimes his learning procured him a situation as clerk in a store. When the Black Hawk war broke out in 1832, he joined a volunteer company, and was made captain. "He was an efficient, faithful officer, watchful of his men, and prompt in the discharge of duty, and his courage and patriotism shrank from no dangers or hardships." Thus the Commander-in-Chief of our armies has not been without a bit of military experience—much more, in fact, than the most of our Brigadier-Generals had had before the commencement of the war.

After his military life was over he looked about for something to do. He ran for the Legislature, but was beaten, though his own precinct gave him 277 votes out of 284. This was the only time he was ever beaten before the people. He bought a store and stock of goods on credit, and was appointed Postmaster. The store proved unprofitable, and he sold out. All this time he pursued his studies. He had already learned grammar, and he had now opportunities for more extensive reading. He wrote out a synopsis of every book he read, and thus fixed it in his memory.

About this time he met John Calhoun, since President of the Lecompton (Kansas) Constitutional Convention. He proposed to Lincoln to take up surveying, and himself aided in his studies. He had plenty of employment as a surveyor, and won a good reputation in this new line of business.

In 1834 he was sent to the Legislature, and the political life commenced which his countrymen's votes have since shown they fully appreciated. When the session of the Legislature was over, he set himself to the study of law in good earnest. In 1836 he obtained a law license, and in April, 1837, he removed to Springfield and commenced the practice of the law in partnership with his friend and former colleague in the Legislature, Hon. John T. Stuart.

One incident of his law practice we cannot refrain from narrating. When Lincoln first went out into the world to earn a living for himself, he worked for a Mr. Armstrong, of Petersburg, Menard Co., who, with his wife, took a great interest in him, lent him books to read, and, after the season for work was over, encouraged him to remain with them until he should find something to "turn his hand to." They also hoped much from his influence over their son, an over-indulged and somewhat unruly boy. We cannot do better than to transcribe the remarks of the Cleveland *Leader* upon this interesting and touching incident.

"Some few years since, the eldest son of Mr. Lincoln's old friend, Armstrong, the chief supporter of his widowed mother—the good old man having some time previously passed from earth,—was arrested on the charge of murder. A young man had been killed during a riotous *mêlée*, in the night time at a camp-meeting, and one of his associates stated that the death-wound was inflicted by young Armstrong. A preliminary examination was gone into, at which the accuser testified so positively, that there seemed no doubt of the guilt of the prisoner, and therefore he was held for trial. As is too often the case, the bloody act caused an undue degree of excitement in the public mind. Every improper incident in the life of the prisoner—each act which bore the least semblance of rowdyism—each schoolboy quarrel,—was suddenly remembered and magnified, until they pictured him as a fiend of the most horrible hue. As these rumors spread abroad they were received as gospel truth, and a feverish desire for vengeance seized upon the infatuated populace, whilst only prison bars prevented a horrible death at the hands of a mob. The events were heralded in the county papers, painted in highest colors, accompanied by rejoicing over the certainty of punishment being meted out to the guilty party. The prisoner, overwhelmed by the circumstances under which he found himself placed, fell into a melancholy condition bordering on despair, and the widowed mother, looking through her tears, saw no cause for hope from earthly aid.

"At this juncture, the widow received a letter from Mr. Lincoln, volunteering his services in an effort to save the youth from the impending stroke. Gladly was his aid accepted, although it seemed impossible for even his sagacity to prevail in such a desperate case; but the heart of the attorney was in his work, and he set about it with a will that knew no such word as fail. Feeling that the poisoned condition of the public mind was such as to preclude the possibility of impanelling an impartial jury in the court having jurisdiction, he procured a change of venue and a postponement of the trial. He then went studiously to work unravelling the history of the case, and satisfied himself that his client was the victim of malice, and that the statements of the accuser were a tissue of falsehoods.

"When the trial was called on, the prisoner, pale and emaciated, with hopelessness written on every feature, and accompanied by his half-hoping, half-despairing mother—whose only hope was in a mother's belief of her son's innocence, in the justice of the God she worshipped, and in the noble counsel, who, without hope of fee or reward upon earth, had undertaken the cause—took his seat in the prisoners' box, and with a 'stony firmness' listened to the reading of the indictment. Lincoln sat quietly by, whilst the large auditory looked on him as though wondering what he could say in defence of one whose guilt they regarded as certain. The examination of the witnesses for the State was begun, and a well-arranged mass of evidence, circumstantial and positive, was introduced, which seemed to impale the prisoner beyond the possibility of extrication. The counsel for the defence propounded but few questions, and those of a character which excited no uneasiness on the part of the prosecutor—merely, in most cases, requiring the main witnesses to be definite as to the time and place. When the evidence of the prosecution was ended, Lincoln introduced a few witnesses to remove some erroneous impressions in regard to the previous character of his client, who, though somewhat rowdyish, had never been known to commit a vicious act; and to show that a greater degree of ill-feeling existed between the accuser and the accused, than the accused and the deceased.

"The prosecutor felt that the case was a clear one, and his opening speech was brief and formal. Lincoln arose, while a deathly silence pervaded the vast audience, and in a clear and moderate tone began his argument. Slowly and carefully he reviewed the testimony, pointing out the hitherto unobserved discrepancies in the statements of the principal witness. That which had seemed plain and plausible he made to appear crooked as a serpent's path. The witness had stated that the affair took place at a certain hour in the evening, and that, by the aid of the brightly shining moon, he saw the prisoner inflict the death-blow with a slung-shot. Mr. Lincoln showed that at the hour referred to the moon had not yet appeared above the horizon, and consequently the whole tale was a fabrication.

"An almost instantaneous change seemed to have been wrought in the minds of his auditors, and the verdict of 'not guilty' was at the end of every tongue. But the advocate was not content with this intellectual achievement. His whole being had for months been bound up in this work of gratitude and mercy, and as the lava of the overcharged crater bursts from its imprisonment, so great thoughts and burning words leaped forth from the soul of the eloquent Lincoln. He drew a picture of the perjurer so horrid and ghastly, that the accuser could sit under it no longer, but reeled and staggered from the court-room, whilst the audience fancied they could see the brand upon his brow. Then in words of thrilling pathos Lincoln appealed to the jurors as fathers of some who might become fatherless, and as husbands of wives who might be widowed, to yield to no previous impressions, no ill-founded prejudice, but to do his client justice; and as he alluded to the debt of gratitude which he owed the boy's sire, tears were seen to fall from many eyes unused to weep.

"It was near night when he concluded, by saying that if justice was done—as he believed it would be—before the sun should set, it would shine upon his client a free man. The jury retired, and the court adjourned for the day. Half an hour had not elapsed, when, as the officers of the court and the volunteer attorney sat at the tea-table of their hotel, a messenger announced that the jury had returned to their seats. All repaired immediately to the court-house, and whilst the prisoner was being brought from the jail, the court-room was filled to overflowing with citizens from the town. When the prisoner and his mother entered, silence reigned as completely as though the house were empty. The foreman of the jury, in answer to the usual inquiry from the court, delivered the verdict of 'Not Guilty!' The widow dropped into the arms of her son, who lifted her up and told her to look upon him as before, free and innocent. Then, with the words, 'Where is Mr. Lincoln?' he rushed across the room and grasped the hand of his deliverer, whilst his heart was too full for utterance. Lincoln turned his eyes towards the West, where the sun still lingered in view, and then, turning to the youth, said, 'It is not yet sundown and you are free.' I confess that my cheeks were not wholly unwet by tears, and I turned from the affecting scene. As I cast a glance behind, I saw Abraham Lincoln obeying the Divine injunction by comforting the widowed and fatherless."

Mr. Lincoln was three times elected to the Legislature; and here commenced his political acquaintance with Stephen A. Douglas. He then remained six years in private life, devoting himself to the practice of the law, displaying remarkable ability, and gaining an enviable reputation. His interest in politics never subsided, and in 1844 he stumped the entire State of Illinois during the Presidential campaign. We have before mentioned that one of his earliest books was the "Life of Henry Clay," and his enthusiastic admiration for that Statesman, aroused in his boyhood, continued in full force during his life. In 1847 Mr. Lincoln took his seat in Congress, and was the only Whig representative from Illinois, which had then seven members in Congress.

The Congress of which Mr. Lincoln was a member, had before it questions of great importance and interest to the country. The Mexican War was then in progress, and Congress had to deal with grave questions arising out of it, besides the many which were to be passed upon as to the means by which it was to be carried on. The irrepressible Slavery Question was there, also, in many of its Protean forms, in questions on the right of petition, in questions as to the District of Columbia, in many questions as to the Territories.

Mr. Lincoln was charged by his enemies in later years, when political enmity was hunting sharply for material out of which to make political capital against him, with lack of patriotism, in that he voted against the war. The charge was sharply and clearly made by Judge Douglas, at the first of their joint discussions in the Senatorial contest of 1858. In his speech at Ottawa, he says of Mr. Lincoln, that "while in Congress he distinguished himself by his opposition to the Mexican war, *taking the side of the common enemy against his own country*, and when he returned home he found that the indignation of the people followed him everywhere."

No better answer can be given to this slander than that which Mr. Lincoln himself made in his reply to this speech. He says: "I was an old Whig, and whenever the Democratic party tried to get me to vote that the war had been righteously begun by the President, I would not do it. But whenever they asked for any money or land-warrants or any thing to pay the soldiers there, during all that time I gave the same vote that Judge Douglas did. You can think as you please as to whether that was consistent. Such is the truth, and the Judge has a right to make all he can out of it. But when he, by a general charge conveys the idea that I withheld supplies from the soldiers who were fighting in the Mexican war, or did any thing else to hinder the soldiers, he is, to say the least, grossly and altogether mistaken, as a consultation of the records will prove to him."

We should need no better proof of the falsity of this charge than this explicit denial. And it is a noticeable fact, that during all the remaining joint debates between Lincoln and Douglas, the latter never repeated the slander until the last half hour of the last debate, to which Mr. Lincoln had no opportunity of replying. Douglas's supporters, however, made vigorous use of the charge everywhere. The whole foundation of it, doubtless, was the fact which Mr. Lincoln states, that, whenever the Democrats tried to get him "to vote that the war had been righteously begun," he would not do it. He might have said more than this. He might have said, as was the fact, that he had been a thorn in their sides on this very point; that he had not only refused to vote that the war was "righteously begun," but had made their efforts to falsify and conceal the facts, and deceive the people into the belief that it was "righteously begun," far more difficult. He showed, in fact, on this point the same clearness and directness, the same keen eye for the important point in a controversy, and the same tenacity in holding it fast and thwarting his opponent's utmost efforts to obscure it and cover it up, to draw attention to other points and raise false issues, which were the marked characteristics of his great controversy with Judge Douglas at a subsequent period of their political history.

He saw that the strength of the position of the administration before the people in reference to the beginning of the war, was in the point, which they lost no opportunity of reiterating, viz., that Mexico had shed the blood of our citizens *on our own soil.* This position he believed to be false, and he accordingly attacked it in a resolution requesting the President to give the House information on that point; which President Polk would have found as difficult to dodge as Douglas found it to dodge the questions which Mr. Lincoln proposed to him.

On the right of petition Mr. Lincoln, of course, held the right side, voting repeatedly against laying on the table without consideration petitions in favor of the abolition of Slavery in the District of Columbia, and against the slave-trade.

On the question of abolishing Slavery in the District, he took rather a prominent part. A Mr. Gott had introduced a resolution directing the committee for the District to introduce a bill abolishing the slave-trade in the District. To this Mr. Lincoln moved an amendment instructing them to introduce a bill for the abolition, not of the slave-trade, but of *Slavery* within the District. The bill which he proposed prevented any slave from ever being brought into the District, except in the case of officers of the Government of the United States, who might bring the necessary servants for themselves and their families while in the District on public business. It prevented any one then resident within the District, or thereafter born within it, from being held in Slavery without the District. It declared that all children of slave mothers born in the District after January 1, 1850, should be free, but should be reasonably supported and educated by the owners of their mothers, and that any owner of slaves in the District might be paid their value from the Treasury, and the slaves should thereupon be free; and it provided also for the submission of the act to the people of the District for their acceptance or rejection.

A bill was afterwards reported by the committee forbidding the introduction of slaves into the District for sale or hire. This bill also Mr. Lincoln supported, but in vain. The time for the success of such measures, involving to an extent attacks upon Slavery, had not yet come.

The question of the Territories came up in many ways. The Wilmot Proviso had made its first appearance in the previous session, in the August before, but it was repeatedly before this Congress also, when efforts were made to apply it to the territory which we procured from Mexico, and to Oregon. On all occasions when it was before the House it was supported by Mr. Lincoln, and he stated during his contest with Judge Douglas that he had voted for it, "in one way and another, about forty times." He thus showed himself in 1847 the same friend of Freedom for the Territories which he was afterwards during the heats of the Kansas struggle.

Another instance in which the Slavery Question was before the House was in the famous Pacheco case. This was a bill to reimburse the heirs of Antonio Pacheco for the value of a slave who was hired by a United States officer in Florida, but ran away and joined the Seminoles, and being taken in arms with them, was sent out of Florida with them when they were transported to the West. The bill was reported to the House by the Committee on Military Affairs.

This committee was composed of nine. Five of these were slaveholders, and these made the majority report. The others, not being slaveholders, reported against the bill. The ground taken by the majority was that slaves were regarded as *property* by the Constitution, and when taken for public service should be paid for as property. The principle involved in the bill, therefore, was the same one which the slaveholders have sought in so many ways to maintain. As they sought afterwards to have it established by a decision of the Supreme Court, so now they sought to have it recognized by Congress, and Mr. Lincoln opposed it in Congress as heartily as he afterwards opposed it when it took the more covert, but no less dangerous shape of a judicial dictum.

On other great questions which came before Congress Mr. Lincoln, being a Whig, took the ground which was held by the great body of his party. He believed in the right of Congress to make appropriations for the improvement of rivers and harbors. He was in favor of giving the public lands, not to speculators, but to actual occupants and cultivators, at as low rates as possible; and he was in favor of a protective tariff, and of abolishing the franking privilege.

In 1848 General Taylor was nominated for the Presidency; Mr. Lincoln was a member of the convention, at Philadelphia, by which he was nominated, and canvassed his own State in his favor. He was also in New England during the campaign, attended the State Convention of Massachusetts, and made a speech at New Bedford, which is still remembered. Illinois, however, cast her vote for General Cass. In 1849 Mr. Lincoln was the Whig candidate in Illinois for United States Senator, but without success—the Democrats having the control of the State, which they retained until the conflict arising out of the Nebraska Bill, in 1854.

During the intervening period Mr. Lincoln took no prominent part in politics, but remained at home in the practice of his profession. We may be sure, however, that he watched closely the course of public events. He had fought Slavery often enough to know what it was, and what the animus of its supporters was. It is not, therefore, likely that he was taken very much by surprise when the Nebraska Bill was introduced, and the proposition was made by Stephen A. Douglas to repeal that very Missouri Compromise which he had declared to be "a sacred thing, which no ruthless hand would ever be reckless enough to disturb."

The Nebraska Bill was passed May 22, 1854, and its passage gave new and increased force to the popular feeling in favor of freedom which the proposition to repeal the Missouri Compromise had excited, and everywhere the friends of freedom gathered themselves together and rallied round her banner, to meet the conflict which was plainly now closely impending, forced upon the people by the grasping ambition of the slaveholders. The political campaign of that year in Illinois was one of the severest ever known. It was intensified by the fact that a United States Senator was to be chosen by the Legislature then to be elected, to fill the place of Shields, who had voted with Douglas in favor of the Nebraska Bill.

Mr. Lincoln took a prominent part in this campaign.

He met Judge Douglas before the people on two occasions, the only ones when the Judge would consent to such a meeting. The first time was at the State Fair at Springfield, on October 4th. This was afterwards considered to have been the greatest event of the whole canvass. Mr. Lincoln opened the discussion, and in his clear and eloquent yet homely way exposed the tergiversations of which his opponent had been guilty, and the fallacy of his pretexts for his present course.

Mr. Douglas had always claimed to have voted for the repeal of the Missouri Compromise because he sustained the "great principle" of Popular Sovereignty, and desired that the inhabitants of Kansas and Nebraska should govern themselves, as they were well able to do. The fallacy of drawing from these premises the conclusion that they therefore should have the right to establish Slavery there was most clearly and conclusively exposed by Mr. Lincoln, so that no one could thereafter be misled by it, unless he was a willing dupe of pro-slavery sophistry.

"My distinguished friend," said he, "says it is an insult to the emigrants of Kansas and Nebraska to suppose that they are not able to govern themselves. We must not slur over an argument of this kind because it happens to tickle the ear. It must be met and answered. I admit that the emigrant to Kansas and Nebraska is competent to govern himself, *but I deny his right to govern any other person without that person's consent.*"

The two opponents met again at Peoria. We believe it is universally admitted that on both of these occasions Mr. Lincoln had decidedly the advantage. The result of the election was the defeat of the Democrats and the election of anti-Nebraska men to the Legislature to secure the election of a United States Senator who would be true to freedom, if they could be brought to unite upon a candidate. Mr. Lincoln was naturally the candidate of those who were of Whig antecedents. Judge Trumbull was as naturally the candidate of some who had really come out from the Democratic party—though they still called themselves Free Democrats.

There was danger, of course, in such a posture of affairs, and Mr. Lincoln, in that spirit of patriotism which he has always shown, by his own personal exertions secured the votes of his friends for Judge Trumbull, who was accordingly chosen Senator. The charge was afterwards made by the enemies of both that there had been in this matter a breach of faith on the part of Judge Trumbull, and that Mr. Lincoln had the right to feel and did feel aggrieved at the result. Mr. Lincoln himself, however, expressly denied in his speech at Charleston, Sept. 18, 1858, that there had been any such breach of faith.

The pressure of the Slavery contest at last fully organized the Republican party, which held its first Convention for the nomination of President and Vice-President at Philadelphia on June 17, 1856. John C. Fremont was nominated for President and William L. Dayton for Vice President. Mr. Lincoln's name was prominent before the Convention for the latter office, and on the informal ballot he stood next to Mr. Dayton, receiving 110 votes. Mr. Lincoln's name headed the Republican Electoral ticket in Illinois, and he took an active part in the canvass, but the Democrats carried the State, though only by a plurality vote.

We now come to the great Senatorial contest of 1858, which established Mr. Lincoln's reputation before the people of the whole conntry, not only as a very able debater and an eloquent orator, but also as a wise politician, wise enough to hold firm to sound-principles, and to yield nothing of them, even against the judgment of earnest friends.

On the 4th of March, 1857, Mr. Buchanan had taken his seat in the Presidential chair. The struggle between Freedom and Slavery for the possession of Kansas was at its height. A few days after his inauguration, the Supreme Court rendered the Dred Scott decision, which was thought by the friends of Slavery to insure their victory by its holding the Missouri Compromise to be unconstitutional, because the Constitution itself carried Slavery over all the Territories of the United States. In spite of this decision, the friends of Freedom in Kansas maintained their ground. The slaveholders, however, pushed forward their schemes, and in November, 1857, their Constitutional Convention, held at Lecompton, adopted the infamous Lecompton Constitution. The trick by which they submitted to the popular vote only a schedule on the Slavery question, instead of the whole Constitution, compelling every voter, however he voted upon this schedule, to vote for their Constitution, which fixed Slavery upon the State just as surely whether the schedule was adopted or not, will be well remembered, as well as the feeling which so villainous a scheme excited throughout the North. Judge Douglas had sustained the Dred

Scott decision, but he could not sustain this attempt to force upon the people of Kansas a Constitution against their will. He declared that he did not care himself whether the people voted the Slavery clause up or down, but he thought they ought to have the chance to vote for or against the Constitution itself.

The Administration had made the measure their own, and this opposition of Douglas at once excited against him the active hostility of the slaveholders and their friends, with whom he had hitherto acted in concert. The bill was finally passed through Congress on April 30th, 1858, under what is known as the English bill, whereby the Constitution was to be submitted to the votes of the people of Kansas, with the offer of heavy bribes to them in the way of donations of land, etc., if they would accept it; and the people, in spite of the bribes, voted it down, by an immense majority.

Judge Douglas's term was on the eve of expiring, and he came home to Illinois after the adjournment of Congress to attend in person to the political campaign, upon the result of which was to depend his re-election to the Senate.

His course on the Lecompton bill had made an open breach between him and the Administration, and he had rendered such good service to the Republicans in their battle with that monstrous infamy, that there were not wanting many among them who were inclined to think it would be wise not to oppose his re-election.

But the Republicans of Illinois thought otherwise. They knew the man. They knew that on the cardinal principle of the Republican party, opposition to the spread of Slavery into the Territories, he was not with them; for he had declared in the most positive way that he "did not care whether Slavery was voted down or up." They believed that in his action on the Lecompton bill, he was actuated fully as much by the certainty that any other action would be followed by his immediate and utter overthrow at home, as from any other considerations. And they therefore determined, in opposition to the views of some influential Republicans at home as well as in other States, to fight the battle through against him, with all the energy that they could bring to the work. And to this end, on the 17th of June, 1858, at their State Convention at Springfield, they nominated Mr. Lincoln as their candidate for the Senate of the United States.

The speech of Mr. Lincoln to the Convention which had nominated him, was the beginning of the campaign. Its opening sentences contained those celebrated words, which have been often quoted both by friends and enemies: "A house divided against itself cannot stand. I believe this Government cannot endure permanently half slave and half free. I do not expect the Union to be dissolved—I do not expect the house to fall, but I do expect it will cease to be divided. It will become all one thing or all the other." Little idea could he have had then how near the time was when the country should be united upon this point. Still less could he have dreamed through what convulsions it was to pass before it reached that wished-for position—into what an abyss of madness and crime the advocates of Slavery would plunge in their efforts to "push it forward till it should become alike lawful in all the States, old as well as new—North as well as South." But there seemed to him to be manifest indications of their design thus to push it forward, and he devoted his speech to showing forth the machinery which they had now almost completed, for the attainment of their purpose; it only needing that the Supreme Court should say that the Constitution carried Slavery over the States, as they had already in the Dred Scott decision declared that it was carried over the Territories. And he closed his speech with a sharp attack upon Douglas, as being a party to this plan to legalize Slavery over the Continent. It was plain from the first that the struggle would take the shape of a personal contest between the two men. Each recognized the other as the embodiment of principles to which he was in deadly hostility. Judge Douglas was the champion of all sympathizers with Slavery at the North, of those who openly advocated it, and still more of those who took the more plausible and dangerous part of not caring whether it "was voted down or up." Mr. Lincoln's soul was on fire with love for freedom and for humanity, and with reverence for the Fathers of the Country, and for the principles of freedom for all under the light of which they marched. He felt that the contest was no mere local one, that it was not of any great consequence what man succeeded in the fight, but that it was all-important that the banner of Freedom should be borne with no faltering step, but "full high advanced." And thus through the whole campaign he sought with all his power to press home to the hearts of the people the principles, the example and the teachings of the men of the Revolution.

The two combatants first met at Chicago, in July.

There was no arrangement then about their speaking against each other, but Judge Douglas having addressed a meeting on the 9th July, it was inevitable that Mr. Lincoln should answer him on the 10th. One week later both spoke in Springfield on the same day, but before different audiences; and one week later Mr. Lincoln addressed a letter to Douglas, challenging him to a series of debates during the campaign.

The challenge was accepted, though not without an attempt to make a little capital out of it, which was quite characteristic. It was also quite characteristic that the terms which Douglas proposed were such as to give him the decided advantage of having four opening and closing speeches to Mr. Lincoln's three; and that Mr. Lincoln, while noticing the inequality, did not hesitate to accept them.

The seven joint debates were held as follows:—at Ottawa on August 21st; at Freeport on August 27th; at Jonesboro on September 15th; at Charleston on September 18th; at Galesburg on October 7th; at Quincy on October 13th; at Alton on October 15th. These seven tournaments raised the greatest excitement throughout the State. They were held in all quarters of the State, from Freeport in the north to Jonesboro in the extreme south. Everywhere the different parties turned out to do honor to their champions. Processions and cavalcades, bands of music and cannon-firing, made every day a day of excitement. But far-greater was the excitement of such oratorical contests between two such skilled debaters, before mixed audiences of friends and foes, to rejoice over every keen thrust at the adversary; to be cast down by each failure to parry the thrust so aimed. We cannot pretend to give more than the barest sketch of these great efforts of Mr. Lincoln's. They are and always will be, to those who are interested in the history of the Slavery contest, most valuable and important documents.

In the first speech at Ottawa, besides defending himself from some points which Douglas had made against him, and among others, explaining and enlarging upon that passage from his Springfield speech, of "A house divided against itself," he took up the charge which he had also made in that speech of the conspiracy to extend Slavery over the northern States, and pressed it home, citing as proof of its existence a speech which Douglas himself had made on the Lecompton bill, in which he had substantially made the same charge upon Buchanan and others. He then showed again that all that was necessary for the accomplishment of the scheme was a decision of the Supreme Court that no State could exclude Slavery, as the Court had already decided that no Territory could exclude it, and the acquiescence of the people in such a decision, and he told the people that Douglas was doing all in his power to bring about such acquiescence in advance, by declaring that the true position was not to care whether Slavery "was voted down or up," and by announcing himself in favor of the Dred Scott decision, not because it was right, but because a decision of the Court is to him a "Thus saith the Lord," and thus committing himself to the next decision just as firmly as to this. He closed his speech with the following eloquent words: "Henry Clay, my beau ideal of a Statesman—the man for whom I fought all my humble life—once said of a class of men who would repress all tendencies to liberty and ultimate emancipation, that they must, if they would do this, go back to the era of our Independence and muzzle the cannon which thunders its annual joyous return; they must blow out the moral lights around us; they must penetrate the human soul and eradicate there the love of liberty; and then, and not till then, could they perpetuate Slavery in this country. To my thinking, Judge Douglas is, by his example and vast influence, doing that very thing in this community, when he says that the negro has nothing in the Declaration of Independence. Henry Clay plainly understood the contrary. Judge Douglas is going back to the era of our Revolution, and to the extent of his ability muzzling the cannon which thunders its annual joyous return. When he invites any people, willing to have Slavery, to establish it, he is blowing out the moral lights around us. When he says he 'cares not whether Slavery is voted down or up'—that it is a sacred right of self-government, he is, in my judgment, penetrating the human soul and eradicating the light of reason and the love of liberty in this American people. And when, by all these means and appliances, he shall succeed in bringing public sentiment to an exact accordance with his own views—when these vast assemblages shall echo back all these sentiments, when they shall come to repeat his views and to avow his principles, and to say all that he says on these mighty questions—then it needs only the formality of the second Dred Scott decision, which he indorses in advance, to make Slavery alike lawful in all the States—old as well as new, North as well as South."

In the second debate at Freeport, Mr. Lincoln gave categorical answers to seven questions which Douglas had proposed to him, and in his turn put four questions to Douglas, to which he got but evasive replies. He also pressed home upon his opponent a charge of quoting resolutions as being adopted at a Republican State Convention, which were never so adopted, and again called Douglas's attention to the conspiracy to nationalize Slavery, and he showed that his pretended desire to leave the people of a Territory free to establish Slavery or exclude it, was really only a desire to allow them to establish it, as was shown by his voting against Mr. Chase's amendment to the Nebraska Bill, which gave them leave to exclude it. In the third debate at Jonesboro, Mr. Lincoln showed that Douglas and his friends were trying to change the position of the country on the Slavery question from what it was when the Constitution was adopted, and that the disturbance of the country had arisen from this pernicious effort. He then cited from Democratic speeches and platforms of former days to show that they occupied then the very opposite ground on the question from that which was taken now, and showed up the evasive character of Douglas's answers to the questions which he had proposed, especially the subterfuge of "unfriendly legislation" which he had set forth as the means by which the people of a Territory could exclude Slavery from its limits in spite of the Dred Scott decision.

When Mr. Lincoln was preparing these questions for Douglas, he was urged by some of his friends not to corner him on that point, because he would surely stand by his doctrine of Squatter Sovereignty in defiance of the Dred Scott decision, "and that," said they, "will make him Senator." "That may be," said Mr. Lincoln, with a twinkle in his eye, "but if he takes that shoot he never can be President."

Mr. Lincoln's sagacity did not fail him here. This position which Douglas took of "unfriendly legislation," was a stumbling-block which he was never able to get over; and if the contest between them had brought out no other good result, the compelling Douglas to take this ground was an immense success.

The fourth speech, at Charleston, was devoted by Mr. Lincoln to enlarging upon the evidence of a charge previously made by Judge Trumbull upon Douglas of being himself responsible for a clause in the Kansas bill which would have deprived the people of Kansas of the right to vote upon their own Constitution—a charge which Douglas could never try to answer without losing his temper.

In the fifth debate, Mr. Lincoln answered the charge that the Republican party was sectional; and after again exploding the fraudulent resolutions and giving strong proof that Douglas himself was a party to the fraud, and again showing that Douglas had failed to answer his question about the acceptance of the new Dred Scott decision, which, he said, was "just as sure to be made as to-morrow is to come, if the Democratic party shall be sustained" in the elections, he discussed the acquisition of further territory and the importance of deciding upon any such acquisition, by the effect which it would have upon the Slavery question among ourselves.

In the next debate, at Quincy, besides making some

personal points as to the mode in which Douglas had conducted the previous discussions, he stated clearly and briefly what were the principles of the Republican party, what they proposed to do, and what they did not propose to do. He said that they looked upon Slavery as "a moral, a social, and a political wrong," and they "proposed a course of conduct which should treat it as a wrong;" did not propose to "disturb it in the States," but did propose to "restrict it to its present limits;" did not propose to decide that Dred Scott was free, but did not believe that the decision in that case was a political rule binding the voters, the Congress, or the President, and proposed "so resisting it as to have it reversed if possible, and a new judicial rule established on the subject."

Mr. Lincoln's last speech, at Alton, was a very full and conclusive argument of the whole Slavery Question. He showed that the present Democratic doctrines were not those held at the time of the Revolution in reference to Slavery; showed how the agitation of the country had come from the attempt to set Slavery upon a different footing, and showed the dangers to the country of this attempt. He brought the whole controversy down to the vital question whether Slavery is wrong or not, and demonstrated that the present Democratic sentiment was that it was not wrong, and that Douglas and those who sympathized with him did not desire or expect ever to see the country freed from this gigantic evil.

It must not be supposed that these seven debates were all of Mr. Lincoln's appearances before the people during the campaign. He made some fifty other speeches all over the State, and everywhere his strong arguments, his forcible language, and his homely way of presenting the great issues, so as to bring them home to the hearts of the people, had a powerful effect. The whole State fairly boiled with the excitement of the contest. Nor this alone, for all over the country the eyes of the people were turned to Illinois as the great battle-ground, and the earnest wishes of almost all who loved freedom followed Mr. Lincoln throughout all the heated struggle. He had, however, other opposition besides that of his political opponents. The action of Judge Douglas on the Lecompton Constitution, and the bitter hostility of the southern wing of the Democratic party towards him, had led very many Republicans, and some of high consideration and influence in other States, to favor his return to the Senate. They deemed this due to the zeal and efficiency with which he had resisted the attempt to force slavery into Kansas against the will of the people, and as important in encouraging other Democratic leaders to imitate the example of Douglas in throwing off the yoke of the slaveholding aristocracy. This feeling proved to be of a good deal of weight against Mr. Lincoln in the canvas

Then, again, the State had been so unfairly districted, that the odds were very heavily against the Republicans, and thus it came about that although on the popular vote Douglas was beaten by more than five thousand votes, he was enabled to carry off the substantial prize of victory by his majority in the Legislature. We say the "substantial prize of victory," and so it was thought to be at the time. But later events showed that the battle which was then fought was after all but the precursor of the Presidential contest, and that it insured to Mr. Lincoln the victory in that more important struggle.

Between the close of this Senatorial contest and the opening of the Presidential campaign, Mr. Lincoln made several visits to other States. In the following year he took an active part in the political campaign in Ohio, still following up his old opponent, who had but recently contributed to Harper's Magazine his famous article on Slavery and the Constitution. He also visited Kansas, and was received with unbounded enthusiasm by the people of that State, whose battle he had fought so well; and in February, 1860, he visited New York, and there made a speech on National Politics before the Young Men's Republican Club at Cooper Institute, the effect of which was to make him better known and still more highly esteemed in New York, where his contest with Douglas had already made him many friends. Indeed, we think we hardly state it too strongly when we say, that their joint effect was to make Mr. Lincoln decidedly the second choice of the great body of the Republicans of New York, as the candidate of the Republican party for the campaign of 1860.

It was, doubtless, during this visit of Mr. Lincoln to New York that the following incident occurred, which is thus narrated by a teacher at the Five Points House of Industry: "Our Sunday School in the Five Points was assembled, one Sabbath morning, when I noticed a tall, remarkable looking man enter the room and take a seat among us. He listened with fixed attention to our exercises, and his countenance expressed such genuine interest that I approached him and suggested that he might be willing to say something to the children. He accepted the invitation with evident pleasure; and coming forward began a simple address, which at once fascinated every little hearer and hushed the room into silence. His language was strikingly beautiful, and his tones musical with intensest feeling. The little faces around him would droop into sad conviction as he uttered sentences of warning, and would brighten into sunshine as he spoke cheerful words of promise. Once or twice he attempted to close his remarks, but the imperative shout of 'Go on!' 'Oh, do go on!' would compel him to resume. As I looked upon the gaunt and sinewy frame of the stranger, and marked his powerful head and determined features, now touched into softness by the impressions of the moment, I felt an irrepressible curiosity to learn something more about him, and when he was quietly leaving the room I begged to know his name. He courteously replied, 'It is Abraham Lincoln, from Illinois.'"

The Republican National Convention of 1860, met on the 16th of May, at Chicago, in an immense building which the people of Chicago had put up for the purpose, called the Wigwam. There were 465 Delegates. The city was filled with earnest men, who had come there to press the claims of their favorite candidates, and the halls and corridors of all the hotels swarmed, and buzzed with an eager crowd, in and out of which darted or pushed or wormed their way the various leaders of party politics. Mr. Chase, Mr. Bates, and Mr. Cameron were spoken of and pressed somewhat as candidates, but from the first it was evident that the contest lay between Mr. Seward and Mr. Lincoln.

Judge Wilmot, of Pennsylvania, was chosen temporary Chairman of the Convention, and in the afternoon of the first day a permanent organization was effected by the choice of George Ashmun, of Massachusetts, as President, with 27 Vice-Presidents and 25 Secretaries. On Thursday, the 17th, the Committee on Resolutions reported the platform, which was enthusiastically adopted. A motion was made to proceed to the nomination at once, and if that had been done the result of the Convention might have proved very different, as at that time it was thought that Mr. Seward's chances were the best. But an adjournment was taken till the morning, and during the night the combinations were made which resulted in the nomination of Mr. Lincoln. The excitement of the Convention and of the audience on the morning of Friday was intense. The Illinoisans had turned out in great numbers, zealous for Lincoln, and though the other States, near and far, had sent many men who were equally zealous for Mr. Seward, it was quite clear that Mr. Lincoln's supporters were in the majority in the audience. The first ballot gave Mr. Seward 173½ votes to 102 for Mr. Lincoln, the rest being scattered. On the second ballot the first indication of the result was felt, when the Chairman of the Vermont Delegation, which had been divided on the previous ballot, announced when the name of Vermont was called, that "Vermont casts her ten votes for the young giant of the West, Abraham Lincoln." On the second ballot, Mr. Seward had 184½ to 181 for Mr. Lincoln, and on the third ballot Mr. Lincoln received 230 votes, being within 1½ of a majority. The vote was not announced, but so many everywhere had kept the count that it was known throughout the Convention at once. Mr. Carter, of Ohio, rose and announced a change in the vote of the Ohio Delegation of four votes in favor of Mr. Lincoln, and the Convention at once boiled over into a state of the wildest excitement. The cheers of the audience within were answered by those of a yet larger crowd without, to whom the result was announced. Cannon roared, and bands played, and banners waved, and the excited Republicans of Chicago cheered themselves hoarse, while on the wings of electricity sped in every direction the news of Mr. Lincoln's nomination, to be greeted everywhere with similar demonstrations. It was long before the Convention could calm itself enough to proceed to business. When it did, other States changed their votes in favor of the successful nominee until it was announced, as the result of the third ballot, that Abraham Lincoln, of Illinois, had received 354 votes and was nominated by the Republican party for the office of President of the United States. The nomination was then, on the motion of Mr. Evarts, of New York, made unanimous, and the Convention adjourned till the afternoon, when they completed their work by nominating Hannibal Hamlin for Vice-President.

Mr. Lincoln was at Springfield at the time. He had been in the telegraph office during the casting of the first and second ballots, but then left, and went over to the office of the State Journal, where he was sitting conversing with friends while the third ballot was being taken. In a few moments came across the wires the announcement of the result. The Superintendent of the Telegraph Company, who was present, wrote on a scrap of paper, "Mr. Lincoln: You are nominated on the third ballot," and a boy ran with the message to Mr. Lincoln. He looked at it in silence amid the shouts of those around him, then rising and putting it in his pocket he said quietly, "There's a little woman down at our house would like to hear this—I'll go down and tell her."

Next day there arrived at Springfield the committee appointed by the Convention to inform Mr. Lincoln officially of his nomination; Mr. Ashmun, President of the Convention, addressing Mr. Lincoln, said:

"I have, sir, the honor, in behalf of the gentlemen who are present—a Committee appointed by the Republican Convention recently assembled at Chicago—to discharge a most pleasant duty. We have come, sir, under a vote of instructions to that Committee, to notify you that you have been selected by the Convention of the Republicans at Chicago for President of the United States. They instruct us, sir, to notify you of that selection, and that Committee deem it not only respectful to yourself, but appropriate to the important matter which they have in hand, that they should come in person, and present to you the authentic evidence of the action of that Convention; and, sir, without any phrase which shall either be considered personally plauditory to yourself, or which shall have any reference to the principles involved in the questions which are connected with your nomination, I desire to present to you the letter which has been prepared, and which informs you of your nomination, and with it the platform resolutions and sentiments which the Convention adopted. Sir, at your convenience we shall be glad to receive from you such a response as it may be your pleasure to give us."

Mr. Lincoln listened to this address with a degree of grave dignity that almost wore the appearance of sadness, and after a brief pause, in which he seemed to be pondering the momentous responsibilities of his position, he thus replied:

"*Mr. Chairman and Gentlemen of the Committee*—I tender to you, and through you to the Republican National Convention, and all the people represented in it, my profoundest thanks for the high honor done me, which you now formally announce. Deeply, and even painfully sensible of the great responsibility which is inseparable from this high honor—a responsibility which I could almost wish had fallen upon some one of the far more eminent men and experienced statesmen whose distinguished names were before the Convention, I shall, by your leave, consider more fully the resolutions of the Convention, denominated the platform, and without any unnecessary or unreasonable delay, respond to you, Mr. Chairman, in writing, not doubting that the platform will be found satisfactory, and the nomination gratefully accepted.

"And now I will not longer defer the pleasure of taking you, and each of you, by the hand"

Tall Judge Kelly, of Pennsylvania, who was one of the Committee, and who is himself a great many feet high, had meanwhile been eyeing Mr. Lincoln's lofty form with a mixture of admiration and very likely jealousy; this had not escaped Mr. Lincoln, and as he shook hands with the judge he inquired, "What is your height?"

"Six feet three; what is yours, Mr. Lincoln?"

"Six feet four."

"Then," said the judge, "Pennsylvania bows to Illinois. My dear man, for years my heart has been aching for a President that I could *look up to*, and I've found him at last in the land where we thought there were none but *little* giants."

Mr. Lincoln's formal reply to the official announcement of his nomination, was as follows:

SPRINGFIELD, ILLINOIS, *May* 23, 1860.

SIR—I accept the nomination tendered me by the Convention over which you presided, of which I am formally apprised in a letter of yourself and others acting as a Committee of the Convention for that purpose. The declaration of principles and sentiments which accompanies your letter meets my approval, and it shall be my care not to violate it, or disregard it in any part. Imploring the assistance of Divine Providence, and with due regard to the views and feelings of all who were represented in the Convention, to the rights of all the states and territories and people of the nation, to the inviolability of the Constitution, and the perpetual union, harmony, and prosperity of all, I am most happy to co-operate for the practical success of the principles declared by the Convention.

Your obliged friend and fellow-citizen,

ABRAHAM LINCOLN.

HON. GEORGE ASHMUN,

President of the Republican Convention.

Mr. Lincoln's nomination proved universally acceptable to the Republican party. They recognized in him a man of firm principles, of ardent love for freedom, of strict integrity and truth, and they went into the political contest with a zeal and enthusiasm which was the guarantee of victory; while the doubt and uncertainty, the divided counsels, and wavering purposes of their opponents were the sure precursors of defeat.

His nomination was the signal to the leaders of the slaveholders' party for pressing upon the Democratic Convention their most ultra views, that by the division of the Democratic forces the victory of Mr. Lincoln might be assured, and the pretext afforded them for carrying into execution the plot against the liberties of the country which they had been for so many years maturing. That they would dare to carry their threat of rebellion into execution, was not believed at the North. If it had been, while it would probably have scared away some votes from Mr. Lincoln, it would have brought to him more votes yet from those who, though following the Democratic banner, had not learned to disregard the good old doctrine that the majority must rule, and would have rushed to its rescue, if they had believed that it was really threatened. The vote which he received was that of a solid phalanx of earnest men, who had resolved that Freedom should be henceforth national, and Slavery should be and remain as it was meant to be when the Constitution was adopted. They formed a body of nearly 2,000,000 voters, who carried for Mr. Lincoln the electoral votes of the States of Maine, New Hampshire, Vermont, Massachusetts, Rhode Island, Connecticut, New York, Pennsylvania, Ohio, Indiana, Illinois, Michigan, Iowa, Wisconsin, Minnesota, California.

That the consequences of that election have been

very different from what was anticipated by the great body of the people is unquestionably true. Few men of any party then understood the secret influences that were conspiring against the peace and integrity of the Union, and fewer still were willing to believe any considerable portion of the people capable of so gigantic a crime as the attempted overthrow of the great Republic of the world, either to revenge a party defeat or to perpetuate the slavery of the negro race. No man can justly be held responsible even for the consequences of his own action, any farther than, in the exercise of a just and fair judgment, he can foresee them. In electing Mr. Lincoln to the Presidency, the American people intended to erect a permanent bulwark against the territorial extension of slavery, and the perpetuation of its political power. If they had foreseen the madness of its defenders, they might have shrunk from the dreadful ordeal through which that madness has compelled the nation to pass, but in this, as in all the affairs of human life, ignorance of the future often proves the basis and guarantee of its wise development: and we believe that even now, with their experience, through three of the stormiest and most terrible years this nation has ever seen, of the sagacity, integrity, and unswerving patriotism with which President Lincoln has performed the duties of his high office, and with their clearer perception of the ultimate issue of that great contest between freedom and slavery, which the progress of events had rendered inevitable, the people look back with entire satisfaction upon the vote which, in 1860, made Mr. Lincoln President of the United States.

THE ADMINISTRATION

OF

ABRAHAM LINCOLN.

PRESIDENT LINCOLN'S ADMINISTRATION.

CHAPTER I.

FROM THE ELECTION, NOV. 6, 1860, TO THE INAUGURATION, MARCH 4, 1861.

ABRAHAM LINCOLN was elected to be President of the United States on the sixth day of November 1860. The preliminary canvass had not been marked by any very extraordinary features. Party lines were a good deal broken up, and four presidential candidates were in the field; but this departure from the ordinary course of party contests had occurred more than once in the previous political history of the country. Mr. LINCOLN was put in nomination by the Republican party, and represented in his life and opinions the precise aim and object for which that party had been formed. He was a native of a slaveholding State; and while he had been opposed to slavery, he had regarded it as a local institution, the creature of local laws, with which the national government of the United States had nothing whatever to do. But in common with all observant public men, he had watched, with distrust and apprehension, the advance of slavery as an element of political power towards ascendency in the government of the nation, and had cordially co-operated with those who thought it absolutely necessary for the future well-being of the country that this tendency should be checked. He had, therefore, opposed very strenuously the extension of slavery into the territories, and had asserted the right and the duty of Congress to exclude it by positive legislation therefrom.

The Chicago Convention, which nominated Mr. LINCOLN, adopted a platform of which this was the cardinal feature; but it also took good care to repel the imputation of its political opponents, and to remove the apprehensions of the South, that the party proposed to interfere with slavery in the States whose laws gave it support and protection. It expressly disavowed all authority and all wish for such interference, and declared its purpose to protect the Southern States in the free enjoyment of all their constitutional rights. The Democratic Convention, originally assembled at Charleston, was disposed to make Mr. DOUGLAS its candidate in opposition to Mr. LINCOLN; but this purpose was thwarted by leading politicians of the slaveholding States, who procured the nomination of Mr. BRECKINRIDGE, with full knowledge of the fact that this would divide the Democratic party, and in all probability secure the election of Mr. LINCOLN. Mr. BRECKINRIDGE represented the pro-slavery element of the Democratic party, and asserted the duty of the national government, by a positive exercise of its legislative and executive power, to protect slavery in the territories, against any legislation either of Congress or of the people of the territories themselves, which should seek to impair in any degree the right, alleged to be recognized in the Constitution, of property in slaves. Mr. DOUGLAS supported the theory that the people of the territories, acting through their territorial legislature, had the same right to decide this question for themselves as they had to decide any other; and he represented this principle in opposition to Mr. LINCOLN on the one hand, and Mr. BRECKINRIDGE on the other, in the Presidential canvass. JOHN BELL, of Tennessee, was also made a candidate by the action mainly of men who were dissatisfied with all the existing political parties, and who were alarmed at the probable results of a

Presidential election which promised to be substantially sectional in its character. They put forth, therefore, no opinions upon the leading points in controversy; and went into the canvass with "the Constitution, the Union, and the enforcement of the laws" as their platform, one upon which they could easily have rallied all the people of all sections of the country, but for the fact which they seemed to overlook, that the widest possible differences of opinion prevailed among the people as to its meaning.

All sections of the country took part in the election. The Southern States were quite as active and quite as zealous as the Northern in carrying on the canvass. Public meetings were held, the newspaper press South as well as North discussed the issues involved with energy and vigor, and every thing on the surface indicated the usual termination of the contest, the triumph of one party and the peaceful acquiescence of all others. The result, however, showed that this was a mistake. The active and controlling politicians of the Southern States had gone into the canvass with the distinct and well-formed purpose of acquiescing in the result only in the event of its giving them the victory. The election took place on the 6th of November. Mr. LINCOLN received the electoral votes of all the free States except New Jersey, which was divided, giving him four votes and Mr. DOUGLAS three. Mr. BRECKINRIDGE received the electoral votes of all the Slave States except Kentucky, Tennessee, and Virginia, which voted for BELL, and Missouri, which voted for DOUGLAS, as did three electors from New Jersey also. Of the popular vote LINCOLN received 1,857,610; DOUGLAS 1,365,976; BRECKINRIDGE 847,953, and BELL 590,631. In the Electoral College LINCOLN received 180 votes, DOUGLAS 12, BRECKINRIDGE 72, and Bell 39.

As soon as the result of the election was known, various movements in the Southern States indicated their purpose of resistance; and it soon became evident that this purpose had been long cherished, and that members of the government under the Presidency of Mr. BUCHANAN had officially given it their sanction and aid. On the 29th of October GENERAL SCOTT sent to the President and JOHN B. FLOYD, his Secretary of War, a letter expressing apprehensions lest the Southern people should seize some of the Federal forts in the Southern States, and advising that they should be immediately garrisoned by way of precaution. The Secretary of War, according to statements subsequently made by one of his eulogists in Virginia, "thwarted, objected, resisted, and forbade" the adoption of those measures, which, according to the same authority, if carried into execution, would have defeated the conspiracy, and rendered impossible the formation of a Southern Confederacy. An official report from the ordnance department, dated January 16, 1861, also shows that during the year 1860, and previous to the Presidential election, 115,000 muskets had been removed from Northern armories and sent to Southern arsenals by a single order of the Secretary of War, issued on the 30th of December, 1859. On the 20th of November the Attorney-General, Hon. JOHN S. BLACK, in reply to inquiries of the President, gave him the official opinion that Congress had no right to carry on war against any State, either to prevent a threatened violation of the Constitution or to enforce an acknowledgment that the Government of the United States is supreme: and it soon became evident that the President adopted this theory as the basis and guide of his Executive action.

South Carolina took the lead in the secession movement. Her legislature assembled on the 4th of November, 1860, and, after casting the electoral vote of the State for JOHN C. BRECKINRIDGE to be President of the United States, passed an act the next day calling a State Convention to meet at Columbia on the 17th of December. On the 10th, F. W. Pickens was elected Governor, and, in his inaugural, declared the determination of the State to secede, on the ground that, "in the recent election for President and Vice-President, the North had carried the election upon principles that make it no longer safe for us to rely upon the powers of the Federal Government or the guarantees of the Federal Compact. This," he added, "is the great overt act of the people of the Northern States, who propose to inaugurate a chief magistrate not to preside over the common interests or destinies of all the States alike, but upon issues of malignant hostility and uncompromising war to be waged upon the rights, the interests, and the peace of half of the States of this Union." The Convention met on the 17th of December, and adjourned the next day to Charleston, on account of the prevalence of small pox at Columbia. On the 20th an ordinance was passed unanimously repealing the ordinance adopted May 23, 1788, whereby the Constitution of the United States was ratified, and "dissolving the union now subsisting between South Carolina and other States under the name of the United States of America;" and on the 24th the Governor issued his proclamation, declaring the State of South Carolina to be a "separate, sovereign, free, and independent State."

This was the first act of secession passed by any State. The debates in the State Convention show clearly enough that it was not taken under the impulse of resentment for any sharp and remediless wrong, nor in apprehension that any such wrong would be inflicted; but in pursuance of a settled and long-cherished purpose. In that debate Mr. Parker said that the movement was "no spasmodic effort—it had been gradually culminating for a long series of years." Mr. Inglis endorsed this remark, and added, "Most of us have had this matter under consideration for the last twenty years." Mr. L. M. Keitt said, "I have been engaged in this movement ever since I entered political life." And Mr. Rhett, who had been for many years in the public service, declared that "the secession of South Carolina was not the event of a day. It is not," said he, "any thing produced by Mr. Lincoln's election, or by the non-execution of the Fugitive Slave Law. It is a matter which has been gathering head for thirty years. The election of Lincoln and Hamlin was the last straw on the back of the camel. But it was not the only one. The back was nearly broken before." So far as South Carolina was concerned there can be no doubt that her action was decided by men who had been plotting disunion for thirty years, not on account of any wrongs her people had sustained at the hands of the Federal Government, but from motives of personal and sectional ambition, and for the purpose of establishing a government which should be permanently and completely in the interest of slavery.

But the disclosures which have since been made, imperfect comparatively as they are, prove clearly that the whole secession movement was in the hands of a few conspirators, who had their head-quarters at the national Capital, and were themselves closely connected with the Government of the United States. A secret meeting of these men was held at Washington on the night of the 5th of January, 1861, at which the Senators from Georgia, Alabama, Louisiana, Arkansas, Texas, Mississippi, and Florida were present. They decided, by resolutions, that each of the Southern States should secede from the Union as soon as possible; that a Convention of seceding States should be held at Montgomery, Alabama, not later than the 15th of February; and that the Senators and Members of Congress from the Southern States ought to remain in their seats as long as possible, in order to defeat measures that might be proposed at Washington hostile to the secession movement. Davis of Mississippi, Slidell of Louisiana, and Mallory of Florida, were appointed a committee to carry these decisions into effect; and, in pursuance of them, Mississippi passed an ordinance of secession January 9th; Alabama and Florida, January 11; Louisiana, January 26, and Texas, February 5th. All these acts, as well as all which followed, were simply the execution of the behests of this secret conclave of conspirators who had resolved upon secession. In all the Conventions of the seceding States, delegates were appointed to meet at Montgomery. In not one of them was the question of secession submitted to a vote of the people; although in some of them the Legislatures had expressly forbidden them to pass any ordinance of secession without making its validity depend on its ratification by the popular vote. The Convention met at Montgomery on the 4th of February, and adopted a provisional constitution, to continue in operation for one year. Under this constitution Jefferson Davis was elected President of the new Confederacy, and Alex. H. Stephens, of Georgia, Vice-President. Both were inaugurated on the 18th. In an address delivered on his arrival at Montgomery, Mr. Davis declared that "the time for compromise has now passed, and the South is determined to maintain her position, and make all who oppose her smell Southern powder and feel Southern steel, if coercion is persisted in." He felt sure of the result; it might be they would "have to encounter inconveniences at the beginning," but he had no doubts of the final issue. The first part of his anticipation has been fully realized; it remains to be seen whether the end will be as peaceful and satisfactory as he predicted.

The policy of the new Confederacy towards the United States was soon officially made known. The government decided to maintain the *status quo* until the expiration of Mr. BUCHANAN's term, feeling assured that, with his declared belief that it would be unconstitutional to coerce a State, they need apprehend from his administration no active hostility to their designs. They had some hope that, by the 4th of March, their new Confederacy would be so far advanced that the new

Administration might waive its purpose of coercion; and they deemed it wise not to do any thing which should rashly forfeit the favor and support of "that very large portion of the North whose moral sense was on their side." Nevertheless, they entered upon prompt and active preparations for war. Contracts were made in various parts of the South for the manufacture of powder, shell, cannon balls, and other munitions of war. Recruiting was set on foot in several of the States. A plan was adopted for the organization of a regular army of the Confederacy, and on the 6th of March Congress passed an act authorizing a military force of 100,000 men.

Thus was opened a new chapter in the history of America. Thus were taken the first steps towards overthrowing the Government and Constitution of the United States, and establishing a new nation, with a new Constitution, resting upon new principles, and aiming at new results. The Constitution of the United States was ordained "in order to form a more perfect Union, establish justice, insure domestic tranquillity, provide for the common defence, promote the general welfare, and secure the blessings of Liberty to ourselves and our posterity." We have the clear and explicit testimony of A. H. Stephens, the Vice-President of the rebel Confederacy, echoing and reaffirming that of the whole civilized world, to the fact, that these high and noble objects—the noblest and the grandest at which human institutions can aim—have been more nearly attained in the practical working of the Government of the United States than anywhere else on the face of the earth. "I look upon this country, with our institutions," said Mr. Stephens before the Legislature of Georgia, on the 14th of November, 1860, after the result of the Presidential election was known, "as the Eden of the world, the paradise of the universe. It may be that out of it we may become greater and more prosperous, but I am candid and sincere in telling you that I fear if we rashly evince passion, and without sufficient cause shall take that step, that instead of becoming greater, or more peaceful, prosperous, and happy—instead of becoming gods we will become demons, and at no distant day commence cutting each other's throats." Mr. Stephens on that occasion went on, in a strain of high patriotism and common sense, to speak of the proposed secession of the State of Georgia, in language which will forever stand as a judicial condemnation of the action of the rebel States. "The first question that presents itself," said Mr. Stephens, "is, shall the people of the South secede from the Union in consequence of the election of Mr. Lincoln to the Presidency of the United States? My countrymen, I tell you candidly, frankly, and earnestly that I do not think that they ought. In my judgment the election of no man, constitutionally chosen to that high office, is sufficient cause for any State to separate from the Union. It ought to stand by and aid still in maintaining the Constitution of the country. To make a point of resistance to the Government, to withdraw from it because a man has been constitutionally elected, puts us in the wrong. * * We went into the election with this people. The result was different from what we wished; but the election has been constitutionally held. Were we to make a point of resistance to the Government, and go out of the Union on this account, the record would be made up hereafter against us."

After the new Confederacy had been organized, and Mr. Stephens had been elected its Vice-President, he made an elaborate speech to the citizens of Savannah, in which he endeavored to vindicate this attempt to establish a new government in place of the government of the United States, and to set forth the new principles upon which it was to rest, and which were to justify the movement in the eyes of the world and of impartial posterity. That exposition is too important to be omitted here. It is the most authoritative and explicit statement of the character and objects of the new government which has ever been made. Mr. Stephens said:

"The new constitution has put at rest forever all agitating questions relating to our peculiar institutions—African slavery as it exists among us—the proper *status* of the negro in our form of civilization. This was the immediate cause of the late rupture and present revolution. Jefferson, in his forecast, had anticipated this, as the 'rock upon which the old Union would split.' He was right. What was conjecture with him, is now a realized fact. But whether he fully comprehended the great truth upon which that rock stood and stands, may be doubted. The prevailing ideas entertained by him and most of the leading statesmen at the time of the formation of the old Constitution were, that the enslavement of the African was in violation of the laws of nature; that it was wrong in principle, socially, morally, and politically. It was an evil they knew not well how to deal with; but the general opinion of the men of that day was, that, somehow or other, in the order of Providence, the institution would be evanescent and pass away. This idea, though not incorporated in the Constitution, was the prevailing idea at the time. The Constitution, it is true, secured every essential guarantee to the institution while it should last, and hence no argument can be justly used against the constitutional guarantees thus secured, because of the common sentiment of the day. Those ideas, however, were fundamentally wrong. They rested upon the assumption of the equality of races. This was an error. It was a sandy foundation, and the idea of a government built upon it was wrong—when the 'storm came and the wind blew, it fell.'

"Our new Government is founded upon exactly the opposite ideas; its foundations are laid, its corner-stone rests upon the great truth that the negro is not equal to the white man; that slavery, subordination to the superior race, is his natural and moral condition. This, our new Government, is the first in the history of the world, based upon this great physical, philosophical, and moral truth. This truth has been slow in the process of its development, like all other truths in the various departments of science. It is even so amongst us. Many who hear me, perhaps, can recollect well that this truth was not generally admitted even within their day. The errors of the past generation still clung to many as late as twenty years ago. Those at the North who still cling to these errors with a zeal above knowledge, we justly denominate fanatics. All fanaticism springs from an aberration of the mind;

from a defect in reasoning. It is a species of insanity. One of the most striking characteristics of insanity, in many instances, is forming correct conclusions from fancied or erroneous premises; so with the anti-slavery fanatics; their conclusions are right if their premises are. They assume that the negro is equal, and hence conclude that he is entitled to equal privileges and rights with the white man. If their premises were correct, their conclusions would be logical and just; but their premises being wrong, their whole argument fails. I recollect once of having heard a gentleman from one of the Northern States, of great power and ability, announce in the House of Representatives, with imposing effect, that we of the South would be compelled, ultimately, to yield upon this subject of slavery; that it was as impossible to war successfully against a principle in politics, as it was in physics or mechanics. That the principle would ultimately prevail. That we, in maintaining slavery as it exists with us, were warring against a principle—a principle founded in nature, the principle of the equality of man. The reply I made to him was, that upon his own grounds we should succeed, and that he and his associates in their crusade against our institutions would ultimately fail. The truth announced, that it was as impossible to war successfully against a principle in politics as well as in physics and mechanics, I admitted, but told him that it was he and those acting with him who were warring against a principle. They were attempting to make things equal which the Creator had made unequal.

"In the conflict thus far, success has been on our side, complete throughout the length and breadth of the Confederate States. It is upon this, as I have stated, our social fabric is firmly planted; and I cannot permit myself to doubt the ultimate success of a full recognition of this principle throughout the civilized and enlightened world."

We have thus traced the course of events in the Southern States during the three months that succeeded the election of President Lincoln. Let us now see what took place in Washington during the same time. Congress met on the 3d of December and the Message of President Buchanan was at once sent in. That document ascribed the discontent of the Southern States to the alleged fact that the violent agitation in the North against slavery had created disaffection among the slaves, and created apprehensions of servile insurrection. The President vindicated the hostile action of the South, assuming that it was prompted by these apprehensions; but went on to show that there was no right on the part of any State to secede from the Union, while at the same time he contended that the General Government had no right to make war on any State for the purpose of preventing it from seceding, and closed this portion of his Message by recommending an amendment of the Constitution which should explicitly recognize the right of property in slaves, and provide for the protection of that right in all the territories of the United States. The belief that the people of South Carolina would make an attempt to seize one or more of the forts in the harbor of Charleston, created considerable uneasiness at Washington; and on the 9th of December the Representatives from that State wrote to the President expressing their "strong convictions" that no such attempt would be made previous to the action of the State Convention, "*provided* that no re-enforcements should be sent into those forts, and their relative military status shall remain as at present." On the 10th of December Howell Cobb resigned his office as Secretary of the Treasury, and on the 14th Gen. Cass resigned as Secretary of State. The latter resigned because the President refused to re-enforce the forts in the harbor of Charleston. On the 20th the State of South Carolina passed the ordinance of secession, and on the 26th Major Anderson transferred his garrison from Fort Moultrie to Fort Sumter. On the 29th John B. Floyd resigned his office as Secretary of War, alleging that the action of Major Anderson was in violation of pledges given by the Government that the military status of the forts at Charleston should remain unchanged, and that the President had declined to allow him to issue an order, for which he had applied on the 27th, to withdraw the garrison from the harbor of Charleston. On the 29th of December, Messrs. Barnwell, Adams, and Orr arrived at Washington, as Commissioners from the State of South Carolina, and at once opened a correspondence with President Buchanan, asking for the delivery of the forts and other government property at Charleston to the authorities of South Carolina. The President replied on the 30th, reviewing the whole question—stating that in removing from Fort Moultrie Major Anderson acted solely on his own responsibility, and that his first impulse on hearing of it was to order him to return, but that the occupation of the fort by South Carolina and the seizure of the arsenal at Charleston had rendered this impossible. The Commissioners replied on the 1st of January, 1861, insisting that the President had pledged himself to maintain the status of affairs in Charleston harbor previous to the removal of Major Anderson from Fort Moultrie, and calling on him to redeem this pledge. This communication the President returned.

On the 8th of January the President sent a Message to Congress, calling their attention to the condition of public affairs, declaring that while he had no right to make aggressive war upon any State, it was his right and his duty to "use military force defensively against those who resist the Federal officers in the execution of their legal functions, and against those who assail the property of the Federal Government;"—but throwing the whole responsibility of meeting the extraordinary emergencies of the occasion upon Congress. On the same day Jacob Thompson, of Mississippi, resigned his office as Secretary of the Interior, because the Star of the West had been sent on the 5th, by order of the Government, with supplies for Fort Sumter, in violation, as he alleged, of the decision of the Cabinet. On the 10th, P. F. Thomas, of Maryland, who had replaced Howell Cobb as Secretary of the Treasury, resigned, and was succeeded by Gen. John A. Dix, of New York.

The debates and the action of Congress throughout the session related mainly to the questions at issue between the two sections. The discussion opened on the 3d of December as soon as the President's Message had been read. The Southern

Senators generally treated the election of the previous November as having been a virtual decision against the equality and rights of the slaveholding States. The Republican members disavowed this construction, and proclaimed their willingness to adopt any just and proper measures which would quiet the apprehensions of the South, while they insisted that the authority of the Constitution should be maintained, and the constitutional election of a President should be respected. At the opening of the session Mr. Powell, of Kentucky, in the Senate moved the reference of that portion of the President's Message which related to the sectional difficulties of the country, to a select committee of thirteen. This resolution being adopted, Mr. Crittenden immediately afterwards introduced a series of joint resolutions, embodying what came to be known afterwards as the Crittenden Compromise—proposing to submit to the action of the people of the several States the following amendments to the Constitution:

1. Prohibiting slavery in all the territory of the United States north of 36° 30′, and protecting it as property in all territory south of that line; and admitting into the Union, with or without slavery as its Constitution might provide, any State that might be formed out of such territory, whenever its population should be sufficient to entitle it to a member of Congress.

2. Prohibiting Congress from abolishing slavery in places under its exclusive jurisdiction within Slave States.

3. Prohibiting Congress from abolishing slavery within the District of Columbia, so long as slavery should exist in Virginia or Maryland; or without the consent of the inhabitants or without just compensation to the owners.

4. Prohibiting Congress from hindering the transportation of slaves from one State to another, or to a territory in which slavery is allowed.

5. Providing that where a fugitive slave is lost to his owner by violent resistance to the execution of the process of the law for his recovery, the United States shall pay to said owner his full value, and may recover the same from the county in which such rescue occurred.

6. These provisions were declared to be unchangeable by any future

amendment of the Constitution, as were also the existing articles relating to the representation of slaves and the surrender of fugitives.

Besides these proposed amendments of the Constitution Mr. Crittenden's resolutions embodied certain declarations in affirmance of the constitutionality and binding force of the fugitive slave law—recommending the repeal by the States of all bills, the effect of which was to hinder the execution of that law, proposing to amend it by equalizing its fees, and urging the effectual execution of the law for the suppression of the African slave trade.

These resolutions were referred to the Committee of Thirteen, ordered on Mr. Powell's motion, and composed of the following Senators:

Messrs. Powell, Hunter, Crittenden, Seward, Toombs, Douglas, Collamer, Davis, Wade, Bigler, Rice, Doolittle, and Grimes.

On the 31st of December, this Committee reported that they "had not been able to agree upon any general plan of adjustment." The whole subject was nevertheless discussed over and over again during the residue of the session; but no final action was taken until the very day of its close. On the 21st of January, Messrs. Yulee and Mallory, of Florida, resigned their seats in the Senate because their State had passed an ordinance of secession, and on the 28th Mr. Iverson, of Georgia, followed their example. Messrs. Clay and Fitzpatrick, of Alabama, and Mr. Davis, of Mississippi, followed next, and on the 4th of February Messrs. Slidell and Benjamin, of Louisiana, also took their leave.

In the House of Representatives the debates took the same general direction as in the Senate. On the first day of the session a resolution was adopted, by a vote of 145 to 38, to refer so much of the President's Message as related to the perilous condition of the country, to a committee of one from each State. This committee was appointed as follows:

Corwin of Ohio.
Millson of Virginia.
Adams of Massachusetts.
Winslow of North Carolina.
Humphrey of New York.
Boyce of South Carolina.
Campbell of Pennsylvania.
Love of Georgia.
Ferry of Connecticut.
Davis of Maryland.
Robinson of Rhode Island.
Whitely of Delaware.
Tappan of New Hampshire.
Stratton of New Jersey.
Bristow of Kentucky.
Morrill of Vermont.
Nelson of Tennessee.
Dunn of Indiana.
Taylor of Louisiana.
Davis of Mississippi.
Kellogg of Illinois.
Houston of Alabama.
Morse of Maine.
Phelps of Missouri.
Rust of Arkansas.
Howard of Michigan.
Hawkins of Florida.
Hamilton of Texas.
Washburn of Wisconsin.
Curtis of Iowa.
Birch of California.
Windom of Minnesota.
Stark of Oregon.

A great variety of resolutions were offered and referred to this committee. In a few days the committee reported the following series of resolutions, and recommended their adoption :

Resolved by the Senate and House of Representatives of the United States of America in Congress assembled, That all attempts on the parts of the Legislatures of any of the States to obstruct or hinder the recovery and surrender of fugitives from service or labor, are in derogation of the Constitution of the United States, inconsistent with the comity and good neighborhood that should prevail among the several States, and dangerous to the peace of the Union.

Resolved, That the several States be respectfully requested to cause their statutes to be revised, with a view to ascertain if any of them are in conflict with or tend to embarrass or hinder the execution of the laws of the United States, made in pursuance of the second section of the fourth article of the Constitution of the United States for the delivering up of persons held to labor by the laws of any State and escaping therefrom; and the Senate and House of Representatives earnestly request that all enactments having such tendency be forthwith repealed, as required by a just sense of constitutional obligations, and by a due regard for the peace of the Republic; and the President of the United States is requested to communicate these resolutions to the

Governors of the several States, with a request that they will lay the same before the Legislatures thereof respectively.

Resolved, That we recognize slavery as now existing in fifteen of the United States by the usages and laws of those States; and we recognize no authority, legally or otherwise, outside of a State where it so exists, to interfere with slaves or slavery in such States, in disregard of the rights of their owners or the peace of society.

Resolved, That we recognize the justice and propriety of a faithful execution of the Constitution, and laws made in pursuance thereof, on the subject of fugitive slaves, or fugitives from service or labor, and discountenance all mobs or hinderances to the execution of such laws, and that citizens of each State shall be entitled to all the privileges and immunities of citizens in the several States.

Resolved, That we recognize no such conflicting elements in its composition, or sufficient cause from any source, for a dissolution of this Government; that we were not sent here to destroy, but to sustain and harmonize the institutions of the country, and to see that equal justice is done to all parts of the same; and finally, to perpetuate its existence on terms of equality and justice to all the States.

Resolved, That a faithful observance, on the part of all the States, of all their constitutional obligations to each other and to the Federal Government, is essential to the peace of the country.

Resolved, That it is the duty of the Federal Government to enforce the Federal laws, protect the Federal property, and preserve the Union of these States.

Resolved, That each State be requested to revise its statutes, and, if necessary, so to amend the same as to secure, without legislation by Congress, to citizens of other States travelling therein, the same protection as citizens of such State enjoy; and also to protect the citizens of other States travelling or sojourning therein against popular violence or illegal summary punishment, without trial in due form of law, for imputed crimes.

Resolved, That each State be also respectfully requested to enact such laws as will prevent and punish any attempt whatever in such State to recognize or set on foot the lawless invasion of any other State or Territory.

Resolved, That the President be requested to transmit copies of the foregoing resolutions to the Governors of the several States, with a request that they be communicated to their respective Legislatures.

These resolutions were intended and admirably calculated to calm the apprehensions of the people of the slaveholding States as to any disposition on the part of the Federal Government to interfere with Slavery, or withhold from them any of their constitutional rights; and in a House controlled by a large Republican majority, they were adopted by a vote of ayes 136, noes 53. Not content with this effort to satisfy all just complaints on the part of the Southern States, the same committee reported the following resolution, recommending such an amendment of the Constitution as should put it forever out of the power of the Government or people of the United States to interfere with Slavery in any of the States:

Be it resolved by the Senate and House of Representatives of the United States of America in Congress assembled (two-thirds of both Houses concurring), That the following article be proposed to the Legislatures of the several States as an amendment to the Constitution of the United States, which, when ratified by three-fourths of said Legislatures, shall be valid, to all intents and purposes, as a part of the said Constitution, namely:

Art. 12. No amendment shall be made to the Constitution which will authorize, or give to Congress the power to abolish or interfere, within any State, with the domestic institutions thereof, including that of persons held to labor or service by the laws of said State.

This resolution was adopted by a vote of 133 to 65—more than *two-thirds* in its favor. This closed the action of the House of Representatives at this session on this important subject, though it had previously adopted, by a unanimous vote, the following declaratory resolution:—

Resolved, That neither the Federal Government nor the people, or the governments of the non-slaveholding States, have the right to legislate upon or interfere with Slavery in any of the slaveholding States in the Union.

The action of the Senate was somewhat modified by the intervening action of a Peace Conference, which assembled at

Washington on the 4th of February, in pursuance of a recommendation of the State of Virginia, embodied in resolutions adopted by the General Assembly of that State on the 19th of January. It consisted of delegates, 133 in number, from 21 States—none of those which had seceded being represented. John Tyler, of Virginia, was appointed president, and a committee, consisting of one from each State, was appointed, with authority to "report what they may deem right, necessary, and proper to restore harmony and preserve the Union." On the 15th of February the committee reported a series of resolutions, in seven sections, which were discussed and amended, one by one, until the afternoon of the 26th, when the vote was taken upon them as amended, in succession, with the following results:

SECTION 1. In all the present territory of the United States, north of the parallel of thirty-six degrees and thirty minutes of north latitude, involuntary servitude, except in punishment of crime, is prohibited. In all the present territory south of that line, the status of persons held to involuntary service or labor, as it now exists, shall not be changed; nor shall any law be passed by Congress or the Territorial Legislature to hinder or prevent the taking of such persons from any of the States of this Union to said territory, nor to impair the rights arising from said relation; but the same shall be subject to judicial cognizance in the Federal Courts, according to the course of the common law. When any territory north or south of said line, within such boundary as Congress may prescribe, shall contain a population equal to that required for a member of Congress, it shall, if its form of government be republican, be admitted into the Union on an equal footing with the original States, with or without involuntary servitude as the constitution of such State may provide.

The vote on the adoption of the section was as follows:

AYES.—Delaware, Kentucky, Maryland, New Jersey, Ohio, Pennsylvania, Rhode Island, Tennessee—8.

NOES.—Connecticut, Illinois, Iowa, Maine, Massachusetts, Missouri, New York, North Carolina, New Hampshire, Vermont, Virginia—11.

So its adoption was not agreed to.

A reconsideration of this vote was called for by the delegates from Illinois and agreed to, 14 to 5. On the next day the question was again taken on the adoption of the section, with the following result:

AYES.—Delaware Illinois, Kentucky, Maryland, New Jersey, Ohio, Pennsylvania, Rhode Island, Tennessee—9.
NOES.—Connecticut, Iowa, Maine, Massachusetts, North Carolina, New Hampshire, Vermont, Virginia—8.

Thus the section was adopted.

It was stated by the members from New York, when the State was called, that one of their number, D. D. Field, was absent, and the delegation was divided. Thus New York, Indiana, and Kansas were divided.

The adoption of the second section was then moved; it was as follows:

SECTION 2. No territory shall be acquired by the United States, except by discovery, and for naval and commercial stations, depots, and transit routes, without the concurrence of a majority of all the Senators from States which allow involuntary servitude, and a majority of all the Senators from States which prohibit that relation; nor shall territory be acquired by treaty, unless the votes of a majority of the Senators from each class of States hereinbefore mentioned be cast as a part of the two-thirds majority necessary to the ratification of such treaty.

The vote on this section was as follows:

AYES.—Delaware, Indiana, Kentucky, Maryland, Missouri, New Jersey, Ohio, Pennsylvania, Rhode Island, Tennessee, Virginia—11.
NOES.—Connecticut, Illinois, Iowa, Maine, Massachusetts, North Carolina, New Hampshire, Vermont—8.

New York and Kansas were divided.

The adoption of section three of the report, with the amendments, was next moved. The amended section was as follows:

SECTION 3. Neither the Constitution nor any amendment thereof shall be construed to give Congress power to regulate, abolish, or control, within any State, the relation established or recognized by the laws thereof touching persons held to labor or involuntary service therein, nor to interfere with or abolish involuntary service in the District of Columbia without the consent of Maryland and without the consent of the owners, or making the owners who do not consent just compensation; nor the power to interfere with or prohibit representatives and others from bringing with them to the District of Columbia, retaining and taking away, persons so held to labor or service; nor the power to interfere with or abolish involuntary service in places under the exclusive jurisdiction of the United States within those States and Territories where the same is established or recognized; nor the power to prohibit the removal or transportation of persons held to labor or involuntary service in any State or territory of the United States to any other State or territory thereof where it is established or recognized by law or usage and the right during transportation, by sea or river, of touching at ports, shores, and landings, and of landing in case of distress, shall exist; but not the right of transit in or through any State or territory, or of sale or traffic, against the law thereof. Nor shall Congress have power to authorize any higher rate of taxation on persons held to labor or service than on land.

The vote on the adoption of the section was as follows:

AYES.—Delaware, Illinois, Kentucky, Maryland, Missouri, New Jersey; North Carolina, Ohio, Pennsylvania, Rhode Island, Tennessee, Virginia—12.

NOES.—Connecticut, Indiana, Iowa, Maine, Massachusetts, New Hampshire, Vermont—7.

So the section was adopted. Kansas and New York were divided.

The adoption of the fourth section of the report, as amended, was then moved; it was as follows:

SECTION 4. The third paragraph of the second section of the fourth article of the Constitution shall not be construed to prevent any of the States, by appropriate legislation, and through the action of their judicial and ministerial officers, from enforcing the delivery of fugitives from labor to the person to whom such service or labor is due.

The vote on the adoption of this section was as follows:

AYES.—Connecticut, Delaware, Illinois, Indiana, Kentucky, Maryland, Missouri, New Jersey, North Carolina, Ohio, Pennsylvania, Rhode Island, Tennessee, Vermont, Virginia—15.

NOES.—Iowa, Maine, Massachusetts, New Hampshire—4.

Thus the section was adopted, Kansas and New York were divided.

The adoption of the fifth section of the report as amended was then moved; it was as follows:

SECTION 5. The foreign slave-trade is hereby forever prohibited, and it shall be the duty of Congress to pass laws to prevent the importation of slaves, coolies, or persons held to service or labor into the United States and the Territories from places beyond the limits thereof.

The vote on the adoption of this section resulted as follows:

AYES.—Connecticut, Delaware, Illinois, Indiana, Kentucky, Maryland, Missouri, New Jersey, New York, New Hampshire, Ohio, Pennsylvania, Rhode Island, Tennessee, Vermont, Kansas—16.

NOES.—Iowa, Maine, Massachusetts, North Carolina, Virginia—5.

The section was thus adopted.

A motion was next made to adopt the sixth section as amended; it was as follows:

SECTION 6. The first, third, and fifth sections, together with this section of these amendments, and the third paragraph of the second section of the first article of the Constitution, and the third paragraph of the second section of the fourth article thereof, shall not be amended or abolished without the consent of all the States.

The vote on this section was as follows:

AYES.—Delaware, Illinois, Kentucky, Maryland, Missouri, New Jersey, Ohio, Pennsylvania, Rhode Island, Tennessee, Kansas—11.

NOES.—Connecticut, Indiana, Iowa, Maine, Massachusetts, North Carolina, New Hampshire, Vermont, Virginia—9.

New York was divided. So this section was adopted.

The motion was then made to adopt the seventh and last section as amended; it was as follows:

SECTION 7. Congress shall provide by law that the United States shall pay to the owner the full value of his fugitive from labor, in all cases where the marshal or other officer whose duty it was to arrest such fugitive, was prevented from doing so by violence or intimidation, from mobs or other riotous assemblages, or when, after arrest, such fugitive was rescued by like violence or intimidation, and the owner thereby deprived of the same; and the acceptance of such payment shall preclude the owner from further claim to such fugitive. Congress shall provide by law for securing to the citizens of each State the privileges and immunities of citizens in the several States.

The vote on this section was as follows:

AYES.—Delaware, Illinois, Indiana, Kentucky, Maryland, New Jersey, New Hampshire, Ohio, Pennsylvania, Rhode Island, Tennessee, Kansas—12.

NOES.—Connecticut, Iowa, Maine, Missouri, North Carolina, Vermont, Virginia—7.

Thus the last section was adopted. New York was divided.

The adoption of the following resolution was then moved by Mr. Franklin, of Pennsylvania:

Resolved, As the sense of this Convention, that the highest political duty of every citizen of the United States is his allegiance to the Federal Government created by the Constitution of the United States, and that no State of this Union has any constitutional right to secede therefrom, or to absolve the citizens of such State from their allegiance to the Government of the United States.

It was moved to lay the resolution on the table. The vote was as follows:

AYES.—Delaware, Kentucky, Maryland, Missouri, New Jersey, North Carolina, Ohio, Tennessee, Virginia—9.

NOES.—Connecticut, Illinois, Indiana, Iowa, Maine, Massachusetts, New York, New Hampshire, Pennsylvania, Rhode Island, Vermont, Kansas—12.

Some amendments were then offered and laid on the table, when its indefinite postponement was moved and carried by the following vote:

AYES.—Delaware, Kentucky, Maryland, Missouri, New Jersey, North Carolina, Ohio, Rhode Island, Tennessee, Virginia—10.

NOES.—Connecticut, Illinois, Indiana, Iowa, Maine, Massachusetts, Pennsylvania—7.

New York was divided.

The following preamble was then offered by Mr. Guthrie, and agreed to:

To the Congress of the United States:

The Convention assembled upon the invitation of the State of Virginia to adjust the unhappy differences which now disturb the peace of the Union and threaten its continuance, make known to the Congress of the United States, that their body convened in the city of Washington on the 4th instant, and continued in session until the 27th.

There were in the body, when action was taken upon that which is here submitted, one hundred and thirty-three commissioners, representing the following States: Maine, New Hampshire, Vermont, Massachusetts, Rhode Island, Connecticut, New York, New Jersey, Pennsylvania, Delaware, Maryland, Virginia, North Carolina, Tennessee, Kentucky, Missouri, Ohio, Indiana, Illinois, Iowa, Kansas.

They have approved what is herewith submitted, and respectfully request that your honorable body will submit it to conventions in the States as an article of amendment to the Constitution of the United States.

In the Senate, on the 2d day of March, a communication was received from the President of the Peace Congress, communicating the resolutions thus adopted in that body. They were at once referred to a committee consisting of Messrs. Crittenden, Bigler, Thomson, Seward, and Trumbull. The next day they were reported to the Senate for its adoption, Messrs. Seward and Trumbull, the minority of the Committee, dissenting from the majority, and proposing the adoption of a resolution calling on the Legislatures of the States to express their will in regard to calling a Convention for amending the Constitution.

The question then came up on adopting the resolutions of the Peace Conference. Mr. Hunter, of Virginia, moved to substitute the first of Mr. Crittenden's resolutions for the first of those reported by the Committee. Mr. Crittenden opposed it, and urged the adoption of the propositions of the Peace Conference in preference to his own. Mr. Mason, of Virginia, opposed the resolutions of the Peace Conference, on the ground that it would not satisfy the South. Mr. Baker, of Oregon, advocated it. Mr. Green, of Missouri, opposed it as surrendering every Southern principle, in which he was seconded by Mr. Lane, of Oregon.

At this stage of the proceedings Mr. Douglas gave a new turn to the form of the proceedings of the Senate, by moving to take up the resolution adopted by the House to amend the Constitution so as to prohibit forever any interference with slavery in the States. This motion was carried. Mr. Pugh moved to amend by substituting for this resolution the resolutions of Mr. Crittenden. This was rejected—ayes 14, noes 25. Mr. Brigham, of Michigan, next moved to substitute a resolution against any amendment of the Constitution, and in favor of enforcing the laws. This was rejected—ayes 13, noes 25. Mr. Grimes, of Iowa, then moved to substitute the resolution of Messrs. Seward and Trumbull, as the minority of the Select Committee, calling on the State Legislatures to express their will in regard to calling a Convention to amend the Constitution. This was rejected—ayes 14, noes 25. The propositions of the Peace Conference were then moved by Mr. Johnson, of Arkansas, and rejected—ayes 3, noes 34. Mr. Crittenden's resolutions were then taken up, and lost by the following vote:

Ayes.—Messrs. Bayard, Bright, Bigler, Crittenden, Douglas, Gwin, Hunter, Johnson of Tenn., Kennedy, Lane, Latham, Mason, Nicholson, Polk, Pugh, Rice, Sebastian, Thomson, and Wigfall—19.

Noes.—Messrs. Anthony, Bingham, Chandler, Clark, Dixon, Doolittle, Durkee, Fessenden, Foote, Foster, Grimes, Harlan, King, Morrill, Sumner, Ten Eyck, Trumbull, Wade, Wilkinson, and Wilson—20.

The resolutions were thus lost in consequence of the withdrawal of Senators from the disaffected States. The question was then taken on the House resolution to amend the Constitution so as to prohibit forever any amendment of the Constitution interfering with slavery in any State, and the resolution was *adopted* by a two-thirds vote—ayes 24, nays 12.

This closed the action of Congress upon this important subject. It was strongly Republican in both branches, yet it had done every thing consistent with its sense of justice and fidelity to the Constitution to disarm the apprehensions of the Southern States, and to remove all provocation for their resistance to the incoming administration. It had given the strongest possible pledge that it had no intention of interfering with slavery in any State, by amending the Constitution so as to make such interference forever impossible. It created governments for three new Territories, Nevada, Dakotah, and Colorado, and passed no law excluding slavery from any one of them. It had severely censured the legislation of some of the Northern States intended to hinder the recovery of fugitives from labor; and in response to its expressed wishes, Rhode Island repealed its laws of that character, and Vermont, Maine, Massachusetts, and Wisconsin, had the subject under consideration, and were ready to take similar action. Yet all this had no effect whatever in changing or checking the secession movement in the Southern States.

CHAPTER II.

FROM SPRINGFIELD TO WASHINGTON.

FROM the date of his election, Mr. LINCOLN maintained silence on the affairs of the country. The government was to remain for three months longer in the hands of Mr. Buchanan, and the new President did not deem it becoming or proper for him to interfere, in any way, with the regular discharge of its duties and responsibilities. On the 11th of February, 1861, he left his home in Springfield, Illinois, accompanied to the railroad dépôt by a large concourse of his friends and neighbors, whom he bade farewell in the following words:

MY FRIENDS: No one not in my position can appreciate the sadness I feel at this parting. To this people I owe all that I am. Here I have lived more than a quarter of a century; here my children were born, and here one of them lies buried. I know not how soon I shall see you again. A duty devolves upon me which is, perhaps, greater than that which has devolved upon any other man since the days of WASHINGTON. He never would have succeeded except for the aid of Divine Providence, upon which he at all times relied. I feel that I cannot succeed without the same Divine aid which sustained him, and on the same Almighty Being I place my reliance for support, and I hope you, my friends, will all pray that I may receive that Divine assistance, without which I cannot succeed, but with which, success is certain. Again I bid you all an affectionate farewell.

As the train passed through the country the President was greeted with hearty cheers and good wishes by the thousands who assembled at the railway stations along the route. Party spirit seemed to have been forgotten, and the cheers were always given for "Lincoln and the Constitution." At Tolono he appeared upon the platform, and in response to the applause which hailed his appearance, he said:

I am leaving you on an errand of national importance, attended, as you are aware, with considerable difficulties. Let us believe, as some poet has expressed it, "Behind the cloud the sun is still shining." I bid you an affectionate farewell.

At Indianapolis the party was welcomed by a salute of thirty-four guns, and the President-elect was received by the Governor of the State in person, and escorted to a carriage in waiting, which proceeded—followed by a procession of the members of both Houses of the Legislature, the municipal authorities, the military, and firemen—to the Bates House. Appearing on the balcony of this hotel, Mr. LINCOLN was greeted by the hearty applause of the large crowd which had assembled in the street, to which he addressed the following remarks:

Gov. Morton and Fellow-Citizens of the State of Indiana:

Most heartily do I thank you for this magnificent reception, and while I cannot take to myself any share of the compliment thus paid, more than that which pertains to a mere instrument, an accidental instrument, perhaps I should say, of a great cause, I yet must look upon it as a most magnificent reception, and as such, most heartily do thank you for it. You have been pleased to address yourself to me chiefly in behalf of this glorious Union in which we live, in all of which you have my hearty sympathy, and, as far as may be within my power, will have, one and inseparably, my hearty consideration; while I do not expect, upon this occasion, or until I get to Washington, to attempt any lengthy speech, I will only say to the salvation of the Union there needs but one single thing, the hearts of a people like yours. [Applause.]

The people, when they rise in mass in behalf of the Union and the liberties of their country, truly may it be said, "The gates of hell cannot prevail against them." [Renewed applause.] In all trying positions in which I shall be placed, and, doubtless, I shall be placed in many such, my reliance will be placed upon you and the people of the United States; and I wish you to remember, now and forever, that it is your business, and not mine; that if the union of these States, and the liberties of this people shall be lost, it is but little to any one man of fifty-two years of age, but a great deal to the thirty millions of people who inhabit these United States, and to their posterity in all coming time. It is your business to rise up and preserve the Union and liberty for yourselves, and not for me.

I desire they should be constitutionally performed. I, as already intimated, am but an accidental instrument, temporary, and to serve but for a limited time, and I appeal to you again to constantly bear in mind that with you, and not with politicians, not with Presidents, not with office-seekers, but with you, is the question, Shall the Union and shall the liberties of this country be preserved to the latest generations? [Cheers.]

In the evening the members of the Legislature waited upon him in a body at his hotel, where one of their number, on behalf of the whole, and in presence of a very large assemblage of the citizens of the place, made a brief address of welcome and congratulation, which Mr. LINCOLN acknowledged in the following terms:

FELLOW-CITIZENS OF THE STATE OF INDIANA: I am here to thank you much for this magnificent welcome, and still more for the generous support given by your State to that political cause which I think is the true and just cause of the whole country and the whole world.

Solomon says there is "a time to keep silence," and when men wrangle by the mouth with no certainty that they *mean* the same *thing*, while using the same *word*, it perhaps were as well if they would keep silence.

The words "coercion" and "invasion" are much used in these days, and often with some temper and hot blood. Let us make sure, if we can, that we do not misunderstand the meaning of those who use them. Let us get exact definitions of these words, not from dictionaries, but from the men themselves, who certainly depreciate the *things* they would represent by the use of words. What, then, is "Coercion?" What is "Invasion?" Would the marching of an army into South Carolina, without the consent of her people, and with hostile intent towards them; be "invasion?" I certainly think it would; and it would be "coercion" also if the South Carolinians were forced to submit. But if the United States should merely hold and retake its own forts and other property, and collect the duties on foreign importations, or even withhold the mails from places where they were habitually violated, would any or all these things be "invasion" or "coercion?" Do our professed lovers of the Union, but who spitefully resolve that they will resist coercion and invasion, understand that such things as these on the part of the United States, would be coercion or invasion of a State? If so, their idea of means to preserve the object of their affection would seem exceedingly thin and airy. If sick, the little pills of the homœopathists would be much too large for it to swallow. In their view, the Union, as a family relation, would seem to be no regular marriage, but a sort of "free love" arrangement, to be maintained only on "passional attraction."

By the way, in what consists the special sacredness of a State? I speak not of the position assigned to a State in the Union, by the Constitution; for that, by the bond, we all recognize. That position, however, a State cannot carry out of the Union with it. I speak of that assumed primary right of a State to rule all which is *less* than itself and ruin all which is larger than itself. If a State and a county in a given case, should be equal in extent of territory, and equal in number of inhabitants, in what, as a matter of principle, is the State better than the county? Would an exchange of names be an exchange of *rights* upon principle? On what rightful principle may a State, being not more than one-fiftieth part of the nation, in soil and population, break up the nation and then coerce a proportionally larger subdivision of itself, in the most arbitrary way? What mysterious right to play tyrant is conferred on a district of country, with its people, by merely calling it a State?

Fellow-citizens, I am not asserting any thing; I am merely asking questions for you to consider. And now allow me to bid you farewell.

On the morning of the 12th, Mr. Lincoln took his departure and arrived at Cincinnati at about noon, having been greeted along the route by the hearty applause of the thousands assembled at the successive stations. His reception at Cincinnati was overwhelming. The streets were so densely crowded that it was with the utmost difficulty the procession could secure a passage. Mr. Lincoln was escorted to the Burnett House, which had been handsomely decorated in honor of his visit. He was welcomed by the Mayor of the city in a few remarks, in response to which he said:

Mr. Mayor and Fellow-Citizens: I have spoken but once before this in Cincinnati. That was a year previous to the late Presidential election.

On that occasion, in a playful manner, but with sincere words, I addressed much of what I said to the Kentuckians. I gave my opinion that we, as Republicans, would ultimately beat them, as Democrats, but that they could postpone that result longer by nominating Senator Douglas for the Presidency than they could in any other way. They did not, in any true sense of the word, nominate Mr. Douglas, and the result has come certainly as soon as ever I expected. I also told them how I expected they would be treated after they should have been beaten; and I now wish to call their attention to what I then said upon that subject. I then said, "When we do as we say, beat you, you perhaps want to know what we will do with you. I will tell you, as far as I am authorized to speak for the opposition, what we mean to do with you. We mean to treat you, as near as we possibly can, as Washington, Jefferson, and Madison treated you. We mean to leave you alone, and in no way to interfere with your institutions; to abide by all and every compromise of the Constitution; and, in a word, coming back to the original proposition, to treat you so far as degenerate men, if we have degenerated, may, according to the example of those noble fathers, WASHINGTON, JEFFERSON, and MADISON. We mean to remember that you are as good as we; that there is no difference between us, other than the difference of circumstances. We mean to recognize and bear in mind always that you have as good hearts in your bosoms as other people, or as we claim to have, and treat you accordingly.

Fellow-citizens of Kentucky! friends! brethren, may I call you in my new position? I see no occasion, and feel no inclination to retract a word of this. If it shall not be made good, be assured the fault shall not be mine.

In the evening the German Republican associations called upon Mr. LINCOLN and presented him an address of congratulation, to which he responded, warmly endorsing the wisdom of the Homestead bill, and speaking of the advantages offered by the soil and institutions of the United States to foreigners who might wish to make it their home. He left Cincinnati on the morning of the 13th, accompanied by a Committee of the Ohio Legislature, which had come from the Capital to meet him. The party reached Columbus at 2 o'clock, and the President was escorted to the hall of the Assembly, where he was formally welcomed by Lieutenant-Governor Kirk on behalf of the Legislature which had assembled in joint session, to which he made the following reply:

MR. PRESIDENT AND MR. SPEAKER, AND GENTLEMEN OF THE GENERAL ASSEMBLY: It is true, as has been said by the President of the Senate, that very great responsibility rests upon me in the position to which the votes of the American people have called me. I am deeply sensible of that weighty responsibility. I cannot but know what you all know, that without a name, perhaps without a reason why I should have a name, there has fallen upon me a task such as did not rest even upon the Father of his country, and so feeling I cannot but turn and look for the support without which it will be impossible for me to perform that great task. I turn, then, and look to the great American people, and to that God who has never forsaken them.

Allusion has been made to the interest felt in relation to the policy of the new Administration. In this I have received from some a degree of credit for having kept silence, and from others some depreciation. I still think that I was right. In the varying and repeatedly shifting scenes of the present, and without a precedent which could enable me to judge by the past, it has seemed fitting that before speaking upon the difficulties of the country, I should have gained a view of the whole field so as to be sure after all—at liberty to modify and change the course of policy as future events may make a change necessary. I have not maintained silence from any want of real anxiety. It is a good thing that there is no more than anxiety, for there is nothing going wrong. It is a consoling circumstance that when we look out, there is nothing that really hurts anybody. We entertain different views upon political questions, but nobody is suffering any thing. This is a most consoling circumstance, and from it we may conclude that all we want is time, patience, and a reliance on that God who has never forsaken this people. Fellow-citizens, what I have said I have said altogether extemporaneously, and will now come to a close.

Both Houses then adjourned. In the evening Mr. LINCOLN held a levée, which was very largely attended. On the morning of the 14th, Mr. LINCOLN left Columbus. At Steubenville he had a formal though brief reception, being addressed by Judge Floyd, to whose remarks he made the following reply:

I fear that the great confidence placed in my ability is unfounded. Indeed, I am sure it is. Encompassed by vast difficulties as I am, nothing shall be wanting on my part, if sustained by the American people and God. I believe the devotion to the Constitution is equally great on both sides of the river. It is only the different understanding of that instrument that causes difficulty. The only dispute on both sides is "What are their rights?" If the majority should not rule, who should be the judge? Where is such a judge to be found? We should all be bound by the majority of the American people—if not, then the minority must control. Would that be right? Would it be just or generous? Assuredly not. I reiterate that the majority should rule. If I adopt a wrong policy, the opportunity for condemnation will occur in four years' time. Then I can be turned out, and a better man with better views put in my place.

The train reached Pittsburg in the evening, and Mr. LINCOLN was received with the utmost enthusiasm at the Monongahela House by a large crowd which had assembled to greet him. He acknowledged their reception briefly:

He said he would not give them a speech, as he thought it more rare, if not more wise, for a public man to abstain from much speaking. He expressed his gratitude and surprise at seeing so great a crowd and such boundless enthusiasm manifested in the night-time and under such untoward circumstances, to greet so unworthy an individual as himself. This was undoubtedly attributable to the position which more by accident than by worth he had attained. He remarked further, that if all those whole-souled people whom he saw this evening before him were for the preservation of the Union, he did not see how it could be in much danger. He had intended to say a few words to the people of Pittsburg—the greatest manufacturing city of the United States—upon such matters as they were interested in; but as he had adopted the plan of holding his tongue for the most part during the last canvass, and since his election, he thought he had perhaps better now still continue to hold his tongue. [Cries of "Go on," "go on."] Well, I am reminded that there is an Alleghany City as well as an Alleghany County, the former the banner town, and the latter the banner county, perhaps, of the world. I am glad to see both of them, and the good people of both. That I may not disappoint these, I will say a few words to you to-morrow as to the peculiar interests of Alleghany County."

On the morning of the 15th, the Mayor and Common Council of the City of Pittsburg waited in a body upon the President-elect. The Mayor made him an address of formal welcome in presence of a very large number of citizens who had assembled to witness the ceremony. After the applause which greeted his appearance had subsided, Mr. LINCOLN made the following remarks:

I most cordially thank his Honor Mayor Wilson and the citizens of Pittsburg generally, for their flattering reception. I am the more grateful because I know that it is not given to me alone, but to the cause I represent, which clearly proves to me their good will, and that sincere feeling is at the bottom of it. And here I may remark, that in every short address I have made to the people, in every crowd through which I have passed, of late, some allusion has been made to the present distracted condition of the country. It is natural to expect that I should say something on this subject; but to touch upon it at all would involve an elaborate discussion of a great many questions and circumstances, requiring more time than I can at present command, and would, perhaps, unnecessarily commit me upon matters which have not yet fully developed themselves. The condition of the country is an extraordinary one, and fills the mind of every patriot with anxiety. It is my intention to give this subject all the consideration I possibly can before specially deciding in regard to it, so that when I do speak it may be as nearly right as possible. When I do speak, I hope I may say nothing in opposition to the spirit of the Constitution, contrary to the integrity of the Union, or which will prove inimical to the liberties of the people or to the peace of the whole country. And, furthermore, when the time arrives for me to speak on this great subject, I hope I may say nothing to disappoint the people generally throughout the country, especially if the expectation has been based upon any thing which I may have heretofore said. Notwithstanding the troubles across the river—(the speaker pointing southwardly across the Monongahela, and smiling)—there is no crisis but an artificial one. What is there now to warrant the condition of affairs presented by our friends over the river? Take even their own view of the questions involved, and there is nothing to justify the course they are pursuing. I repeat, then, there is no crisis, excepting such a one as may be gotten up at any time by turbulent men, aided by designing politicians. My advice to them, under such circumstances, is to keep cool. If the great American people only keep their temper on both sides of the line, the troubles will come to an end, and the question which now distracts the country will be settled, just as surely as all other difficulties of a like character which have originated in this Government have been adjusted. Let the people on both sides keep their self-possession, and just as other clouds have cleared away in due time, so will this great nation continue to prosper as heretofore. But, fellow-citizens, I have spoken longer on this subject than I intended at the outset.

It is often said that the Tariff is the specialty of Pennsylvania. Assuming that direct taxation is not to be adopted, the Tariff question must be as durable as the Government itself. It is a question of national housekeeping. It is to the Government what replenishing the meal-tub is to the family. Every varying circumstance will require frequent modifications as to the amount needed, and the sources of supply. So far there is little difference of opinion among the people. It is only whether, and how far, the duties on imports shall be adjusted to favor home productions. In the home market that controversy begins. One party insists that too much protection oppresses one class for the advantage of another, while the other party argues that with all its incidents, in the long run, all classes are benefited. In the Chicago Platform there is a plank upon this subject, which should be a general law to the incoming Administration. We should do neither more nor less than we gave the people reason to believe we would when they gave us their votes. That plank is as I now read:

Mr. LINCOLN'S private secretary then read section twelfth of the Chicago Platform, as follows:

> That while providing revenue for the support of the General Government, by duties upon imports, sound policy requires such an adjustment of these imports as will encourage the development of the industrial interest of the whole country; and we commend that policy of national exchanges which secures to working-men liberal wages—to agriculture remunerating prices—to mechanics and manufacturers adequate reward for their skill, labor, and enterprise; and to the nation commercial prosperity and independence.

Mr. LINCOLN resumed: As with all general propositions, doubtless there will be shades of difference in construing this. I have by no means a thoroughly matured judgment upon this subject, especially as to details; some general ideas are about all. I have long thought to produce any necessary article at home which can be made of as good quality and with as little labor at home as abroad, would be better policy, at least by the difference of the carrying from abroad. In such a case the carrying is demonstrably a dead loss of labor. For instance, labor being the true standard of value, is it not plain that if equal labor gets a bar of railroad iron out of a mine in England, and another out of a mine in Pennsylvania, each can be laid down in a track at home cheaper than they could exchange countries, at least by the cost of carriage? If there be a present cause why one can be both made and carried cheaper in money price than the other can be made without carrying, that cause is an unnatural and injurious one, and ought naturally if not rapidly to be removed. The condition of the treasury at this time would seem to render an early revision of the Tariff indispensable. The Morrill Tariff bill, now pending before Congress, may or may not become a law. I am not posted as to its particular provisions, but if they are generally satisfactory and the bill shall now pass, there will be an end of the matter for the present. If, however, it shall not pass, I suppose the whole subject will be one of the most pressing and important for the next Congress. By the Constitution, the Executive may recommend measures which he may think proper, and he may veto those he thinks improper, and it is supposed that he may add to these certain indirect influences to affect the action of Congress. My political education strongly inclines me against a very free use of any of these means by the Executive to control the legislation of the country. As a rule, I think it better that Congress should originate as well as perfect its measures without external bias. I, therefore, would rather recommend to every gentleman who knows he is to be a member of the next Congress, to take an enlarged view, and inform himself thoroughly, so as to contribute his part to such an adjustment of the tariff as shall produce a sufficient revenue, and in its other bearings, so far as possible, be just and equal to all sections of the country and all classes of the people.

Mr. LINCOLN left Pittsburg immediately after the delivery of this speech, being accompanied to the dépôt by a long procession of the people of the city. The train reached Cleveland at half-past four in the afternoon, and the President-elect was received by a long procession, which marched, amidst the roar of artillery, through the principal streets to the Weddell House, where Mr. LINCOLN, in reply to an address of welcome from the Mayor, made the following remarks:

MR. CHAIRMAN AND FELLOW-CITIZENS OF CLEVELAND: We have been marching about two miles through snow, rain, and deep mud. The large numbers that have turned out under these circumstances testify that you are in earnest about something or other. But do I think so meanly of you as to suppose that that earnestness is about me personally? I would be doing you injustice to suppose it was. You have assembled to testify your respect to the Union and the Constitution and the laws. And here let me state that it is with you, the people, to advance the great cause of the Union and the Constitution, and not with any one man. It rests with you alone. This fact is strongly impressed on my mind at present. In a community like this, whose appearance testifies to their intelligence, I am convinced that the cause of liberty and the Union can never be in danger. Frequent allusion is made to the excitement at present existing in our national politics, and it is as well that I should also allude to it here. I think that there is no occasion for any excitement. The crisis, as it is called, is altogether an artificial crisis. In all parts of the nation there are differences of opinion on politics. There are differences of opinion even here. You did not all vote for the person who now addresses you. What is happening now will not hurt those who are further away from here. Have they not all their rights now as they ever have had? Do not they have their fugitive slaves returned now as ever? Have they not the same Constitution that they have lived under for seventy odd years? Have they not a position as citizens of this common country, and have we any power to change that position? [Cries of "No."] What, then, is the matter with them? Why all this excitement? Why all these complaints? As I said before, this crisis is all artificial! It has no foundation in fact. It was not "argued up," as the saying is, and cannot therefore be argued down. Let it alone, and it will go down of itself. [Laughter.] Mr. LINCOLN said that they must be content with but a few words from him. He was very much fatigued, and had spoken so much that he was already hoarse. He thanked them for the cordial and magnificent reception they had given him. Not less did he thank them for the votes they gave him last fall; and quite as much he thanked them for the efficient aid they had given the cause which he represented—a cause which he would say was a good one.

He had one more word to say. He was given to understand that this reception was tendered not only by his own party supporters, but by men of all parties. This is as it should be. If Judge Douglas had been elected, and had been here, on his way to Washington, as I am to-night, the Republicans should have joined his supporters in welcoming him, just as his friends have joined with mine to-night. If all do not join now to save the good old ship of the Union on this voyage, nobody will have a chance to pilot her on another voyage. He concluded by thanking all present for the devotion they had shown to the cause of the Union.

On the morning of the 16th the Presidential party left Cleveland for Buffalo. At Erie, where they dined, loud calls were made upon Mr. LINCOLN for a speech, in response to which he made a few remarks, excusing himself for not expressing his opinions on the exciting questions of the day. He trusted that when the time for speaking should come, he should find it necessary to say nothing not in accordance with the Constitution, as well as with the interests of the people of the whole country. At Northeast Station he took occasion to state that during the campaign he had received a letter from a young girl of the place, in which he was kindly admonished to do certain things, and among others to let his whiskers grow; and, as he had acted upon that piece of advice, he would now be glad to welcome his fair correspondent, if she was among the crowd. In response to the call a lassie made her way through the crowd, was helped on the platform, and was kissed by the President.

Arriving at Buffalo, Mr. LINCOLN had the utmost difficulty to make his way through the dense crowd which had assembled in anticipation of his arrival. On reaching the American Hotel, he was welcomed in a brief speech by Acting-Mayor Bemis, to which he responded as follows:

MR. MAYOR AND FELLOW-CITIZENS OF BUFFALO AND THE STATE OF NEW YORK: I am here to thank you briefly for this grand reception given to me, not personally, but as the representative of our great and beloved country. [Cheers.] Your worthy Mayor has been pleased to mention, in his address to me, the fortunate and agreeable journey which I have had from home, only it is a rather circuitous route to the Federal capital. I am very happy that he was enabled in truth to congratulate myself and company on that fact. It is true we have had nothing thus far to mar the pleasure of the trip. We have not been met alone by those who assisted in giving the election to me; I say not alone by them, but by the whole population of the country through which we have passed. This is as it should be. Had the election fallen to any other of the distinguished candidates instead of myself, under the peculiar circumstances, to say the least, it would have been proper for all citizens to have greeted him as you now greet me. It is an evidence of the devotion of the whole people to the Constitution, the Union, and the perpetuity of the liberties of this country. [Cheers.] I am unwilling on any occasion that I should be so meanly thought of as to have it supposed for a moment that these demonstrations are tendered to me personally. They are tendered to the country, to the institutions of the country, and to the perpetuity of the liberties of the country, for which these institutions were made and created.

Your worthy Mayor has thought fit to express the hope that I may be able to relieve the country from the present, or, I should say, the threatened difficulties. I am sure I bring a heart true to the work. [Tremendous applause.] For the ability to perform it, I must trust in that Supreme Being who has never forsaken this favored land, through the instrumentality of this great and intelligent people. Without that assistance I shall surely fail; with it I cannot fail. When we speak of threatened difficulties to the country, it is natural that it should be expected that something should be said by myself with regard to particular measures. Upon more mature reflection, however—and others will agree with me—that, when it is considered that these difficulties are without precedent, and never have been acted upon by any individual situated as I am, it is most proper I should wait and see the developments, and get all the light possible, so that when I do speak authoritatively, I may be as near right as possible. [Cheers.] When I shall speak authoritatively, I hope to say nothing inconsistent with the Constitution, the Union, the rights of all the States, of each State, and of each section of the country, and not to disappoint the reasonable expectations of those who have confided to me their votes. In this connection allow me to say that you, as a portion of the great American people, need only to maintain your composure, stand up to your sober convictions of right, to your obligations to the Constitution, and act in accordance with those sober convictions, and the clouds which now arise in the horizon will be dispelled, and we shall have a bright and glorious future; and when this generation has passed away, tens of thousands will inhabit this country where only thousands inhabit it now. I do not propose to address you at length; I have no voice for it. Allow me again to thank you for this magnificent reception, and bid you farewell.

Mr. LINCOLN remained at Buffalo over Sunday, the 17th, and on the morning of the 18th left for Albany. On reaching Rochester he was introduced by the Mayor to a crowd of several thousands, to whom he said:

I confess myself, after having seen many large audiences since leaving home, overwhelmed with this vast number of faces at this hour of the morning. I am not vain enough to believe that you are here from any wish to see me as an individual, but because I am for the time being the representative of the American people. I could not, if I would, address you at any length. I have not the strength, even if I had the time, for a speech at each of these many interviews that are afforded me on my way to Washington. I appear merely to see you, and to let you see me, and to bid you farewell. I hope it will be understood that it is from no disinclination to oblige anybody that I do not address you at greater length."

At Syracuse, where preparations had been made to give him a formal reception, he made the following remarks in reply to an address of welcome from the Mayor:

LADIES AND GENTLEMEN: I see you have erected a very fine and handsome platform here for me, and I presume you expected me to speak from it. If I should go upon it, you would imagine that I was about to deliver you a much longer speech than I am. I wish you to understand that I mean no discourtesy to you by thus declining. I intend discourtesy to no one. But I wish you to understand that, though I am unwilling to go upon this platform, you are not at liberty to draw any inferences concerning any other platform with which my name has been or is connected. [Laughter and applause.] I wish you long life and prosperity individually, and pray that with the perpetuity of those institutions under which we have all so long lived and prospered, our happiness may be secured, our future made brilliant, and the glorious destiny of our country established forever. I bid you a kind farewell.

At Utica, where an immense and most enthusiastic assemblage of people from the surrounding country had gathered to see him, Mr. LINCOLN contented himself by saying:

LADIES AND GENTLEMEN: I have no speech to make to you, and no time to speak in. I appear before you that I may see you, and that you may see me; and I am willing to admit, that so far as the ladies are concerned, I have the best of the bargain, though I wish it to be understood that I do not make the same acknowledgment concerning the men. [Laughter and applause.]

The train reached Albany at half-past two in the afternoon, where Mr. LINCOLN was formally received by the Mayor in a complimentary address, to which he thus replied:

MR. MAYOR: I can hardly appropriate to myself the flattering terms in which you communicate the tender of this reception, as personal to myself. I most gratefully accept the hospitalities tendered to me, and will not detain you or the audience with any extended remarks at this time. I presume that in the two or three courses through which I shall have to go, I shall have to repeat somewhat, and I will therefore only repeat to you my thanks for this kind reception.

A procession was then formed, which escorted Mr. LINCOLN to the steps of the Capitol, where he was welcomed by the Governor, in presence of an immense mass of the people, whom he addressed as follows:

MR. GOVERNOR: I was pleased to receive an invitation to visit the capital of the great Empire State of the nation, on my way to the Federal Capital, and I now thank you, Mr. Governor, and the people of this capital, and the people of the State of New York, for this most hearty and magnificent welcome. If I am not at fault, the great Empire State at this time contains a greater population than did the United States of America at the time she achieved her national independence. I am proud to be invited to pass through your capital and meet them, as I now have the honor to do.

I am notified by your Governor that this reception is given without distinction of party. I accept it the more gladly because it is so. Almost all men in this country, and in any country where freedom of thought is tolerated, attach themselves to political parties. It is but ordinary charity to attribute this to the fact that in so attaching himself to the party which his judgment prefers, the citizen believes he thereby promotes the best interests of the whole country; and when an election is passed, it is altogether befitting a free people that, until the next election, they should be as one people. The reception you have extended to me to-day is not given to me personally. It should not be so, but as the representative for the time being of the majority of the nation. If the election had resulted in the selection of either of the other candidates, the same cordiality should have been extended to him as is extended to me this day, in testimony of the devotion of the whole people to the Constitution and the whole Union, and of their desire to perpetuate our institutions, and to hand them down in their perfection to succeeding generations.

I have neither the voice nor the strength to address you at any greater length. I beg you will accept my most grateful thanks for this devotion—not to me, but to this great and glorious free country.

Mr. LINCOLN was then escorted to the Hall of Assembly, and was formally received on behalf of the members of the Legislature, to whom he made the following address:

MR. PRESIDENT AND GENTLEMEN OF THE LEGISLATURE OF THE STATE OF NEW YORK: It is with feelings of great diffidence, and, I may say, with feelings of awe, perhaps greater than I have recently experienced, that I meet you here in this place. The history of this great State, the renown of those great men who have stood here, and spoke here, and been heard here, all crowd around my fancy, and incline me to shrink from any attempt to address you. Yet I have some confidence given me by the generous manner in which you have invited me, and by the still more generous manner in which you have received me, to speak further. You have invited and received me without distinction of party. I cannot for a moment suppose that this has been done in any considerable degree with reference to my personal services, but that it is done in so far as I am regarded at this time as the representative of the majesty of this great nation. I doubt not this is the truth, and the whole truth, of the case, and this is as it should be. It is much more gratifying to me that this reception has been given to me as the representative of a free people, than it could possibly be if tendered as an evidence of devotion to me, or to any one man personally. And now I think it were more fitting that I should close these hasty remarks. It is true that, while I hold myself, without mock modesty, the humblest of all individuals that have ever been elevated to the Presidency, I have a more difficult task to perform than any one of them. You have generously tendered me the united support of the great Empire State. For this, in behalf of the nation—in behalf of the present and future of the nation—in behalf of civil and religious liberty for all time to come, most gratefully do I thank you. I do not propose to enter into an explanation of any particular line of policy, as to our present difficulties, to be adopted by the incoming Administration. I deem it just to you, to myself, and to all, that I should see every thing, that I should hear every thing, that I should have every light that can be brought within my reach, in order that when I do so speak, I shall have enjoyed every opportunity to take correct and true grounds; and for this reason I don't propose to speak, at this time, of the policy of the Government. But when the time comes I shall speak, as well as I am able, for the good of the present and future of this country—for the good both of the North and the South of this country—for the good of the one and the other, and of all sections of the country. [Rounds of applause.] In the mean time, if we have patience, if we restrain ourselves, if we allow ourselves not to run off in a passion, I still have confidence that the Almighty, the Maker of the Universe, will, through the instrumentality of this great and intelligent people, bring us through this as he has through all the other difficulties of our country. Relying on this, I again thank you for this generous reception." [Applause and cheers.]

On the morning of the 19th Mr. Lincoln went to Troy, and, in reply to the welcome of the Mayor, said:

"Mr. Mayor and Citizens of Troy: I thank you very kindly for this great reception. Since I left my home it has not been my fortune to meet an assemblage more numerous and more orderly than this. I am the more gratified at this mark of your regard since you assure me it is tendered, not to the individual, but to the high office you have called me to fill. I have neither strength nor time to make any extended remarks, and I can only repeat to you my sincere thanks for the kind reception you have thought proper to extend to me."

On the route to New York, by the Hudson River Railroad, very large crowds of people had assembled at the various stations, to welcome him. At Hudson he spoke as follows:

FELLOW-CITIZENS: I see that you have provided a platform, but I shall have to decline standing on it. [Laughter and applause.] The superintendent tells me I have not time during our brief stay to leave the train. I had to decline standing on some very handsome platforms prepared for me yesterday. But I say to you, as I said to them, you must not on this account draw the inference that I have any intention to desert any platform I have a legitimate right to stand on. I do not appear before you for the purpose of making a speech. I come only to see you, and to give you the opportunity to see me, and I say to you, as I have before said to crowds where there are so many handsome ladies as there are here, I think I have decidedly the best of the bargain. I have only, therefore, to thank you most cordially for this kind reception, and bid you all farewell.

At Poughkeepsie, where great preparations had been made for his reception, he responded thus to an address from the Mayor:

FELLOW-CITIZENS: It is altogether impossible I should make myself heard by any considerable portion of this vast assemblage; but, although I appear before you mainly for the purpose of seeing you, and to let you see, rather than hear me, I cannot refrain from saying that I am highly gratified,—as much here, indeed, under the circumstances, as I have been anywhere on my route,—to witness this noble demonstration—made, not in honor of an individual, but of the man who at this time humbly, but earnestly, represents the majesty of the nation. This reception, like all others that have been tendered to me, doubtless emanates from all the political parties, and not from one alone. As such I accept it the more gratefully, since it indicates an earnest desire on the part of the whole people, without regard to political differences, to save—not the country, because the country will save itself—but to save the institutions of the country—those institutions under which, in the last three-quarters of a century, we have grown to be a great, an intelligent, and a happy people—the greatest, the most intelligent, and the happiest people in the world. These noble manifestations indicate, with unerring certainty, that the whole people are willing to make common cause for this object; that if, as it ever must be, some have been successful in the recent election, and some have been beaten,—if some are satisfied, and some are dissatisfied, the defeated party are not in favor of sinking the ship, but are desirous of running it through the tempest in safety, and willing, if they think the people have committed an error in their verdict now, to wait in the hope of reversing it, and setting it right next time. I do not say that in the recent election the people did the wisest thing that could have been done; indeed, I do not think they did; but I do say, that in accepting the great trust committed to me, which I do with a determination to endeavor to prove worthy of it, I must rely upon you, upon the people of the whole country, for support; and with their sustaining aid, even I, humble as I am, cannot fail to carry the ship of State safely through the storm.

I have now only to thank you warmly for your kind attendance, and bid you all an affectionate farewell.

At Peekskill, in reply to a brief address from Judge Nelson, he said:

LADIES AND GENTLEMEN: I have but a moment to stand before you, to listen to and return your kind greeting. I thank you for this reception and for the pleasant manner in which it is tendered to me, by our mutual friend. I will say in a single sentence, in regard to the difficulties that lie before me and our beloved country, that if I can only be as generously and unanimously sustained, as the demonstrations I have witnessed indicate I shall be, I shall not fail; but without your sustaining hands I am sure that neither I, nor any other man, can hope to surmount these difficulties. I trust that in the course I shall pursue I shall be sustained, not only by the party that elected me, but by the patriotic people of the whole country.

The President-elect reached New York at 3 o'clock, and was received by an immense demonstration of popular enthusiasm. Places of business were generally closed, and the streets were filled with people, eager to catch a glimpse of his person. On reaching the Astor House, he was compelled by the importunity of the assembled crowd to appear on the balcony, from which he said:

FELLOW-CITIZENS: I have stepped before you merely in compliance with what appears to be your wish, and not with the purpose of making a speech. I do not propose making a speech this afternoon. I could not be heard by any but a small fraction of you at best; but, what is still worse than that, I have nothing just now to say that is worthy of your hearing. [Applause.] I beg you to believe that I do not now refuse to address you from any disposition to disoblige you, but to the contrary. But, at the same time, I beg of you to excuse me for the present.

In the evening, Mr. LINCOLN received a large deputation from the various Republican associations which had taken an active part in the election canvass, and in reply to a brief welcome from Mr. E. D. Smith, on their behalf, he thus addressed them:

MR. CHAIRMAN AND GENTLEMEN: I am rather an old man to avail myself of such an excuse as I am now about to do. Yet the truth is so distinct, and presses itself so distinctly upon me, that I cannot well avoid it—and that is, that I did not understand when I was brought into this room that I was brought here to make a speech. It was not intimated to me that I was brought into the room where DANIEL WEBSTER and HENRY CLAY had made speeches, and where, in my position, I might be expected to do something like those men, or do something worthy of myself or my audience. I, therefore, will beg you to make very great allowance for the circumstances in which I have been by surprise brought before you. Now, I have been in the habit of thinking and speaking sometimes upon political questions that have for some years past agitated the country; and, if I were disposed to do so, and we could take up some one of the issues, as the lawyers call them, and I were called upon to make an argument about it to the best of my ability, I could do so without much preparation. But, that is not what you desire to be done here to-night.

I have been occupying a position since the Presidential election of silence, of avoiding public speaking, of avoiding public writing. I have been doing so, because I thought, upon full consideration, that was the proper course for me to take. [Great applause.] I am brought before you now, and required to make a speech, when you all approve more than any thing else of the fact that I have been keeping silence. [Great laughter, cries of "Good," and applause.] And now it seems to me that the response you give to that remark ought to justify me in closing just here. [Great laughter.] I have not kept silence since the Presidential election from any party wantonness, or from any indifference to the anxiety that pervades the minds of men about the aspect of the political affairs of this country. I have kept silence for the reason that I supposed it was peculiarly proper that I should do so until the time came when, according to the custom of the country, I could speak officially.

A Voice—The custom of the country?

I heard some gentleman say "According to the custom of the country." I alluded to the custom of the President-elect, at the time of taking the oath of office. That is what I meant by "the custom of the country." I do suppose that, while the political drama being enacted in this country, at this time, is rapidly shifting its scenes—forbidding an anticipation, with any degree of certainty, to-day, what we shall see to-morrow—it was peculiarly fitting that I should see it all, up to the last minute, before I should take ground that I might be disposed (by the shifting of the scenes afterwards) also to shift. [Applause.] I have said, several times, upon this journey, and I now repeat it to you, that when the time does come, I shall then take the ground that I think is right—[applause]—the ground that I think is right—[applause, and cries of "Good, good"]—right for the North, for the South, for the East, for the West, for the whole country. [Cries of "Good," "Hurrah for LINCOLN," and applause.] And in doing so, I hope to feel no necessity pressing upon me to say any thing in conflict with the Constitution; in conflict with the continued union of these States—[applause]—in conflict with the perpetuation of the liberties of this people—[applause]—or any thing in conflict with any thing whatever that I have ever given you reason to expect from me. [Applause.] And now, my friends, have I said enough? [Loud cries of "No, no," and three cheers for LINCOLN.] Now, my friends, there appears to be a difference of opinion between you and me, and I really feel called upon to decide the question myself. [Applause, during which Mr. LINCOLN descended from the table.]

On the morning of the 20th Mr. LINCOLN proceeded to the City Hall, where it had been arranged that he should have an official reception. He was there addressed by Mayor Wood in the following terms:

MR. LINCOLN: As Mayor of New York, it becomes my duty to extend to you an official welcome in behalf of the Corporation. In doing so permit me to say, that this city has never offered hospitality to a man clothed with more exalted powers, or resting under graver responsibilities, than those which circumstances have devolved upon you.

Coming into office with a dismembered Government to reconstruct, and a disconnected and hostile people to reconcile, it will require a high patriotism, and an elevated comprehension of the whole country and its varied interests, opinions, and prejudices, to so conduct public affairs as to bring it back again to its former harmonious, consolidated, and prosperous condition. If I refer to this topic, sir, it is because New York is deeply interested. The present political divisions have sorely afflicted her people. All her material interests are paralyzed. Her commercial greatness is endangered. She is the child of the American Union. She has grown up under its maternal care, and been fostered by its paternal bounty, and we fear that if the Union dies, the present supremacy of New York may perish with it. To you, therefore, chosen under the forms of the Constitution as the head of the Confederacy, we look for a restoration of fraternal relations between the States—only to be accomplished by peaceful and conciliatory means, aided by the wisdom of Almighty God.

To this address Mr. LINCOLN made the following reply:

MR. MAYOR: It is with feelings of deep gratitude that I make my acknowledgments for the reception that has been given me in the great commercial city of New York. I cannot but remember that it is done by the people, who do not, by a large majority, agree with me in political sentiment. It is the more grateful to me, because in this I see that for the great principles of our Government the people are pretty nearly or quite unanimous. In regard to the difficulties that confront us at this time, and of which you have seen fit to speak so becomingly and so justly, I can only say that I agree with the sentiments expressed. In my devotion to the Union I hope I am behind no man in the nation. As to my wisdom in conducting affairs so as to tend to the preservation of the Union, I fear too great confidence may have been placed in me. I am sure I bring a heart devoted to the work. There is nothing that could ever bring me to consent—willingly to consent—to the destruction of this Union (in which not only the great city of New York, but the whole country, has acquired its greatness), unless it would be that thing for which the Union itself was made. I understand that the ship is made for the carrying and preservation of the cargo; and so long as the ship is safe with the cargo, it shall not be abandoned. This Union shall never be abandoned, unless the possibility of its existence shall cease to exist, without the necessity of throwing passengers and cargo overboard. So long, then, as it is possible that the prosperity and liberties of this people can be preserved within this Union, it shall be my purpose at all times to preserve it. And now, Mr. Mayor, renewing my thanks for this cordial reception, allow me to come to a close. [Applause.]

On the morning of Thursday, the 21st, Mr. LINCOLN left New York for Philadelphia, and on reaching Jersey City was met and welcomed, on behalf of the State, by the Hon. W. L. Dayton, to whose remarks he made this reply:

MR. DAYTON AND GENTLEMEN OF THE STATE OF NEW JERSEY: I shall only thank you briefly for this very kind reception given me, not personally, but as the temporary representative of the majesty of the nation. [Applause.] To the kindness of your hearts, and of the hearts of your brethren in your State, I should be very proud to respond, but I shall not have strength to address you or other assemblages at length, even if I had the time to do so. I appear before you, therefore, for little else than to greet you, and to briefly say farewell. You have done me the very high honor to present your reception courtesies to me through your great man—a man with whom it is an honor to be associated anywhere, and in owning whom no State can be poor. [Applause.] He has said enough, and by the saying of it suggested enough, to require a response of an hour well considered. [Applause.] I could not in an hour make a worthy response to it. I therefore, ladies and gentlemen of New Jersey, content myself with saying, most heartily do I indorse all the sentiments he has expressed. [Applause.] Allow me, most gratefully, to bid you farewell. [Applause.]

At Newark he was welcomed by the Mayor, to whom he said:

MR. MAYOR: I thank you for this reception at the city of Newark. With regard to the great work of which you speak, I will say that I bring to it a heart filled with love for my country, and an honest desire to do what is right. I am sure, however, that I have not the ability to do any thing unaided of God, and that without his support, and that of this free, happy, prosperous, and intelligent people, no man can succeed in doing that the importance of which we all comprehend. Again thanking you for the reception you have given me, I will now bid you farewell, and proceed upon my journey.

At Trenton he was received by a committee of the Legislature, and escorted to both branches, which were in session. The President of the Senate welcomed him in a brief address, to which he made the following reply:

MR. PRESIDENT AND GENTLEMEN OF THE SENATE OF THE STATE OF NEW JERSEY: I am very grateful to you for the honorable reception of which I have been the object. I cannot but remember the place that New Jersey holds in our early history. In the early revolutionary struggle few of the States among the old thirteen had more of the battle-fields of the country within their limits than old New Jersey. May I be pardoned if, upon this occasion, I mention that away back in my childhood, the earliest days of my being able to read, I got hold of a small book, such a one as few of the younger members have ever seen, "WEEM'S *Life of Washington.*" I remember all the accounts there given of the battle-fields and struggles for the liberties of the country, and none fixed themselves upon my imagination so deeply as the struggle here at Trenton, New Jersey. The crossing of the river; the contest with the Hessians; the great hardships endured at that time, all fixed themselves on my memory, more than any single revolutionary event; and you all know, for you have all been boys, how these early impressions last longer than any others. I recollect thinking then, boy even though I was, that there must have been something more than common that these men struggled for. I am exceedingly anxious that that thing which they struggled for; that something even more than National Independence; that something that held out a great promise to all the people of the world to all time to come—I am exceedingly anxious that this Union, the Constitution, and the liberties of the people shall be perpetuated in accordance with the original idea for which that struggle was made, and I shall be most happy indeed if I shall be an humble instrument in the hands of the Almighty and of this, his most chosen people, as the chosen instrument—also in the hands of the Almighty—for perpetuating the object of that great struggle. You give me this reception, as I understand, without distinction of party. I learn that this body is composed of a majority of gentlemen who, in the exercise of their best judgment in the choice of a Chief Magistrate, did not think I was the man. I understand, nevertheless, that they come forward here to greet me as the constitutional President of the United States—as citizens of the United States to meet the man who, for the time being, is the representative man of the nation—united by a purpose to perpetuate the Union and liberties of the people. As such, I accept this reception more gratefully than I could do did I believe it was tendered to me as an individual.

Mr. LINCOLN then passed to the Assembly Chamber, where, in reply to the Speaker, he said:

MR. SPEAKER AND GENTLEMEN: I have just enjoyed the honor of a reception by the other branch of this Legislature, and I return to you and them my thanks for the reception which the people of New Jersey have given through their chosen representatives to me as the representative, for the time being, of the majesty of the people of the United States. I appropriate to myself very little of the demonstrations of respect with which I have been greeted. I think little should be given to any man, but that it should be a manifestation of adherence to the Union and the Constitution. I understand myself to be received here by the representatives of the people of New Jersey, a majority of whom differ in opinion from those with whom I have acted. This manifestation is, therefore, to be regarded by me as expressing their devotion to the Union, the Constitution, and the liberties of the people. You, Mr. Speaker, have well said that this is a time when the bravest and wisest look with doubt and awe upon the aspect presented by our national affairs. Under these circumstances, you will readily see why I should not speak in detail of the course I shall deem it best to pursue. It is proper that I should avail myself of all the information and all the time at my command, in order that when the time arrives in which I must speak officially, I shall be able to take the ground which I deem the best and safest, and from which I may have no occasion to swerve. I shall endeavor to take the ground I deem most just to the North, the East, the West, the South, and the whole country. I take it, I hope, in good temper, certainly with no malice towards any section. I shall do all that may be in my power to promote a peaceful settlement of all our difficulties. The man does not live who is more devoted to peace than I am. [Cheers.] None who would do more to preserve it, but it may be necessary to put the foot down firmly. [Here the audience broke out into cheers so loud and long, that for some moments it was impossible to hear Mr. LINCOLN's voice.] And if I do my duty and do right you will sustain me, will you not? [Loud cheers, and cries of "Yes, yes, we will."] Received, as I am, by the members of a Legislature, the majority of whom do not agree with me in political sentiments, I trust that I may have their assistance in piloting the ship of State through this voyage, surrounded by perils as it is, for if it should suffer wreck now, there will be no pilot ever needed for another voyage. Gentlemen, I have already spoken longer than I intended, and must beg leave to stop here.

The procession then moved to the Trenton House, where the President-elect made the following speech to the crowd outside:

I have been invited by your representatives to the Legislature, to visit this, the Capital of your honored State, and in acknowledging their kind invitation, compelled to respond to the welcome of the presiding officers of each body, and I suppose they intended I should speak to you through them, as they are the representatives of all of you; and if I was to speak again here, I should only have to repeat, in a great measure, much that I have said, which would be disgusting to my friends around me who have met here. I have no speech to make, but merely appear to see you and let you look at me, and as to the latter I think I have greatly the best of the bargain. [Laughter.] My friends, allow me to bid you farewell.

The party arrived at Philadelphia at 4 o'clock, and the President-elect, proceeding immediately to the Continental Hotel, was welcomed in a brief speech from Mayor Henry, to which he replied as follows:

Mr. Mayor and Fellow-Citizens of Philadelphia: I appear before you to make no lengthy speech, but to thank you for this reception, The reception you have given me to-night is not to me, the man, the individual, but to the man who temporarily represents, or should represent the majesty of the nation. [Cheers.] It is true, as your worthy Mayor has said, that there is anxiety amongst the citizens of the United States at this time. I deem it a happy circumstance that this dissatisfied position of our fellow-citizens does not point us to any thing in which they are being injured, or about to be injured, for which reason I have felt all the while justified in concluding that the crisis, the panic, the anxiety of the country at this time, is artificial. If there be those who differ with we upon this subject, they have not pointed out the substantial difficulty that exists. I do not mean to say that an artificial panic may not do considerable harm: that it has done such I do not deny. The hope that has been expressed by your Mayor, that I may be able to restore peace, harmony, and prosperity to the country, is most worthy of him; and happy, indeed, will I be if I shall be able to verify and fulfil that hope. [Tremendous cheering.] I promise you, in all sincerity, that I bring to the work a sincere heart. Whether I will bring a head equal to that heart will be for future times to determine. It were useless for me to speak of details of plans now; I shall speak officially next Monday week, if ever. If I should not speak then it were useless for me to do so now. If I do speak then it is useless for me to do so now. When I do speak I shall take such ground as I deem best calculated to restore peace, harmony, and prosperity to the country, and tend to the perpetuity of the nation and the liberty of these States and these people. Your worthy Mayor has expressed the wish, in which I join with him, that it were convenient for me to remain in your city long enough to consult your merchants and manufacturers; or as it were, to listen to those breathings rising within the consecrated walls wherein the Constitution of the United States, and I will add the Declaration of Independence, were originally framed and adopted. [Enthusiastic applause.] I assure you and your Mayor that I had hoped on this occasion, and upon all occasions during my life, that I shall do nothing inconsistent with the teachings of these holy and most sacred walls. I never asked any thing that does not breathe from those walls. All my political warfare has been in favor of the teachings that came forth from these sacred walls. May my right hand forget its cunning, and my tongue cleave to the roof of my mouth, if ever I prove false to those teachings. Fellow-citizens, I have addressed you longer than I expected to do, and now allow me to bid you good night.

On the 21st Mr. LINCOLN visited the old Independence Hall, from which was originally issued the Declaration of Independence. He was received in a cordial speech by Mr. Theodore Cuyler, to which he made the following response:

MR. CUYLER: I am filled with deep emotion at finding myself standing here in this place, where were collected together the wisdom, the patriotism, the devotion to principle from which sprang the institutions under which we live. You have kindly suggested to me that in my hands is the task of restoring peace to the present distracted condition of the country. I can say in return, sir, that all the political sentiments

I entertain have been drawn, so far as I have been able to draw them, from the sentiments which originated in and were given to the world from this hall. I have never had a feeling, politically, that did not spring from the sentiments embodied in the Declaration of Independence. I have often pondered over the dangers which were incurred by the men who assembled here, and framed and adopted that Declaration of Independence. I have pondered over the toils that were endured by the officers and soldiers of the army who achieved that Independence. I have often inquired of myself what great principle or idea it was that kept this Confederacy so long together. It was not the mere matter of the separation of the Colonies from the mother land, but that sentiment in the Declaration of Independence which gave liberty, not alone to the people of this country, but, I hope, to the world, for all future time. [Great applause.] It was that which gave promise that in due time the weight would be lifted from the shoulders of all men. This is the sentiment embodied in the Declaration of Independence. Now, my friends, can this country be saved upon that basis? If it can, I will consider myself one of the happiest men in the world if I can help to save it. If it cannot be saved upon that principle it will be truly awful. But if this country cannot be saved without giving up that principle, I was about to say I would rather be assassinated on this spot than surrender it. [Applause.] Now, in my view of the present aspect of affairs, there need be no bloodshed or war. There is no necessity for it. I am not in favor of such a course, and I may say in advance that there will be no bloodshed, unless it be forced upon the Government, and then it will be compelled to act in self-defence. [Applause.]

My friends, this is wholly an unexpected speech, and I did not expect to be called upon to say a word when I came here. I supposed it was merely to do something towards raising the flag—I may, therefore, have said something indiscreet. [Cries of "No, no."] I have said nothing but what I am willing to live by, and if it be the pleasure of Almighty God, die by.

One object of the visit to the Hall was, to have Mr. LINCOLN assist in raising the national flag over the Hall. Arrangements had been made for the performance of this ceremony, and Mr. Lincoln was escorted to the platform prepared for the purpose, and was invited, in a brief address, to raise the flag. He responded in a patriotic speech, announcing his cheerful compliance with the request. He alluded to the original flag of thirteen stars, saying that the number had increased as time rolled on and we became a happy, powerful people, each star adding to its prosperity. The future is in the hands of the people. It was on such an occasion we could reason together, reaffirm our devotion to the country and the principles of the Declaration of Independence. Let us make up our minds, said he, that whenever we do put a new star upon our banner, it shall be a fixed one, never to be dimmed by the horrors of war, but brightened by the contentment and prosperity of peace. Let us go on to extend the area of our usefulness, and add star upon star until their light shall shine over five hundred millions of free and happy people. He then performed his part in the ceremony, amidst a thundering discharge of artillery.

In the afternoon he left for the West. On reaching Lancaster he was received with a salute, and replied to an address of welcome in the following words:

LADIES AND GENTLEMEN OF OLD LANCASTER: I appear not to make a speech. I have not time to make a speech at length, and not strength to make them on every occasion, and worse than all I have none to make. There is plenty of matter to speak about in these times, but it is well known that the more a man speaks the less he is understood—the more he says one thing, the more his adversaries contend he meant something else. I shall soon have occasion to speak officially, and then I will endeavor to put my thoughts just as plain as I can express myself—true to the Constitution and Union of all the States, and to the perpetual liberty of all the people. Until I so speak, there is no need to enter upon details. In conclusion, I greet you most heartily, and bid you an affectionate farewell.

On reaching Harrisburg, on the 22d, Mr. LINCOLN was escorted to the Legislature, and was welcomed by the presiding officers of the two houses, to whom he replied as follows:

I appear before you only for a very few, brief remarks, in response to what has been said to me. I thank you most sincerely for this reception and the generous words in which support has been promised me upon this occasion. I thank your great Commonwealth for the overwhelming support it recently gave, not me personally, but the cause which I think a just one, in the late election. [Loud applause.] Allusion has been made to the fact—the interesting fact, perhaps, we should say—that I for the first time appear at the Capital of the great Commonwealth of Pennsylvania upon the birthday of the Father of his Country, in connection with that beloved anniversary connected with the history of this country. I have already gone through one exceedingly interesting scene this morning in the ceremonies at Philadelphia. Under the high conduct of gentlemen there, I was for the first time allowed the privilege of standing in old Independence Hall [Enthusiastic cheering], to have a few words addressed to me there, and opening up to me an opportunity of expressing, with much regret, that I had not more time to express something of my own feelings, excited by the occasion, somewhat to harmonize and give shape to the feelings that had been really the feelings of my whole life, Besides this, our friends there had provided a magnificent flag of the country. They had arranged it so that I was given the honor of raising it to the head of its staff. [Applause.] And when it went up I was pleased that it went to its place by the strength of my own feeble arm, when, according to the arrangement, the cord was pulled, and it floated gloriously to the wind, without an accident, in the light, glowing sunshine of the morning. I could not help hoping that there was, in the entire success of that beautiful ceremony, at least something of an omen of what is to come. [Loud applause.] How could I help feeling then as I often have felt? In the whole of that proceeding I was a very humble instrument. I had not provided the flag; I had not made the arrangements for elevating it to its place; I had applied but a very small portion of my feeble strength in raising it. In the whole transaction I was in the hands of the people who had arranged it, and if I can have the same generous co-operation of the people of the nation, I think the flag of our country may yet be kept flaunting gloriously. [Loud, enthusiastic, and continued cheers.] I recur for a moment but to repeat some words uttered at the hotel, in regard to what has been said about the military support which the General Government may expect from the Commonwealth of Pennsylvania in a proper emergency. To guard against any possible mistake do I recur to this. It is not with any pleasure that I contemplate the possibility that a necessity may arise in this country for the use of the military arm. [Applause.] While I am exceedingly gratified to see the manifestation upon your streets of your military force here, and exceedingly gratified at your promises here to use that force upon a proper emergency—while I make these acknowledgments, I desire to repeat, in order to preclude any possible misconstruction, that I do most sincerely hope that we shall have no use for them. [Applause.] That it will never become their duty to shed blood, and most especially never to shed fraternal blood. I promise that, so far as I may have wisdom to direct, if so painful a result shall in anywise be brought about, it shall be through no fault of mine. [Cheers.] Allusion has also been made by one of your honored speakers to some remarks recently made by myself at Pittsburg, in regard to what is supposed to be the especial interest of this great Commonwealth of Pennsylvania. I now wish only to say, in regard to that matter, that the few remarks which I uttered on that occasion were rather carefully worded. I took pains that they should be so. I have seen no occasion since to add to them, or subtract from them. I leave them precisely as they stand [applause], adding only now that I am pleased to have an expression from you, gentlemen of Pennsylvania, significant that they are satisfactory to you. And now, gentlemen of the General Assembly of the Commonwealth of Pennsylvania, allow me to return you again my most sincere thanks.

After the delivery of this address, Mr. LINCOLN devoted some hours to the reception of visitors, and at six o'clock retired to his room. The next morning the whole country was surprised to learn that he had arrived in Washington—twelve hours sooner than he had originally intended. His sudden departure proved to have been a measure of precaution for which events subsequently disclosed afforded a full justification. For some time previous to his departure from home, the rumor had been current that he would never reach the Capital alive. An attempt was made on the Toledo and Western Railroad, on the 11th of February, to throw from the track the train on which he was journeying, and just as he was leaving Cincinnati a hand grenade was found to have been secreted on board the cars. These and other circumstances led to an organized and thorough investigation, under the direction of a police detective, carried on with great skill and perseverance at Baltimore, and which resulted in disclosing the fact that a small gang of assassins, under the leadership of an Italian who assumed the name of Orsini, had arranged to take his life during his passage through Baltimore. Gen. Scott and Mr. Seward had both been apprised of the same fact through another source, and they had sent Mr. F. W. Seward as a special messenger to Philadelphia, to meet the President-elect there, previous to his departure for Harrisburg, and give him notice of these circumstances. Mr. LINCOLN did not deviate from the programme he had marked out for himself, in consequence of these communications; except that, under the advice of friends, he deemed it prudent to anticipate by one train the time he was expected to arrive in Washington. He reached there on the morning of Saturday, the 23d.

On Wednesday, the 27th, the Mayor and Common Council of the city waited upon Mr. LINCOLN, and tendered him a welcome. He replied to them as follows:

MR. MAYOR: I thank you, and through you the municipal authorities of this city who accompany you, for this welcome. And as it is the first time in my life since the present phase of politics has presented itself in this country, that I have said any thing publicly within a region of country where the institution of slavery exists, I will take this occasion to say, that I think very much of the ill-feeling that has existed and still exists between the people in the sections from which I came and the people here, is dependent upon a misunderstanding of one another. I therefore avail myself of this opportunity to assure you, Mr. Mayor, and all the gentlemen present, that I have not now, and never have had, any other than as kindly feelings towards you as the people of my own section. I have not now, and never have had, any disposition to treat you in any respect otherwise than as my own neighbors. I have not now any purpose to withhold from you any of the benefits of the Constitution, under any circumstances, that I would not feel myself constrained to withhold from my own neighbors; and I hope, in a word, that when we shall become better acquainted, and I say it with great confidence, we shall like each other the more. I thank you for the kindness of this reception.

On the next evening a serenade was given to Mr. LINCOLN

by the members of the Republican Association, and he then addressed the crowd which the occasion had brought together, as follows:

MY FRIENDS: I suppose that I may take this as a compliment paid to me, and as such please accept my thanks for it. I have reached this city of Washington under circumstances considerably differing from those under which any other man has ever reached it. I am here for the purpose of taking an official position amongst the people, almost all of whom were politically opposed to me, and are yet opposed to me, as I suppose.

I propose no lengthy address to you. I only propose to say, as I did on yesterday, when your worthy Mayor and Board of Aldermen called upon me, that I thought much of the ill feeling that has existed between you and the people of your surroundings and that people from among whom I came, has depended, and now depends, upon a misunderstanding.

I hope that, if things shall go along as prosperously as I believe we all desire they may, I may have it in my power to remove something of this misunderstanding; that I may be enabled to convince you, and the people of your section of the country, that we regard you as in all things our equals, and in all things entitled to the same respect and the same treatment that we claim for ourselves; that we are in nowise disposed, if it were in our power, to oppress you, to deprive you of any of your rights under the Constitution of the United States, or even narrowly to split hairs with you in regard to these rights, but are determined to give you, as far as lies in our hands, all your rights under the Constitution—not grudgingly, but fully and fairly. [Applause.] I hope that, by thus dealing with you, we will become better acquainted, and be better friends.

And now, my friends, with these few remarks, and again returning my thanks for this compliment, and expressing my desire to hear a little more of your good music, I bid you good night.

This closed Mr. LINCOLN'S public speeches down to the date of his inauguration.

CHAPTER III.

FROM THE INAUGURATION TO THE MEETING OF CONGRESS, JULY 4, 1861.

On the 4th of March, 1861, Mr. Lincoln took the oath and assumed the duties of the Presidential office. He was quite right in saying, on the eve of his departure from his home in Springfield, that those duties were greater than had devolved upon any other man since the days of Washington. A conspiracy which had been on foot for thirty years had reached its crisis. Yet in spite of all that had been done by the leading spirits in this movement, the people of the slaveholding States were by no means a unit in its support. Seven of those States, South Carolina, Georgia, Alabama, Mississippi, Texas, Florida, and Louisiana, had passed secession ordinances and united in the establishment of a hostile Confederacy; but in nearly all of them a considerable portion of the people were opposed to the movement, while in all the remaining slaveholding States a very active canvass was carried on between the friends and the opponents of secession. In Maryland, Virginia, Kentucky, and Tennessee especially, the Government of the United States was vindicated and its authority sustained by men of pre-eminent ability and of commanding reputation, and there seemed abundant reason for hoping that, by the adoption of prudent measures, the slaveholding section might be divided and the Border Slave States retained in the Union. The authorities of the rebel Confederacy saw the importance of pushing the issue to an instant decision. Under their directions nearly all the forts, arsenals, dock-yards, custom-houses, etc., belonging to the United States, within the limits of the seceded States, had been seized and were held by representatives of the rebel government. The only forts in the South which remained in possession of the Union, were Forts Pickens, Taylor, and Jefferson on the Florida coast, and Fort Sumter in Charleston harbor, and preparations were far advanced for the reduction and capture of these. Officers of the army and navy from the South had resigned their commissions and entered the rebel service. Civil officers representing the United States within the limits of the Southern States could no longer discharge their functions, and all the powers of that Government were practically paralyzed.

It was under these circumstances that Mr. LINCOLN entered upon the duties of his office, and addressed himself to the task, first, of withholding the Border States from joining the Confederacy, as an indispensable preliminary to the great work of quelling the rebellion and restoring the authority of the Constitution.

The ceremony of inauguration took place as usual in front of the Capitol and in presence of an immense multitude of spectators. A large military force was in attendance under the immediate command of General Scott, but nothing occurred to interrupt the harmony of the occasion. Before taking the oath of office Mr. LINCOLN delivered the following

INAUGURAL ADDRESS.

Fellow-Citizens of the United States:

In compliance with a custom as old as the Government itself, I appear before you to address you briefly, and to take in your presence the oath prescribed by the Constitution of the United States to be taken by the President "before he enters on the execution of his office."

I do not consider it necessary at present for me to discuss those matters of administration about which there is no special anxiety or excitement.

Apprehension seems to exist among the people of the Southern States that by the accession of a Republican Administration their property and their peace and personal security are to be endangered.

There has never been any reasonable cause for such apprehension. Indeed, the most ample evidence to the contrary has all the while existed and been open to their inspection. It is found in nearly all the published speeches of him who now addresses you. I do but quote from one of those speeches when I declare that "I have no purpose, directly or indirectly, to interfere with the institution of slavery in the States where it exists. I believe I have no lawful right to do so, and I have no inclination to do so." Those who nominated and elected me did so with full knowledge that I had made this and many similar declarations, and had never recanted them. And more than this, they placed in the platform for my acceptance, and as a law to themselves and to me, the clear and emphatic resolution which I now read:

Resolved, That the maintenance inviolate of the rights of the States, and especially the right of each State, to order and control its own domestic institutions according to its own judgment exclusively, is essential to the balance of power on which the perfection and endurance of our political fabric depend, and we denounce the lawless invasion by armed force of the soil of any State or Territory, no matter under what pretext, as among the gravest of crimes.

I now reiterate these sentiments; and, in doing so, I only press upon the public attention the most conclusive evidence of which the case is susceptible, that the property, peace, and security of no section are to be in anywise endangered by the now incoming Administration. I add, too, that all the protection which, consistently with the Constitution and the laws, can be given, will be cheerfully given to all the States, when lawfully demanded, for whatever cause—as cheerfully to one section as to another.

There is much controversy about the delivering up of fugitives from service or labor. The clause I now read is as plainly written in the Constitution as any other of its provisions:

No person held to service or labor in one State, under the laws thereof, escaping into another, shall, in consequence of any law or regulation therein, be discharged from such service or labor, but shall be delivered up on claim of the party to whom such service or labor may be due.

It is scarcely questioned that this provision was intended by those who made it for the reclaiming of what we call fugitive slaves; and the intention of the lawgiver is the law. All members of Congress swear their support to the whole Constitution—to this provision as much as any other. To the proposition, then, that slaves, whose cases come within the terms of this clause, "shall be delivered up," their oaths are unanimous. Now, if they would make the effort in good temper, could they not, with nearly equal unanimity, frame and pass a law by means of which to keep good that unanimous oath?

There is some difference of opinion whether this clause should be enforced by National or by State authority; but surely that difference is not a very material one. If the slave is to be surrendered, it can be of but little consequence to him, or to others, by which authority it is done. And should any one, in any case, be content that his oath shall go unkept, on a mere unsubstantial controversy as to how it shall be kept?

Again, in any law upon this subject, ought not all the safeguards of liberty known in civilized and humane jurisprudence to be introduced, so that a free man be not, in any case, surrendered as a slave? And might it not be well, at the same time, to provide by law for the enforcement of that clause in the Constitution which guarantees that "the citizens of each State shall be entitled to all privileges and immunities of citizens in the several States?"

I take the official oath to-day with no mental reservations, and with no purpose to construe the Constitution or laws by any hypercritical rules. And while I do not choose now to specify particular acts of Congress as proper to be enforced, I do suggest that it will be much safer for all, both in official and private stations, to conform to and abide by all those acts which stand unrepealed, than to violate any of them, trusting to find impunity in having them held to be unconstitutional.

It is seventy-two years since the first inauguration of a President under our National Constitution. During that period, fifteen different and greatly distinguished citizens have, in succession, administered the Executive branch of the Government. They have conducted it through many perils, and generally with great success. Yet, with all this scope for precedent, I now enter upon the same task for the brief constitutional term of four years, under great and peculiar difficulty. A disruption of the Federal Union, heretofore only menaced, is now formidably attempted.

I hold that, in contemplation of universal law, and of the Constitution, *the Union of these States is perpetual.* Perpetuity is implied, if not expressed, in the fundamental law of all National Governments. It is safe to assert that no Government proper ever had a provision in its organic law for its own termination. Continue to execute all the express provisions of our National Constitution, and the Union will endure forever—

it being impossible to destroy it, except by some action not provided for in the instrument itself.

Again, if the United States be not a Government proper, but an association of States in the nature of contract merely, can it, as a contract, be peaceably unmade by less than all the parties who made it? One party to a contract may violate it—break it, so to speak; but does it not require all to lawfully rescind it?

Descending from these general principles, we find the proposition that, in legal contemplation, the Union is perpetual, confirmed by the history of the Union itself. The Union is much older than the Constitution. It was formed, in fact, by the Articles of Association in 1774. It was matured and continued by the Declaration of Independence in 1776. It was further matured, and the faith of all the then Thirteen States expressly plighted and engaged that it should be perpetual, by the Articles of Confederation in 1778. And, finally, in 1787, one of the declared objects for ordaining and establishing the Constitution was "to form a more perfect union."

But if destruction of the Union, by one, or by a part only, of the States, be lawfully possible, the Union is less perfect than before, the Constitution having lost the vital element of perpetuity.

It follows, from these views, that no State, upon its own mere motion, can lawfully get out of the Union; that resolves and ordinances to that effect are legally void; and that acts of violence within any State or States, against the authority of the United States, are insurrectionary or revolutionary, according to circumstances.

I, therefore, consider that, in view of the Constitution and the laws, the Union is unbroken, and to the extent of my ability I shall take care, as the Constitution itself expressly enjoins upon me, that the laws of the Union be faithfully executed in all the States. Doing this I deem to be only a simple duty on my part; and I shall perform it, so far as practicable, unless my rightful masters, the American people, shall withhold the requisite means, or, in some authoritative manner, direct the contrary. I trust this will not be regarded as a menace, but only as the declared purpose of the Union that it will constitutionally defend and maintain itself.

In doing this there need be no bloodshed or violence; and there shall be none, unless it be forced upon the national authority. The power confided to me will be used to hold, occupy, and possess the property and places belonging to the Government, and to collect the duties and imposts; but beyond what may be but necessary for these objects, there will be no invasion, no using of force against or among the people anywhere. Where hostility to the United States, in any interior locality, shall be so great and universal as to prevent competent resident citizens from holding the Federal offices, there will be no attempt to force obnoxious strangers among the people for that object. While the strict legal right may exist in the Government to enforce the exercise of these offices, the attempt to do so would be so irritating, and so nearly impracticable withal, I deem it better to forego, for the time, the uses of such offices.

The mails, unless repelled, will continue to be furnished in all parts of the Union. So far as possible, the people everywhere shall have that sense of perfect security which is most favorable to calm thought and reflection. The course here indicated will be followed, unless current events and experience shall show a modification or change to be proper, and in every case and exigency my best discretion will be exercised, according to circumstances actually existing, and with a view and a hope of a peaceful solution of the national troubles, and the restoration of fraternal sympathies and affections.

That there are persons in one section or another who seek to destroy the Union at all events, and are glad of any pretext to do it, I will neither affirm nor deny; but if there be such, I need address no word to them. To those, however, who really love the Union, may I not speak?

Before entering upon so grave a matter as the destruction of our national fabric, with all its benefits, its memories, and its hopes, would it not be wise to ascertain precisely why we do it? Will you hazard so desperate a step while there is any possibility that any portion of the ills you fly from have no real existence? Will you, while the certain ills you fly to are greater than all the real ones you fly from—will you risk the commission of so fearful a mistake?

All profess to be content in the Union, if all constitutional rights can be maintained. Is it true, then, that any right, plainly written in the Constitution, has been denied? I think not. Happily the human mind is so constituted that no party can reach to the audacity of doing this. Think, if you can, of a single instance in which a plainly written provision of the Constitution has ever been denied. If, by the mere force of numbers, a majority should deprive a minority of any clearly written constitutional right, it might, in a moral point of view, justify revolution—certainly would if such right were a vital one. But such is not our case. All the vital rights of minorities and of individuals are so plainly assured to them by affirmations and negations, guarantees and prohibitions in the Constitution, that controversies never arise concerning them. But no organic law can ever be framed with a provision specifically applicable to every question which may occur in practical administration. No foresight can anticipate, nor any document of reasonable length contain, express provisions for all possible questions. Shall fugitives from labor be surrendered by National or by State authority? The Constitution does not expressly say. May Congress prohibit slavery in the Territories? The Constitution does not expressly say. Must Congress protect slavery in the Territories? The Constitution does not expressly say.

From questions of this class spring all our constitutional controversies, and we divide upon them into majorities and minorities. If the minority will not acquiesce the majority must, or the Government must cease. There is no other alternative; for continuing the Government is acquiescence on one side or the other. If a minority in such case will secede rather than acquiesce, they make a precedent which, in turn, will divide and ruin them; for a minority of their own will secede from them whenever a majority refuses to be controlled by such minority. For instance, why may not any portion of a new Confederacy, a year or two hence, arbitrarily secede again, precisely as portions of the present Union now claim to secede from it? All who cherish disunion sentiments are now being educated to the exact temper of doing this.

Is there such perfect identity of interests among the States to compose a new Union, as to produce harmony only, and prevent renewed secession?

Plainly, the central idea of secession is the essence of anarchy. A majority held in restraint by constitutional checks and limitations, and always changing easily with deliberate changes of popular opinions and sentiments, is the only true sovereign of a free people. Whoever rejects it, does, of necessity, fly to anarchy or to depotism. Unanimity is impossible; the rule of a minority, as a permanent arrangement, is wholly inadmissible; so that, rejecting the majority principle, anarchy or despotism in some form is all that is left.

I do not forget the position assumed by some, that constitutional questions are to be decided by the Supreme Court; nor do I deny that such decisions must be binding, in any case, upon the parties to a suit as to the object of that suit, while they are also entitled to very high respect and consideration in all parallel cases by all other departments of the Government. And while it is obviously possible that such decisions may be erroneous in any given case, still the evil effect following it being limited to that particular case, with the chance that it may be overruled, and never become a precedent for other cases, can better be borne than could the evils of a different practice. At the same time the candid citizen must confess that if the policy of the Government upon vital questions affecting the whole people, is to be irrevocably fixed by decisions of the Supreme Court, the instant they are made in ordinary litigation between parties in personal actions the people will have ceased to be their own rulers, having to that extent practically resigned their government into the hands of that eminent tribunal.

Nor is there is this view any assault upon the Court of the Judges. It is a duty from which they may not shrink to decide cases properly brought before them, and it is no fault of theirs if others seek to turn their decisions to political purposes. One section of our country believes slavery is right, and ought to be extended, while the other believes it is wrong, and ought not to be extended. This is the only substantial dispute. The fugitive slave clause of the Constitution, and the law for the suppression of the foreign slave-trade, are each as well enforced, perhaps, as any law can ever be in a community where the moral sense of the people imperfectly supports the law itself. The great body of the people abide by the dry legal obligation in both cases, and a few break over in each. This, I think, cannot be perfectly cured; and it would be worse in both cases after the separation of the sections than before. The foreign slave-trade, now imperfectly suppressed, would be ultimately revived without restriction in one section; while fugitive slaves, now only partially surrendered, would not be surrendered at all by the other.

Physically speaking, we cannot separate. We cannot remove our respective sections from each other, nor build an impassable wall between them. A husband and wife may be divorced, and go out of the presence and beyond the reach of each other; but the different parts of our country cannot do this. They cannot but remain face to face; and intercourse, either amicable or hostile, must continue between them. It is impossible, then, to make that intercourse more advantageous or more satisfactory after separation than before? Can aliens make treaties easier than friends can make laws? Can treaties be more faithfully enforced between aliens than laws can among friends? Suppose you go to war, you cannot fight always; and when, after much loss on both sides, and no gain on either, you cease fighting, the identical old questions, as to terms of intercourse, are again upon you.

This country, with its institutions, belongs to the people who inhabit it. Whenever they shall grow weary of the existing Government, they can exercise their constitutional right of amending it, or their revolutionary right to dismember or overthrow it. I cannot be ignorant of the fact that many worthy and patriotic citizens are desirous of having the national Constitution amended. While I make no recommendation of amendments, I fully recognize the rightful authority of the people over the whole subject, to be exercised in either of the modes prescribed in the instrument itself; and I should, under existing circumstances, favor rather than oppose a fair opportunity being afforded the people to act upon it. I will venture to add, that to me the convention mode seems preferable, in that it allows amendments to originate with the people themselves, instead of only permitting them to take or reject propositions originated by others not especially chosen for the purpose, and which might not be precisely such as they would wish to either accept or refuse. I understand a proposed amendment to the Constitution—which amendment, however, I have not seen—has passed Congress, to the effect that the Federal Government shall never interfere with the domestic institutions of the States, including that of persons held to service. To avoid misconstruction of what I have said, I depart from my purpose not to speak of particular amendments so far as to say that, holding such a provision now to be implied constitutional law, I have no objections to its being made express and irrevocable.

The Chief Magistrate derives all his authority from the people, and they have conferred none upon him to fix terms for the separation of the States. The people themselves can do this also if they choose; but the Executive, as such, has nothing to do with it. His duty is to administer the present Government as it came to his hands, and to transmit it, unimpaired by him, to his successor.

Why should there not be a patient confidence in the ultimate justice of the people? Is there any better or equal hope in the world? In our present differences, is either party without faith of being in the right? If the Almighty Ruler of Nations, with his eternal truth and justice, be on your side of the North, or on yours of the South, that truth and that justice will surely prevail, by the judgment of this great tribunal of the American people.

By the frame of the Government under which we live, the same people have wisely given their public servants but little power for mischief; and have, with equal wisdom, provided for the return of that little to their own hands at very short intervals. While the people retain their virtue and vigilance, no Administration, by any extreme of wickedness or folly, can very seriously injure the Government in the short space of four years.

My countrymen, one and all, think calmly and well upon this whole subject. Nothing valuable can be lost by taking time. If there be an object to hurry any of you in hot haste to a step which you would never take deliberately, that object will be frustrated by taking time; but no good object can be frustrated by it. Such of you as are now dissatisfied still have the old Constitution unimpaired, and, on the sensitive point, the laws of your own framing under it; while the new Administration will have no immediate power, if it would, to change either. If it were admitted that you who are dissatisfied hold the right side in the dispute, there still is no single good reason for precipitate action. Intelligence, patriotism, Christianity, and a firm reliance on Him who has never yet forsaken this favored land, are still competent to adjust, in the best way, all our present difficulty.

In your hands, my dissatisfied fellow-countrymen, and not in mine, is the momentous issue of civil war. The Government will not assail you.

You can have no conflict without being yourselves the aggressors. You have no oath registered in heaven to destroy the Government; while I shall have the most solemn one to "preserve, protect, and defend" it.

I am loth to close. We are not enemies, but friends. We must not be enemies. Though passion may have strained, it must not break our bonds of affection.

The mystic cord of memory, stretching from every battle-field and patriot grave to every living heart and hearthstone all over this broad land, will yet swell the chorus of the Union, when again touched, as surely they will be, by the better angels of our nature.

The declarations of the Inaugural, as a general thing, gave satisfaction to the loyal people of the whole country. It was seen, everywhere, that while President Lincoln felt constrained, by the most solemn obligations of duty, to maintain the authority of the Government of the United States over all the territory within its jurisdiction, whenever that authority should be disputed by the actual exercise of armed force, he would nevertheless do nothing whatever to provoke such a demonstration, and would take no step which could look like violence or offensive warfare upon the seceded States. In the Border States its reception was in the main satisfactory. But, as a matter of course, in those States, as elsewhere throughout the South, the secession leaders gave it the most hostile construction. No effort was spared to inflame the public mind by representing the Inaugural as embodying the purpose of the President to make war upon the Southern States for their attempt to secure a redress of wrongs.

The President's first act was to construct his Cabinet, which was done by the appointment of William H. Seward, of New York, Secretary of State; Salmon P. Chase, of Ohio, Secretary of the Treasury; Simon Cameron, of Pennsylvania, Secretary of War; Gideon Welles, of Connecticut, Secretary of the Navy; Caleb B. Smith, of Indiana, Secretary of the Interior; Montgomery Blair, of Maryland, Postmaster-General; and Edward Bates, of Missouri, Attorney-General. These nominations were all confirmed by the Senate, and these gentlemen entered upon the discharge of the duties of their several offices.

On the 12th of March, Messrs. John Forsyth, of Alabama, and Crawford, of Georgia, requested an unofficial interview with the Secretary of State, which the latter declined. On the 13th they sent to him a communication informing him that they were in Washington as Commissioners from a government composed of seven States which had withdrawn from the American Union, and that they desired to enter upon negotiations for the adjustment of all questions growing out of this separation. Mr. Seward, by direction of the President, declined to receive them, because it "could not be admitted that the States referred to had, in law or fact, withdrawn from the Federal Union, or that they could do so in any other manner than with the consent and concert of the people of the United States, to be given through a National Convention to be assembled in conformity with the provisions of the Constitution of the United States." This communication, though written on the 15th of March, was withheld, with the consent of the Commissioners, until the 8th of April, when it was delivered. The fact of its receipt, and its character, were instantly telegraphed to Charleston, and it was made the occasion for precipitating the revolution by an act which, it was believed, would unite all the Southern States in support of the Confederacy. On the day of its receipt, the 8th of April, Gen. Beauregard, at Charleston, telegraphed to L. P. Walker, the rebel Secretary of War, at Montgomery, that "an authorized messenger from President Lincoln had just informed Gov. Pickens and himself that provisions would be sent to Fort Sumter peaceably, or, otherwise, by force." Gen. B. was instructed to demand the surrender of the fort, which he did on the 11th, and was at once informed by Major Anderson, who was in command, that his "sense of honor and his obligations to his Government prevented his compliance." On the night of the same day Gen. Beauregard wrote to Major Anderson, by orders of his government, that if he "would state the time at which he would evacuate Fort Sumter" (as it was known that it must soon be evacuated for lack of provisions) "and will agree that, in the mean time, you will not use your guns against us unless ours shall be employed against Fort Sumter, we will abstain from opening fire upon you." At half-past two in the morning of the 12th, Major Anderson replied that he would evacuate the fort by noon on the 15th, abiding, mean time, by the terms proposed, unless he should "receive, prior to that, controlling instructions from his Government, or additional supplies." In reply to this note he was notified, at half-past three, that the rebels would open their batteries upon the fort in one hour from that time. This they did, and, after a bombardment of thirty-three hours, Major Anderson agreed to evacuate the fort, which he carried into effect on Sunday morning, the 14th.

The effect of this open act of war was, in some respects, precisely what had been anticipated by the rebel authorities: in other respects, it was very different. Upon the Southern States it had the effect of arousing public sentiment to the highest pitch of enthusiasm, and of strengthening the rebel cause. At the North, it broke down, for the moment, all party distinctions and united the people in a cordial and hearty support of the Government.

The President regarded it as an armed attack upon the Government of the United States, in support of the combination which had been organized into a Confederacy to resist and destroy its authority, and he saw, at once, that it could be met and defeated only by the force placed in his hands for the maintenance of that authority. He, accordingly, on the 15th of April, issued the following

PROCLAMATION.

By the President of the United States.

WHEREAS, the laws of the United States have been for some time past and now are opposed, and the execution thereof obstructed, in the States of South Carolina, Georgia, Alabama, Florida, Mississippi, Louisiana, and Texas, by combinations too powerful to be suppressed by the ordinary course of judicial proceedings, or by the powers vested in the marshals by law: now, therefore, I, ABRAHAM LINCOLN, President of the United States, in virtue of the power in me vested by the Constitution and the laws, have thought fit to call forth, and hereby do call forth, the militia of the several States of the Union to the aggregate number of 75,000, in order to suppress said combinations, and to cause the laws to be duly executed.

The details for this object will be immediately communicated to the State authorities through the War Department. I appeal to all loyal citizens to favor, facilitate, and aid this effort to maintain the honor, the integrity, and existence of our national Union, and the perpetuity of popular government, and to redress wrongs already long enough endured. I deem it proper to say that the first service assigned to the forces hereby called forth, will probably be to repossess the forts, places, and property which have been seized from the Union; and in every event the utmost care will be observed, consistently with the objects aforesaid, to avoid any devastation, any destruction of, or interference with, property, or any disturbance of peaceful citizens of any part of the country; and I hereby command the persons composing the combinations aforesaid, to disperse and retire peaceably to their respective abodes, within twenty days from this date.

Deeming that the present condition of public affairs presents an extraordinary occasion, I do hereby, in virtue of the power in me vested by the Constitution, convene both houses of Congress. The Senators and Representatives are, therefore, summoned to assemble at their respective Chambers at twelve o'clock, noon, on Thursday, the fourth day of July next, then and there to consider and determine such measures as, in their wisdom, the public safety and interest may seem to demand.

In witness whereof, I have hereunto set my hand, and caused the seal of the United States to be affixed.

Done at the City of Washington, this fifteenth day of April, in the year of our Lord one thousand eight hundred and sixty-one, and of the independence of the United States the eighty-fifth.

ABRAHAM LINCOLN.

By tne President.

WILLIAM H. SEWARD, Secretary of State.

The issue of this Proclamation created the most intense enthusiasm throughout the country. Scarcely a voice was raised in any of the Northern States against this measure, which was seen to be one of absolute necessity and of self-defence on tho part of the Government. Every Northern State responded promptly to the President's demand, and from private persons, as well as by the Legislatures, men, arms, and money were offered, in unstinted profusion and with the most zealous alacrity, in support of the Government. Massachusetts was first in the field: and on the first day after the issue of the Proclamation, her Sixth Regiment, completely equipped, started from Boston for the National Capital. Two more regiments were also made ready, and took their departure within forty-eight hours. The Sixth Regiment, on its way to Washington, on the 19th, was attacked by a mob in Baltimore, carrying a secession flag, and several of its members were killed or severely wounded. This inflamed to a still higher point the excitement which already pervaded the country. The whole Northern section of the Union felt outraged that troops should be assailed and murdered on their way to protect the capital of the nation. In Maryland, where the Secession party was strong, there was also great excitement, and the Governor of the State and the Mayor of Baltimore united in urging, for prudential reasons, that no more troops should be brought through that city. To their representation the President made the following reply:

WASHINGTON, *April* 29, 1861.

Governor Hicks and Mayor Brown:

GENTLEMEN: Your letter by Messrs. Bond, Dobbin, and Brune is received. I tender you both my sincere thanks for your efforts to keep the peace in the trying situation in which you are placed.

For the future, troops must be brought here, but I make no point of bringing them through Baltimore. Without any military knowledge myself, of course I must leave details to General Scott. He hastily said this morning in the presence of these gentlemen, "March them around Baltimore and not through it." I sincerely hope the General, on fuller reflection, will consider this practical and proper, and that you will not object to it. By this a collision of the people of Baltimore with the troops will be avoided, unless they go out of their way to seek it. I hope you will exert your influence to prevent this.

Now and ever I shall do all in my power for peace consistently with the maintenance of the Government.

Your obedient servant,

A. LINCOLN.

And in further response to the same request from Governor Hicks, followed by a suggestion that the controversy between the North and South might be referred to Lord Lyons, the British minister, for arbitration, President Lincoln, through the Secretary of State, made the following reply:

DEPARTMENT OF STATE, *April* 22, 1861.

His Excellency Thos. H. Hicks, Governor of Maryland:

SIR: I have had the honor to receive your communication of this morning, in which you inform me that you have felt it to be your duty to advise the President of the United States to order elsewhere the troops then off Annapolis, and also that no more may be sent through Maryland; and that you have further suggested that Lord Lyons be requested to act as mediator between the contending parties in our country, to prevent the effusion of blood.

The President directs me to acknowledge the receipt of that communication, and to assure you that he has weighed the counsels it contains with the respect which he habitually cherishes for the Chief Magistrates of the several States, and especially for yourself. He regrets, as deeply as any magistrate or citizen of this country can, that demonstrations against the safety of the United States, with very extensive preparations for the effusion of blood, have made it his duty to call out the forces to which you allude.

The force now sought to be brought through Maryland, is intended for nothing but the defence of the capital. The President has necessarily confided the choice of the national highway which that force shall take in coming to this city to the Lieutenant-General commanding the Army of the United States, who, like his only predecessor, is not less distinguished for his humanity, than for his loyalty, patriotism, and distinguished public service.

The President instructs me to add, that the national highway thus selected by the Lieutenant-General, has been chosen by him, upon consultation with prominent magistrates and citizens of Maryland, as the one which, while a route is absolutely necessary, is farthest removed from the populous cities of the State, and with the expectation that it would therefore be the least objectionable one.

The President cannot but remember that there has been a time in the history of our country when a general of the American Union, with forces designed for the defence of its capital, was not unwelcome anywhere in the State of Maryland, and certainly not at Annapolis, then, as now, the capital of that patriotic State, and then, also, one of the capitals of the Union.

If eighty years could have obliterated all the other noble sentiments of that age in Maryland, the President would be hopeful, nevertheless, that there is one that would forever remain there and everywhere. That sentiment is, that no domestic contention whatever that may arise among the parties of this Republic, ought in any case to be referred to any foreign arbitrament, least of all to the arbitrament of a European monarchy.

I have the honor to be, with distinguished consideration, your Excellency's most obedient servant,

WILLIAM H. SEWARD.

At the President's request, the mayor of Baltimore, and a number of the leading influential citizens of Maryland, waited upon him at Washington, and had an open conference upon the condition of affairs in that State. The Mayor subsequently made the following report of the interview:

The President, upon his part, recognized the good faith of the city and State authorities, and insisted upon his own. He admitted the excited state of feeling in Baltimore, and his desire and duty to avoid the fatal consequences of a collision with the people. He urged, on the other hand, the absolute, irresistible necessity of having a transit through the State for such troops as might be necessary for the protection of the Federal Capital. *The protection of Washington*, he asseverated with great earnestness, was the sole object of concentrating troops there; and he protested that none of the troops brought through Maryland were intended for any purposes hostile to the State, or *aggressive* as against the Southern States. Being now unable to bring them up the Potomac in security, the Government must either bring them through Maryland or abandon the capital.

He called on General Scott for his opinion, which the General gave at length, to the effect that troops might be brought through Maryland, without going through Baltimore, by either carrying them from Perrysville to Annapolis, and thence by rail to Washington, or by bringing them to the Relay House on the Northern Central Railroad, and marching them to the Relay House on the Washington Railroad, and thence by rail to the Capital. If the people would permit them to go by either of those routes uninterruptedly, the necessity of their passing through Baltimore would be avoided. If the people would not permit them a transit thus remote from the city, they must select their own best route, and, if need be, fight their way through Baltimore—a result which the General earnestly deprecated.

The President expressed his hearty concurrence in the desire to avoid a collision, and said that no more troops should be ordered through Baltimore, if they were permitted to go interruptedly by either of the other routes suggested. In this disposition the Secretary of War expressed his participation.

Mayor Brown assured the President that the city authorities would use all lawful means to prevent their citizens from leaving Baltimore to attack the troops in passing at a distance; but he urged, at the same time, the impossibility of their being able to promise any thing more than their best efforts in that direction. The excitement was great, he told the President; the people of all classes were fully aroused, and it was impossible for any one to answer for the consequences of the presence of Northern troops anywhere within our borders. He reminded the President, also, that the jurisdiction of the city authorities was confined to their own population, and that he could give no promises for the people elsewhere, because he would be unable to keep them if given. The President frankly acknowledged this difficulty, and said that the Government would only ask the city authorities to use their best efforts with respect to those under their jurisdiction.

The interview terminated with the distinct assurance, on the part of the President, that no more troops would be sent through Baltimore unless obstructed in their transit in other directions, and with the understanding that the city authorities should do their best to restrain their own people.

In accordance with this understanding, troops were forwarded to Washington by way of Annapolis, until peace and order were restored in Baltimore, when the regular use of the highway through that city was resumed, and has been continued without interruption to the present time.

On the 19th of April the President issued the following proclamation, blockading the ports of the seceded States:

A PROCLAMATION, BY THE PRESIDENT OF THE UNITED STATES.

Whereas, an insurrection against the Government of the United States has broken out in the States of South Carolina, Georgia, Alabama, Florida, Mississippi, Louisiana, and Texas, and the laws of the United States for the collection of the revenue cannot be efficiently executed therein conformable to that provision of the Constitution which required duties to be uniform throughout the United States:

And *whereas* a combination of persons, engaged in such insurrection, have threatened to grant pretended letters of marque, to authorize the bearers thereof to commit assaults on the lives, vessels, and property of the good citizens of the country, lawfully engaged in commerce on the high seas, and in waters of the United States:

And *whereas* an Executive Proclamation has been already issued, requiring the persons engaged in these disorderly proceedings to desist therefrom, calling out a militia force for the purpose of repressing the same, and convening Congress in extraordinary session to deliberate and determine thereon:

Now, therefore, I, ABRAHAM LINCOLN, President of the United States, with a view to the same purposes before mentioned, and to the protection of the public peace, and the lives and property of quiet and orderly citizens pursuing their lawful occupations, until Congress shall have assembled and deliberated on the said unlawful proceedings, or until the same shall have ceased, have further deemed it advisable to set on foot a blockade of the ports within the States aforesaid, in pursuance of the laws of the United States and of the laws of nations in such cases provided. For this purpose, a competent force will be posted so as to prevent entrance and exit of vessels from the ports aforesaid. If, therefore, with a view to violate such blockade, a vessel shall approach, or shall attempt to leave any of the said ports, she will be duly warned by the commander of one of the blockading vessels, who will endorse on her register the fact and date of such warning; and if the same vessel shall again attempt to enter or leave the blockaded port, she will be captured and sent to the nearest convenient port, for such proceedings against her and her cargo as prize as may be deemed advisable.

And I hereby proclaim and declare, that if any person, under the pretended authority of such States, or under any other pretence, shall molest a vessel of the United States, or the persons or cargo on board of her, such persons will be held amenable to the laws of the United States for the prevention and punishment of piracy.

By the President, ABRAHAM LINCOLN.

WILLIAM H. SEWARD, *Secretary of State.*

WASHINGTON, *April* 19, 1861.

These were the initial steps by which the Government sought to repel the attempt of the rebel Confederacy to overthrow its authority by force of arms. Its action was at that time wholly defensive. The declarations of rebel officials, as well as the language of the Southern press, indicated very clearly their intention to push the war begun at Sumter into the North. Jefferson Davis had himself declared, more than a month previous, that whenever the war should open, the North and not the South should be the field of battle. At a popular demonstration held at Montgomery, Ala., on hearing that fire had been opened upon Sumter, L. P. Walker, the rebel Secretary of War, had said, that while "no man could tell where the war would end, he would prophesy that the flag which now flaunts the breeze here, would float over the dome of the old capitol at Washington before the first of May," and that it "might float eventually over Faneuil Hall itself."

The rebel Government had gone forward with great vigor to prepare the means for making good these predictions. Volunteers was summoned to the field. Besides garrisoning the fortresses in their possession along the Southern coast, a force of nearly 20,000 men was pushed rapidly forward to Virginia. A loan of eight millions of dollars was raised, and Davis issued a proclamation offering letters of marque to all persons who might desire to aid the rebel Government and enrich themselves by depredations upon the rich and extended commerce of the United States. The South thus plunged openly and boldly into a war of aggression; and the President, in strict conformity with the declaration of his Inaugural, put the Government upon the defensive, and limited the military operations of the moment to the protection of the capital.

The effect of these preliminary movements upon the Border Slave States was very decided. The assault upon Sumter greatly excited the public mind throughout those States. In Virginia it was made to enure to the benefit of the rebels. The State Convention, which had been in session since the 13th of February, was composed of 152 delegates, a large majority of whom were Union men. The Inaugural of President Lincoln had created a good deal of excitement among the members, and a very animated contest had followed as to its proper meaning. The secessionists insisted that it announced a policy of coercion towards the South, and had seized the occasion to urge the immediate passage of an ordi nance of secession. This gave rise to a stormy debate, in which the friends of the Union maintained their ascendency. The news of the attack upon Sumter created a whirlwind of excitement, which checked somewhat the Union movement; and, on the 13th of April, Messrs. Preston, Stuart, and Randolph, who had been sent to Washington to ascertain the President's intentions towards the South, sent in their report, which was received just after Governor Pickens of South

Carolina had announced the attack upon Sumter, and had demanded to know what Virginia intended to do in the war they had just commenced, and in which they were determined to triumph or perish. The Commissioners reported that the President had made the following reply to their inquiries:

To Hon. Messrs. Preston, Stuart, and Randolph:

GENTLEMEN: As a committee of the Virginia Convention, now in session, you present me a preamble and resolution in these words:

Whereas, In the opinion of this Convention, the uncertainty which prevails in the public mind as to the policy which the Federal Executive intends to pursue towards the seceded States, is extremely injurious to the industrial and commercial interests of the country, tends to keep up an excitement which is unfavorable to the adjustment of the pending difficulties, and threatens a disturbance of the public peace; therefore,

Resolved, That a committee of three delegates be appointed to wait on the President of the United States, present to him this preamble, and respectfully ask him to communicate to this Convention the policy which the Federal Executive intends to pursue in regard to the Confederate States.

In answer I have to say, that having, at the beginning of my official term, expressed my intended policy as plainly as I was able, it is with deep regret and mortification I now learn there is great and injurious uncertainty in the public mind as to what that policy is, and what course I intend to pursue. Not having as yet seen occasion to change, it is now my purpose to pursue the course marked out in the Inaugural Address. I commend a careful consideration of the whole document as the best expression I can give to my purposes. As I then and therein said, I now repeat, "The power confided in me will be used to hold, occupy, and possess property and places belonging to the Government, and to collect the duties and imposts; but beyond what is necessary for these objects there will be no invasion, no using of force against or among the people anywhere." By the words "property and places belonging to the Government," I chiefly allude to the military posts and property which were in possession of the Government when it came into my hands. But if, as now appears to be true, in pursuit of a purpose to drive the United States authority from these places, an unprovoked assault has been made upon Fort Sumter, I shall hold myself at liberty to repossess it, if I can, like places which had been seized before the Government was devolved upon me; and in any event I shall, to the best of my ability, repel force by force. In case it proves true that Fort Sumter has been assaulted, as is reported, I shall, perhaps, cause the United States mails to be withdrawn from all the States which claim to have seceded, believing that the commencement of actual war against the Government justifies and possibly demands it. I scarcely need to say that I consider the military posts and property situated within the States which claim to have seceded, as yet belonging to the Government of the United States as much as they did before the supposed secession. Whatever else I may do for the purpose, I shall not attempt to collect the duties and imposts by any armed invasion of any part of the country; not meaning by this, however, that I may not land a force deemed necessary to relieve a fort upon the border of the country. From the fact that I have quoted a part of the Inaugural Address, it must not be inferred that I repudiate any other part, the whole of which I reaffirm, except so far as what I now say of the mails may be regarded as a modification.

ABRAHAM LINCOLN.

On the 17th, two days after this report was presented, and immediately after receiving the President's proclamation calling for troops, the Convention passed an ordinance of secession by a vote of 88 to 55; and Virginia, being thus the most advanced member of the rebel Confederacy, became the battle-field of all the earlier contests which ensued, and on the 21st of May the capital of the rebel government was transferred to Richmond. Very strenuous efforts were made by the rebel authorities to secure the adhesion of Maryland, Kentucky, Tennessee, and Missouri to the Confederacy; but the wise forbearance of the President in his earlier measures had checked these endeavors, and held all those States but Tennessee aloof from active participation in the secession movement.

The months of May and June were devoted to the most active and vigorous preparations on both sides for the contest which was seen to be inevitable. Over a hundred thousand troops had been raised and organized in the rebel States, and the great mass of them had been pushed forward toward the Northern border. On the 20th of April the Government of the United States seized all the despatches which had accumulated in the telegraph offices during the preceding year, for the purpose of detecting movements in aid of the rebel conspiracy. On the 27th of April the blockade of rebel ports was extended by proclamation to the ports of North Carolina and Virginia. On the 3d of May the President issued a proclamation calling into the service of the United States 42,034 volunteers for three years, and ordering an addition of 22,114 officers and men to the regular army, and 18,000 seamen to the navy. And on the 16th, by another proclamation, he directed the commander of the United States forces in Florida to "permit no person to exercise any office or authority upon the islands of Key West, the Tortugas, and Santa Rosa, which may be inconsistent with the laws and Constitution of the United States, authorizing him, at the same time, if he shall find it necessary, to suspend the writ of *habeas corpus*, and to remove from the vicinity of the United States fortresses all dangerous or suspected persons."

One of the first duties of the new Administration was to define the position to be taken by the Government of the United States towards foreign nations in view of the rebellion. While it is impossible to enter here upon this very wide branch of the general subject at any considerable length, this history would be incomplete if it did not state, in official language, the attitude which the President decided to assume. That is very distinctly set forth in the letter of instructions prepared by the Secretary of State for Mr. Adams, on the eve of his departure for the court of St. James, and dated April 10, in the following terms:

Before considering the arguments you are to use, it is important to indicate those which you are not to employ in executing that mission:

First. The President has noticed, as the whole American people have, with much emotion, the expressions of good-will and friendship towards the United States, and of concern for their present embarrassments, which have been made on apt occasions, by her Majesty and her ministers. You will make due acknowledgment for these manifestations, but at the same time you will not rely on any mere sympathies or national kindness. You will make no admissions of weakness in our Constitution, or of apprehension on the part of the Government. You will rather prove, as you easily can, by comparing the history of our country with that of other States, that its Constitution and Government are really the strongest and surest which have ever been erected for the safety of any people. You will in no case listen to any suggestions of compromise by this Government, under foreign auspices, with its discontented citizens. If, as the President does not at all apprehend, you shall unhappily find her Majesty's Government tolerating the application of the so-called seceding States, or wavering about it, you will not leave them to suppose for a moment that they can grant that application and remain the friends of the United States. You may even assure them promptly, in that case, that if they determine to recognize, they may at the same time prepare to enter into alliance with the enemies of this republic. You alone will represent your country at London, and you will represent the whole of it there. When you are asked to divide that duty with others, diplomatic relations between the Government of Great Britain and this Government will be suspended, and will remain so until it shall be seen which of the two is most strongly intrenched in the confidence of their respective nations and of mankind.

You will not be allowed, however, even if you were disposed, as the President is sure you will not be, to rest your opposition to the application of the Confederate States on the ground of any favor this Administration, or the party which chiefly called it into existence, proposes to show to Great Britain, or claims that Great Britain ought to show them. You will not consent to draw into debate before the British Government any opposing moral principles which may be supposed to lie at the foundation of the controversy between those States and the Federal Union.

You will indulge in no expressions of harshness or disrespect, or even impatience, concerning the seceding States, their agents, or their people. But you will, on the contrary, all the while remember that those States are now, as they always heretofore have been, and, notwithstanding their temporary self-delusion, they must always continue to be, equal and honored members of this Federal Union, and that their citizens throughout all political misunderstandings and alienations still are and always must be our kindred and countrymen. In short, all your arguments must belong to one of three classes, namely: *First.* Arguments drawn from the principles of public law and natural justice, which regulate the intercourse of equal States. *Secondly.* Arguments which concern equally the honor, welfare, and happiness of the discontented States, and the honor, welfare, and happiness of the whole Union. *Thirdly.* Arguments which are equally conservative of the rights and interests, and even sentiments of the United States, and just in their bearing upon the rights, interests, and sentiments of Great Britain and all other nations.

Just previous to the arrival of Mr. Adams at his post, the British Government determined, acting in concert with that of France, to recognize the rebels as a belligerent power. Against this recognition our Government directed Mr. Adams to make a decided and energetic protest. On the 15th of June the British and French ministers at Washington requested an interview with the Secretary of State for the purpose of reading to him certain instructions they had received on this subject from their respective governments. Mr. Seward declined to hear them officially until he knew the nature of the document, which was accordingly left with him for perusal, and he afterwards declined altogether to hear it read, or receive official notice of it. In a letter to Mr. Adams, on the 19th, he thus states its character and contents:

That paper purports to contain a decision at which the British Government has arrived, to the effect that this country is divided into two belligerent parties, of which this Government represents one, and that Great Britain assumes the attitude of a neutral between them.

This Government could not, consistently with a just regard for the sovereignty of the United States, permit itself to debate these novel and extraordinary positions with the Government of her Britannic Majesty; much less can we consent that that Government shall announce to us a decision derogating from that sovereignty, at which it has arrived without previously conferring with us upon the question. The United States are still solely and exclusively sovereign within the territories they have lawfully acquired and long possessed, as they have always been. They are at peace with all the world, as, with unimportant exceptions, they have always been. They are living under the obligations of the law of nations, and of treaties with Great Britain, just the same now as heretofore; they are, of course, the friend of Great Britain, and they insist that Great Britain shall remain their friend now, just as she has hitherto been. Great Britain, by virtue of these relations, is a stranger to parties and sections in this country, whether they are loyal to the United States or not, and Great Britain can neither rightfully qualify the sovereignty of the United States, nor concede, nor recognize any rights or interests or power of any party, State, or section, in contravention to the unbroken sovereignty of the Federal Union. What is now seen in this country is the occurrence, by no means peculiar, but frequent in all countries, more frequent even in Great Britain than here, of an armed insurrection engaged in attempting to overthrow the regularly constituted and established Government. There is, of course, the employment of force by the Government to suppress the insurrection, as every other government necessarily employs force in such cases. But these incidents by no means constitute a state of war impairing the sovereignty of the Government, creating belligerent sections, and entitling foreign States to intervene, or to act as neutrals between them, or in any other way to cast off their lawful obligations to the nation thus for the moment disturbed. Any other principle than this would be to resolve government everywhere into a thing of accident and caprice, and ultimately all human society into a state of perpetual war.

We do not go into any argument of fact or of law in support of the positions we have thus assumed. They are simply the suggestions of the instinct of self-defence, the primary law of human action—not more the law of individual than of national life.

Similar views were presented for the consideration of the French Emperor, and, indeed, of all the foreign governments with which we held diplomatic intercourse. The action of the seceding States was treated as rebellion, purely domestic in its character, upon the nature or merits of which it would be unbecoming in us to hold any discussion with any foreign power. The President pressed upon all those governments the duty of accepting this view of the question, and of abstaining, consequently, from every act which could be construed into any recognition of the rebel Confederacy, or which could embarrass the Government of the United States in its endeavors to re-establish its rightful authority. Especial pains were taken, by the most emphatic declarations, to leave no doubt in the mind of any foreign statesman as to the purpose of the people of the United States to accomplish that result. "You cannot be too decided or explicit," was the uniform language of the Secretary, "in making known to the government that there is not now, nor has there been, nor will there be, any the least idea existing in this Government of suffering a dissolution of this Union to take place in any way whatever." Efforts were also made by our Government to define, with the precision which the novel features of the case required, the law of nations in regard to neutral rights, and also to secure a general concurrence of the maritime powers in the principles of the Paris Convention of 1859: the latter object was, however, thwarted by the demand made by both

France and England, that they should not be required to abide by these principles in their application to the internal conflict which was going on in the United States. This demand the President pronounced inadmissible.

CHAPTER IV.

THE EXTRA SESSION OF CONGRESS, AND THE MILITARY EVENTS OF THE SUMMER OF 1861.

In pursuance of the President's proclamation of the 15th of April, Congress met in extra session on the 4th of July, 1861. The Republicans had control of both houses, counting 31 votes out of 48 in the Senate, and 106 out of 178 in the House, there being, moreover, 5 in the Senate and 28 in the House who, without belonging to the Republican party, supported the Administration in its efforts to preserve the Union. Hon. G. A. Grow was elected Speaker of the House; and, on the 5th, the President communicated to Congress his first annual message as follows:

Fellow-Citizens of the Senate and
House of Representatives:

Having been convened on an extraordinary occasion, as authorized by the Constitution, your attention is not called to any ordinary subject of legislation.

At the beginning of the present presidential term, four months ago, the functions of the Federal Government were found to be generally suspended within the several States of South Carolina, Georgia, Alabama, Mississippi, Louisiana, and Florida, excepting only those of the Post-Office Department.

Within these States all the forts, arsenals, dock-yards, custom-houses and the like, including the movable and stationary property in and about them, had been seized, and were held in open hostility to this Government, excepting only Forts Pickens, Taylor, and Jefferson, on and near the Florida coast, and Fort Sumter, in Charleston harbor, South Carolina. The forts thus seized had been put in improved condition, new ones had been built, and armed forces had been organized and were organizing, all avowedly with the same hostile purpose.

The forts remaining in the possession of the Federal Government in and near these States were either besieged or menaced by warlike preparations, and especially Fort Sumter was nearly surrounded by well-protected hostile batteries, with guns equal in quality to the best of its own, and outnumbering the latter as perhaps ten to one. A disproportionate share of the Federal muskets and rifles had somehow found their way into these States, and had been seized to be used against the Government. Accumulations of the public revenue, lying within them, had been seized for the same object. The Navy was scattered in distant seas, leaving but a very small part of it within the immediate reach of the Government. Officers of the Federal Army and Navy had resigned in great numbers; and of those resigning, a large proportion had taken up arms against the Government. Simultaneously, and in connection with all this, the purpose to sever the Federal Union was openly avowed. In accordance with this purpose, an ordinance had been adopted in each of these States, declaring the States, respectively, to be separated from the National Union. A formula for instituting a combined government of these States had been promulgated; and this illegal organization, in the character of Confederate States, was already invoking recognition, aid, and intervention from foreign Powers.

Finding this condition of things, and believing it to be an imperative duty upon the incoming Executive to prevent, if possible, the consummation of such attempt to destroy the Federal Union, a choice of means to that end became indispensable. This choice was made, and was declared in the Inaugural Address. The policy chosen looked to the exhaustion of all peaceful measures before a resort to any stronger ones. It sought only to hold the public places and property not already wrested from the Government, and to collect the revenue, relying for the rest on time, discussion, and the ballot-box. It promised a continuance of the mails, at Government expense, to the very people who were resisting the Government; and it gave repeated pledges against any disturbance to any of the people, or any of their rights. Of all that which a President might constitutionally and justifiably do in such a case, every thing was forborne, without which it was believed possible to keep the Government on foot.

On the 5th of March (the present incumbent's first full day in office, a letter of Major Anderson, commanding at Fort Sumter, written on the 28th of February, and received at the War Department on the 4th of March, was by that Department placed in his hands. This letter expressed the professional opinion of the writer, that re-enforcements could not be thrown into that fort within the time for his relief, rendered necessary by the limited supply of provisions, and with a view of holding possession of the same, with a force of less than twenty thousand good and well-disciplined men. This opinion was concurred in by all the officers of his command, and their *memoranda* on the subject were made enclosures of Major Anderson's letter. The whole was immediately laid before Lieutenant-General Scott, who at once concurred with Major Anderson in opinion. On reflection, however, he took full time, consulting with other officers, both of the army and the navy; and at the end of four days came reluctantly, but decidedly, to the same conclusion as before. He also stated at the same time that no such sufficient force was then at the control of the Government, or could be raised and brought to the ground within the time when the provisions in the fort would be exhausted. In a purely military point of view, this reduced the duty of the Administration in the case to the mere matter of getting the garrison safely out of the fort.

It was believed, however, that to so abandon that position, under the circumstances, would be utterly ruinous; that the necessity under which it was to be done would not be fully understood; that by many it would be construed as a part of a voluntary policy; that at home it would discourage the friends of the Union, embolden its adversaries, and go far to insure to the latter a recognition abroad; that, in fact, it would be our national destruction consummated. This could not be allowed. Starvation was not yet upon the garrison; and ere it would be reached Fort Pickens might be re-enforced. This would be a clear indication of policy, and would better enable the country to accept the evacuation of Fort Sumter as a military necessity. An order was at once directed to be sent for the landing of the troops from the steamship Brooklyn into Fort Pickens. This order could not go by land, but must take the longer and slower route by sea. The first return news from the order was received just one week before the fall of Fort Sumter. The news itself was that the officer commanding the Sabine, to which vessel the troops had been transferred from the Brooklyn, acting upon some *quasi* armistice of the late Administration (and of the existence of which the present Administration, up to the time the order was despatched, had only too vague and uncertain rumors to fix attention), had refused to land the troops. To now re-enforce Fort Pickens before a crisis would be reached at Fort Sumter was impossible—rendered so by the near exhaustion of provisions in the latter-named fort. In precaution against such a conjuncture, the Government had a few days before commenced preparing an expedition, as well adapted as might be, to relieve Fort Sumter, which expedition was intended to be ultimately used or not, according to circumstances. The strongest anticipated case for using it was now presented, and it was resolved to send it forward. As had been intended in this contingency, it was also resolved to notify the Governor of South Carolina that he might expect an attempt would be made to provision the fort; and that, if the attempt should not be resisted, there would be no effort to throw in men, arms, or ammunition, without further notice, or in case of an attack upon the fort. This notice was accordingly given; whereupon the fort was attacked and bombarded to its fall, without even awaiting the arrival of the provisioning expedition.

It is thus seen that the assault upon and reduction of Fort Sumter was in no sense a matter of self-defence upon the part of the assailants. They well knew that the garrison in the fort could by no possibility commit aggression upon them. They knew—they were expressly notified—that the giving of bread to the few brave and hungry men of the garrison was all which would on that occasion be attempted, unless themselves, by resisting so much, should provoke more. They knew that this Government desired to keep the garrison in the fort, not to assail them, but to maintain visible possession, and thus to preserve the Union from actual and immediate dissolution—trusting, as hereinbefore stated, to time, discussion, and the ballot-box for final adjustment; and they assailed and reduced the fort for precisely the reverse object—to drive out the visible authority of the Federal Union, and thus force it to immediate dissolution. That this was their object the Executive well understood; and having said to them in the Inaugural Address, "You can have no conflict without being yourselves the aggressors," he took pains not only to keep this declaration good, but also to keep the case so free from the power of ingenious sophistry that the world should not be able to misunderstand it. By the affair at Fort Sumter, with its surrounding circumstances, that point was reached. Then and thereby the assailants of the Government began the conflict of arms, without a gun in sight, or in expectancy to return their fire, save only the few in the fort, sent to that harbor years before for their own protection, and still ready to give that protection in whatever was lawful. In this act, discarding all else, they have forced upon the country the distinct issue, "immediate dissolution or blood."

And this issue embraces more than the fate of these United States. It presents to the whole family of man the question, whether a constitutional republic or democracy—a government of the people by the same people—can or cannot maintain its territorial integrity against its own domestic foes. It presents the question, whether discontented individuals, too few in numbers to control administration, according to organic law, in any case, can always, upon the pretences made in this case, or on any other pretences, or arbitrarily, without any pretence, break up their Government, and thus practically put an end to free government upon the earth. It forces us to ask, "Is there, in all republics, this inherent and fatal weakness?" "Must a government, of necessity, be too strong for the liberties of its own people, or too weak to maintain its own existence?"

So viewing the issue, no choice was left but to call out the war power of the Government; and so to resist force employed for its destruction, by force for its preservation.

The call was made, and the response of the country was most gratifying, surpassing in unanimity and spirit the most sanguine expectation. Yet none of the States commonly called Slave States, except Delaware, gave a regiment through regular State organization. A few regiments have been organized within some others of those States by individual enterprise, and received into the Government service. Of course, the seceded States, so called (and to which Texas had been joined about the time of the inauguration), gave no troops to the cause of the Union. The Border States, so called, were not uniform in their action, some of them being almost for the Union, while in others—as Virginia, North Carolina, Tennessee, and Arkansas—the Union sentiment was nearly repressed and silenced. The course taken in Virginia was the most remarkable—perhaps the most important. A convention, elected by the people of that State to consider this very question of disrupting the Federal Union, was in session at the capital of Virginia when Fort Sumter fell. To this body the people had chosen a large majority of professed Union men. Almost immediately after the fall of Sumter many members of that majority went over to the original disunion minority, and with them adopted an ordinance for withdrawing the State from the Union. Whether this change was wrought by their great approval of the assault upon Sumter, or their great resentment at the Government's resistance to that assault, is not definitely known. Although they submitted the ordinance for ratification to a vote of the people, to be taken on a day then somewhat more than a month distant, the Convention and the Legislature (which was also in session at the same time and place), with leading men of the State not members of either, immediately commenced acting as if the State were already out of the Union. They pushed military preparations vigorously forward all over the State. They seized the United States armory at Harper's Ferry, and the navy-yard at Gosport, near Norfolk. They received—perhaps invited—into their State large bodies of troops, with their warlike appointments, from the so-called seceded States. They formally entered into a treaty of temporary alliance and co-operation with the so-called "Confederate States," and sent members to their Congress at Montgomery; and, finally, they permitted the insurrectionary Government to be transferred to their capital at Richmond.

The people of Virginia have thus allowed this giant insurrection to make its nest within her borders; and this Government has no choice left but to deal with it where it finds it. And it has the less regret, as the loyal citizens have in due form claimed its protection. Those loyal citizens this Government is bound to recognize and protect as being Virginia.

In the Border States, so-called—in fact, the Middle States—there are those who favor a policy which they call "armed neutrality"—that is, an arming of those States to prevent the Union forces passing one way, or the disunion the other, over their soil. This would be disunion completed. Figuratively speaking, it would be the building of an impassable wall along the line of separation—and yet not quite an impassable one, for, under the guise of neutrality, it would tie the hands of Union men, and freely pass supplies from among them to the insurrectionists, which it could not do as an open enemy. At a stroke it would take all the trouble off the hands of secession, except only what proceeds from the external blockade. It would do for the disunionists that which of all things they most desire—feed them well, and give them disunion without a struggle of their own. It recognizes no fidelity to the Constitution, no obligation to maintain the Union; and while very many who have favored it are doubtless loyal citizens, it is, nevertheless, very injurious in effect.

Recurring to the action of the Government, it may be stated that at first a call was made for seventy five thousand militia; and rapidly following this, a proclamation was issued for closing the ports of the insurrectionary districts by proceedings in the nature of a blockade. So far all was believed to be strictly legal. At this point the insurrectionists announced their purpose to enter upon the practice of privateering.

Other calls were made for volunteers to serve for three years, unless sooner discharged, and also for large additions to the regular army and navy. These measures, whether strictly legal or not, were ventured upon under what appeared to be a popular demand and a public necessity; trusting then, as now, that Congress would readily ratify them. It is believed that nothing has been done beyond the constitutional competency of Congress.

Soon after the first call for militia, it was considered a duty to authorize the Commanding-General, in proper cases, according to his discretion, to suspend the privilege of the writ of habeas corpus, or, in other words, to arrest and detain, without resort to the ordinary processes and forms of law, such individuals as he might deem dangerous to the public safety. This authority has purposely been exercised but very sparingly. Nevertheless, the legality and propriety of what has been done under it are questioned, and the attention of the country has been called to the proposition, that one who has sworn to "take care that the laws be faithfully executed," should not himself violate them. Of course, some consideration was given to the question of power and propriety before this matter was acted upon. The whole of the laws which were required to be faithfully executed were being resisted, and failing of execution in nearly one-third of the States. Must they be allowed to finally fail of execution, even had it been perfectly clear that by the use of the means necessary to their execution some single law, made in such extreme tenderness of the citizen's liberty that practically it relieves more of the guilty than of the innocent, should to a very limited extent be violated? To state the question more directly: Are all the laws but one to go unexecuted, and the Government itself go to pieces, lest that one be violated? Even in such a case, would not the official oath be broken if the Government should be overthrown, when it was believed that disregarding the single law would tend to preserve it? But it was not believed that this question was presented. It was not believed that any law was violated. The provision of the Constitution that "the privilege of the writ of habeas corpus shall not be suspended unless when, in cases of rebellion or invasion, the public safety may require it," is equivalent to a provision—is a provision—that such privilege may be suspended when, in case of rebellion or invasion, the public safety does require it. It was decided that we have a case of rebellion, and that the public safety does require the qualified suspension of the privilege of the writ which was authorized to be made. Now, it is insisted that Congress, and not the Executive, is vested with this power. But the Constitution itself is silent as to which or who is to exercise the power; and as the provision was plainly made for a dangerous emergency, it cannot be believed the framers of the instrument intended that in every case the danger should run its course until Congress could be called together, the very assembling of which might be prevented, as was intended in this case, by the rebellion.

No more extended argument is now offered, as an opinion, at some length, will probably be presented by the Attorney-General. Whether there shall be any legislation on the subject, and, if any, what, is submitted entirely to the better judgment of Congress.

The forbearance of this Government had been so extraordinary, and so long continued, as to lead some foreign nations to shape their action as if they supposed the early destruction of our national Union was probable. While this, on discovery, gave the Executive some concern, he is now happy to say that the sovereignty and rights of the United States are now everywhere practically respected by foreign powers; and a general sympathy with the country is manifested throughout the world.

The reports of the Secretaries of the Treasury, War, and the Navy, will give the information in detail deemed necessary and convenient for your deliberation and action; while the Executive and all the Departments will stand ready to supply omissions, or to communicate new facts considered important for you to know.

It is now recommended that you give the legal means for making this contest a short and decisive one; that you place at the control of the Government, for the work, as least four hundred thousand men and $400,000,000. That number of men is about one-tenth of those of proper ages within the regions where, apparently, all are willing to engage; and the sum is less than a twenty-third part of the money value owned by the men who seem ready to devote the whole. A debt of $600,000,000 now, is a less sum per head than was the debt of our Revolution when we came out of that struggle; and the money value in the country now bears even a greater proportion to what it was then, than does the population. Surely each man has as strong a motive now to preserve our liberties, as each had then to establish them.

A right result, at this time, will be worth more to the world than ten times the men and ten times the money. The evidence reaching us from the country leaves no doubt that the material for the work is abundant, and that it needs only the hand of legislation to give it legal sanction, and the hand of the Executive to give it practical shape and efficiency. One of the greatest perplexities of the Government is to avoid receiving troops faster than it can provide for them. In a word, the people will save their Government, if the Government itself will do its part only indifferently well.

It might seem, at first thought, to be of little difference whether the present movement at the South be called "secession," or "rebellion." The movers, however, will understand the difference. At the beginning, they knew they could never raise their treason to any respectable magnitude by any name which implies violation of law. They knew their people possessed as much of moral sense, as much of devotion to law and order, and as much pride in, and reverence for the history and Government of their common country, as any other civilized and patriotic people. They knew they could make no advancement directly in the teeth of these strong and noble sentiments. Accordingly, they commenced by an insidious debauching of the public mind. They invented an ingenious sophism, which, if conceded, was followed by perfectly logical steps, through all the incidents, to the complete destruction of the Union. The sophism itself is, that any State of the Union may, consistently with the national Constitution, and therefore lawfully and peacefully, withdraw from the Union without the consent of the Union, or of any other State. The little disguise that the supposed right is to be exercised only for just cause, themselves to be the sole judges of its justice, is too thin too merit any notice.

With rebellion thus sugar-coated they have been drugging the public mind of their section for more than thirty years, and until at length they have brought many good men to a willingness to take up arms against the Government the day after some assemblage of men have enacted the farcical pretence of taking their State out of the Union, who could have been brought to no such thing the day before.

This sophism derives much, perhaps the whole, of its currency from the assumption that there is some omnipotent and sacred supremacy pertaining to a State—to each State of our Federal Union. Our States have neither more nor less power than that reserved to them in the

Union by the Constitution—no one of them ever having been a State out of the Union. The original ones passed into the Union even before they cast off their British colonial dependence; and the new ones each came into the Union directly from a condition of dependence, excepting Texas. And even Texas, in its temporary independence, was never designated a State. The new ones only took the designation of States on coming into the Union, while that name was first adopted by the old ones in and by the Declaration of Independence. Therein the "United Colonies" were declared to be "free and independent States;" but, even then, the object plainly was not to declare their independence of one another, or of the Union, but directly the contrary; as their mutual pledge and their mutual action before, at the time, and afterwards, abundantly show. The express plighting of faith by each and all of the original thirteen in the Articles of Confederation, two years later, that the Union shall be perpetual, is most conclusive. Having never been States, either in substance or in name, outside of the Union, whence this magical omnipotence of "State rights," asserting a claim of power to lawfully destroy the Union itself? Much is said about the "sovereignty" of the States; but the word even is not in the national Constitution; nor, as is believed, in any of the State constitutions. What is "sovereignty" in the political sense of the term? Would it be far wrong to define it "a political community without a political superior?" Tested by this, no one of our States, except Texas, ever was a sovereignty. And even Texas gave up the character on coming into the Union; by which act she acknowledged the Constitution of the United States and the laws and treaties of the United States made in pursuance of the Constitution, to be for her the supreme law of the land. The States have their *status* in the Union, and they have no other legal *status*. If they break from this, they can only do so against law and by revolution. The Union, and not themselves separately, procured their independence and their liberty. By conquest or purchase the Union gave each of them whatever of independence or liberty it has. The Union is older than any of the States, and, in fact, it created them as States. Originally some dependent colonies made the Union, and, in turn, the Union threw off their old dependence for them, and made them States, such as they are. Not one of them ever had a State constitution independent of the Union. Of course, it is not forgotten that all the new States framed their constitutions before they entered the Union; nevertheless dependent upon, and preparatory to, coming into the Union.

Unquestionably the States have the powers and rights reserved to them in and by the national Constitution; but among these, surely, are not included all conceivable powers, however mischievous or destructive; but, at most, such only as were known in the world, at the time, as governmental powers; and, certainly, a power to destroy the Government itself had never been known as a governmental—as a merely administrative power. This relative matter of national power and State rights, as a principle, is no other than the principle of generality and locality. Whatever concerns the whole should be confided to the whole—to the General Government; while whatever concerns only the State should be left exclusively to the State. This is all there is of original principle about it. Whether the national Constitution in defining boundaries between the two has applied the principle with exact accuracy, is not to be questioned. We are all bound by that defining, without question.

What is now combated, is the position that secession is consistent with the Constitution—is lawful and peaceful. It is not contended that there is any express law for it; and nothing should ever be implied as law which leads to unjust or absurd consequences. The nation purchased with money the countries out of which several of these States were formed; is it just that they shall go off without leave and without refunding? The nation paid very large sums (in the aggregate, I believe, nearly a hundred millions) to relieve Florida of the aboriginal tribes; is it just that she shall now be off without consent, or without making any return? The nation is now in debt for money applied to the benefit of these so-called seceding States in common with the rest; is it just either that creditors shall go unpaid, or the remaining States pay the whole? A part of the present national debt was contracted to pay the old debts of Texas; is it just that she shall leave and pay no part of this herself?

Again, if one State may secede, so may another; and when all shall have seceded, none is left to pay the debts. Is this quite just to creditors? Did we notify them of this sage view of ours when we borrowed their money? If we now recognize this doctrine by allowing the seceders to go in peace, it is difficult to see what we can do if others choose to go, or to extort terms upon which they will promise to remain.

The seceders insist that our constitution admits of secession. They have assumed to make a national constitution of their own, in which, of necessity, they have either discarded or retained the right of secession, as they insist it exists in ours. If they have discarded it, they thereby admit that, on principle, it ought not to be in ours. If they have retained it, by their own construction of ours, they show that to be consistent they must secede from one another whenever they shall find it the easiest way of settling their debts, or effecting any other selfish or unjust object. The principle itself is one of disintegration, and upon which no Government can possibly endure.

If all the States save one should assert the power to drive that one out of the Union, it is presumed the whole class of seceder politicians would at once deny the power, and denounce the act as the greatest outrage upon State rights. But suppose that precisely the same act, instead of being called "driving the one out," should be called "the seceding of the others from that one," it would be exactly what the seceders claim to do; unless, indeed, they make the point that the one, because it is a minority, may rightfully do what the others, because they are a majority, may not rightfully do. These politicians are subtile and profound on the rights of minorities. They are not partial to that power which made the Constitution, and speaks from the preamble, calling itself "We, the People."

It may well be questioned whether there is to-day a majority of the legally qualified voters of any State, except, perhaps, South Carolina, in favor of disunion. There is much reason to believe that the Union men are the majority in many, if not in every other one, of the so-called seceded States. The contrary has not been demonstrated in any one of them. It is ventured to affirm this even of Virginia and Tennessee; for the result of an election held in military camps, where the bayonets are all on one side of the question voted upon, can scarcely be considered as demonstrating popular sentiment. At such an election, all that large class who are at once for the Union and against coercion would be coerced to vote against the Union.

It may be affirmed, without extravagance, that the free institutions we enjoy have developed the powers and improved the condition of our whole people beyond any example in the world. Of this we now have a striking and an impressive illustration. So large an army as the Government has now on foot was never before known without a soldier in it but who had taken his place there of his own free choice. But more than this; there are many single regiments whose members, one and another, possess full practical knowledge of all the arts, sciences, professions, and whatever else, whether useful or elegant, is known in the world; and there is scarcely one from which there could not be selected a President, a Cabinet, a Congress and perhaps a court, abundantly competent to administer the Government itself. Nor do I say this is not true also in the army of our late friends, now adversaries in this contest; but if it is, so much better the reason why the Government which has conferred such benefits on both them and us should not be broken up. Whoever, in any section, proposes to abandon such a Government, would do well to consider in deference to what principle it is that he does it; what better he is likely to get in its stead; whether the substitute will give, or be intended to give, so much of good to the people? There are some foreshadowings on this subject. Our adversaries have adopted some declarations of independence, in which, unlike the good old one, penned by Jefferson, they omit the words, "all men are created equal." Why? They have adopted a temporary national constitution, in the preamble of which, unlike our good old one, signed by Washington, they omit "We, the People," and substitute, "We, the deputies of the sovereign and independent States." Why? Why this deliberate pressing out of view the rights of men and the authority of the people?

This is essentially a people's contest. On the side of the Union it is a struggle for maintaining in the world that form and substance of government whose leading object is to elevate the condition of men; to lift artificial weights from all shoulders; to clear the paths of laudable pursuits for all; to afford all an unfettered start and a fair chance in the race of life. Yielding to partial and temporary departures, from necessity, this is the leading object of the Government for whose existence we contend.

I am most happy to believe that the plain people understand and appreciate this. It is worthy of note, that while in this the Government's hour of trial, large numbers of those in the army and navy who have been favored with the offices have resigned and proved false to the hand which had pampered them, not one common soldier or common sailor is known to have deserted his flag.

Great honor is due to those officers who remained true, despite the example of their treacherous associates; but the greatest honor, and most important fact of all, is the unanimous firmness of the common soldiers and common sailors. To the last man, so far as known, they have successfully resisted the traitorous efforts of those whose commands but an hour before they obeyed as absolute law. This is the patriotic instinct of plain people. They understand, without an argument, that the destroying the Government which was made by Washington means no good to them.

Our popular Government has often been called an experiment. Two points in it our people have already settled—the successful establishing and the successful administering of it. One still remains—its successful maintenance against a formidable internal attempt to overthrow it. It is now for them to demonstrate to the world that those who can fairly carry an election can also suppress a rebellion; that ballots are the rightful and peaceful successors of bullets; and that when ballots have fairly and constitutionally decided, there can be no successful appeal back to bullets; that there can be no successful appeal, except to ballots themselves, at succeeding elections. Such will be a great lesson of peace; teaching men that what they cannot take by an election, neither can they take by a war; teaching all the folly of being the beginners of a war.

Lest there be some uneasiness in the minds of candid men as to what is to be the course of the Government towards the Southern States after the rebellion shall have been suppressed, the Executive deems it proper to say, it will be his purpose then, as ever, to be guided by the Constitution and the laws; and that he probably will have no different understanding of the powers and duties of the Federal Government relatively to the rights of the States and the people under the Constitution than that expressed in the inaugural address.

He desires to preserve the Government, that it may be administered for all, as it was administered by the men who made it. Loyal citizens everywhere have the right to claim this of their Government, and the

Government has no right to withhold or neglect it. It is not perceived that in giving it there is any coercion, any conquest, or any subjugation, in any just sense of those terms.

The Constitution provides, and all the States have accepted the provision, that "the United States shall guarantee to every State in this Union a republican form of Government." But if a State may lawfully go out of the Union, having done so it may also discard the republican form of Government; so that to prevent its going out is an indispensable means to the end of maintaining the guarantee mentioned; and when an end is lawful and obligatory, the indispensable means to it are also lawful and obligatory.

It was with the deepest regret that the Executive found the duty of employing the war power in defence of the Government forced upon him. He could but perform this duty or surrender the existence of the Government. No compromise by public servants could in this case be a cure; not that compromises are not often proper, but that no popular Government can long survive a marked precedent that those who carry an election can only save the Government from immediate destruction by giving up the main point upon which the people gave the election. The people themselves, and not their servants, can safely reverse their own deliberate decisions.

As a private citizen the Executive could not have consented that these institutions shall perish; much less could he, in betrayal of so vast and so sacred a trust as these free people have confided to him. He felt that he had no moral right to shrink, or even to count the chances of his own life, in what might follow. In full view of his great responsibility he has so far done what he has deemed his duty. You will now, according to your own judgment, perform yours. He sincerely hopes that your views and your action may so accord with his as to assure all faithful citizens who have been disturbed in their rights of a certain and speedy restoration to them, under the Constitution and the laws.

And having thus chosen our course, without guile and with pure purpose, let us renew our trust in God, and go forward without fear and with manly hearts.

ABRAHAM LINCOLN.

July 4, 1861.

Congress imitated the President in confining its attention exclusively to the rebellion and the means for its suppression. The zealous and enthusiastic loyalty of the people met a prompt response from their representatives. The Judiciary Committee in the House was instructed on the 8th to prepare a bill to confiscate the property of rebels against the Government, and on the 9th a resolution was adopted (ayes 93, noes 55), declaring it to be "no part of the duty of the soldiers of the United States to capture and return fugitive slaves." A bill was promptly introduced to declare valid all the acts of the President for the suppression of the rebellion previous to the meeting of Congress, and it brought on a general discussion of the principles involved and the interests concerned in the contest. There were a few in both Houses, with John C. Breckinridge, of Kentucky, at their head, who still insisted that any resort by the Government to the use of the war power against the rebels was unconstitutional, and could only end in the destruction of the Union; but the general sentiment of both Houses fully sustained the President in the steps he had taken. The subject of slavery was introduced into the discussion commenced by Senator Powell, of Kentucky, who proposed on the 18th to amend the Army Bill by adding a section that no part of the army should be employed "in subjecting or holding as a conquered province any sovereign state now or lately one of the United States, or in abolishing or interfering with African slavery in any of the States." The debate which ensued elicited the sentiments of members on this subject. Mr. Sherman, of Ohio, concurred in the sentiment that the war was "not to be waged for the purpose of subjugating any state or freeing any slave, or to interfere with the social or domestic institutions of any State or any people; it was to preserve this Union, to maintain the Constitution as it is in all its clauses, in all its guarantees, without change or limitation." Mr. Dixon, of Connecticut, assented to this, but also declared that if the South should protract the war, and "it should turn out that either this Government or slavery must be destroyed, then the people of the North—the Conservative people of the North—would say, rather than let the Government perish, let slavery perish." Mr. Lane, of Kansas, did not believe that slavery could survive in any state the march of the Union armies. These seemed to be the sentiments of both branches of Congress. The amendment was rejected and bills were passed ratifying the acts of the President, authorizing him to accept the services of half a million of vollunteers, and placing five hundred millions of dollars at the disposal of the Government for the prosecution of the war.

On the 15th of July, Mr. McClernand, a democrat from Illinois, offered a resolution pledging the House to vote any amount of money and any number of men necessary to suppress the rebellion, and restore the authority of the Government, which was adopted with but five opposing votes; and on the 22d of July, Mr. Crittenden, of Kentucky, offered the following resolution, defining the objects of the war:

Resolved by the House of Representatives of the Congress of the United States, That the present deplorable civil war has been forced upon the country by the disunionists of the Southern States, now in arms against the constitutional Government, and in arms around the capital; that in this national emergency, Congress, banishing all feelings of mere passion or resentment, will recollect only its duty to the whole country; that this war is not waged on their part in any spirit of oppression, or for any purpose of conquest or subjugation, or purpose of overthrowing or interfering with the rights or established institutions of those States, but to defend and maintain the *supremacy* of the Constitution, and to preserve the Union with all the dignity, equality, and rights of the several States unimpaired; and that as soon as these objects are accomplished the war ought to cease.

This resolution was adopted with but two dissenting votes. It was accepted by the whole country as defining the objects and limiting the continuance of the war, and was regarded with special favor by the loyal citizens of the Border States, whose sensitiveness on the subject of slavery had been skilfully and zealously played upon by the agents and allies of the rebel confederacy. The war was universally represented by these men as waged for the destruction of slavery, and as aiming, not at the preservation of the Union, but the emancipation of the slaves; and there was great danger that these appeals to the pride, the interest, and the prejudices of the Border Slave States might bring them to join their fortunes to those of the rebellion. The passage of this resolution, with so great a degree of unanimity, had a very soothing effect upon the apprehensions of these states, and contributed largely to strengthen the Government in its contest with the rebellion.

The sentiments of Congress on this matter, as well as on the general subject of the war, were still further developed in the debates which followed the introduction to the House of a bill passed by the Senate to "confiscate property used for insurrectionary purposes." It was referred to the Judiciary Committee and reported back with an amendment, providing that whenever any slave should be required or permitted by his master to take up arms, or be employed in any fort, dock-yard, or in any military service in aid of the rebellion, he should become entitled to his freedom. Mr. Wickliffe and Mr. Burnett of Kentucky at once contested the passage of the bill on the ground that the Government had no right to interfere in any way with the relation existing between a master and his slave;—and they were answered by the northern members with the argument that the Government certainly had a right to confiscate property of any kind employed in the rebellion, and that there was no more reason for protecting slavery against the consequences of exercising this right, than for shielding any other interest that might be thus involved. The advocates of the bill denied that it was the intention of the law to emancipate the slaves, or that it would bear any such construction in the courts of justice. They repudiated the idea that men in arms against the Union and Constitution could claim the protection of the Constitution, and thus derive from that instrument increased ability to secure its destruction; but they based their proposed confiscation of slave property solely on the ground that it was a necessary means to the prosecution of the war, and not in any sense the object for which the war was waged. After a protracted debate, that section of the bill which related to this subject was passed—ayes 60, noes 48, in the following form:

That whenever hereafter, during the present insurrection against the Government of the United States, any person claimed to be held to labor or service, under the laws of any State, shall be required or permitted by the person to whom such labor or service is claimed to be due, or by the lawful agent of such person, to take up arms against the United States, or shall be required or permitted by the person to whom such service or labor is claimed to be due, or his lawful agent, to work or to be employed in or upon any fort, navy-yard, dock, armory, ship, or intrenchment, or in any military or naval service whatever, against the Government and lawful authority of the United States, then, and in every such case, the person to whom such service is claimed to be due, shall forfeit his claim to such labor, any law of the State, or of the United States, to the contrary notwithstanding; and whenever thereafter the person claiming such labor or service shall seek to enforce his claim, it shall be a full and sufficient answer to such claim that the person whose service or labor is claimed, had been employed in hostile service against the Government of the United States, contrary to the provisions of this act.

Congress closed its extra session on the 6th of August. It had taken the most vigorous and effective measures for the suppression of the rebellion, having clothed the President with even greater power than he had asked for in the prosecution of the war, and avoided with just fidelity all points which could divide and weaken the loyal sentiment of the country. The people responded with hearty applause to the patriotic action of their representatives. The universal temper of the country was one of buoyancy and hope. Throughout the early part of the summer the rebels had been steadily pushing troops through Virginia to the borders of the Potomac, menacing the national capital with capture, until in the latter part of June they had an army of not far from 35,000 men, holding a strong position along the Bull Run creek,—its left posted at Winchester, and its right resting at Manassas. It was determined to attack this force and drive it from the vicinity of Washington, and the general belief of the country was that this would substantially end the war. The national army, numbering about 30,000 men, moved from the Potomac, on the 16th of July, under General McDowell, and the main attack was made on the 21st. It resulted in the defeat, with a loss of 480 killed and 1,000 wounded, of our forces, and their falling back, in the utmost disorder and confusion, upon Washington. Our army was completely routed, and if the rebel forces had known the extent of their success, and had been in condition to avail themselves of it with vigor and energy, the Capital would easily have fallen into their hands.

The result of this battle took the whole country by surprise. The most sanguine expectations of a prompt and decisive victory had been universally entertained; and the actual issue first revealed to the people the prospect of a long and bloody war. But the public heart was not in the least discouraged. On the contrary, the effect was to rouse still higher the courage and determination of the people. No one dreamed for an instant of submission. The most vigorous efforts were made to reorganize the army, to increase its numbers by volunteering, and to establish a footing for national troops at various points along the rebel coast. On the 28th of August Fort Hatteras was surrendered to the National forces, and on the 31st of October Port Royal, on the coast of South Carolina, fell into possession of the United States. On the 3d of December Ship Island, lying between Mobile and New Orleans, was occupied. Preparations were also made for an expedition against New Orleans, and by a series of combined movements the rebel forces were driven out of Western Virginia, Kentucky and Missouri—States in which the population had from the beginning of the contest been divided in sentiment and in action.

On the 31st of October General Scott, finding himself unable, in consequence of illness and advancing age, to take the field or discharge the duties imposed by the enlarging contest, resigned his position as commander of the army, in the following letter to the Secretary of War:

HEAD-QUARTERS OF THE ARMY,
WASHINGTON, *October* 31, 1861.

The Hon. S. CAMERON, Secretary of War:

SIR: For more than three years I have been unable, from a hurt, to mount a horse, or to walk more than a few paces at a time, and that with much pain. Other and new infirmities—dropsy and vertigo—admonish me that repose of mind and body, with the appliances of surgery and medicine, are necessary to add a little more to a life already protracted much beyond the usual span of man.

It is under such circumstances—made doubly painful by the unnatural and unjust rebellion now raging in the Southern States of our (so late) prosperous and happy Union—that I am compelled to request that my name be placed on the list of army officers retired from active service.

As this request is founded on an absolute right, granted by a recent act of Congress, I am entirely at liberty to say it is with deep regret that I withdraw myself, in these momentous times, from the orders of a President who has treated me with distinguished kindness and courtesy; whom I know, upon much personal intercourse, to be patriotic, without sectional partialities or prejudices; to be highly conscientious in the performance of every duty, and of unrivalled activity and perseverance.

And to you, Mr. Secretary, whom I now officially address for the last time, I beg to acknowledge my many obligations, for the uniform high consideration I have received at your hands; and have the honor to remain, sir, with high respect, your obedient servant,

WINFIELD SCOTT.

President LINCOLN waited upon General Scott at his residence, accompanied by his Cabinet, and made personal expression to him of the deep regret which he, in common with the whole country, felt in parting with a public servant so venerable in years and so illustrious for the services he had rendered. He also issued the following order:

On the first day of November, 1861, upon his own application to the President of the United States, Brevet Lieutenant-General Winfield Scott is ordered to be placed, and hereby is placed, upon the list of retired officers of the army of the United States, without reduction of his current pay, subsistence, or allowances.

The American people will hear with sadness and deep emotion that General Scott has withdrawn from the active control of the army, while the President and unanimous Cabinet express their own and the nation's sympathy in his personal affliction, and their profound sense of the important public services rendered by him to his country during his long and brilliant career, among which will ever be gratefully distinguished his faithful devotion to the Constitution, the Union, and the Flag, when assailed by parricidal rebellion.

ABRAHAM LINCOLN.

The command of the army then devolved by appointment upon Major-General McClellan, who had been recalled from Western Virginia after the battle of Bull Run, and had devoted himself to the task of recruiting the army in front of Washington, and preparing it for the defence of the capital, and for a fresh advance upon the forces of the rebellion.

It cannot have escaped attention that thus far, in its policy concerning the war, the government had been very greatly influenced by a desire to prevent the Border Slave States from joining the rebel confederacy. Their accession would have added immensely to the forces of the rebellion, and would have increased very greatly the labor and difficulty of its suppression. The administration and Congress had, therefore, avoided, so far as possible, any measures in regard to slavery which could needlessly excite the hostile prejudices of the people of the Border States. The Confiscation Act affected only those slaves who should be "required or permitted" by their masters to render service to the rebel cause. It did not in any respect change the condition of any others. The President, in the executive department, acted upon the same principle. The question first arose in Virginia, simultaneously at Fortress Monroe and in the western part of the state. On the 26th of May, General McClellan issued an address to the people of the district under his command, in which he said to them, "Understand one thing clearly: not only will we abstain from all interference with your slaves, but we will, on the contrary, with an iron hand crush any attempt at insurrection on their part." On the 27th of May, General Butler, in command at Fortress Monroe, wrote to the Secretary of War that he was greatly embarrassed by the number of slaves that were coming in from the surrounding country and seeking protection within the lines of his camp. He had determined to regard them as *contraband* of war, and to employ their labor at a fair compensation, against which should be charged the expense of their support—the relative value to be adjusted afterwards. The Secretary of War, in a letter dated May 30th, expressed the approval by the Government of the course adopted by General Butler, and directed him, on the one hand, to "permit no interference by the persons under his command with the relations of persons held to service under the laws of any state," and on the other, to "refrain from surrendering to alleged masters any such persons who might come within his lines."

On the 8th of August, after the passage of the Confiscation Act by Congress, the Secretary of War again wrote to General Butler, setting forth somewhat more fully the views of the President and the administration upon this subject, as follows:

It is the desire of the President that *all existing rights in all the States be fully respected and maintained.* The war now prosecuted on the part of the Federal Government is a war for the Union and for the preservation of all constitutional rights of States and the citizens of the States in the Union. Hence no question can arise as to fugitives from service within the States and territories in which the authority of the Union is fully acknowledged. The ordinary forms of judicial proceeding, which must be respected by military and civil authorities alike, will suffice for the enforcement of all legal claims. But in States wholly or partially under insurrectionary control, where the laws of the United States are so far opposed and resisted that they cannot be effectually enforced, it is obvious that rights dependent on the execution of those laws must temporarily fail; and it is equally obvious that rights dependent on the laws of the States within which military operations are conducted must be necessarily subordinated to the military exigencies created by the insurrection, if not wholly forfeited by the treasonable conduct of parties claiming them. To this general rule rights to services can form no exception.

The act of Congress approved August 6th, 1861, declares that if persons held to service shall be employed in hostility to the United States, the right to their services shall be forfeited, and such persons shall be discharged therefrom. It follows of necessity that no claim can be recognized by the military authorities of the Union to the services of such persons when fugitives.

A more difficult question is presented in respect to persons escaping from the service of loyal masters. It is quite apparent that the laws of the State, under which only the services of such fugitives can be claimed, must needs be wholly, or almost wholly suspended, as to remedies, by the insurrection and the military measures necessitated by it, and it is equally apparent that the substitution of military for judicial measures, for the enforcement of such claims, must be attended by great inconveniences, embarrassments, and injuries.

Under these circumstances it seems quite clear that the substantial rights of loyal masters will be best protected by receiving such fugitives, as well as fugitives from disloyal masters, into the service of the United States, and employing them under such organizations and in such occupations as circumstances may suggest or require. Of course a record should be kept, showing the name and description of the fugitives, the name and the character, as loyal or disloyal, of the master, and such facts as may be necessary to a correct understanding of the circumstances of each case after tranquillity shall have been restored. Upon the return of peace, Congress will doubtless properly provide for all the persons thus received into the service of the Union, and for just compensation to loyal masters. In this way only, it would seem, can the duty and safety of the Government, and the just rights of all, be fully reconciled and harmonized.

You will therefore consider yourself as instructed to govern your future action, in respect to fugitives from service, by the principles herein stated, and will report from time to time, and at least twice in each month, your action in the premises to this Department. You will, however, neither authorize nor permit any interference, by the troops under your command, with the servants of peaceful citizens, in house or field, nor will you, in any way, encourage such servants to leave the lawful service of their masters; nor will you, except in cases where the public safety may seem to require it, prevent the voluntary return of any fugitive to the service from which he may have escaped.

The same policy was adopted in every part of the country, All interference with the internal institutions of any state was expressly forbidden; but the Government would avail itself of the services of a portion of the slaves, taking carefully to provide for compensation to loyal masters. On the 16th of August, Hon. C. B. Smith, Secretary of the Interior, in a speech made at Providence, R. I., took occasion to declare the policy of the administration upon this subject. Its theory, said he, is that "the states are sovereign within their spheres; the Government of the United States has no more right to interfere with the institution of slavery in South Carolina than it has to interfere with the peculiar institution of Rhode Island whose benefits I have enjoyed."

On the 31st of August, General Fremont, commanding the western department, which embraced Missouri and a part of Kentucky, issued an order "extending and declaring established martial law throughout the state of Missouri," and declaring that "the property, real and personal, of all persons in the State of Missouri, who shall take up arms against the United States, or who shall be directly proven to have taken an active part with their enemies in the field, is declared to be confiscated to the public use, and *their slaves*, if any they have, *are hereby declared free men*." The President regarded this order as transcending the authority vested in him by the Act of Congress, and wrote to General Fremont, calling his attention to this point, and requesting him to modify his proclamation so as to make it conform to the law. General Fremont, desiring to throw off from himself the responsibility of changing his action, desired an explicit order—whereupon the President thus addressed him:—

WASHINGTON, D. C., *September* 11, 1861.

Major-General JOHN C. FREMONT:

SIR: Yours of the 8th, in answer to mine of the 2d inst., was just received. Assured that you upon the ground could better judge of the necessities of your position than I could at this distance, on seeing your proclamation of August 30, I perceived no general objection to it; the particular clause, however, in relation to the confiscation of property and the liberation of slaves appeared to me to be objectionable in its non-conformity to the act of Congress, passed the 6th of last August, upon the same subjects, and hence I wrote you expressing my wish that that clause should be modified accordingly. Your answer just received expresses the preference on your part that I should make an open order for the modification, which I very cheerfully do. It is therefore ordered that the said clause of said proclamation be so modified, held and construed as to conform with, and not to transcend, the provisions on the same subject contained in the act of Congress entitled "An act to confiscate property used for insurrectionary purposes," approved August 6, 1861, and the said act be published at length with this order. Your obedient servant,

A. LINCOLN.

These views of the Government were still farther enforced in a letter from the Secretary of War to General T. W. Sherman, who commanded the expedition to Port Royal, and in orders issued by General Dix in Virginia on the 17th of November, and by General Halleck, who succeeded General Fremont in the western department, prohibiting fugitive slaves from being received within the lines of the army. During all this time strenuous efforts were made in various quarters to induce the President to depart from this policy, and not only to proclaim a general emancipation of all the slaves, but to put arms in their hands and employ them in the field against the rebels. But they were ineffectual. The President adhered firmly and steadily to the policy which the then existing circumstances of the country, in his judgment, rendered wise and necessary; and he was sustained in this action by the public sentiment of the loyal States, and by the great body of the people in the slave States along the border. The course which he pursued at that time contributed largely, beyond doubt, to strengthen the cause of the Union in those Border States, and especially to withdraw Tennessee from her hastily formed connection with the rebel confederacy.

In the early part of November an incident occurred which threatened for a time to involve the country in open war with England. On the 7th of that month the British mail steamer *Trent* left Havana for St. Thomas, having on board Messrs. J. M. Mason and John Slidell, on their way as commissioners from the Confederate States to England and France. On the 8th the *Trent* was hailed from the U. S. frigate *San Jacinto*, Captain Wilkes, and brought to by a shot across her bows. Two officers and about twenty armed men from the latter then went on board the *Trent*, searched her, and took from her by force and against the protest of the British officers, the two rebel commissioners, with Messrs. Eustis and McFarland, their secretaries, who were brought to the United States and lodged in Fort Warren, the *Trent* being released and proceeding on her way. The most intense excitement pervaded the country when news of this affair was received. The feeling was one of admiration at the boldness of Captain Wilkes, and of exultation at the capture of the rebel emissaries. In England the most intense and passionate resentment took possession of the public mind. The demand for instant redress was universal, and, in obedience to it, the Government at once ordered troops to Canada and the outfit of vessels of war.

Our Government met the matter with prompt and self-possessed decision. On the 30th of November Mr. Seward wrote to Mr. Adams a general statement of the facts of the case, accompanied by the assurance that "in the capture of Messrs. Mason and Slidell Captain Wilkes had acted without any instructions from the Government," and that our Government was prepared to discuss the matter in a perfectly fair and friendly spirit as soon as the ground taken by the British Government should be made known. Earl Russell, under the same date, wrote to Lord Lyons, rehearsing the facts of the case, and saying that the British Government was "willing to believe that the naval officer who committed the aggression was not acting in compliance with any authority from his Government," because the Government of the United States "must be fully aware that the British Government could not allow such an affront to the national honor to pass without full reparation." Earl Russell trusted, therefore, that when the matter should be brought under its notice the United States Government would, "of its own accord, offer to the British Government such redress as alone could satisfy the British nation, namely, the liberation of the four gentlemen and their delivery to the British minister, that they may again be placed under British protection, and a suitable apology for the aggression which has been committed." In a subsequent note Lord Lyons was instructed to wait seven days after its delivery for a reply to this demand, and in case no answer, or any other answer than a compliance with its terms, should be given by the expiration of that time, he was to leave Washington with the archives of the legation, and repair immediately to London.

On the 26th of December the Secretary of State, by direction of the President, sent a reply to this dispatch, in which the whole question was discussed at length, and with conspicuous ability. The Government decided that the detention of the vessel and the removal from her of the emissaries of the rebel confederacy, was justifiable by the laws of war and the practice and precedents of the British Government; but that in assuming to decide upon the liability of these persons to capture for himself, instead of sending them before a legal tribunal where a regular trial could be had, Captain Wilkes had departed from the rule of international law uniformly asserted by the American Government, and forming part of its most cherished policy. The Government decided, therefore, that the four persons in question would be "cheerfully liberated." This decision, sustained by the reasoning advanced in its support, commanded the immediate and universal acquiescence of the American people; while in England it was received with hearty applause by the friends of this country, especially as it silenced the clamors and disappointed the hostile hopes of its enemies. The French Government had joined that of England in its representations upon this subject, and the decision of our Government was received there with equal satisfaction. The effect of the incident, under the just and judicious course adopted by the Administration, was eminently favorable to the United States, increasing the general respect for its adherence to sound principles of public law, and silencing effectually the slander that its Government was too weak to disappoint or thwart a popular clamor. One of the immediate fruits of the discussion was the prompt rejection of all demands for recognizing the independence of the Confederate States.

CHAPTER V.

THE REGULAR SESSION OF CONGRESS, DEC. 1861.—THE MESSAGE.—DEBATES, ETC.

CONGRESS met in regular session (the second of the thirty-seventh Congress) on the 2d of December, 1861. On the next day the President sent in his Annual Message, as follows:

FELLOW-CITIZENS OF THE SENATE AND HOUSE OF REPRESENTATIVES:

In the midst of unprecedented political troubles, we have cause of great gratitude to God for unusual good health, and most abundant harvests.

You will not be surprised to learn that, in the peculiar exigencies of the times, our intercourse with foreign nations has been attended with profound solicitude, chiefly turning upon our own domestic affairs.

A disloyal portion of the American people have, during the whole year, been engaged in an attempt to divide and destroy the Union. A nation which endures factious domestic division, is exposed to disrespect abroad; and one party, if not both, is sure, sooner or later, to invoke foreign intervention.

Nations thus tempted to interfere are not always able to resist the counsels of seeming expediency and ungenerous ambition, although measures adopted under such influences seldom fail to be unfortunate and injurious to those adopting them.

The disloyal citizens of the United States who have offered the ruin of our country, in return for the aid and comfort which they have invoked abroad, have received less patronage and encouragement than they probably expected. If it were just to suppose, as the insurgents have seemed to assume, that foreign nations, in this case, discarding all moral, social, and treaty obligations, would act solely and selfishly for the most speedy restoration of commerce, including especially the acquisition of cotton, those nations appear, as yet, not to have seen their way to their object more directly, or clearly, through the destruction, than through the preservation, of the Union. If we could dare to believe that foreign nations are actuated by no higher principle than this,

I am quite sure a sound argument could be made to show them that they can reach their aim more readily and easily by aiding to crush this rebellion, than by giving encouragement to it.

The principal lever relied on by the insurgents for exciting foreign nations to hostility against us, as already intimated, is the embarrassment of commerce. Those nations, however, not improbably, saw from the first, that it was the Union which made, as well our foreign as our domestic commerce. They can scarcely have failed to perceive that the effort for disunion produced the existing difficulty; and that one strong nation promises more durable peace, and a more extensive, valuable, and reliable commerce, than can the same nation broken into hostile fragments.

It is not my purpose to review our discussions with foreign States; because whatever might be their wishes or dispositions, the integrity of our country and the stability of our Government mainly depend, not upon them, but on the loyalty, virtue, patriotism, and intelligence of the American people. The correspondence itself, with the usual reservations, is herewith submitted.

I venture to hope it will appear that we have practised prudence and liberality towards foreign powers, averting causes of irritation; and with firmness maintaining our own rights and honor.

Since, however, it is apparent that here, as in every other State, foreign dangers necessarily attend domestic difficulties, I recommend that adequate and ample measures be adopted for maintaining the public defences on every side. While, under this general recommendation, provision for defending our sea-coast line readily occurs to the mind, I also, in the same connection, ask the attention of Congress to our great lakes and rivers. It is believed that some fortifications and dépôts of arms and munitions, with harbor and navigation improvements, all at well-selected points upon these, would be of great importance to the national defence and preservation. I ask attention to the views of the Secretary of War, expressed in his report upon the same general subject.

I deem it of importance that the loyal regions of East Tennessee and Western North Carolina should be connected with Kentucky and other faithful parts of the Union by railroad. I, therefore, recommend, as a military measure, that Congress provide for the construction of such road as speedily as possible.

Kentucky will no doubt co-operate, and, through her Legislature, make the most judicious selection of a line. The northern terminus must connect with some existing railroad, and whether the route shall be from Lexington or Nicholasville to the Cumberland Gap, or from Lebanon to the Tennessee line, in the direction of Knoxville, or on some still different line, can easily be determined. Kentucky and the General Government co-operating, the work can be completed in a very short time, and when done it will be not only of vast present usefulness, but also a valuable permanent improvement worth its cost in all the future.

Some treaties, designed chiefly for the interests of commerce, and having no grave political importance, have been negotiated, and will be submitted to the Senate for their consideration. Although we have failed to induce some of the commercial Powers to adopt a desirable melioration of the rigor of maritime war, we have removed all obstructions from the way of this humane reform, except such as are merely of temporary and accidental occurrence.

I invite your attention to the correspondence between her Britannic Majesty's Minister, accredited to this Government, and the Secretary of State, relative to the detention of the British ship *Perthshire* in June last by the United States steamer *Massachusetts*, for a supposed breach of the blockade. As this detention was occasioned by an obvious misapprehension of the facts, and as justice requires that we should commit no belligerent act not founded in strict right as sanctioned by public law, I recommend that an appropriation be made to satisfy the reasonable demand of the owners of the vessel for her detention.

I repeat the recommendation of my predecessor in his annual message to Congress in December last in regard to the disposition of the surplus which will probably remain after satisfying the claims of American citizens against China, pursuant to the awards of the commissioners under the act of the 3d of March, 1859.

If, however, it should not be deemed advisable to carry that recommendation into effect, I would suggest that authority be given for investing the principal over the proceeds of the surplus referred to in good securities, with a view to the satisfaction of such other just claim of our citizens against China as are not unlikely to arise hereafter in the course of our extensive trade with that Empire.

By the act of the 5th of August last, Congress authorized the President to instruct the commanders of suitable vessels to defend themselves against and to capture pirates. This authority has been exercised in a single instance only.

For the more effectual protection of our extensive and valuable commerce in the Eastern seas, especially, it seems to me that it would also be advisable to authorize the commanders of sailing-vessels to recapture any prizes which pirates may make of the United States vessels and their cargoes, and the Consular Courts established by law in Eastern countries to adjudicate the cases in the event that this should not be objected to by the local authorities.

If any good reason exists why we should persevere longer in withholding our recognition of the independence and sovereignty of Hayti and Liberia, I am unable to discern it. Unwilling, however, to inaugurate a novel policy in regard to them without the approbation of Congress, I submit for your consideration the expediency of an appropriation for maintaining a *Chargé d'Affaires* near each of those new States. It does not admit of doubt that important commercial advantages might be secured by favorable treaties with them.

The operations of the Treasury during the period which has elapsed since your adjournment have been conducted with signal success. The patriotism of the people has placed at the disposal of the Government the large means demanded by the public exigencies. Much of the national loan has been taken by citizens of the industrial classes, whose confidence in their country's faith, and zeal for their country's deliverance from its present peril, have induced them to contribute to the support of the Government the whole of their limited acquisitions. This fact imposes peculiar obligations to economy and disbursement and energy in action. The revenue from all sources, including loans for the financial year ending on the 30th of June, 1861, was $86,835,900 27; and the expenditures for the same period, including payments on account of the public debt, were $84,578,034 47, leaving a balance in the treasury, on the 1st of July, of $2,257,065 80 for the first quarter of the financial year ending on September 30, 1861. The receipts from all sources, including the balance of July 1, were $102,532,509 27, and the expenses $98,239,733 09, leaving a balance, on the 1st of October, 1861, of $4,292,776 18.

Estimates for the remaining three-quarters of the year and for the financial year of 1863, together with his views of the ways and means for meeting the demands contemplated by them, will be submitted to Congress by the Secretary of the Treasury. It is gratifying to know that the expenses made necessary by the rebellion are not beyond the resources of the loyal people, and to believe that the same patriotism which has thus far sustained the Government will continue to sustain it till peace and union shall again bless the land. I respectfully refer to the report of the Secretary of War for information respecting the numerical strength of the army, and for recommendations having in view an increase of its efficiency, and the well-being of the various branches of the service intrusted to his care. It is gratifying to know that the patriotism of the people has proved equal to the occasion, and that the number of troops tendered greatly exceed the force which Congress authorized me to call into the field. I refer with pleasure to these portions of his report which make allusion to the creditable degree of discipline already attained by our troops, and to the excellent sanitary condition of the entire army. The recommendation of the Secretary for an organization of the militia upon a uniform basis is a subject of vital importance to the future safety of the country, and is commended to the serious attention of Congress. The large addition to the regular army, in connection with the defection that has so considerably diminished the number of its officers, gives peculiar importance to his recommendation for increasing the corps of cadets to the greatest capacity of the Military Academy.

By mere omission I presume Congress has failed to provide chaplains for the hospitals occupied by the volunteers. This subject was brought to my notice, and I was induced to draw up the form of a letter, one copy of which, properly addressed, has been delivered to each of the persons, and at the dates respectively named and stated in a schedule, containing, also, the form of the letter marked A, and herewith transmitted. These gentlemen, I understand, entered upon the duties designated at the times respectively stated in the schedule, and have labored faithfully therein ever since. I therefore recommend that they be compensated at the same rate as chaplains in the army. I further suggest that general provision be made for chaplains to serve at hospitals, as well as with regiments.

The report of the Secretary of the Navy presents, in detail, the operations of that branch of the service, the activity and energy which have characterized its administration, and the results of measures to increase its efficiency and power. Such have been the additions, by construction and purchase, that it may almost be said a navy has been created and brought into service since our difficulties commenced.

Besides blockading our extensive coast, squadrons larger than ever before assembled under our flag have been put afloat, and performed deeds which have increased our naval renown.

I would invite special attention to the recommendation of the Secretary for a more perfect organization of the navy, by introducing additional grades in the service.

The present organization is defective and unsatisfactory, and the suggestions submitted by the department will, it is believed, if adopted, obviate the difficulties alluded to, promote harmony, and increase the efficiency of the navy.

There are three vacancies on the bench of the Supreme Court—two by the decease of Justices Daniel and McLean, and one by the resignation of Justice Campbell. I have so far forborne making nominations to fill these vacancies for reasons which I will now state. Two of the outgoing judges resided within the States now overrun by revolt; so that if successors were appointed in the same localities, they could not now serve upon their circuits; and many of the most competent men there probably would not take the personal hazard of accepting to serve, even here, upon the supreme bench. I have been unwilling to throw all the appointments northward, thus disabling myself from doing justice to the South on the return of peace; although I may remark that to transfer to the North one which has heretofore been in the South, would not, with reference to territory and population, be unjust.

During the long and brilliant judicial career of Judge McLean, his circuit grew into an empire—altogether too large for any one judge to give the courts therein more than a nominal attendance—rising in population from one million four hundred and seventy thousand and eighteen, in 1830, to six million one hundred and fifty-one thousand four hundred and five, in 1860.

Besides this, the country generally has outgrown our present judicial system. If uniformity was at all intended, the system requires that all the States shall be accommodated with Circuit Courts, attended by supreme judges, while, in fact, Wisconsin, Minnesota, Iowa, Kansas, Florida, Texas, California, and Oregon, have never had any such courts. Nor can this well be remedied without a change of the system; because the adding of judges to the Supreme Court, enough for the accommodation of all parts of the country with Circuit Courts, would create a court altogether too numerous for a judicial body of any sort. And the evil, if it be one, will increase as new States come into the Union. Circuit Courts are useful, or they are not useful. If useful, no State should be denied them; if not useful, no State should have them. Let them be provided for all, or abolished as to all.

Three modifications occur to me, either of which, I think, would be an improvement upon our present system. Let the Supreme Court be of convenient number in every event. Then, first, let the whole country be divided into circuits of convenient size, the supreme judges to serve in a number of them corresponding to their own number, and independent circuit judges be provided for all the rest. Or, secondly, let the supreme judges be relieved from circuit duties, and circuit judges provided for all the circuits. Or, thirdly, dispense with circuit courts altogether, leaving the judicial functions wholly to the district courts and an independent Supreme Court.

I respectfully recommend to the consideration of Congress the present condition of the statute laws, with the hope that Congress will be able to find an easy remedy for many of the inconveniences and evils which constantly embarrass those engaged in the practical administration of them. Since the organization of the Government, Congress has enacted some five thousand acts and joint resolutions, which fill more than six thousand closely-printed pages, and are scattered through many volumes. Many of these acts have been drawn in haste and without sufficient caution, so that their provisions are often obscure in themselves, or in conflict with each other, or at least so doubtful as to render it very difficult for even the best-informed persons to ascertain precisely what the statute law really is.

It seems to me very important that the statute laws should be made as plain and intelligible as possible, and be reduced to as small a compass as may consist with the fulness and precision of the will of the legislature and the perspicuity of its language. This, well done, would, I think, greatly facilitate the labors of those whose duty it is to assist in the administration of the laws, and would be a lasting benefit to the people, by placing before them, in a more accessible and intelligible form, the laws which so deeply concern their interests and their duties.

I am informed by some whose opinions I respect, that all the acts of Congress now in force, and of a permanent and general nature, might be revised and re-written, so as to be embraced in one volume (or, at most, two volumes) of ordinary and convenient size. And I respectfully recommend to Congress to consider of the subject, and, if my suggestion be approved, to devise such plan as to their wisdom shall seem most proper for the attainment of the end proposed.

One of the unavoidable consequences of the present insurrection is the entire suppression, in many places, of all the ordinary means of administering civil justice by the officers, and in the forms of existing law. This is the case, in whole or in part, in all the insurgent States; and as our armies advance upon and take possession of parts of those States, the practical evil becomes more apparent. There are no courts nor officers to whom the citizens of other States may apply for the enforcement of their lawful claims against citizens of the insurgent States; and there is a vast amount of debt constituting such claims. Some have estimated it as high as two hundred million dollars, due, in large part, from insurgents in open rebellion to loyal citizens who are, even now, making great sacrifices in the discharge of their patriotic duty to support the Government.

Under these circumstances, I have been urgently solicited to establish, by military power, courts to administer summary justice in such cases. I have thus far declined to do it, not because I had any doubt that the end proposed—the collection of the debts—was just and right in itself, but because I have been unwilling to go beyond the pressure of necessity in the unusual exercise of power. But the powers of Congress, I suppose, are equal to the anomalous occasion, and therefore I refer the whole matter to Congress, with the hope that a plan may be devised for the administration of justice in all such parts of the insurgent States and Territories as may be under the control of this Government, whether by a voluntary return to allegiance and order, or by the power of our arms; this, however, not to be a permanent institution, but a temporary substitute, and to cease as soon as the ordinary courts can be re-established in peace.

It is important that some more convenient means should be provided, if possible, for the adjustment of claims against the Government, especially in view of their increased number by reason of the war. It is as much the duty of Government to render prompt justice against itself, in favor of citizens, as it is to administer the same between private individuals. The investigation and adjudication of claims, in their nature belong to the judicial department; besides, it is apparent that the attention of Congress will be more than usually engaged, for some time to come, with great national questions. It was intended, by the organization of the Court of Claims, mainly to remove this branch of business from the halls of Congress; but while the court has proved to be an effective and valuable means of investigation, it in great degree fails to effect the object of its creation, for want of power to make its judgments final.

Fully aware of the delicacy, not to say the danger, of the subject, I commend to your careful consideration whether this power of making judgments final may not properly be given to the court, reserving the right of appeal on questions of law to the Supreme Court, with such other provisions as experience may have shown to be necessary.

I ask attention to the report of the Postmaster-General, the following being a summary statement of the condition of the department:

The revenue from all sources during the fiscal year ending June 30, 1861, including the annual permanent appropriation of seven hundred thousand dollars for the transportation of "free mail matter," was nine million, forty-nine thousand, two hundred and ninety-six dollars and forty cents, being about two per cent. less than the revenue for 1860.

The expenditures were thirteen million, six hundred and six thousand, seven hundred and fifty-nine dollars and eleven cents, showing a decrease of more than eight per cent. as compared with those of the previous year, and leaving an excess of expenditure over the revenue for the last fiscal year of four million, five hundred and fifty-seven thousand, four hundred and sixty-two dollars and seventy-one cents.

The gross revenue for the year ending June 30, 1863, is estimated at an increase of four per cent. on that of 1861, making eight million, six hundred and eighty-three thousand dollars, to which should be added the earnings of the department in carrying free matter, viz.: seven hundred thousand dollars, making nine millions three hundred and eighty-three thousand dollars.

The total expenditures for 1863 are estimated at twelve million, five hundred and twenty-eight thousand dollars, leaving an estimated deficiency of three million, one hundred and forty-five thousand dollars to be supplied from the Treasury, in addition to the permanent appropriation.

The present insurrection shows, I think, that the extension of this district across the Potomac River, at the time of establishing the Capitol here, was eminently wise, and consequently that the relinquishment of that portion of it which lies within the State of Virginia was unwise and dangerous. I submit for your consideration the expediency of regaining that part of the district, and the restoration of the original boundaries thereof, through negotiations with the State of Virginia.

The report of the Secretary of the Interior, with the accompanying documents, exhibits the condition of the several branches of the public business pertaining to that department. The depressing influences of the insurrection have been especially felt in the operations of the Patent and General Land Offices. The cash receipts from the sales of public lands during the past year have exceeded the expenses of our land system only about two hundred thousand dollars. The sales have been entirely suspended in the Southern States, while the interruptions to the business of the country, and the diversion of large numbers of men from labor to military service, have obstructed settlements in the new States and territories of the Northwest.

The receipts of the Patent Office have declined in nine months about one hundred thousand dollars, rendering a large reduction of the force employed necessary to make it self-sustaining.

The demands upon the Pension Office will be largely increased by the insurrection. Numerous applications for pensions, based upon the casualties of the existing war, have already been made. There is reason to believe that many who are now upon the pension rolls, and in receipt of the bounty of the Government, are in the ranks of the insurgent army, or giving them aid and comfort. The Secretary of the Interior has directed a suspension of the payment of the pensions of such persons upon proof of their disloyalty. I recommend that Congress authorize that officer to cause the names of such persons to be stricken from the pension rolls.

The relations of the Government with the Indian tribes have been greatly disturbed by the insurrection, especially in the southern superintendency and in that of New Mexico. The Indian country south of Kansas is in the possession of insurgents from Texas and Arkansas. The agents of the United States appointed since the 4th of March for this superintendency have been unable to reach their posts, while the most of those who were in office before that time have espoused the insurrectionary cause, and assume to exercise the powers of agents by virtue of commissions from the insurrectionists. It has been stated in the public press that a portion of those Indians have been organized as a military force, and are attached to the army of the insurgents. Although the Government has no official information upon this subject, letters have been written to the Commissioner of Indian Affairs by several prominent chiefs, giving assurance of their loyalty to the United States, and expressing a wish for the presence of Federal troops to protect them. It is believed that upon the repossession of the country by the Federal forces, the Indians will readily cease all hostile demonstrations, and resume their former relations to the Government.

Agriculture, confessedly the largest interest of the nation, has not a department, nor a bureau, but a clerkship only, assigned to it in the Government. While it is fortunate that this great interest is so independent in its nature as to not have demanded and extorted more from the Government, I respectfully ask Congress to consider whether something more cannot be given voluntarily with general advantage.

Annual reports exhibiting the condition of our agriculture, commerce, and manufactures, would present a fund of information of great practical value to the country. While I make no suggestion as to details, I venture the opinion that an agricultural and statistical bureau might profitably be organized.

The execution of the laws for the suppression of the African slave-trade has been confided to the Department of the Interior, It is a subject of gratulation that the efforts which have been made for the suppression of this inhuman traffic have been recently attended with unusual success. Five vessels being fitted out for the slave-trade have been seized and condemned. Two mates of vessels engaged in the trade, and one person in equipping a vessel as a slaver, have been convicted and subjected to the penalty of fine and imprisonment, and one captain, taken with a cargo of Africans on board his vessel, has been convicted of the highest grade of offence under our laws, the punishment of which is death.

The Territories of Colorado, Dakotah, and Nevada, created by the last Congress, have been organized, and civil administration has been inaugurated therein under auspices especially gratifying, when it is considered that the leaven of treason was found existing in some of these new countries when the Federal officers arrived there.

The abundant natural resources of these Territories, with the security and protection afforded by organized government, will doubtless invite to them a large immigation when peace shall restore the business of the country to its accustomed channels. I submit the resolutions of the Legislature of Colorado, which evidence the patriotic spirit of the people of the Territory. So far the authority of the United States has been upheld in all the Territories, as it is hoped it will be in the future. I commend their interests and defence to the enlightened and generous care of Congress.

I recommend to the favorable consideration of Congress the interests of the District of Columbia. The insurrection has been the cause of much suffering and sacrifice to its inhabitants, and as they have no representative in Congress, that body should not overlook their just claims upon the Government.

At your late session a joint resolution was adopted authorizing the President to take measures for facilitating a proper representation of the industrial interests of the United States at the exhibition of the industry of all nations to be holden at London in the year 1862. I regret to say I have been unable to give personal attention to this subject—a subject at once so interesting in itself, and so extensively and intimately connected with the material prosperity of the world. Through the Secretaries of State and of the Interior a plan or system has been devised and partly matured, and which will be laid before you.

Under and by virtue of the act of Congress entitled "An act to confiscate property used for insurrectionary purposes," approved August 6, 1861, the legal claims of certain persons to the labor and service of certain other persons have become forfeited; and numbers of the latter, thus liberated, are already dependent on the United States, and must be provided for in some way. Besides this, it is not impossible that some of the States will pass similar enactments for their own benefit respectively, and by operation of which persons of the same class will be thrown upon them for disposal. In such case I recommend that Congress provide for accepting such persons from such States, according to some mode of valuation, in lieu, *pro tanto*, of direct taxes, or upon some other plan to be agreed on with such States respectively; that such persons, on such acceptance by the General Government, be at once deemed free; and that, in any event, steps be taken for colonizing both classes (or the one first mentioned, if the other shall not be brought into existence) at some place or places in a climate congenial to them. It might be well to consider, too, whether the free colored people already in the United States could not, so far as individuals may desire, be included in such colonization.

To carry out the plan of colonization may involve the acquiring of territory, and also the appropriation of money beyond that to be expended in the territorial acquisition. Having practised the acquisition of territory for nearly sixty years, the question of constitutional power to do so is no longer an open one with us. The power was questioned at first by Mr. Jefferson, who, however, in the purchase of Louisiana, yielded his scruples on the plea of great expediency. If it be said that the only legitimate object of acquiring territory is to furnish homes for white men, this measure effects that object; for the emigration of colored men leaves additional room for white men remaining or coming here. Mr. Jefferson, however, placed the importance of procuring Louisiana more on political and commercial grounds than on providing room for population.

On this whole proposition, including the appropriation of money with the acquisition of territory, does not the expediency amount to absolute necessity—that, without which the Government itself cannot be perpetuated?

The war continues. In considering the policy to be adopted for suppressing the insurrection, I have been anxious and careful that the inevitable conflict for this purpose shall not degenerate into a violent and remorseless revolutionary struggle.

In the exercise of my best discretion I have adhered to the blockade of the ports held by the insurgents, instead of putting in force by proclamation the law of Congress enacted at the late session for closing those ports.

So, also, obeying the dictates of prudence, as well as the obligations of law, instead of transcending I have adhered to the act of Congress to confiscate property used for insurrectionary purposes. If a new law upon the same subject shall be proposed, its propriety will be duly considered. The Union must be preserved; and hence all indispensable means must be employed. We should not be in haste to determine that radical and extreme measures, which may reach the loyal as well as the disloyal, are indispensable.

The inaugural address at the beginning of the Administration, and the message to Congress at the late special session, were both mainly devoted to the domestic controversy out of which the insurrection and consequent war have sprung. Nothing now occurs to add or subtract to or from the principles or general purposes stated and expressed in those documents.

The last ray of hope for preserving the Union peaceably expired at the assault upon Fort Sumter; and a general review of what has occurred since may not be unprofitable. What was painfully uncertain then is much better defined and more distinct now; and the progress of events is plainly in the right direction. The insurgents confidently claimed a strong support from north of Mason and Dixon's line; and the friends of the Union were not free from apprehension on the point. This, however, was soon settled definitely, and on the right side. South of the line, noble little Delaware led off right from the first. Maryland was made to seem against the Union. Our soldiers were assaulted, bridges were burned, and railroads torn up within her limits; and we were many days, at one time, without the ability to bring a single regiment over her soil to the capital. Now her bridges and railroads are repaired and open to the Government; she already gives seven regiments to the cause of the Union, and none to the enemy; and her people, at a regular election, have sustained the Union by a larger majority and a larger aggregate vote than they ever before gave to any candidate or any question. Kentucky, too, for some time in doubt, is now decidedly and, I think, unchangeably ranged on the side of the Union. Missouri is comparatively quiet, and, I believe, cannot again be overrun by the insurrectionists. These three States of Maryland, Kentucky, and Missouri, neither of which would promise a single soldier at first, have now an aggregate of not less than forty thousand in the field for the Union; while of their citizens, certainly not more than a third of that number, and they of doubtful whereabouts and doubtful existence, are in arms against it. After a somewhat bloody struggle of months, winter closes on the Union people of Western Virginia, leaving them masters of their own country.

An insurgent force of about fifteen hundred, for months dominating the narrow peninsular region constituting the counties of Accomac and Northampton, and known as Eastern Shore of Virginia, together with some contiguous parts of Maryland, have laid down their arms; and the people there have renewed their allegiance to, and accepted the protection of, the old flag. This leaves no armed insurrectionist north of the Potomac, or east of the Chesapeake.

Also we have obtained a footing at each of the isolated points on the southern coast of Hatteras, Port Royal, Tybee Island, near Savannah, and Ship Island; and we likewise have some general accounts of popular movements in behalf of the Union in North Carolina and Tennessee.

These things demonstrate that the cause of the Union is advancing steadily and certainly southward.

Since your last adjournment Lieutenant-General Scott has retired from the head of the army. During his long life the nation has not been unmindful of his merit; yet, on calling to mind how faithfully, ably, and brilliantly he has served the country, from a time far back in our history, when few of the now living had been born, and thenceforward continually, I cannot but think we are still his debtors. I submit, therefore, for your consideration what further mark of recognition is due to him, and to ourselves as a grateful people.

With the retirement of General Scott came the executive duty of appointing in his stead a general-in-chief of the army. It is a fortunate circumstance that neither in council nor country was there, so far as I know, any difference of opinion as to the proper person to be selected. The retiring chief repeatedly expressed his judgment in favor of General McClellan for the position; and in this the nation seemed to give a unanimous concurrence. The designation of General McClellan is, therefore, in considerable degree, the selection of the country as well as of the Executive; and hence there is better reason to hope there will be given him the confidence and cordial support thus, by fair implication, promised, and without which he cannot, with so full efficiency, serve the country.

It has been said that one bad general is better than two good ones;

and the saying is true, if taken to mean no more than that an army is better directed by a single mind, though inferior, than by two superior ones at variance and cross-purposes with each other.

And the same is true in all joint operations wherein those engaged can have none but a common end in view, and can differ only as to the choice of means. In a storm at sea, no one on board can wish the ship to sink; and yet not unfrequently all go down together, because too many will direct, and no single mind can be allowed to control.

It continues to develop that the insurrection is largely, if not exclusively a war upon the first principle of popular government—the rights of the people. Conclusive evidence of this is found in the most grave and maturely-considered public documents, as well as in the general tone of the insurgents. In those documents we find the abridgment of the existing right of suffrage, and the denial to the people of all right to participate in the selection of public officers, except the legislative, boldly advocated, with labored arguments to prove that large control of the people in government is the source of all political evil. Monarchy itself is sometimes hinted at as a possible refuge from the power of the people.

In my present position, I could scarcely be justified were I to omit raising a warning voice against this approach of returning despotism.

It is not needed, nor fitting here, that a general argument should be made in favor of popular institutions; but there is one point, with its connections, not so hackneyed as most others, to which I ask a brief attention. It is the effort to place capital on an equal footing with, if not above, labor, in the structure of government. It is assumed that labor is available only in connection with capital; that nobody labors unless somebody else, owning capital, somehow by the use of it induces him to labor. This assumed, it is next considered whether it is best that capital shall hire laborers, and thus induce them to work by their own consent, or buy them, and drive them to it without their consent. Having proceeded so far, it is naturally concluded that all laborers are either hired laborers, or what we call slaves. And further, it is assumed that whoever is once a hired laborer is fixed in that condition for life.

Now, there is no such relation between capital and labor as assumed; nor is there any such thing as a free man being fixed for life in the condition of a hired laborer. Both these assumptions are false, and all inferences from them are groundless.

Labor is prior to and independent of capital. Capital is only the fruit of labor, and could never have existed if labor had not first existed. Labor is the superior of capital, and deserves much the higher consideration. Capital has its rights, which are as worthy of protection as any other rights. Nor is it denied that there is, and probably always will be, a relation between labor and capital, producing mutual benefits. The error is in assuming that the whole labor of community exists within that relation. A few men own capital, and those few avoid labor themselves, and, with their capital, hire or buy another few to labor for them. A large majority belong to neither class—neither work for others, nor have others working for them. In most of the Southern States, a majority of the whole people of all colors are neither slaves nor masters; while in the Northern, a large majority are neither hirers nor hired. Men, with their families—wives, sons, and daughters—work for themselves, on their farms, in their houses, and in their shops, taking the whole product to themselves, and asking no favors of capital on the one hand, nor of hired laborers or slaves on the other. It is not forgotten that a considerable number of persons mingle their own labor with capital—that is, they labor with their own hands, and also buy or hire others to labor for them; but this is only a mixed, and not a distinct class. No principle stated is disturbed by the existence of this mixed class.

Again: as has already been said, there is not of necessity any such thing as the free hired laborer being fixed to that condition for life. Many independent men everywhere in these States, a few years back in their lives, were hired laborers. The prudent, penniless beginner in the world labors for wages awhile, saves a surplus with which to buy tools or land for himself, then labors on his own account another while, and at length hires another new beginner to help him. This is the just, and generous, and prosperous system, which opens the way to all, gives hope to all, and consequent energy, and progress, and improvement of condition to all. No men living are more worthy to be trusted than those who toil up from poverty—none less inclined to take or touch aught which they have not honestly earned. Let them beware of surrendering a political power which they already possess, and which, if surrendered, will surely be used to close the door of advancement against such as they, and to fix new disabilities and burdens upon them, till all of liberty shall be lost.

From the first taking of our national census to the last are seventy years; and we find our population, at the end of the period, eight times as great as it was at the beginning. The increase of those other things which men deem desirable has been even greater. We thus have, at one view, what the popular principle, applied to Government through the machinery of the States and the Union, has produced in a given time; and also what, if firmly maintained, it promises for the future. There are already among us those who, if the Union be preserved, will live to see it contain two hundred and fifty millions. The struggle of to-day is not altogether for to-day; it is for a vast future also. With a reliance on Providence, all the more firm and earnest, let us proceed in the great task which events have devolved upon us.

ABRAHAM LINCOLN.

The actual condition of the country and the progress of the war, at the opening of the session, are very clearly stated in this document; and the principles upon which the President had based his conduct of public affairs are set forth with great distinctness and precision. On the subject of interfering with slavery, the President had adhered strictly to the letter and spirit of the act passed by Congress at its extra session; but he very distinctly foresaw that it might become necessary, as a means of quelling the rebellion and preserving the Union, to resort to a much more vigorous policy than was contemplated by that act. While he threw out a timely caution against undue haste in the adoption of extreme measures, he promised full and careful consideration of any new law which Congress might consider it wise and expedient to pass.

It very soon became evident that Congress was disposed to make very considerable advances upon the legislation of the extra session. The resistance of the rebels had been more vigorous and effective than was anticipated, and the defeat at Bull Run had exasperated, as well as aroused, the public mind. The forbearance of the Government in regard to slavery had not only failed to soften the hostility of the rebels, but had been represented to Europe by the rebel authorities as proving a determination on the part of the United States to protect and perpetuate slavery by restoring the authority of the Constitution which guaranteed its safety; and the acts of the extra session, especially the Crittenden resolution, defining and limiting the objects of the war, were quoted in rebel dispatches to England, for that purpose. It was known also that within the lines of the rebel army, slaves were freely employed in the construction of fortifications, and that they contributed, in this and other ways, very largely to the strength of the insurrection. The whole country, under the iufluence of these facts, began to regard slavery as not only the cause of the rebellion, but as the main strength of its armies and the bond of union for the rebel forces;—and Congress, representing and sharing this feeling, entered promptly and zealously upon such measures as it would naturally suggest. Resolutions at the very outset of the session were offered, calling on the President to emancipate slaves whenever and wherever such action would tend to weaken the rebellion; and the general policy of the Government upon this subject became the theme of protracted and animated debate. The orders issued by the generals of the army, especially McClellan, Halleck, and Dix, by which fugitive slaves were prohibited from coming within the army lines, were severely censured. All the resolutions upon these topics were, however, referred to appropriate committees, generally without specific instructions as to the character of their action upon them.

Early in the session a strong disposition was evinced in some quarters to censure the Government for its arbitrary arrests of persons in the loyal States, suspected of aiding the rebels, its suppression of disloyal presses, and other acts which it had deemed essential to the safety of the country: and a sharp debate took place in the Senate upon a resolution of inquiry and implied censure offered by Mr. Trumbull, of Illinois. The general feeling, however, was so decidedly in favor of sustaining the President, that the resolution was referred to the Judiciary Committee, by a vote of 25 to 17.

On the 19th of December, in the Senate, a debate on the

relation of slavery to the rebellion arose upon a resolution offered by Mr. Willey, of Virginia, who contested the opinion that slavery was the cause of the war, and insisted that the rebellion had its origin in the hostility of the Southern political leaders to the democratic principle of government; he believed that when the great body of the Southern people came to see the real purpose and aim of the rebellion, they would withdraw their support, and restore the Union. No action was taken on the resolution, which merely gave occasion for debate. A resolution was adopted in the House, forbidding the employment of the army to return fugitive slaves to their owners; and a bill was passed in both Houses, declaring that hereafter there shall be "neither slavery nor involuntary servitude in any of the Territories of the United States, now existing, or which may at any time be formed or acquired by the United States, otherwise than in the punishment of crimes whereof the party shall have been duly convicted."

In the Senate, on the 18th of March, a bill was taken up to abolish slavery in the District of Columbia; and an amendment was offered, directing that those thus set free should be colonized out of the United States. The policy of colonization was fully discussed in connection with the general subject, the senators from the Border States opposing the bill itself, mainly on grounds of expediency, as calculated to do harm under the existing circumstances of the country. The bill was passed, with an amendment appropriating money to be used by the President in colonizing such of the emancipated slaves as might wish to leave the country. It received in the Senate 29 votes in its favor and 14 against it. In the House it passed by a vote of 92 to 38.

President Lincoln sent in the following Message, announcing his approval of the bill:

FELLOW-CITIZENS OF THE SENATE AND HOUSE OF REPRESENTATIVES:

The act entitled "An act for the release of certain persons held to service or labor in this District of Columbia," has this day been approved and signed.

I have never doubted the constitutional authority of Congress to abolish slavery in this District; and I have ever desired to see the national capital freed from the institution in some satisfactory way. Hence there has never been in my mind any question upon the subject except the one of expediency, arising in view of all the circumstances. If there be matters within and about this act which might have taken a course or shape more satisfactory to my judgment, I do not attempt to specify them. I am gratified that the two principles of compensation and colonization are both recognized and practically applied in the act.

In the matter of compensation, it is provided that claims may be presented within ninety days from the passage of the act, "but not thereafter;" and there is no saving for minors, *femmes covert*, insane, or absent persons. I presume this is an omission by mere oversight, and I recommend that it be supplied by an amendatory or supplemental act.

ABRAHAM LINCOLN.

April 16, 1862.

On the 6th of March the President sent to Congress the following Message on the subject of aiding such slaveholding States as might take measures to emancipate their slaves:

WASHINGTON, *March* 6, 1862.

FELLOW-CITIZENS OF THE SENATE AND HOUSE OF REPRESENTATIVES:

I recommend the adoption of a joint resolution by your honorable body, which shall be, substantially, as follows:

Resolved, That the United States, in order to co-operate with any State which may adopt gradual abolition of slavery, give to such State pecuniary aid, to be used by such State, in its discretion, to compensate it for the inconvenience, public and private, produced by such change of system.

If the proposition contained in the resolution does not meet the approval of Congress and the country, there is an end of it. But if it does command such approval, I deem it of importance that the States and people immediately interested should be at once distinctly notified of the fact, so that they may begin to consider whether to accept or reject it.

The Federal Government would find its highest interest in such a measure as one of the most important means of self-preservation. The leaders of the existing rebellion entertain the hope that this Government will ultimately be forced to acknowledge the independence of some part of the disaffected region, and that all the Slave States north of such part will then say, "The Union for which we have struggled being already gone, we now choose to go with the Southern section." To deprive them of this hope substantially ends the rebellion; and the initiation of emancipation deprives them of it, and of all the States initiating it.

The point is not that all the States tolerating slavery would very soon, if at all, initiate emancipation; but while the offer is equally made to all, the more Northern shall, by such initiation, make it certain to the more Southern that in no event will the former ever join the latter in their proposed Confederacy. I say initiation, because, in my judgment, gradual and not sudden emancipation is better for all.

In the mere financial or pecuniary view, any member of Congress with the census or an abstract of the Treasury report before him, can, readily see for himself how very soon the current expenditures of this war would purchase, at a fair valuation, all the slaves in any named State.

Such a proposition on the part of the General Government sets up no claim of a right by the Federal authority to interfere with slavery within State limits—referring as it does the absolute control of the subject, in each case, to the State and the people immediately interested. It is proposed as a matter of perfectly free choice to them.

In the annual Message, last December, I thought fit to say "the Union must be preserved, and hence all indispensable means must be employed." I said this, not hastily but deliberately. War has been made, and continues to be an indispensable means to this end. A practical reacknowledgment of the national authority would render the war unnecessary, and it would at once cease. But resistance continues, and the war must also continue; and it is impossible to foresee all the incidents which may attend, and all the ruin which may follow it. Such as may seem indispensable, or may obviously promise great efficiency towards ending the struggle, must and will come.

The proposition now made (though an offer only) I hope it may be esteemed no offence to ask whether the pecuniary consideration tendered would not be of more value to the States and private persons concerned than would the institution and property in it, in the present aspect of affairs. While it is true that the adoption of the proposed resolution would be merely initiatory, and not within itself a practical measure, it is recommended in the hope that it would lead to important practical results.

In full view of my great responsibility to my God and my country, I earnestly beg the attention of Congress and the people to the subject.

ABRAHAM LINCOLN.

This Message indicates very clearly the tendency of the President's reflections upon the general relations of slavery to the rebellion. He had most earnestly endeavored to arouse the people of the Southern States to a contemplation of the fact that, if they persisted in their effort to overthrow the Government of the United States, the fate of slavery would sooner or later inevitably be involved in the conflict. The time was steadily approaching when, in consequence of their obstinate persistence in the rebellion, this result would follow; and the President, with wise forethought, sought anxiously to reconcile the shock which the contest would involve, with the order of the country and the permanent prosperity of all classes of the people. The general feeling of the country at that time was in harmony with this endeavor. The people were still disposed to exhaust every means which justice would sanction, to withdraw the people of the Southern States from the disastrous war into which they had been plunged by their leaders, and they welcomed this suggestion of the President as likely to produce that result, if any effort in that direction could.

In pursuance of the recommendation of the Message, Mr. R. Conkling, of New York, introduced, in the House of Representatives, on the 10th of March, the following resolution:

Resolved by the Senate and House of Representatives of the United States in Congress assembled, That the United States ought to co-operate with any State which may adopt gradual abolishment of slavery, giving to such State pecuniary aid, to be used by such State in its discretion, to compensate for the inconveniences, public and private, produced by such a change of system.

The debate on this resolution illustrated the feelings of the country on the subject. It was vehemently opposed by the sympathizers with secession from both sections, as an unconstitutional interference with slavery, and hesitatingly supported by the anti-slavery men of the North, as less decided in its hostility than they had a right to expect. The sentiment of the more moderate portion of the community was expressed by Mr. Fisher, of Delaware, who regarded it as an olive-branch of peace and harmony and good faith presented by the North, and as well calculated to bring about a peaceful solution and settlement of the slavery question. It was adopted in the House by a vote of 89 to 31. Coming up in the Senate on the 24th of March, it was denounced in strong terms by Mr. Saulsbury, of Delaware, and others—Mr. Davis, of Kentucky, opposing the terms in which it was couched, but approving its general tenor. It subsequently passed, receiving 32 votes in its favor, and but 10 against it. This resolution was approved by the President on the 10th of April. It was generally regarded by the people and by the President himself as rather an experiment than as a fixed policy—as intended to test the temper of the people of the Southern States, and offer them a way of escape from the evils and embarrassments with which slavery had surrounded them, rather than set forth a distinct line of conduct which was to be pressed upon the country at all hazards. This character, indeed, was stamped upon it by the fact that its practical execution was made to depend wholly on the people of the Southern States themselves. It recognized their complete control over slavery, within their own limits, and simply tendered them the aid of the General Government in any steps they might feel inclined to take to rid themselves of it.

The President was resolved that the experiment should have a full and a fair trial; and while he would not, on the one hand, permit its effect to be impaired by the natural impatience of those among his friends who were warmest and most extreme in their hostility to slavery, he, on the other hand, lost no opportunity to press the proposition on the favorable consideration of the people of the Border Slave States.

On the 9th of May, General Hunter, who commanded the department of South Carolina, which included also the States of Georgia and Florida, issued an order declaring all the slaves within that department to be thenceforth "forever free." This was done not from any alleged military necessity, growing out of the operations in his department, but upon a theoretical incompatibility between slavery and martial law. The President thereupon at once issued the following proclamation:

Whereas, There appears in the public prints what purports to be a proclamation of Major-General Hunter, in the words and figures following:

HEAD-QUARTERS DEPARTMENT OF THE SOUTH,
HILTON HEAD, S. C., *May* 9, 1862.

General Order, *No.* 11.

The three States of Georgia, Florida, and South Carolina, comprising the Military Department of the South, having deliberately declared themselves no longer under the United States of America, and having taken up arms against the United States, it becomes a military necessity to declare them under martial law.

This was accordingly done on the 25th day of April, 1862. Slavery and martial law in a free country are altogether incompatible. The persons in these States—Georgia, Florida, and South Carolina—heretofore held as slaves, are therefore declared forever free.

[OFFICIAL.]

Signed, DAVID HUNTER,
Major-General Commanding.

ED. W. SMITH, Acting Assistant Adj't General.

And, whereas, the same is producing some excitement and misunderstanding, therefore I, Abraham Lincoln, President of the United States, proclaim and declare that the Government of the United States had no knowledge or belief of an intention on the part of General Hunter to issue such proclamation, nor has it yet any authentic information that the document is genuine; and, further, that neither General Hunter nor any other commander or person has been authorized by the Government of the United States to make proclamation declaring the slaves of any State free, and that the supposed proclamation now in question, whether genuine or false, is altogether void so far as respects such declaration.

I further make known that, whether it be competent for me, as Commander-in-Chief of the Army and Navy, to declare the slaves of any State or States free; and whether at any time, or in any case, it shall have become a necessity indispensable to the maintenance of the Government to exercise such supposed power, are questions which, under my responsibility, I reserve to myself, and which I cannot feel justified in leaving to the decision of commanders in the field.

These are totally different questions from those of police regulations in armies or in camps.

On the sixth day of March last, by a special Message, I recommended to Congress the adoption of a joint resolution, to be substantially as follows:

> *Resolved*, That the United States ought to co-operate with any State which may adopt a gradual abolishment of slavery, giving to such State earnest expression to compensate for its inconveniences, public and private, produced by such change of system.

The resolution in the language above quoted was adopted by large majorities in both branches of Congress, and now stands an authentic, definite, and solemn proposal of the Nation to the States and people most interested in the subject matter. To the people of these States now, I mostly appeal. I do not argue—I beseech you to make the arguments for yourselves. You cannot, if you would, be blind to the signs of the times.

I beg of you a calm and enlarged consideration of them, ranging, if it may be, far above partisan and personal politics.

This proposal makes common cause for a common object, casting no reproaches upon any. It acts not the Pharisee. The change it contemplates would come gently as the dews of Heaven, not rending or wrecking any thing. Will you not embrace it? So much good has not been done by one effort in all past time, as in the Providence of God it is now your high privilege to do. May the vast future not have to lament that you have neglected it.

In witness whereof, I have hereunto set my hand and caused the seal of the United States to be hereunto affixed.

Done at the city of Washington this 19th day of May, in the year of our Lord one thousand eight hundred and sixty-two, and of the independence of the United States the eighty-sixth.

(Signed) ABRAHAM LINCOLN.

By the President:

W. H. SEWARD, Secretary of State.

This proclamation silenced the clamorous denunciation by which its enemies had assailed the Administration on the strength of General Hunter's order, and renewed the confidence, which for the moment had been somewhat impaired, in the President's adherence to the principles of action he had laid down. Nothing practical, however, was done in any of the Border States indicating any disposition to act upon his suggestions and avail themselves of the aid which Congress had offered. The members of Congress from those States had taken no steps towards inducing action in regard to it on the part of their constituents. Feeling the deepest interest in the adoption of some measure which should permanently detach the Border Slave States from the rebel Confederacy, and believing that the plan he had recommended would tend to accomplish that object, President LINCOLN sought a conference with the members of Congress from those States, and on the 12th of July, when they waited upon him at the executive mansion, he addressed them as follows:

GENTLEMEN: After the adjournment of Congress, now near, I shall have no opportunity of seeing you for several months. Believing that you of the Border States hold more power for good than any other equal number of members, I feel it a duty which I cannot justifiably waive to make this appeal to you.

I intend no reproach or complaint when I assure you that, in my opinion, if you all had voted for the resolution in the gradual emancipation Message of last March the war would now be substantially ended. And the plan therein proposed is yet one of the most potent and swift means of ending it. Let the States which are in rebellion see definitely and certainly that in no event will the States you represent ever join their proposed Confederacy, and they cannot much longer maintain the contest. But you cannot divest them of their hope to ultimately have you with them so long as you show a determination to perpetuate the institution within your own States. Beat them at elections, as you have overwhelmingly done, and, nothing daunted, they still claim you as their own. You and I know what the lever of their power is. Break that lever before their faces, and they can shake you no more forever.

Most of you have treated me with kindness and consideration, and I trust you will not now think I improperly touch what is exclusively your own, when, for the sake of the whole country, I ask, Can you, for your States, do better than to take the course I urge? Discarding *punctilio* and maxims adapted to more manageable times, and looking only to the unprecedentedly stern facts of our case, can you do better in any possible event? You prefer that the constitutional relation of the States to the nation shall be practically restored without disturbance of the institution: and if this were done, my whole duty, in this respect, under the Constitution and my oath of office, would be performed. But it is not done, and we are trying to accomplish it by war. The incidents of the war cannot be avoided. If the war continues long, as it must if the object be not sooner attained, the institution in your States will be extinguished by mere friction and abrasion—by the mere incidents of the war. It will be gone, and you will have nothing valuable in lieu of it. Much of its value is gone already. How much better for you and for your people to take the step which at once shortens the war, and secures substantial compensation for that which is sure to be wholly lost in any other event! How much better to thus save the money which else we sink forever in the war! How much better to do it while we can, lest the war ere long render us pecuniarily unable to do it! How much better for you, as seller, and the nation, as buyer, to sell out and buy out that without which the war could never have been, than to sink both the thing to be sold and the price of it in cutting one another's throats!

I do not speak of emancipation at once, but of a decision at once to emancipate gradually. Room in South America for colonization can be obtained cheaply, and in abundance, and when numbers shall be large enough to be company and encouragement for one another, the freed people will not be so reluctant to go.

I am pressed with a difficulty not yet mentioned—one which threatens division among those who, united, are none too strong. An instance of it is known to you. General Hunter is an honest man. He was, and I hope still is, my friend. I valued him none the less for his agreeing with me in the general wish that all men everywhere could be free. He proclaimed all men free within certain States, and I repudiated the proclamation. He expected more good and less harm from the measure than I could believe would follow. Yet, in repudiating it, I gave dissatisfaction, if not offence, to many whose support the country cannot afford to lose. And this is not the end of it. The pressure in this direction is still upon me, and is increasing. By conceding what I now ask you can relieve me, and, much more, can relieve the country in this important point.

Upon these considerations I have again begged your attention to the Message of March last. Before leaving the Capitol, consider and discuss it among yourselves. You are patriots and statesmen, and as such I pray you consider this proposition; and at the least commend it to the consideration of your States and people. As you would perpetuate popular government for the best people in the world, I beseech you that you do in nowise omit this. Our common country is in great peril, demanding the loftiest views and boldest action to bring a speedy relief. Once relieved, its form of government is saved to the world; its beloved history and cherished memories are vindicated, and its happy future fully assured and rendered inconceivably grand. To you, more than to any others, the privilege is given to assure that happiness and swell that grandeur, and to link your own names therewith forever.

The members to whom the President thus appealed were divided in opinion as to the merits of the proposition which he had laid before them. A majority of them submitted an elaborate reply, in which they dissented from the President's opinion that the adoption of this policy would terminate the war or serve the Union cause. They held it to be his duty to avoid all interference, direct or indirect, with slavery in the Southern States, and attributed much of the stubborn hostility which the South had shown in prosecuting the war, to the fact that Congress had departed in various instances from the spirit and objects for which the war ought to be prosecuted by the Government. A minority of those members, not being able to concur in this reply, submitted one of their own, in which they thus set forth their view of the motives of the President in the course he had adopted, and expressed their substantial concurrence in its justice and wisdom:

We believe that the whole power of the Government, upheld and sustained by all the influences and means of all loyal men in all sections and of all parties, is essentially necessary to put down the rebellion and preserve the Union and the Constitution. We understand your appeal to us to have been made for the purpose of securing this result. A very large portion of the people in the Northern States believe that slavery is the "lever power of the rebellion." It matters not whether this opinion is well-founded or not. The belief does exist, and we have to deal with things as they are, and not as we would have them be. In consequence of the existence of this belief, we understand that an immense pressure is brought to bear for the purpose of striking down this institution through the exercise of military authority. The Government cannot maintain this great struggle if the support and influence of the men who entertain these opinions be withdrawn. Neither can the Government hope for early success if the support of that element called "conservative" be withdrawn.

Such being the condition of things, the President appeals to the Border State men to step forward and prove their patriotism by making the first sacrifice. No doubt, like appeals have been made to extreme men in the North to meet us half way, in order that the whole moral, political, pecuniary, and physical force of the nation may be firmly and earnestly united in one grand effort to save the Union and the Constitution.

Believing that such were the motives that prompted your address, and such the results to which it looked, we cannot reconcile it to our sense of duty, in this trying hour, to respond in a spirit of fault-finding or querulousness over the things that are past. We are not disposed to seek for the cause of present misfortunes in the errors and wrongs of others who propose to unite with us in a common purpose. But, on the other hand, we meet your address in the spirit in which it was made, and, as loyal Americans, declare to you and to the world, that there is no sacrifice that we are not ready to make to save the Government and institutions of our fathers. That we, few of us though there may be, will permit no men, from the North or from the South, to go further than we in the accomplishment of the great work before us. That, in order to carry out these views, we will, so far as may be in our power, ask the people of the Border States calmly, deliberately, and fairly to consider your recommendations. We are the more emboldened to assume this position from the fact now become history, that the leaders of the Southern rebellion have offered to abolish slavery amongst them as a condition to foreign intervention in favor of their independence as a nation.

If they can give up slavery to destroy the Union, we can surely ask our people to consider the question of emancipation to save the Union.

9

Hon. Horace Maynard, of Tennessee, on the 16th of July submitted to the President his views of the question, in which he thus set forth his appreciation of the motives which had induced him to make the proposition in question to the Southern States :

Your whole administration gives the highest assurance that you are moved, not so much from a desire to see all men everywhere made free, as from a desire to preserve free institutions for the benefit of men already free ; not to make slaves free men, but to prevent free men from being made slaves ; not to destroy an institution which a portion of us only consider bad, but to save an institution which we all alike consider good. I am satisfied that you would not ask from any of your fellow-citizens a sacrifice not in your judgment imperatively required by the safety of the country. This is the spirit of your appeal, and I respond to it in the same spirit.

Determined to leave undone nothing which it was in his power to do to effect the object he had so much at heart, the President on the 12th of July sent into Congress a Message transmitting the draft of a bill upon the subject, as follows :

Fellow-Citizens of the Senate and House of Representatives :—Herewith is the draft of the bill to compensate any State which may abolish slavery within its limits, the passage of which, substantially as presented, I respectfully and earnestly recommend.

ABRAHAM LINCOLN.

Be it enacted by the Senate and House of Representatives of the United States of America in Congress assembled :—That whenever the President of the United States shall be satisfied that any State shall have lawfully abolished slavery within and throughout such State, either immediately or gradually, it shall be the duty of the President, assisted by the Secretary of the Treasury, to prepare and deliver to each State an amount of six per cent. interest-bearing bonds of the United States, equal to the aggregate value at — dollars per head of all the slaves within such State as reported by the census of 1860 ; the whole amount for any one State to be delivered at once, if the abolishment be immediate, or in equal annual installments, if it be gradual, interest to begin running on each bond at the time of delivery, and not before.

And be it further enacted, That if any State, having so received any such bonds, shall at any time afterwards by law reintroduce or tolerate slavery within its limits, contrary to the act of abolishment upon which such bonds shall have been received, said bonds so received by said State shall at once be null and void, in whosesoever hands they may be, and such State shall refund to the United States all interest which may have been paid on such bonds.

The bill was referred to a Committee, but no action was taken upon it in Congress, nor did any of the Border States respond to the President's invitation. The proposition, however, served a most excellent purpose in testing the sentiment of both sections of the country, and in preparing the way for the more vigorous treatment of the subject of slavery which the blind and stubborn prejudices of the slaveholding communities were rapidly rendering inevitable.

Two other subjects of importance engaged the attention and received the action of Congress during this session; the provision of a currency, and the amendment of the law to confiscate the property of rebels. A bill authorizing the issue of Treasury notes to the amount of $150,000,000, and making them a legal tender in all business transactions, was reported in the House by the Finance Committee, of which Hon. E. G. Spaulding, of New York, was Chairman, and taken up for discussion on the 17th of June. It was advocated mainly on the score of necessity, and was opposed on the ground of its alleged unconstitutionality. The division of sentiment on the subject was not a party one, some of the warmest friends and supporters of the administration doubting whether Congress had the power to make any thing but silver and gold a legal tender in the payment of debts. The same bill provided for a direct tax, involving stamp duties, taxes upon incomes, etc., sufficient with the duties upon imports to raise $150,000,000 per annum, and also for the establishment of a system of free banking by which bank notes to be circulated as currency might be issued upon the basis of stocks of the United States deposited as security. The bill was discussed at length, and was finally adopted by a vote 93 to 59. In the Senate it encountered a similar opposition, but passed by a vote of 30 to 7, a motion to strike out the legal tender clause having been previously rejected, 17 voting in favor of striking it out, and 22 against it.

The subject of confiscating the property of rebels excited still deeper interest. A bill for that purpose was taken up in the Senate, on the 25th of February, for discussion. By one of its sections all the slaves of any person, anywhere in the United States, aiding the rebellion, were declared to be forever free, and subsequent sections provided for colonizing slaves thus enfranchised. The bill was advocated on the ground that in no other way could the property of rebels, in those States where the judicial authority of the United States had been overborne, be reached; while it was opposed on the ground that it was unconstitutional, and that it would tend to render the Southern people still more united and desperate in their rebellion. By the confiscation act of the previous session, a slave who had been employed in aiding the rebellion was declared to be free, but the fact that he had been thus employed must be shown by due judicial process; by this bill all the slaves of any person who had been thus engaged were set free without the intervention of any judicial process whatever. This feature of the bill was warmly opposed by some of the ablest and most reliable of the supporters of the Administration as a departure from all recognized rules of proceeding, and as a direct interference with slavery in the States, in violation of the most solemn pledge of the Government, the Republican party, and individual supporters of the Administration. Senator Collamer, of Vermont, urged this view of the case with great cogency, citing Mr. Sumner's opinion expressed on the 25th of February, 1861, when, on presenting a memorial to the Senate in favor of abolishing slavery, he had added: "In offering it, I take this occasion to declare most explicitly that I do not think that Congress has any right to interfere with slavery in a State;" and quoting also Senator Fessenden's declaration in the debate on abolishing slavery in the District of Columbia, when he said: "I have held, and I hold to-day, and I say to-day what I have said in my place before, that the Congress of the United States, or the people of the United States through the Congress, under the Constitution as it now exists, have no right whatever to touch by legislation the institution of slavery in the States where it exists by law." Mr. Sherman's opinion, expressed in the same debate, that "we ought religiously to adhere to the promises we made to the people of this country when Mr. LINCOLN was elected President—we ought to abstain religiously from all interference with the domestic institutions of the Slave or the Free States," was also quoted, and Mr. Collamer said he did not see how it was possible to pass the bill in its present form without giving the world to understand that they *had* violated those pledges, and *had* interfered with slavery in the States. Mr. Collamer accordingly offered an amendment to the bill, obviating the objections he had urged against it; and this, with other amendments offered by other Senators, was referred to a Select Committee, which subsequently reported a bill designed, as the Chairman, Mr. Clark, of New Hampshire, explained, to harmonize the various shades of opinion upon the subject, and secure the passage of some measure which should meet the expectations of the country and the emergency of the case. The first section of this bill provided, that every person who should hereafter commit the crime of treason against the United States, *and be adjudged guilty thereof*, should suffer death, and all his slaves, if any, be declared and made free; or he should be imprisoned not less than five years, and fined not less than ten thousand dollars, and all his slaves, if any, be declared and made free.

The distinctive feature of this section, as distinguished from the corresponding section of the original bill, consisted in the fact that a trial and conviction were required before any person guilty of treason could be punished, either by death, imprisonment, or the forfeiture of his property. It was opposed on the one hand, by Mr. Trumbull, of Illinois, on the ground that it "made treason easy"—and on the other, by Mr. Davis, of Kentucky, because it set slaves free. Mr. Sumner offered a substitute to the whole bill, which in his judgment did not go far enough in giving the country the advantage of the "opportunity which God, in his beneficence, had afforded" it for securing universal emancipation. Mr. Powell, of Kentucky, moved to strike out the eleventh section, which authorized the President to "employ as many persons of African descent as he might deem necessary and proper for the suppression of the rebellion, and to organize and use them in such manner as he might judge best for the public welfare,"—but his motion was rejected by a vote of 11 to 25. While the bill was thus denounced by one class of Senators as too violent in its method of dealing with the rebels, it was resisted with still greater vehemence by another class as entirely defective in that respect. Mr. Sumner was especially severe in his censure of Senators who proposed, he said, "when the life of our Republic is struck at, to proceed as if by an indictment in a criminal court." His remarks gave rise to considerable personal discussion—which was interrupted by the receipt of a similar bill which had been passed by the House of Representatives, and which was decidedly more in harmony with the extreme views of Mr. Sumner and his friends, than the Senate bill. It assumed that the rebels were to be treated like a foreign enemy, without regard to the limitations and requirements of the Constitution, and that Congress, instead of the President, had the supreme and exclusive control of the operations of the war. This bill on coming before the Senate was set aside, and the bill which had been reported by the Senate Committee substituted in its place, by a vote of 21 to 17, and the latter was finally passed; ayes 28, noes 13. The House did not concur in this amendment to its own bill; but on receiving the report of a Committee of Conference which made some amendments to the Senate bill, it was passed, as amended, by both Houses and sent to the President for his signature.

The provisions of this bill were as follows:

SECTION 1 enacted that every person who should after its passage commit the crime of treason against the United States, and be adjudged guilty thereof, should suffer death, and all his slaves, if any, should be declared and made free; or he should be imprisoned for not less than five years, and fined not less than $10,000, and all his slaves made free.

SECTION 2 declared that if any person shall hereafter incite, assist, or engage in any rebellion against the authority of the United States or the laws thereof, or give aid or comfort thereto, or to any existing rebellion, and be convicted thereof, he shall be imprisoned for ten years or less, fined not more than $10,000, and all his slaves shall be set free.

SECTION 3. Every person guilty of these offences shall be forever disqualified to hold any office under the United States.

SECTION 4. This act was not to affect the prosecution, conviction, or punishment of any person guilty of treason before the passage of the act, unless convicted under it.

SECTION 5 made it the duty of the President to seize and apply to the use of the army of the United States, all the property of persons who had served as officers of the rebel army, or had held certain civil offices under the rebel Government, or in the rebel States, provided they had taken an oath of allegiance to the rebel authorities, and also of persons who, having property in any of the loyal States, shall hereafter give aid to the rebellion.

SECTION 6 prescribed that if any other persons being engaged in the rebellion should not, within sixty days after public proclamation duly made by the President, cease to aid the rebellion, all their property should be confiscated in the same manner.

SECTION 7 directed that proceedings *in rem* should be instituted in the name of the United States in the court of the district within which such property might be found, and if said property, whether real or personal, should be found to belong to any person engaged in rebellion, it should be condemned as enemies' property, and become the property of the United States.

SECTION 8 gave the several District Courts of the United States authority and power to make such orders as these proceedings might require.

SECTION 9 enacted that all slaves of persons who shall hereafter be engaged in rebellion against the Government of the United States, or who shall in any way give aid or comfort thereto, escaping from such persons, and taking refuge within the lines of the army, and all slaves captured from such persons or deserted by them and coming under the control of the Government of the United States, and all slaves of such persons found, or being within any place occupied by rebel forces, and afterwards occupied by the forces of the United States, shall be deemed captives of war, and shall be forever free of their servitude, and not again held as slaves.

SECTION 10 enacted that no slave escaping into another State should be delivered up, unless the claimant should make oath that the owner or master of such slave had never borne arms against the United States, or given any aid and comfort to the rebellion; and every person in the military service of the United States was prohibited from deciding on the validity of any claim to the services of any escaped slave, on pain of dismissal.

SECTION 11 authorized the President to employ as many persons of African descent as he might deem necessary and proper for the suppression of the rebellion, and to organize and use them as he might deem best for the public welfare.

SECTION 12 authorized the President to make provision for the colonization, with their own consent, of persons freed under this act, to some country beyond the limits of the United States, having first obtained the consent of the Government of said country to their protection and settlement, with all the privileges of free men.

SECTION 13 authorized the President at any time hereafter, by proclamation, to extend to persons who may have participated in this Rebellion, pardon and amnesty, with such exceptions, and at such time, and on such conditions as he might deem expedient for the public welfare.

SECTION 14 gave the Courts of the United States authority to institute such proceedings, and issue such orders as might be necessary to carry this act into effect.

It soon came to be understood that the President had objections to certain portions of the bill which would probably prevent him from signing it. A joint resolution was at once passed in the House, providing that the bill should be so construed "as not to apply to any acts done prior to its passage; nor to include any member of a State legislature, or judge of any State court who has not, in accepting or entering upon his office, taken an oath to support the constitution of the so-called Confederate States of America." When this reached the Senate, Mr. Clark, of New Hampshire, offered the following, to be added to the resolution:

> Nor shall any punishment or proceedings under said act be so construed as to work a forfeiture of the real estate of the offender beyond his natural life.

This provision encountered a sharp opposition, Mr. Trumbull, of Illinois, insisting that the forfeiture of real estate for life only would amount to nothing, and other Senators objecting to being influenced in their action by the supposed opinions of the President. Mr. Clark also proposed another amendment, authorizing the President, in granting an amnesty, to restore to the offender any property which might have been seized and condemned under this act. The resolutions and amendments were passed by the Senate, and received the concurrence of the House. On the 17th of July President LINCOLN sent in the following message, announcing that he had signed the bill, and specifying his objections to the act in its original shape:

Fellow-Citizens of the Senate and House of Representatives:

Considering the bill for "An act to suppress insurrection, to punish treason and rebellion, to seize and confiscate the property of rebels, and for other purposes," and the joint resolution explanatory of said act as being substantially one, I have approved and signed both.

Before I was informed of the resolution, I had prepared the draft of a message, stating objections to the bill becoming a law, a copy of which draft is herewith submitted. ABRAHAM LINCOLN.

July 12, 1862.

[Copy.]

Fellow-Citizens of the House of Representatives:

I herewith return to the honorable body, in which it originated, the bill for an act entitled "An act to suppress treason and rebellion, to seize and confiscate the property of rebels, and for other purposes," together with my objections to its becoming a law.

Their is much in the bill to which I perceive no objection. It is wholly prospective; and it touches neither person nor property of any loyal citizen, in which particular it is just and proper.

The first and second sections provide for the conviction and punishment of persons who shall be guilty of treason, and persons who shall "incite, set on foot, assist, or engage in any rebellion or insurrection against the authority of the United States, or the laws thereof, or shall give aid or comfort thereto, or shall engage in or give aid and comfort to any such existing rebellion or insurrection." By fair construction, persons within those sections are not punished without regular trials in duly constituted courts, under the forms and all the substantial provisions of law and the Constitution applicable to their several cases. To this I perceive no objection; especially as such persons would be within the general pardoning power, and also the special provision for pardon and amnesty contained in this act.

It is also provided that the slaves of persons convicted under these sections shall be free. I think there is an unfortunate form of expression, rather than a substantial objection, in this. It is startling to say that Congress can free a slave within a State, and yet if it were said the ownership of a slave had first been transferred to the nation, and Congress had then liberated him, the difficulty would at once vanish. And this is the real case. The traitor against the General Government forfeits his slave at least as justly as he does any other property; and he forfeits both to the Government against which he offends. The Government, so far as there can be ownership, thus owns the forfeited slaves, and the question for Congress in regard to them is, "Shall they be made free or sold to new masters?" I perceive no objection to Congress deciding in advance that they shall be free. To the high honor of Kentucky, as I am informed, she is the owner of some slaves by *escheat*, and has sold none, but liberated all. I hope the same is true of some other States. Indeed, I do not believe it will be physically possible for the General Government to return persons so circumstanced to actual slavery. I believe there would be physical resistance to it, which could neither be turned aside by argument nor driven away by force. In this view I have no objection to this feature of the bill. Another matter involved in these two sections, and running through other parts of the act, will be noticed hereafter.

I perceive no objections to the third or fourth sections.

So far as I wish to notice the fifth and sixth sections, they may be considered together. That the enforcement of these sections would do no injustice to the persons embraced within them is clear. That those who make a causeless war should be compelled to pay the cost of it is too obviously just to be called in question. To give governmental protection to the property of persons who have abandoned it, and gone on a crusade to overthrow the same Government, is absurd, if considered in the mere light of justice. The severest justice may not always be the best policy. The principle of seizing and appropriating the property of the person embraced within these sections is certainly not very objectionable, but a justly discriminating application of it would be very difficult, and, to a great extent, impossible. And would it not be wise to place a power of remission somewhere, so that these persons may know they have something to lose by persisting and something to gain by desisting? I am not sure whether such power of remission is or is not in section thirteen. Without any special act of Congress, I think our military commanders, when, in military phrase, "they are within the enemy's country," should, in an orderly manner, seize and use whatever of real or personal property may be necessary or convenient for their commands; at the same time preserving, in some way, the evidence of what they do.

What I have said in regard to slaves, while commenting on the first and second sections, is applicable to the ninth, with the difference that no provision is made in the whole act for determining whether a particular individual slave does or does not fall within the classes defined in that section. He is to be free upon certain conditions; but whether those conditions do or do not pertain to him, no mode of ascertaining is provided. This could be easily supplied.

To the tenth section I make no objection. The oath therein required seems to be proper, and the remainder of the section is substantially identical with a law already existing.

The eleventh section simply assumes to confer discretionary power upon the Executive. Without the law, I have no hesitation to go as far in the direction indicated as I may at any time deem expedient. And I am ready to say now, I think it is proper for our military commanders to employ, as laborers, as many persons of African descent as can be used to advantage.

The twelfth and thirteenth sections are something better than unobjectionable; and the fourteenth is entirely proper, if all other parts of the Act shall stand.

That to which I chiefly object pervades most part of the Act, but more distinctly appears in the first, second, seventh, and eighth sections. It is the sum of those provisions which results in the divesting of title forever.

For the causes of treason and ingredients of treason, not amounting to the full crime, it declares forfeiture extending beyond the lives of the guilty parties; whereas the Constitution of the United States declares that "no attainder of treason shall work corruption of blood or forfeiture except during the life of the person attainted." True, there is to be no formal attainder in this case; still, I think, the greater punishment cannot be constitutionally inflicted, in a different form, for the same offence.

With great respect I am constrained to say I think this feature of the Act is unconstitutional. It would not be difficult to modify it.

I may remark that the provision of the Constitution, put in language borrowed from Great Britain, applies only in this country, as I understand, to real or landed estate.

Again, this Act, *in rem*, forfeits property for the ingredients of treason without a conviction of the supposed criminal, or a personal hearing given him in any proceeding. That we may not touch property lying within our reach, because we cannot give personal notice to an owner who is absent endeavoring to destroy the Government, is certainly satisfactory. Still, the owner may not be thus engaged; and I think a reasonable time should be provided for such parties to appear and have personal hearings. Similar provisions are not uncommon in connection with proceedings *in rem*.

For the reasons stated, I return the Bill to the House in which it originated.

The passage of this bill constituted a very important step in the prosecution of the war for the suppression of the Rebellion. It prescribed definite penalties for the crime of treason, and thus supplied a defect in the laws as they then existed. It gave the rebels distinctly to understand that one of these penalties, if they persisted in their resistance to the authority of the United States, would be the emancipation of their slaves. And it also authorized the employment by the President of persons of African descent, to aid in the suppression of the Rebellion in any way which he might deem most conducive to the public welfare. Yet throughout the bill, it was clearly made evident that the object and purpose of these measures was not the abolition of slavery, but the preservation of the Union and the restoration of the authority of the Constitution.

On the 14th of January SIMON CAMERON resigned his position as Secretary of War. On the 30th of April the House of Representatives passed, by a vote of 75 to 45, a resolution, censuring certain official acts performed by him while acting as Secretary of War; whereupon, on the 27th of May, President Lincoln transmitted to the House the following message:

TO THE SENATE AND HOUSE OF REPRESENTATIVES:

The insurrection which is yet existing in the United States, and aims at the overthrow of the Federal Constitution and the Union, was clandestinely prepared during the winter of 1860 and 1861, and assumed an open organization in the form of a treasonable provisional government at Montgomery, Alabama, on the eighteenth day of February, 1861. On the twelfth day of April, 1861, the insurgents committed the flagrant act of civil war by the bombardment and capture of Fort Sumter, which cut off the hope of immediate conciliation. Immediately afterwards all the roads and avenues to this city were obstructed, and the capital was put into the condition of a siege. The mails in every direction were stopped and the lines of telegraph cut off by the insurgents, and military and naval forces which had been called out by the Government for the defence of Washington were prevented from reaching the city by organized and combined treasonable resistance in the State of Maryland. There was no adequate and effective organization for the public defence. Congress had indefinitely adjourned. There was no time to convene them. It became necessary for me to choose whether, using only the existing means, agencies, and processes which Congress had provided, I should let the government fall into ruin, or whether, availing myself of the broader powers conferred by the Constitution in cases of insurrection, I would make an effort to save it, with all its blessings, for the present age and for posterity. I thereupon summoned my constitutional advisers, the heads of all the departments, to meet on Sunday, the twentieth day of April, 1861, at the office of the Navy Department, and then and there, with their unanimous concurrence, I directed that an armed revenue cutter should proceed to sea to afford protection to the commercial marine, especially to the California treasure-ships, then on their way to this coast. I also directed the Commandant of the Navy Yard at Boston to purchase or charter, and arm, as quickly as possible, five steamships for purposes of public defence. I directed the Commandant of the Navy Yard at Philadelphia to purchase or charter, and arm an equal number for the same purpose. I directed the Commandant at New York to purchase or charter, and arm an equal number. I directed Commander Gillis to purchase or charter, and arm and put to sea two other vessels. Similar directions were given to Commodore Du Pont, with a view to the opening of passages by water to and from the capital. I directed the several officers to take the advice and obtain the aid and efficient services in the matter of his Excellency Edwin D. Morgan, the Governor of New York, or, in his absence, George D. Morgan, Wm. M. Evarts, R. M. Blatchford, and Moses H. Grinnell, who were, by my directions, especially empowered by the Secretary of the Navy to act for his department in that crisis, in matters pertaining to the forwarding of troops and supplies for the public defence. On the same occasion I directed that Gov. Morgan and Alexander Cummings, of the city of New York, should be authorized by the Secretary of War, Simon Cameron, to make all necessary arrangements for the transportation of troops and munitions of war in aid and assistance of the officers of the army of the United States, until communication by mails and telegraph should be completely re-established between the cities of Washington and New York. No security was required to be given by them, and either of them was authorized to act in case of inability to consult with the other. On the same occasion I authorized and directed the Secretary of the Treasury to advance, without requiring securing, two millions of dollars of public money to John A. Dix, George Opdyke, and Richard M. Blatchford, of New York, to be used by them in meeting such requisitions as should be directly consequent upon the military and naval measures for the defence and support of the Government, requiring them only to act without compensation, and to report their transactions when duly called upon. The several departments of the Government at that time contained so large a number of disloyal persons that it would have been impossible to provide safely through official agents only, for the performance of the duties thus confided to citizens favorably known for their ability, loyalty, and patriotism. The several orders issued upon these occurrences were transmitted by private messengers, who pursued a circuitous way to the seaboard cities, inland across the States of Pennsylvania and Ohio, and the northern lakes. I believe that by these and other similar measures taken in *that* crisis, some of which were without any authority of law, the Government was saved from overthrow. I am not aware that a dollar of the public funds thus confided without authority of law, to unofficial persons, was either lost or wasted, although apprehensions of such misdirections occurred to me as objections to these extraordinary proceedings, and were necessarily overruled. I recall these transactions now because my attention has been directed to a resolution which was passed by the House of Representatives on the thirtieth of last month, which is in these words:

> *Resolved*, that Simon Cameron, late Secretary of War, by intrusting Alexander Cummings with the control of large sums of the public money, and authority to purchase military supplies without restriction, without requiring from him any guarantee for the faithful performance of his duties, while the services of competent public officers were available, and by involving the government in a vast number of contracts with persons not legitimately engaged in the business pertaining to the subject matter of such contracts, especially in the purchase of arms for future delivery, has adopted a policy highly injurious to the public service, and deserves the censure of the House.

Congress will see that I should be wanting in candor and in justice if I should leave the censure expressed in this resolution to rest exclusively or chiefly upon Mr. Cameron. The same sentiment is unanimously entertained by the heads of the departments, who participated in the proceedings which the House of Representatives has censured. It is due to Mr. Cameron to say that although he fully approved the proceedings, they were not moved nor suggested by himself, and that not only the President, but all the other heads of departments were at least equally responsible with him for whatever error, wrong or fault was committed in the premises. ABRAHAM LINCOLN.

This letter was in strict conformity with the position uniformly held by the President in regard to the responsibility of members of his cabinet for acts of the Administration. He always maintained that the proper duty of each Secretary was, to direct the details of every thing done within his own department, and to tender such suggestions, information, and advice to the President as he might solicit at his hands. But the duty and responsibility of deciding what line of policy should be pursued, or what steps should be taken in any specific case, in his judgment, belonged exclusively to the President; and he was always willing and ready to assume it. This position has been widely and sharply assailed in various quarters as contrary to the precedents of our early history: but we believe it to be substantially in accordance with the theory of the Constitution upon this subject.

The progress of our armies in certain portions of the Southern States had warranted the suspension, at several ports, of the restrictions placed upon commerce by the blockade. On the 12th of May the President accordingly issued a proclamation declaring that the blockade of the ports of Beaufort, Port Royal, and New Orleans, should so far cease from the 1st of June, that commercial intercourse from those ports, except as to contraband of war, might be resumed, subject to the laws of the United States and the regulations of the Treasury Department.

On the 1st of July he issued another proclamation, in pursuance of the law of June 7th, designating the States and parts of States that were then in insurrection, so that the laws of the United States concerning the collection of taxes could not be enforced within their limits, and declaring that "the taxes legally chargeable upon real estate, under the act referred to, lying within the States or parts of States thus designated, together with a penalty of fifty per cent. of said taxes, should be a lien upon the tracts or lots of the same, severally charged, till paid."

On the 20th of October, finding it absolutely necessary to provide judicial proceedings for the State of Louisiana, a part of which was in our military possession, the President issued an order establishing a Provisional Court in the City of New Orleans, of which Charles A. Peabody was made Judge, with authority to try all causes, civil and criminal, in law, equity, revenue, and admiralty, and particularly to exercise all such power and jurisdiction as belongs to the Circuit and District Courts of the United States. His proceedings were to be conformed, so far as possible, to the course of proceedings and practice usual in the Courts of the United States of Louisiana, and his judgment was to be final and conclusive.

Congress adjourned on the 17th of July, having adopted many measures of marked though minor importance, besides those to which we have referred, to aid in the prosecution of the war. Several Senators were expelled for adherence, direct or indirect, to the rebel cause; measures were taken to remove from the several departments of the Government *employés* more or less openly in sympathy with secession; Hayti and Liberia were recognized as independent republics; a treaty was negotiated and ratified with Great Britain which conceded the right, within certain limits, of searching suspected slavers carrying the American flag, and the most liberal grants in men and money were made to the Government for the prosecution of the war. The President had appointed military Governors for several of the Border States, where public sentiment was divided, enjoining them to protect the loyal citizens and to regard them as alone entitled to a voice in the direction of civil affairs.

Public sentiment throughout the loyal States sustained the action of Congress and the President as adapted to the emergency and well calculated to aid in the suppression of the rebellion. At the same time it was very evident that the conviction was rapidly gaining ground that Slavery was the cause of the Rebellion; that the paramount object of the conspirators against the Union was to obtain new guaranties for the institution; and that it was this interest alone which gave unity and vigor to the rebel cause. A very active and influential party at the North had insisted from the outset that the most direct way of crushing the Rebellion was by crushing Slavery, and they had urged upon the President the adoption of a policy of immediate and unconditional emancipation, as the only thing necessary to bring into the ranks of the Union armies hundreds of thousands of enfranchised slaves, as well as the great mass of the people of the Northern States who needed this stimulus of an appeal to their moral sentiment. After the adjournment of Congress these demands became still more clamorous and importunate. The President was summoned to avail himself of the opportunity offered by the passage of the Confiscation Bill, and to decree the instant liberation of every slave belonging to a rebel master. These demands soon assumed, with the more impatient and intemperate portion of the friends of the Administration, a tone of complaint and condemnation, and the President was charged with gross and culpable remissness in the discharge of duties imposed upon him by the Act of Congress. They were embodied with force and effect in a letter addressed to the President by Hon. Horace Greeley, and published in the *N. Y. Tribune* of the 19th of August, to which President LINCOLN made the following reply:

EXECUTIVE MANSION, WASHINGTON, *Aug.* 22, 1862.

HON. HORACE GREELEY:

DEAR SIR—I have just read yours of the 19th instant, addressed to myself through the New York *Tribune.*

If there be in it any statements or assumptions of fact which I may know to be erroneous, I do not now and here controvert them.

If there be any inferences which I may believe to be falsely drawn, I do not now and here argue against them.

If there be perceptible in it an impatient and dictatorial tone, I waive it in deference to an old friend whose heart I have always supposed to be right.

As to the policy I "seem to be pursuing," as you say, I have not meant to leave any one in doubt. I would save the Union. I would save it in the shortest way under the Constitution.

The sooner the national authority can be restored the nearer the Union will be—the Union as it was.

If there be those who would not save the Union unless they could at the same time save slavery, I do not agree with them.

If there be those who would not save the Union unless they could at the same time destroy slavery, I do not agree with them.

My paramount object is to save the Union, and not either to save or destroy slavery.

If I could save the Union without freeing any slave, I would do it—if I could save it by freeing all the slaves, I would do it—and if I could do it by freeing some and leaving others alone, I would also do that.

What I do about slavery and the colored race, I do because I believe it helps to save this Union, and what I forbear, I forbear because I do not believe it would help to save the Union.

I shall do less whenever I shall believe what I am doing hurts the cause, and I shall do more whenever I believe doing more will help the cause.

I shall try to correct errors when shown to be errors, and I shall adopt new views so fast as they shall appear to be true views.

I have here stated my purpose according to my views of official duty, and I intend no modification of my oft-expressed personal wish that all men everywhere could be free.

Yours,

A. Lincoln.

It was impossible to mistake the President's meaning after this letter, or to have any doubt as to the policy by which he expected to re-establish the authority of the Constitution over the whole territory of the United States. His "paramount object," in every thing he did and in every thing he abstained from doing, was to "save the Union." He regarded all the power conferred on him by Congress in regard to slavery, as having been conferred to aid him in the accomplishment of that object—and he was resolved to wield those powers so as best, according to his own judgment, to aid in its attainment. He forebore, therefore, for a long time, the issue of such a proclamation as he was authorized to make by the sixth section of the Confiscation act of Congress—awaiting the developments of public sentiment on the subject, and being especially anxious that when it was issued it should receive the moral support of the great body of the people of the whole country, without regard to party distinctions. He sought, therefore, with assiduous care, every opportunity of informing himself as to the drift of public sentiment on this subject. He received and conversed freely with all who came to see him and to urge upon him the adoption of their peculiar views; and on the 13th of September gave formal audience to a deputation from all the religious denominations of the city of Chicago, which had been appointed on the 7th, to wait upon him. The Committee presented a memorial requesting him at once to issue a proclamation of universal emancipation, and the chairman followed it by some remarks in support of this request.

The President listened attentively to the memorial, and then made to those who had presented it the following reply:'

The subject presented in the memorial is one upon which I have thought much for weeks past, and I may even say for months. I am approached with the most opposite opinions and advice, and that by religious men, who are equally certain that they represent the Divine will. I am sure that either the one or the other class is mistaken in that belief, and perhaps in some respect both. I hope it will not be irreverent for me to say that if it is probable that God would reveal his will to others, on a point so connected with my duty, it might be supposed he would reveal it directly to me; for, unless I am more deceived in myself than I often am, it is my earnest desire to know the will of Providence in this matter. And if I can learn what it is I will do it! These are not, however, the days of miracles, and I suppose it will be granted that I am not to expect a direct revelation. I must study the plain physical facts of the case, ascertain what is possible, and learn what appears to be wise and right.

The subject is difficult, and good men do not agree. For instance, the other day, four gentlemen of standing and intelligence from New York called as a delegation on business connected with the war; but before leaving two of them earnestly besought me to proclaim general emancipation, upon which the other two at once attacked them. You know also that the last session of Congress had a decided majority of anti-slavery men, yet they could not unite on this policy. And the same is true of the religious people. Why, the rebel soldiers are praying with a great deal more earnestness, I fear, than our own troops, and expecting God to favor their side: for one of our soldiers who had been taken prisoner told Senator Wilson a few days since that he met nothing so discouraging as the evident sincerity of those he was among in their prayers. But we will talk over the merits of the case.

What good would a proclamation of emancipation from me do, especially as we are now situated? I do not want to issue a document that the whole world will see must necessarily be inoperative, like the Pope's bull against the comet! Would my word free the slaves, when I cannot even enforce the Constitution in the rebel States? Is there a single court, or magistrate, or individual that would be influenced by it there? And what reason is there to think it would have any greater effect upon the slaves than the late law of Congress, which I approved, and which offers protection and freedom to the slaves of rebel masters who come within our lines? Yet I cannot learn that that law has caused a single slave to come over to us. And suppose they could be induced by a proclamation of freedom from me to throw themselves upon us, what should we do with them? How can we feed and care for such a multitude? General Butler wrote me a few days since that he was issuing more rations to the slaves who have rushed to him than to all the white troops under his command. They eat, and that is all; though it is true General Butler is feeding the whites also by the thousand; for it nearly amounts to a famine there. If, now, the pressure of the war should call off our forces from New Orleans to defend some other point, what is to prevent the masters from reducing the blacks to slavery again; for I am told that whenever the rebels take any black prisoners, free or slave, they immediately auction them off! They did so with those they took from a boat that was aground in the Tennessee River a few days ago. And then I am very ungenerously attacked for it! For instance, when, after the late battles at and near Bull Run, an expedition went out from Washington under a flag of truce to bury the dead and bring in the wounded, and the rebels seized the blacks who went along to help, and sent them into slavery, Horace Greeley said in his paper that the Government would probably do nothing about it. What could I do?

Now, then, tell me, if you please, what possible result of good would follow the issuing of such a proclamation as you desire? Understand, I raise no objections against it on legal or constitutional grounds, for, as commander-in-chief of the army and navy, in time of war I suppose I have a right to take any measure which may best subdue the enemy, nor do I urge objections of a moral nature, in view of possible consequences of insurrection and massacre at the South. I view this matter as a practical war measure, to be decided on according to the advantages or disadvantages it may offer to the suppression of the rebellion.

The Committee replied to these remarks, insisting that a proclamation of emancipation would secure at once the sympathy of Europe and the civilized world; and that as slavery was clearly the cause and origin of the rebellion, it was simply just, and in accordance with the word of God, that it should be abolished. To these remarks the President responded as follows:

I admit that slavery is at the root of the rebellion, or at least its *sine qua non*. The ambition of politicians may have instigated them to act, but they would have been impotent without slavery as their instrument. I will also concede that emancipation would help us in Europe, and convince them that we are incited by something more than ambition. I grant, further, that it would help somewhat at the North, though not so much, I fear, as you and those you represent imagine. Still, some additional strength would be added in that way to the war, and then, unquestionably, it would weaken the rebels by drawing off their laborers, which is of great importance; but I am not so sure we could do much with the blacks. If we were to arm them, I fear that in a few weeks the arms would be in the hands of the rebels; and, indeed, thus far, we have not had arms enough to equip our white troops. I will mention another thing, though it meet only your scorn and contempt. There are 50,000 bayonets in the Union army from the Border Slave States. It would be a serious matter if, in consequence of a proclamation such as you desire, they should go over to the rebels. I do not think they all would—not so many, indeed, as a year ago, or as six months ago—not so many to-day as yesterday. Every day increases their Union feeling. They are also getting their pride enlisted, and want to beat the rebels. Let me say one thing more: I think you should admit that we already have an important principle to rally and unite the people, in the fact that constitutional government is at stake. This is a fundamental idea going down about as deep as any thing.

The Committee replied to this in some brief remarks, to which the President made the following response:

Do not misunderstand me because I have mentioned these objections. They indicate the difficulties that have thus far prevented my action in some such way as you desire. I have not decided against a proclamation of liberty to the slaves, but hold the matter under advisement. And I can assure you that the subject is on my mind, by day and night, more than any other. Whatever shall appear to be God's will I will do. I trust that in the freedom with which I have canvassed your views I have not in any respect injured your feelings.

After free deliberation, and being satisfied that the public welfare would be promoted by such a step, and that public sentiment would sustain it, on the 22d of September the President issued the following preliminary

PROCLAMATION OF EMANCIPATION.

I, Abraham Lincoln, President of the United States of America, and Commander-in-Chief of the army and navy thereof, do hereby proclaim and declare that hereafter, as heretofore, the war will be prosecuted for the object of practically restoring the constitutional relation between the United States and each of the States, and the people thereof, in which States that relation is or may be suspended or disturbed.

That it is my purpose, upon the next meeting of Congress, to again recommend the adoption of a practical measure tendering pecuniary aid to the free acceptance or rejection of all Slave States so-called, the people whereof may not then be in rebellion against the United States, and which States may then have voluntarily adopted, or thereafter may voluntarily adopt, immediate or gradual abolishment of slavery within their respective limits; and that the effort to colonize persons of African descent, with their consent, upon this continent or elsewhere, with the previously obtained consent of the governments existing there, will be continued.

That on the first day of January, in the year of our Lord one thousand eight hundred and sixty three, all persons held as slaves within any State, or designated part of a State, the people whereof shall then be in rebellion against the United States, shall be then, thenceforward, and forever free; and the Executive Government of the United States, including the military and naval authority thereof, will recognize and maintain the freedom of such persons, and will do no act or acts to repress such persons, or any of them, in any efforts they may make for their actual freedom.

That the Executive will, on the first day of January aforesaid, by proclamation, designate the States and parts of States, if any, in which the people thereof respectively shall then be in rebellion against the United States; and the fact that any State, or the people thereof, shall on that day be in good faith represented in the Congress of the United States, by members chosen thereto at elections wherein a majority of the qualified voters of such State shall have participated, shall, in the absence of strong countervailing testimony, be deemed conclusive evidence that such State, and the people thereof, are not then in rebellion against the United States.

That attention is hereby called to an act of Congress entitled "An Act to make an additional Article of War," approved March 13th, 1862, and which act is in the words and figures following:

Be it enacted by the Senate and House of Representatives of the United States of America in Congress assembled, That hereafter the following shall be promulgated as an additional article of war for the government of the army of the United States, and shall be obeyed and observed as such:

ARTICLE.—All officers or persons in the military or naval service of the United States are prohibited from employing any of the forces under their respective commands for the purpose of returning fugitives from service or labor who may have escaped from any persons to whom such service or labor is claimed to be due; and any officer who shall be found guilty by a court-martial of violating this article shall be dismissed from the service.

SEC. 2. *And be it further enacted*, That this act shall take effect from and after its passage.

Also, to the ninth and tenth sections of an act entitled "An Act to Suppress Insurrection, to Punish Treason and Rebellion, to seize and Confiscate Property of Rebels, and for other Purposes," approved July 16, 1862, and which sections are in the words and figures following:

SEC. 9. *And be it further enacted*, That all slaves of persons who shall hereafter be engaged in rebellion against the Government of the United States, or who shall in any way give aid or comfort thereto, escaping from such persons and taking refuge within the lines of the army; and all slaves captured from such persons, or deserted by them and coming under the control of the Government of the United States; and all slaves of such persons found *on* [or] being within any place occupied by rebel forces and afterward occupied by forces of the United States, shall be deemed captives of war, and shall be forever free of their servitude, and not again held as slaves.

SEC. 10. *And be it further enacted*, That no slave escaping into any State, Territory, or the District of Columbia, from any other State, shall be delivered up, or in any way impeded or hindered of his liberty, except for crime, or some offence against the laws, unless the person claiming said fugitive shall first make oath that the person to whom the labor or service of such fugitive is alleged to be due is his lawful owner, and has not borne arms against the United States in the present rebellion, nor in any way given aid and comfort thereto; and no person engaged in the military or naval service of the United States shall, under any pretence whatever, assume to decide on the validity of the claim of any person to the service or labor of any other person, or surrender up any such person to the claimant, on pain of being dismissed from the service.

And I do hereby enjoin upon and order all persons engaged in the military and naval service of the United States to observe, obey, and enforce, within their respective spheres of service, the act and sections above recited.

And the Executive will in due time recommend that all citizens of the United States who shall have remained loyal thereto throughout the rebellion, shall (upon the restoration of the constitutional relation between the United States and their respective States and people, if that relation shall have been suspended or disturbed) be compensated for all losses by acts of the United States, including the loss of slaves.

In witness whereof, I have hereunto set my hand and caused the seal of the United States to be affixed.

Done at the city of Washington, this twenty-second day of September, in the year of our Lord one thousand eight hundred [L. S.] and sixty-two, and of the Independence of the United States the eighty-seventh.

ABRAHAM LINCOLN.

By the President:

WILLIAM H. SEWARD, Secretary of State.

The issuing of this proclamation created the deepest interest, not unmixed with anxiety, in the public mind. The opponents of the Administration in the loyal States, as well as the sympathizers with secession everywhere, insisted that it afforded unmistakable evidence that the object of the war was, what they had always declared it to be, the abolition of slavery, and not the restoration of the Union; and they put forth the most vigorous efforts to arouse public sentiment against the Administration on this ground. They were met, however, by the clear and explicit declaration of the document itself, in which the President "proclaimed and declared" that "hereafter, as heretofore, the war will be prosecuted for the object of practically restoring the constitutional relation between the United States and each of the States and the people thereof, in which that relation is or may be suspended or disturbed." This at once made it evident that emancipation, as provided for in the Proclamation, as a war measure, was subsidiary and subordinate to the paramount object of the war—the restoration of the Union, and the re-establishment of the authority of the Constitution; and in this sense it was favorably received by the great body of the loyal people of the United States.

It only remains to be added, in this connection, that on the first of January, 1863, the President followed this measure by issuing the following

PROCLAMATION.

Whereas, on the 22d day of September, in the year of our Lord one thousand eight hundred and sixty-two, a proclamation was issued by the President of the United States, containing, among other things, the following, to wit:

That on the first day of January, in the year of our Lord one thousand eight hundred and sixty-three, all persons held as slaves within any States or designated part of a State, the people whereof shall then be in rebellion against the United States, shall be then, thenceforward, and forever free; and the Executive Government of the United States, including the military and naval authority thereof, will recognize and maintain the freedom of such persons, and will do no act or acts to repress such persons, or any of them, in any efforts they may make for their actual freedom.

That the Executive will, on the first day of January aforesaid, by proclamation, designate the States and parts of States, if any, in which the people thereof respectively shall then be in rebellion against the United States; and the fact that any State, or the people thereof, shall on that day be in good faith represented in the Congress of the United States, by members chosen thereto at elections wherein a majority of the qualified voters of such State shall have participated, shall, in the absence of strong countervailing testimony, be deemed conclusive evidence that such State, and the people thereof, are not then in rebellion against the United States.

Now, therefore, I, ABRAHAM LINCOLN, President of the United States, by virtue of the power in me vested as Commander-in-Chief of the Army and Navy of the United States in time of actual armed rebellion against the authority and Government of the United States, and as a fit and necessary war measure for suppressing said rebellion, do, on this first day of January, in the year of our Lord one thousand eight hundred and sixty-three, and in accordance with my purpose so to do, publicly proclaimed for the full period of one hundred days, from the day first above mentioned, order and designate as the States and parts of States wherein the people thereof respectively are this day in rebellion against the United States, the following, to wit:

Arkansas, Texas, Louisiana (except the parishes of St. Bernard, Plaquemines, Jefferson, St. John, St. Charles, St. James, Ascension, Assumption, Terre Bonne, Lafourche, Ste. Marie, St. Martin, and Orleans, including the city of New Orleans), Mississippi, Alabama, Florida, Georgia, South Carolina, North Carolina, and Virginia (except the forty-eight counties designated as West Virginia, and also the counties of Berkeley, Accomac, Northampton, Elizabeth City, York, Princess Anne, and Norfolk, including the cities of Norfolk and Portsmouth), and which excepted parts are for the present left precisely as if this proclamation were not issued.

And by virtue of the power and for the purpose aforesaid, I do order and declare that all persons held as slaves within said designated States and parts of States are and henceforward shall be free; and that the Executive Government of the United States, including the military and naval authorities thereof, will recognize and maintain the freedom of said persons.

And I hereby enjoin upon the people so declared to be free to abstain from all violence, unless in necessary self-defence; and I recommend to them that, in all cases when allowed, they labor faithfully for reasonable wages.

And I further declare and make known that such persons, of suitable condition, will be received into the armed service of the United States to garrison forts, positions, stations, and other places, and to man vessels of all sorts in said service.

And upon this act, sincerely believed to be an act of justice, warranted by the Constitution upon military necessity, I invoke the considerate judgment of mankind, and the gracious favor of Almighty God.

In testimony whereof, I have hereunto set my name, and caused the seal of the United States to be affixed.

Done at the city of Washington, this first day of January, in the year of our Lord one thousand eight hundred and sixty-three, and of the independence of the United States the eighty-seventh.

[L. S.]

By the President: ABRAHAM LINCOLN.

WILLIAM H. SEWARD, Secretary of State.

CHAPTER VI.

THE MILITARY ADMINISTRATION OF 1862—THE PRESIDENT AND GENERAL M'CLELLAN.

The repulse of the national forces at the battle of Bull Run in July, 1861, aroused the people of the loyal States to a sense of the magnitude of the contest which had been forced upon them. It stimulated to intoxication the pride and ambition of the rebels, and gave infinite encouragement to their efforts to raise fresh troops, and increase the military resources of their Confederation. Nor did the reverse the national cause had sustained for an instant damp the ardor, or check the determination, of the Government and people of the loyal States. General McDowell, the able and accomplished officer who commanded the army of the United States in that engagement, conducted the operations of the day with signal ability; and his defeat was due, as subsequent disclosures have clearly shown, far more to accidents for which others were responsible, than to any lack of skill in planning the battle, or of courage and generalship on the field. But it was the first considerable engagement of the war, and its loss was a serious and startling disappointment to the sanguine expectations of the people: it was deemed necessary, therefore, to place a new commander at the head of the army in front of Washington. General McClellan, who had been charged, at the outset of the war, with operations in the department of the Ohio, and who had achieved marked success in clearing Western Virginia of the rebel troops, was summoned to Washington on the 22d of July, and on the 27th assumed command of the Army of the Potomac.

Although then in command only of a department, General McClellan, with an ambition and a presumption natural, perhaps, to his age and the circumstances of his advancement, addressed his attention to the general conduct of the war in all sections of the country, and favored the Government and Lieutenant-General Scott with several elaborate and meritorious letters of advice, as to the method most proper to be pursued for the suppression of the rebellion. He soon, however, found it necessary to attend to the preparation of the army under his command for an immediate resumption of hostilities. Fresh troops in great numbers speedily poured in from the Northern States, and were organized and disciplined for prompt and effective service. The number of troops in and about the capital when General McClellan assumed command, was a little over 50,000, and the brigade organization of General McDowell formed the basis for the distribution of these new forces. By the middle of October this army had been raised to over 150,000 men, with an artillery force of nearly 500 pieces—all in a state of excellent discipline, under skilful officers, and animated by a zealous and impatient eagerness to renew the contest for the preservation of the Constitution and Government of the United States. The President and Secretary of War had urged the division of the army into *corps d'armée*, for the purpose of more effective service; but General McClellan had discouraged and thwarted their endeavors in this direction, mainly on the ground that there were not officers enough of tried ability in the army to be intrusted with such high commands as this division would create.

On the 22d of October, a portion of our forces which had been ordered to cross the Potomac above Washington, in the direction of Leesburgh, were met by a heavy force of the enemy at Ball's Bluff, repulsed with severe loss, and compelled to return. The circumstances of this disaster excited a great deal of dissatisfaction in the public mind, and this was still further aggravated by the fact that the rebels had obtained, and been allowed to hold, complete control of the Potomac below Washington, so as to establish a virtual and effective blockade of the capital from that direction. Special efforts were repeatedly made by the President and the Navy Department to clear the banks of the river of the rebel forces, known to be small in number, which held them, but it was found impossible to induce General McClellan to take any steps to aid in the accomplishment of this result. In October he had promised that on a day named, 4,000 troops should be ready to proceed down the river to co-operate with the Potomac flotilla under Captain Craven; but at the time appointed the troops did not arrive, and General McClellan alleged, as a reason for having changed his mind, that his engineers had informed him that so large a body of troops could not be landed. The Secretary of the Navy replied that the landing of the troops was a matter of which that department assumed the responsibility; and it was then agreed that the troops should be sent down the next night. They were not sent, however, either then or at any other time, for which General McClellan assigned as a reason the fear that such an attempt might bring on a general engagement. Captain Craven upon this threw up his command, and the Potomac remained closed to the vessels and transports of the United States until it was opened in March of the next year by the voluntary withdrawal of the rebel forces.

On the 1st of November, General McClellan was appointed by the President to succeed General Scott in the command of all the armies of the Union, remaining in personal command of the Army of the Potomac. His attention was then of necessity turned to the direction of army movements, and to the conduct of political affairs, so far as they came under military control, in the more distant sections of the country. But no movement took place in the Army of the Potomac.

The season had been unusually favorable for military operations—the troops were admirably organized and disciplined, and in the highest state of efficiency—in numbers they were known to be far superior to those of the rebels opposed to them, who were nevertheless permitted steadily to push their approaches towards Washington, while from the highest officer to the humblest private our forces were all animated with an eager desire to be led against the enemies of their country. As winter approached without any indications of an intended movement of our armies, the public impatience rose to the highest point of discontent. The Administration was everywhere held responsible for these unaccountable delays, and was freely charged by its opponents with a design to protract the war for selfish political purposes of its own: and at the fall election the public dissatisfaction made itself manifest by adverse votes in every considerable State where elections were held.

Unable longer to endure this state of things, President Lincoln put an end to it on the 27th of January, 1862, by issuing the following order:

EXECUTIVE MANSION, WASHINGTON, *January* 27, 1862.

Ordered, That the twenty-second day of February, 1862, be the day for a general movement of the land and naval forces of the United States against the insurgent forces. That especially the army at and about Fortress Monroe, the army of the Potomac, the army of Western Virginia, the army near Munfordsville, Kentucky, the army and flotilla at Cairo, and a naval force in the Gulf of Mexico, be ready to move on that day.

That all other forces, both land and naval, with their respective commanders, obey existing orders for the time, and be ready to obey additional orders when duly given.

That the heads of departments, and especially the Secretaries of War and of the Navy, with all their subordinates, and the General-in-Chief, with all other commanders and subordinates of land and naval forces, will severally be held to their strict and full responsibilities for prompt execution of this order.

ABRAHAM LINCOLN.

This order, which applied to all the armies of the United States, was followed four days afterwards by the following special order directed to General McClellan:

EXECUTIVE MANSION, WASHINGTON, *January* 31, 1862.

Ordered, That all the disposable force of the Army of the Potomac, after providing safely for the defence of Washington, be formed into an expedition for the immediate object of seizing and occupying a point upon the railroad southwestward of what is known as Manassas Junction, all details to be in the discretion of the Commander-inChief, and the expedition to move before or on the twenty-second day of February next.

ABRAHAM LINCOLN.

The object of this order was to engage the rebel army in front of Washington by a flank attack, and by its defeat relieve the capital, put Richmond at our mercy, and break the main strength of the rebellion by destroying the principal army arrayed in its support. Instead of obeying it, General McClellan remonstrated against its execution, and urged the adoption of a different plan of attack, which was to move upon Richmond by way of the Chesapeake Bay, the Rappahannock River, and a land march across the country from Urbana, leaving the rebel forces in position at Manassas to be held in check, if they should attempt a forward movement, only by the troops in the fortifications around Washington. As the result of several conferences with the President, he obtained permission to state in writing his objections to his plan—the President meantime sending him the following letter of inquiry:

EXECUTIVE MANSION, WASHINGTON, *February* 3, 1862.

MY DEAR SIR: You and I have distinct and different plans for a movement of the Army of the Potomac; yours to be done by the Chesapeake, up the Rappahannock to Urbana, and across land to the terminus of the railroad on the York River; mine to move directly to a point on the railroad southwest of Manassas.

If you will give satisfactory answers to the following questions, I shall gladly yield my plan to yours:

1st. Does not your plan involve a greatly larger expenditure of *time* and *money* than mine?

2d. Wherein is a victory *more certain* by your plan than mine?

3d. Wherein is a victory *more valuable* by your plan than mine?

4th. In fact, would it not be *less* valuable in this: that it would break no great line of the enemy's communications, while mine would?

5th. In case of disaster, would not a retreat be more difficult by your plan than mine?

Yours, truly, ABRAHAM LINCOLN.

Major-General McCLELLAN.

General McClellan sent to the Secretary of War, under date of February 3d, a very long letter, presenting strongly the advantage possessed by the rebels in holding a central defensive position, from which they could with a small force resist any attack on either flank, concentrating their main strength upon the other for a decisive action. The uncertainties of the weather, the necessity of having long lines of communication, and the probable indecisiveness even of a victory, if one should be gained, were urged against the President's plan. So strongly was General McClellan in favor of his own plan of operations, that he said he "should prefer the move from Fortress Monroe as a base, to an attack upon Manassas." The President was by no means convinced by General McClellan's reasoning; but in consequence of his steady resistance and unwillingness to enter upon the execution of any other plan, he assented to a submission of the matter to a council of twelve officers held late in February, at head-quarters. The result of that council was, a decision in favor of moving by way of the lower Chesapeake and the Rappahannock—seven of the Generals present, viz., Fitz-John Porter, Franklin, W. F. Smith, McCall, Blenker, Andrew Porter, and Naglee, voting in favor of it, as did Keyes also, with the qualification that the army should not move until the rebels were driven from the Potomac, and Generals McDowell, Sumner, Heintzelman, and Barnard, voting against it.

In this decision the President acquiesced, and on the 8th of March, issued two general war orders, the first directing the Major-General commanding the Army of the Potomac to proceed forthwith to organize that part of said army destined to enter upon active operations into four army corps, to be commanded, the first by General McDowell, the second by General Sumner, the third by General Heintzelman, and the fourth by General Keyes. General Banks was assigned to the command of a fifth corps. It also appointed General Wadsworth Military Governor of Washington, and directed the order to be "executed with such promptness and dispatch as not to delay the commencement of the operations already directed to be undertaken by the Army of the Potomac."

The second of these orders was as follows:

EXECUTIVE MANSION, WASHINGTON, *March* 8, 1862.

Ordered, That no change of the base of operations of the Army of the Potomac shall be made without leaving in and about Washington such a force as, in the opinion of the General-in-Chief and the commanders of army corps, shall leave said city entirely secure.

That no more than two army corps (about fifty thousand troops) of said Army of the Potomac shall be moved *en route* for a new base of operations until the navigation of the Potomac, from Washington to the Chesapeake Bay, shall be freed from the enemy's batteries, and other obstructions, or until the President shall hereafter give express permission.

That any movement as aforesaid, *en route* for a new base of operations, which may be ordered by the General-in-Chief, and which may be intended to move upon the Chesapeake Bay, shall begin to move upon the bay as early as the eighteenth March instant, and the General-in-Chief shall be responsible that it moves as early as that day.

Ordered, That the army and navy co-operate in an immediate effort to capture the enemy's batteries upon the Potomac between Washington and the Chesapeake Bay.

ABRAHAM LINCOLN.

L. THOMAS, *Adjutant-General.*

This order was issued on the 8th of March. On the 9th, information was received by General McClellan, at Washington, that the enemy had abandoned his position in front of that city. He at once crossed the Potomac, and on the same night issued orders for an immediate advance of the whole army towards Manassas,—not with any intention, as he has since explained, of pursuing the rebels, and taking advantage of their retreat, but to "get rid of superfluous baggage and other impediments which accumulate so easily around an army encamped for a long time in one locality"—to give the troops "some experience on the march and bivouac preparatory to the campaign," and to afford them also a "good intermediate step between the quiet and comparative comfort of the camps around Washington and the vigor of active operations."* These objects, in General McClellan's opinion, were sufficiently accomplished by what the Prince de Joinville, of his staff, styles a "promenade" of the army to Manassas, where they learned, from personal inspection, that the rebels had actually evacuated that position; and on the 15th, orders were issued for a return of the forces to Alexandria.

On the 11th of March, the President issued another order, stating that "Major-General McClellan having personally taken the field at the head of the Army of the Potomac, until otherwise ordered, he is relieved from the command of the other military departments, retaining command of the department of the Potomac." Major-General Halleck was assigned to the command of the department of the Mississippi, and the Mountain department was created for Major-General Fremont. All the commanders of departments were also required to report directly to the Secretary of War.

On the 13th of March, a council of war was held at head-quarters, then at Fairfax Court-House, by which it was decided that, as the enemy had retreated behind the Rappahannock, operations against Richmond could best be conducted from Fortress Monroe, *provided :*

* See General McClellan's Report, dated August 4, 1863.

1st. That the enemy's vessel, Merrimac, can be neutralized.

2d. That the means of transportation, sufficient for an immediate transfer of the force to its new base, can be ready at Washington and Alexandria to move down the Potomac; and,

3d. That a naval auxiliary force can be had to silence, or aid in silencing, the enemy's batteries on the York River.

4th. That the force to be left to cover Washington shall be such as to give an entire feeling of security for its safety from menace.

NOTE.—That with the forts on the right bank of the Potomac fully garrisoned, and those on the left bank occupied, a covering force in front of the Virginia line of twenty-five thousand men would suffice. (Keyes, Heintzelman, and McDowell.)

A total of forty thousand men for the defence of the city would suffice. (Sumner.)

Upon receiving a report of this decision, the following communication was at once addressed to the commanding general:

WAR DEPARTMENT, *March* 13, 1862.

The President having considered the plan of operations agreed upon by yourself and the commanders of army corps, makes no objection to the same, but gives the following directions as to its execution:

1. Leave such force at Manassas Junction as shall make it entirely certain that the enemy shall not repossess himself of that position and line of communication.

2. Leave Washington entirely secure.

3. Move the remainder of the force down the Potomac, choosing a new base at Fortress Monroe, or anywhere between here and there, or, *at all events, move such remainder of the army at once in pursuit of the enemy by some route.*

EDWIN M. STANTON,
Secretary of War.

Major-General GEORGE B. McCLELLAN.

It will readily be seen, from these successive orders, that the President, in common with the whole country, had been greatly pained by the long delay of the Army of the Potomac to move against the enemy while encamped at Manassas, and that this feeling was converted into chagrin and mortification when the rebels were allowed to withdraw from that position without the slightest molestation, and without their design being even suspected until it had been carried into complete and successful execution. He was impatiently anxious, therefore, that no more time should be lost in delays. In reply to the Secretary of War, General McClellan, before embarking for the Peninsula, communicated his intention of reaching, without loss of time, the field of what he believed would be a decisive battle, which he expected to fight between West Point and Richmond. On the 31st of March, the President, out of deference to the importunities of General Fremont and his friends, and from a belief that this officer could make good use of a larger force than he then had at his command in the mountain department, ordered General Blenker's division to leave the Army of the Potomac and join him, a decision which he announced to General McClellan in the following letter:

EXECUTIVE MANSION,
WASHINGTON, *March* 31, 1862.

MY DEAR SIR: This morning I felt constrained to order Blenker's division to Fremont, and I write this to assure you that I did so with great pain, understanding that you would wish it otherwise. If you could know the full pressure of the case, I am confident that you would justify it, even beyond a mere acknowledgment that the Commander-in-Chief may order what he pleases.

Yours, very truly, A. LINCOLN.

Major-General MCCLELLAN.

General Banks, who had at first been ordered by General McClellan to occupy Manassas, and thus cover Washington, was directed by him, on the 1st of April, to throw the rebel General Jackson well back from Winchester, and then move on Staunton at a time "nearly coincident with his own move on Richmond;" though General McClellan expressed the fear that General Banks "could not be ready in time" for that movement. The four corps of the Army of the Potomac, destined for active operations by way of the Peninsula, were ordered to embark, and forwarded as rapidly as possible to Fortress Monroe. On the 1st of April, General McClellan wrote to the Secretary of War, giving a report of the dispositions he had made for the defence of Washington; and on the 2d, General Wadsworth submitted a statement of the forces under his command, which he regarded as entirely inadequate to the service required of them. The President referred the matter to Adjutant-General Thomas and General E. A. Hitchcock, who made a report on the same day, in which they decided that the force left by General McClellan was not sufficient to make Washington "entirely secure," as the President had required in his order of March 13; nor was it as large as the council of officers held at Fairfax Court-House on the same day had adjudged to be necessary. In accordance with this decision, and for the purpose of rendering the capital safe, the army corps of General McDowell was detached from General McClellan's immediate command, and ordered to report to the Secretary of War.

On reaching Fortress Monroe, General McClellan found Commodore Goldsborough, who commanded on that naval station, unwilling to send any considerable portion of his force up the York River, as he was employed in watching the Merrimac, which had closed the James River against us. He had, therefore, landed at the Fortress and commenced his march up the Peninsula, having reached the Warwick River, in the immediate vicinity of Yorktown, which had been fortified, and was held by a rebel force of about 11,000 men, under General Magruder—a part of them, however, being across the river at Gloucester. He here halted to reconnoitre the position; and on the 6th, wrote to the President that he had but 85,000 men fit for duty—that the whole line of the Warwick River was strongly fortified—that it was pretty certain he was to "have the whole force of the enemy on his hands, probably not less than 100,000 men, and probably more," and that he should commence siege operations as soon as he could get up his train. He entered, accordingly, upon this work, telegraphing from time to time complaints that he was not properly supported by the Government, and asking for re-enforcements.

On the 9th of April, President LINCOLN addressed him the following letter:

WASHINGTON, *April* 9, 1862.

MY DEAR SIR: Your dispatches, complaining that you are not properly sustained, while they do not offend me, do pain me very much.

Blenker's division was withdrawn from you before you left here, and you know the pressure under which I did it, and, as I thought, acquiesced in it—certainly not without reluctance.

After you left, I ascertained that less than twenty thousand unorganized men, without a single field battery, were all you designed to be left for the defence of Washington and Manassas Junction, and part of this even was to go to General Hooker's old position. General Banks's corps, once designed for Manassas Junction, was diverted and tied up on the line of Winchester and Strasburg, and could not leave it without again exposing the Upper Potomac and the Baltimore and Ohio Railroad. This presented, or would present, when McDowell and Sumner should be gone, a great temptation to the enemy to turn back from the Rappahannock and sack Washington. My implicit order that Washington should, by the judgment of all the commanders of army corps, be left entirely secure, had been neglected. It was precisely this that drove me to detain McDowell.

I do not forget that I was satisfied with your arrangement to leave Banks at Manassas Junction: but when that arrangement was broken up, and nothing was substituted for it, of course I was constrained to substitute something for it myself. And allow me to ask, do you really think I should permit the line from Richmond, *via* Manassas Junction, to this city, to be entirely open, except what resistance could be presented by less than twenty thousand unorganized troops? This is a question which the country will not allow me to evade.

There is a curious mystery about the number of troops now with you. When I telegraphed you on the sixth, saying you had over a hundred thousand with you, I had just obtained from the Secretary of War a statement taken, as he said, from your own returns, making one hundred and eight thousand then with you and *en route* to you. You now say you will have but eighty-five thousand when all *en route* to you shall have reached you. How can the discrepancy of twenty-three thousand be accounted for?

As to General Wool's command, I understand it is doing for you precisely what a like number of your own would have to do if that command was away.

I suppose the whole force which has gone forward for you is with you by this time. And if so, I think it is the precise time for you to strike a blow. By delay, the enemy will relatively gain upon you—that is, he will gain faster by fortifications and re-enforcements than you can by re-enforcements alone. And once more let me tell you, it is indispensable to you that you strike a blow. I am powerless to help this. You will do me the justice to remember I always insisted that going down the bay in search of a field, instead of fighting at or near Manassas, was only shifting, and not surmounting, a difficulty; that we would find the same enemy, and the same or equal intrenchments, at either place. The country will not fail to note, is now noting, that the present hesitation to move upon an intrenched enemy is but the story of Manassas repeated.

I beg to assure you that I have never written you or spoken to you in greater kindness of feeling than now, nor with a fuller purpose to sustain you, so far as, in my most anxious judgment, I consistently can. But you must act.

Yours, very truly,
A. LINCOLN.

Major-General McCLELLAN.

In this letter the President only echoed the impatience and eagerness of the whole country. The most careful inquiries which General Wool, in command at Fortress Monroe, had been able to make, satisfied him that Yorktown was not held by any considerable force; and subsequent disclosures have made it quite certain that this force was so utterly inadequate to the defence of the position that a prompt movement upon it would have caused its immediate surrender, and enabled our army to advance at once upon Richmond. General McClellan decided, however, to approach it by a regular siege; and it was not until this design had become apparent, that the rebel Government began to re-enforce Magruder.* He continued his

* The following extract from the official report of Major-General Magruder, dated May 3d, 1862, and published by order of the Confederate Congress, is conclusive as to the real strength of the force which General McClellan had in front of him at Yorktown:

HEAD-QUARTERS, DEPARTMENT OF THE PENINSULA,
LEE'S FARM, May 3, 1862.

General S. COOPER, A. and I. G. C. S. A.:

GENERAL: Deeming it of vital importance to hold Yorktown on York River, and Mulberry Island on James River, and to keep the enemy in check by an intervening line until the authorities might take such steps as should be deemed necessary to meet a serious advance of the enemy in the Peninsula, I felt compelled to dispose my forces in such a manner as to accomplish these objects with the least risk possible under the circumstances of great hazard which surrounded the little army I commanded.

I had prepared as my real line of defence, positions in advance at Harwood's and Young's Mills. Both flanks of this line were defended by boggy and difficult streams and swamps. * * In my opinion this advanced line, with its flank defences, might have been held by 20,000 troops. * * *Finding my forces too weak to attempt the defence of this line*, I was compelled to prepare to receive the enemy on a second line on Warwick River. This line was incomplete in its preparations. Keeping then only small bodies of troops at Harwood's and Young's Mills, and on Ship Point, I distributed my remaining forces along the Warwick line, embracing a front from Yorktown to Minor's farm of twelve miles, and from the latter place to Mulberry Island Point one and a half miles. I was compelled to place in Gloucester Point, Yorktown, and Mulberry Island, fixed garrisons amounting to 6,000 men, *my whole force being 11,000, so that it will be seen that the balance of the line, embracing a length of thirteen miles, was defended by about 5,000 men.*

After the reconnoissances in great force from Fortress Monroe and Newport News, the enemy, on the 3d of April, advanced and took possession of Harwood's Mill. He advanced in two heavy columns, one along the old York road, and the other along the Warwick road, and on the 5th of April appeared simultaneously along the whole part of our line from Minor's farm to Yorktown. I have no accurate data upon which to base an exact statement of his force; but from various sources of information I was satisfied that I had before me the enemy's Army of the Potomac, under the command of General McClellan, with the exception of the two *corps d'armee* of Banks and McDowell respectively—forming an aggregate number certainly of not less than 100,000, since ascertained to have been 120,000 men.

On every portion of my lines he attacked us with a furious cannonading and musketry, which was responded to with effect by our batteries and troops of the line. His skirmishers also were well thrown forward on this and the succeeding day, and energetically felt our whole line, but were everywhere repulsed by the steadiness of our troops. *Thus with 5,000 men, exclusive of the garrisons, we stopped and held in check over one hundred thousand of the enemy.* Every preparation was made in anticipation of another attack by the enemy. The men slept in the trenches and applications to the Government for more troops, more cannon, more transportation—all which were sent forward to him as rapidly as possible, being taken mainly from McDowell's corps. On the 14th of April, General Franklin, detached from that corps, reported to General McClellan, near Yorktown, but his troops remained on board the transports. A month was spent in this way, the President urging action in the most earnest manner, and the commanding general delaying from day to day his reiterated promises to commence operations immediately. At last, on the morning of the 4th of May, it was discovered that the rebels had been busy for a day or two in evacuating Yorktown, and that the last of their columns had left that place, all their supply-trains having been previously removed on the day and night preceding. General McClellan, in announcing this event to the Government, added that "no time would be lost" in the pursuit, and that he should "push the enemy to the wall." General Stoneman, with a column of cavalry, was at once sent forward to overtake the retreating enemy, which he succeeded in doing on the same day, and was repulsed. On the 5th, the forces ordered forward by General McClellan came up, and found a very strong rear-guard of the rebels strongly fortified, about two miles east of Williamsburg, and prepared to dispute the advance of the pursuing troops. It had been known from the beginning that a very formidable line of forts had been erected here, and it ought to have been equally well known by the commanding general that the retreating enemy would avail

under arms, *but, to my utter surprise, he permitted day after day to elapse without an assault.*

In a few days the object of his delay was apparent. *In every direction in front of our lines, through the intervening woods and along the open fields, earthworks began to appear.* Through the energetic action of the government re-enforcements began to pour in, and *each hour the army of the Peninsula grew stronger and stronger, until anxiety passed from my mind as to the result of an attack upon us.*

* * * *

J. BANKHEAD MAGRUDER, *Major-General.*

himself of them to delay the pursuit. General McClellan, however, had evidently anticipated no resistance. He remained at his head-quarters, two miles in the rear of Yorktown, until summoned by special messenger in the afternoon of the 5th, who announced to him that our troops had encountered the enemy strongly posted, that a bloody battle was in progress, and that his presence on the field was imperatively required. Replying to the messenger that he had supposed our troops in front "could attend to that little matter," General McClellan left his head-quarters at about half-past two, P. M., and reached the field at five. General Hooker, General Heintzelman, and General Sumner, had been fighting under enormous difficulties, and with heavy losses, during all the early part of the day; and just as the commanding general arrived, General Kearney had re-enforced General Hooker, and General Hancock had executed a brilliant flank movement, which turned the fortunes of the day, and left our forces in possession of the field.

General McClellan does not seem to have understood that this affair was simply an attempt of the rebel rear-guard to cover the retreat of the main force, and that when it had delayed the pursuit it had accomplished its whole purpose. He countermanded an order for the advance of two divisions, and ordered them back to Yorktown; and in a dispatch sent to the War Department the same night, he treats the battle as an engagement with the whole rebel army. "I find," he says, "General Joe Johnson in front of me in strong force, probably greater, a good deal, than my own." He again complains of the inferiority of his command, says he will do all he can "with the force at his disposal," and that he should "run the *risk* of at least *holding them in check* here (at Williamsburg) while he resumed the original plan"—which was to send Franklin to West Point by water. But the direct pursuit of the retreating rebel army was abandoned—owing, as the general said, to the bad state of the roads, which rendered it impracticable. Some five days were spent at Williamsburg, which enabled the rebels, notwithstanding the "state of the roads," to withdraw their whole force across the Chickahominy, and establish themselves within the fortifications in front of Richmond. On the morning of the 7th, General Franklin landed at West Point, but too late to intercept the main body of the retreating army: he was met by a strong rear-guard, with whom he had a sharp but fruitless engagement.

The York River had been selected as the base of operations, in preference to the James, because it "was in a better position to effect a junction with any troops that might move from Washington on the Fredericksburg line;"* and arrangements were made to procure supplies for the army by that route. On the 9th, Norfolk was evacuated by the rebels, all the troops withdrawing in safety to Richmond; and the city, on the next day, was occupied by General Wool. On the 11th, the formidable steamer Merrimac, which had held our whole naval force at Fortress Monroe completely in check, was blown up by the rebels themselves, and our vessels attempted to reopen the navigation of the James River, but were repulsed by a heavy battery at Drury's bluff, eight miles below Richmond. After waiting for several days for the roads to improve, the main body of the army was put in motion on the road towards Richmond, which was about forty miles from Williamsburg; and, on the 16th, head-quarters were established at White House, at the point where the Richmond railroad crosses the Pamunkey, an affluent of the York River—the main body of the army lying along the south bank of the Chickahominy, a swampy stream, behind which the rebel army had intrenched itself for the defence of Richmond.

* See General McClellan's testimony—Report of Committee on Conduct of the War, Vol. i., p. 431.

General McClellan began again to prepare for fighting the "decisive battle" which he had been predicting ever since the rebels withdrew from Manassas, but which they had so far succeeded in avoiding. A good deal of his attention, however, was devoted to making out a case of neglect against the Government. On the 10th of May, when he had advanced but three miles beyond Williamsburg, he sent a long dispatch to the War Department, reiterating his conviction that the rebels were about to dispute his advance with their whole force, and asking for "every man" the Government could send him. If not re-enforced he said he should probably be "obliged to fight nearly double his numbers strongly intrenched." Ten days previously the official returns showed that he had 160,000 men under his command. On the 14th, he telegraphed the President, reiterating his fears that he was to be met by overwhelming numbers, saying that he could not bring more than 80,000 men into the field, and again asking for "every man" that the War Department could send him. Even if more troops should not be needed for military purposes, he thought a great display of imposing force in the capital of the rebel government would have the best moral effect. To these repeated demands the President, through the Secretary of War, on the 18th of May, made the following reply:

WASHINGTON, May 18—2 P. M.

GENERAL: Your dispatch to the President, asking re-enforcements, has been received and carefully considered.

The President is not willing to uncover the capital entirely; and it is believed that even if this were prudent, it would require more time to effect a junction between your army and that of the Rappahannock by the way of the Potomac and York River, than by a land march. In order, therefore, to increase the strength of the attack upon Richmond at the earliest moment, General McDowell has been ordered to march upon that city by the shortest route. He is ordered, keeping himself always in position to save the capital from all possible attack, so to operate as to put his left wing in communication with your right wing, and you are instructed to co-operate so as to establish this communication as soon as possible by extending your right wing to the north of Richmond.

It is believed that this communication can be safely established either north or south of the Pamunkey River.

In any event, you will be able to prevent the main body of the enemy's forces from leaving Richmond, and falling in overwhelming force upon General McDowell. He will move with between thirty-five and forty thousand men.

A copy of the instructions to General McDowell are with this. The specific task assigned to his command has been to provide against any danger to the capital of the nation.

At your earnest call for re-enforcements, he is sent forward to co-operate in the reduction of Richmond, but charged, in attempting this, not to uncover the city of Washington, and you will give no order, either before or after your junction, which can put him out of position to cover this city. You and he will communicate with each other by telegraph or otherwise, as frequently as may be necessary for sufficient co-operation. When General McDowell is in position on your right, his supplies must be drawn from West Point, and you will instruct your staff officers to be prepared to supply him by that route.

The President desires that General McDowell retain the command of the department of the Rappahannock, and of the forces with which he moves forward.

By order of the President. EDWIN M. STANTON.

In reply to this, on the 21st of May, General McClellan repeated his declarations of the overwhelming force of the rebels, and urged that General McDowell should join him *by water* instead of by land, going down the Rappahannock and the Bay to Fortress Monroe, and then ascending the York and Pamunkey Rivers. He feared there was "little hope that he could join him overland in time for the coming battle. Delays," he says, "on my part will be dangerous: I fear sickness and demoralization. This region is unhealthy for Northern men, and unless kept moving, I fear that our soldiers may become discouraged"—a fear that was partially justified by the experience of the whole month succeeding, during which he kept them idle. He complained also that McDowell was not put more completely under his command, and declared that a movement by land would uncover Washington quite as completely as one by water. He was busy at that time in bridging the Chickahominy, and gave no instructions, as required, for supplying McDowell's forces on their arrival at West Point.

To these representations, he received from the President the following reply:

WASHINGTON, *May* 24, 1862.

I left General McDowell's camp at dark last evening. Shields's command is there, but it is so worn that he cannot move before Monday morning, the 26th. We have so thinned our line to get troops for other places that it was broken yesterday at Front Royal, with a probable loss to us of one regiment infantry, two companies cavalry, putting General Banks in some peril.

The enemy's forces, under General Anderson, now opposing General McDowell's advance, have, as their line of supply and retreat, the road to Richmond.

If, in conjunction with McDowell's movement against Anderson, you could send a force from your right to cut off the enemy's supplies from Richmond, preserve the railroad bridge across the two forks of the Pamunkey, and intercept the enemy's retreat, you will prevent the army now opposed to you from receiving an accession of numbers of nearly 15,000 men; and if you succeed in saving the bridges, you will secure a line of railroad for supplies in addition to the one you now have. Can you not do this almost as well as not, while you are building the Chickahominy bridges? McDowell and Shields both say they can, and positively will move Monday morning. I wish you to move cautiously and safely.

You will have command of McDowell, after he joins you, precisely as you indicated in your long dispatch to us of the 21st.

A. LINCOLN, *President.*

Major-General G. B. McCLELLAN.

General Banks, it will be remembered, had been sent by General McClellan on the 1st of April, to guard the approaches to Washington by the valley of the Shenandoah, which were even then menaced by Jackson with a considerable rebel force. A conviction of the entire insufficiency of the forces left for the protection of the capital, had led to the retention of McDowell, from whose command, however, upon General McClellan's urgent and impatient applications, General Franklin's division had been detached. On the 23d, as stated in the above letter from the President, there were indications of a purpose on Jackson's part to move in force against Banks; and this purpose was so clearly developed, and his situation became so critical, that the President was compelled to re-enforce him, a movement which he announced in the following dispatch to General McClellan:

May 24, 1862.—(From Washington, 4 P. M.)

In consequence of General Banks's critical position, I have been compelled to suspend General McDowell's movements to join you. The enemy are making a desperate push upon Harper's Ferry, and we are trying to throw General Fremont's force, and part of General McDowell's, in their rear.

A. LINCOLN, *President.*

Major-General G. B. McCLELLAN.

Unable apparently, or unwilling to concede any thing whatever to emergencies existing elsewhere, General McClellan remonstrated against the diversion of McDowell, in reply to which he received, on the 26th, the following more full explanation from the President:

WASHINGTON, *May* 25, 1862.

Your dispatch received. General Banks was at Strasburg with about 6,000 men, Shields having been taken from him to swell a column for McDowell to aid you at Richmond, and the rest of his force scattered at various places. On the 23d, a rebel force, of 7,000 to 10,000, fell upon one regiment and two companies guarding the bridge at Port Royal, destroying it entirely; crossed the Shenandoah, and on the 24th, yesterday, pushed on to get north of Banks on the road to Winchester. General Banks ran a race with them, beating them into Winchester yesterday evening. This morning a battle ensued between the two forces, in which General Banks was beaten back into full retreat toward Martinsburg, and probably is broken up into a total rout. Geary, on the Manassas Gap Railroad, just now reports that Jackson is now near

Front Royal with 10,000 troops, following up and supporting, as I understand, the force now pursuing Banks. Also, that another force of ten thousand is near Orleans, following on in the same direction. Stripped bare, as we are here, I will do all we can to prevent them crossing the Potomac at Harper's Ferry or above. McDowell has about twenty thousand of his forces moving back to the vicinity of Port Royal, and Fremont, who was at Franklin, is moving to Harrisonburg, both these movements intended to get in the enemy's rear.

One more of McDowell's brigades is ordered through here to Harper's Ferry; the rest of his forces remain for the present at Fredericksburg. We are sending such regiments and dribs from here and Baltimore as we can spare to Harper's Ferry, supplying their places in some sort, calling in militia from the adjacent States. We also have eighteen cannon on the road to Harper's Ferry, of which arm there is not a single one at that point. This is now our situation.

If McDowell's force was now beyond our reach, we should be entirely helpless. Apprehensions of something like this, and no unwillingness to sustain you, has always been my reason for withholding McDowell's forces from you.

Please understand this, and do the best you can with the forces you have.

A. LINCOLN, *President.*

Major-General McCLELLAN.

Jackson continued his triumphant march through the Shenandoah valley, and for a time it seemed as if nothing could prevent his crossing the Potomac, and making his appearance in rear of Washington. The President promptly announced this state of things to General McClellan in the following dispatch:

WASHINGTON, *May* 25, 1862—2 P. M.

The enemy is moving north in sufficient force to drive General Banks before him; precisely in what force we cannot tell. He is also threatening Leesburg and Geary on the Manassas Gap Railroad, from both north and south; in precisely what force we cannot tell. I think the movement is a general and concerted one. Such as would not be if he was acting upon the purpose of a very desperate defence of Richmond. I think the time is near when you must either attack Richmond or give up the job, and come to the defence of Washington. Let me hear from you instantly.

A. LINCOLN.

To this General McClellan replied that, independently of the President's letter, "The time *was* very near when he *should* attack Richmond." He knew nothing of Banks's position and force, but thought Jackson's movement was designed to prevent re-enforcements being sent to *him.*

On the 26th, the President announced to General McClellan the safety of Banks at Williamsport, and then turned his attention, with renewed anxiety, to the movement against Richmond, urging General McClellan, if possible, to cut the railroad between that city and the Rappahannock, over which the enemy obtained their supplies. The general, on the evening of the 26th, informed him that he was "quietly closing in upon the enemy preparatory to the last struggle"—that he felt forced to take every possible precaution against disaster, and that his "arrangements for the morrow were very important, and if successful would leave him free to strike on the return of the force attacked." The movement here referred to was one against a portion of the rebel forces at Hanover Court-House, which threatened McDowell, and was in position to re-enforce Jackson. The expedition was under command of General Fitz-John Porter, and proved a success. General McClellan on the 28th announced it to the Government as a "complete rout" of the rebels, and as entitling Porter to the highest honors. In the same dispatch he said he would do his best to cut off Jackson from returning to Richmond, but doubted if he could. The great battle was about to be fought before Richmond, and he adds: "It is the policy and the duty of the Government to send me *by water* all the well-drilled troops available. All unavailable troops should be collected *here.*" Porter, he said, had cut all the railroads but the one from Richmond to Fredericksburg, which was the one concerning which the President had evinced the most anxiety. Another expedition was sent to the South Anna River and Ashland, which destroyed some bridges without opposition. This was announced to the Government by

General McClellan as another "complete victory" achieved by the heroism of Porter,—accompanied by the statement that the enemy were even in greater force than he had supposed. "I will do," said the dispatch, "all that quick movements can accomplish, and you must send me all the troops you can, and leave to me full latitude as to choice of commanders." In reply, the President sent him the following:

WASHINGTON, *May* 28, 1862.

I am very glad of General F. J. Porter's victory; still, if it was a total rout of the enemy, I am puzzled to know why the Richmond and Fredericksburg Railroad was not seized again, as you say you have all the railroads but the Richmond and Fredericksburg. I am puzzled to see how, lacking that, you can have any, except the scrap from Richmond to West Point. The scrap of the Virginia Central, from Richmond to Hanover Junction, without more, is simply nothing. That the whole of the enemy is concentrating on Richmond, I think, cannot be certainly known to you or me. Saxton, at Harper's Ferry, informs us that large forces, supposed to be Jackson's and Ewell's, forced his advance from Charlestown to-day. General King telegraphs us from Fredericksburg that contrabands give certain information that fifteen thousand left Hanover Junction Monday morning to re-enforce Jackson. I am painfully impressed with the importance of the struggle before you, and shall aid you all I can consistently with my view of the due regard to all points.

A. LINCOLN.

Major-General MCCLELLAN.

To a dispatch reporting the destruction of the South Anna Railroad bridge, the President replied thus:

WASHINGTON, *May* 29, 1862.

Your dispatches as to the South Anna and Ashland being seized by our forces this morning is received. Understanding these points to be on the Richmond and Fredericksburg Railroad, I heartily congratulate the country, and thank General McClellan and his army for their seizure.

A. LINCOLN.

On the 30th, General McClellan telegraphed to the Secretary of War, complaining that the Government did not seem to appreciate the magnitude of Porter's victory, and saying that his army was now well in hand, and that "*another day* will make the probable field of battle passable for artillery."

On the 25th of May, General Keyes with the Fourth Corps had been ordered across the Chickahominy, and was followed by the Third, under General Heintzelman—one Division of the Fourth, under General Casey, being pushed forward within seven miles of Richmond, to Seven Pines, which he was ordered to hold at all hazards. On the 28th, General Keyes was ordered to advance Casey's Division three-quarters of a mile to Fair Oaks. General Keyes obeyed the order, but made strong representations to head-quarters of the extreme danger of pushing these troops so far in advance without adequate support, and requested that General Heintzelman might be brought within supporting distance, and that a stronger force might be crossed over the Chickahominy to be in readiness for the general engagement which these advances would be very likely to bring on. These requests were neglected, and General Keyes was regarded and treated as an alarmist. On the afternoon of the 30th he made a personal examination of his front, and reported that he was menaced by an overwhelming force of the enemy in front and on both flanks, and he again urged the necessity for support, to which he received a very abrupt reply that no more troops would be crossed over, and that the Third Corps would not be advanced unless he was attacked. At about noon the next day he was attacked on both flanks and in front, General Casey's Division driven back with heavy loss, and in spite of a stubborn and gallant resistance on the part of his corps, General Keyes was compelled to fall back with severe losses, some two miles, when the enemy was checked, and night put an end to the engagement. On hearing the firing at head-quarters, some four miles distant, General McClellan ordered General Sumner to hold his command in readiness to move. General Sumner not only did so, but moved them at once to the bridge, and on receiving authority crossed over, and, by the greatest exertions over muddy roads, reached the field of battle in time to aid in checking the rebel advance for the night. Early the next morning the enemy renewed the attack with great vigor, but the arrival of General Sumner, and the advance of General Heintzelman's Corps, enabled our forces, though still greatly inferior, not only to repel the assault, but to inflict upon the enemy a signal defeat. They were driven back in the utmost confusion and with terrible losses upon Richmond, where their arrival created the utmost consternation, as it was taken for granted they would be immediately followed by our whole army.

General McClellan, who had remained with the main body of the army on the other side of the Chickahominy during the whole of the engagements of both days, crossed the river after the battle was over, and visited the field. "The state of the roads," he says, "and the impossibility of manœuvring artillery, prevented pursuit." He returned to head-quarters in the afternoon. On the next day, June 2d, General Heintzelman sent forward a strong reconnoitering party under General Hooker, which went within four miles of Richmond without finding any enemy. Upon being informed of this fact, General McClellan ordered the force to fall back to its old position, assigning the bad state of the roads as the reason for not attempting either to march upon Richmond or even to hold the ground already gained. In a dispatch to Washington on the 2d, he states that he "only waits for the river to fall to cross with the rest of the army and *make a general attack.* The *morale* of my troops," he adds, "is now such that I can venture much. I do not fear for odds against me." It seems to have been his intention then, to concentrate his forces for an immediate advance upon the rebel capital, though in his report, written more than a year afterwards, he says the idea of uniting the two wings of the army at that time for a vigorous move upon Richmond was "simply absurd, and was probably never seriously entertained by any one connected with the Army of the Potomac." *

The Government at once took measures to strengthen the army by all the means available. An order was issued, placing at his command all the disposable forces at Fortress Monroe, and another ordering McDowell to send McCall's division to him by water from Fredericksburg. McDowell or Fremont was expected to fight Jackson at Front Royal, after which, part of their troops would become available for the Army of the Potomac. On the 4th, General McClellan telegraphed that it was raining, that the river was still high, that he had "to be very cautious," that he expected another severe battle, and hoped, after our heavy losses, he "should no longer be regarded as an alarmist." On the 5th, the Secretary of War sent him word that troops had been embarked for him at Baltimore, to which he replied on the 7th, "*I shall be in perfect readiness to move forward and take Richmond the moment McCall reaches here, and the ground will admit the passage of artillery.*" On the 10th, General McCall's forces began to arrive at White House, and on the same day General McClellan telegraphed to the Department that a rumor had reached him that the rebels had been re-enforced by Beauregard,—that he thought a portion of Halleck's army from Tennessee should be sent to strengthen him, but that he should "attack with what force he had, as soon as the weather and ground will permit—but there will be a delay," he added, "the extent of which no one can foresee, for the season is altogether abnormal." The Secretary of War replied that Halleck would be urged to comply with his request if he could safely do so—that neither Beauregard nor his army was in Richmond, that McDowell's force would join him as soon as possible, that Fremont had had an engagement, not

* See Gen. McClellan's Report, August 4, 1863.

wholly successful, with Jackson, and closing with this strong and cordial assurance of confidence and support:

Be assured, General, that there never has been a moment when my desire has been otherwise than to aid you with my whole heart, mind, and strength, since the hour we first met; and whatever others may say for their own purposes, you have never had, and never can have, any one more truly your friend, or more anxious to support you, or more joyful than I shall be at the success which I have no doubt will soon be achieved by your arms.

On the 14th, General McClellan wrote to the War Department that the weather was favorable, and that *two days* more would make the ground practicable. He still urges the propriety of sending him more troops, but finds a new subject of complaint in a telegram he had received from McDowell. The latter, on the 8th, had received the following orders:

The Secretary of War directs that, having first provided adequately for the defence of the city of Washington and for holding the position at Fredericksburg, you operate with the residue of your force as speedily as possible in the direction of Richmond to co-operate with Major-General McClellan in accordance with the instructions heretofore given you. *McCall's Division*, which has been by previous order directed towards Richmond by water, *will still form a part of the Army of the Rappahannock, and will come under your orders when you are in a position to co-operate with General McClellan.*

General McDowell had telegraphed McClellan as follows on the 10th of June:

For the third time I am ordered to join you, and hope this time to get through. In view of the remarks made with reference to my leaving you, and not joining you before, by your friends, and of something I have heard as coming from you on that subject, I wish to say I go with the greatest satisfaction, and hope to arrive with my main body in time to be of service. McCall goes in advance by water. I will be with you in ten days with the remainder by Fredericksburg.

And again, June 12th:

The delay of Major-General Banks to relieve the Division of my command in the valley beyond the time I had calculated on, will prevent my joining you with the remainder of the troops I am to take below at as early a day as I named. My Third Division (McCall's) is now on the way. *Please do me the favor to so place it that it may be in a position to join the others as they come down from Fredericksburg.*

These telegrams, it will be seen, are in accordance with the orders to McDowell of the 8th, which directed that McCall's Division should continue to form part of the Army of the Rappahannock, and required that McDowell should operate in the direction of Richmond, to co-operate with McClellan *in accordance with instructions heretofore given him.*

These instructions are those of the 17th and 18th of May, concerning which McClellan sent the President his long telegram of the 21st, in which he says:

This fact (McDowell's forces coming within his Department), my superior rank, and the express language of the sixty-second article of war, will place his command under my orders, unless it is otherwise specially directed by your Excellency, and I consider that he will be under my command, except that I am not to detach any portion of his forces, or give any orders which can put him out of position to cover Washington.

To this the President answered:

You will have command of McDowell after he joins you, precisely as you indicated in your long dispatch to us of the 21st.

In regard to this, McClellan, in his report (August 4th, 1863), says:

This information, that McDowell's Corps would march from Fredericksburg on the following Monday—the 26th—and that he would be under my command as indicated in my telegram of the 21st, was cheering news, and I now felt confident that we would on his arrival be sufficiently strong to overpower the large army confronting us.

Yet in the simple request of McDowell, as to the posting of his Third (McCall's) Division—made to carry out the plan—the news of which, McClellan says, was so cheering, and inspired him with such confidence, McClellan sees nothing but personal ambition on McDowell's part, and protests against that "spirit" in the following terms:

> That request does not breathe the proper spirit. Whatever troops come to me must be disposed of so as to do the most good. I do not feel that, in such circumstances as those in which I am now placed, General McDowell should wish the general interests to be sacrificed for the purpose of increasing his command.
>
> *If I cannot fully control all his troops, I want none of them, but would prefer to fight the battle with what I have, and let others be responsible for the results.*
>
> The department lines should not be allowed to interfere with me; but General McD., and all other troops sent to me, should be placed *completely at my disposal,* to do with them as I think best. In no other way can they be of assistance to me. I therefore request that I may have entire and full control. The stake at issue is too great to allow personal considerations to be entertained: *you know that I have none.*

It had been suggested, in some of the journals of the day, that General McDowell might possibly advance upon Richmond from the north, without waiting for McClellan: it is scarcely possible, however, that any suspicion of such a purpose could have had any thing to do with General McClellan's reiterated and emphatic desire that McDowell should join him by water, so as to be in his rear, and not by land, which would bring him on his front,—with his peremptory demand that all McDowell's troops should be "completely at his disposal," with his indignant protest against McDowell's personal ambition, or with his conviction of the propriety and necessity of disavowing all personal considerations for himself. But it is certainly a little singular that a commander, intrusted with an enterprise of such transcendent importance to his army and country, who had been so urgently calling for reenforcements as absolutely indispensable to success, should have preferred not to receive them, but to fight the battle with what he had, rather than have the co-operation of McDowell under the two conditions fixed by the President, (1), that he should not deprive him of his troops, or, (2), post them so as to prevent their being kept interposed between the enemy and Washington. Even if he could leave "others to be responsible for the results," it is not easy to see how he could reconcile the possibility of adverse results with his professedly paramount concern for the welfare of his country.

On the 20th of June, he telegraphed the President that troops to the number probably of 10,000 had left Richmond to re-enforce Jackson; that his defensive works on the Chickahominy, made necessary by his "inferiority of numbers," would be completed the next day; and that he would be glad to learn the "disposition, as to numbers and position, of the troops not under his command, in Virginia and elsewhere," as also to lay before his Excellency, "by letter or telegraph, his views as to the present state of military affairs *throughout the whole country.*" To this he received the following reply:

WASHINGTON, *June* 21, 1862—6 P. M.

Your dispatch of yesterday, two P. M., was received this morning. If it would not divert too much of your time and attention from the army under your immediate command, I would be glad to have your views as to the present state of military affairs throughout the whole country, as you say you would be glad to give them. I would rather it should be by letter than by telegraph, because of the better chance of secrecy. As to the numbers and positions of the troops not under your command, in Virginia and elsewhere, even if I could do it with accuracy, which I cannot, I would rather not transmit either by telegraph or letter, because of the chances of its reaching the enemy. I would be very glad to talk with you, but you cannot leave your camp, and I cannot well leave here. A. LINCOLN, *President.*

Major-General GEORGE B. MCCLELLAN.

The President also stated that the news of Jackson's having been re-enforced from Richmond was confirmed by Gen. King at Fredericksburg, and added, "If this is true, it is as good as a re-enforcement to you of an equal force." In acknowledging the first dispatch, Gen. McClellan said, he "perceived that it would be better to defer the communication he desired to make" on the condition of the country at large; he soon, indeed, had occasion to give all his attention to the army under his command.

Gen. McClellan had been, for nearly a month, declaring his intention to advance upon Richmond immediately. At times as has been seen from his dispatches, the movement was fixed for specific days, though in every instance something occurred, when the decisive moment arrived, to cause a further postponement. On the 18th, again announcing his intention to advance, he said that a "general engagement might take place at *any hour*, as an advance by us involves a battle more or less decisive." But in the same dispatch he said, "After to-morrow we shall fight the rebel army as soon as Providence will permit." But in this case, as in every other, in spite of his good intentions, and the apparent permission of Providence, Gen. McClellan made no movement in advance, but waited until he was attacked. He had placed his army astride the Chickahominy—the left wing being much the strongest and most compact, the right being comparatively weak and very extended. He had expended, however, a great deal of labor in bridging the stream, so that either wing could have been thrown across with great ease and celerity. Up to the 24th of June, Gen. McClellan believed Jackson to be in strong force at Gordonsville, where he was receiving re-enforcements from Richmond with a view to operations in that quarter. But on that day he was told by a deserter that Jackson was planning a movement to attack his right and rear on the 28th, and this information was confirmed by advices from the War Department on the 25th. On that day, being convinced that he is to be attacked, and will therefore be compelled to fight, he writes to the Department to throw upon others the responsibility of an anticipated defeat. He declares the rebel force to be some 200,000, regrets his "great inferiority of numbers," but protests that he is not responsible for it, as he has repeatedly and constantly called for re-enforcements, and declares that if the result of the action is a disaster, the "responsibility cannot be thrown on his shoulders, but must rest where it belongs." He closes by announcing that a reconnoissance which he had ordered had proved successful, that he should probably be attacked the next day, and that he felt "that there was no use in again asking for re-enforcements." To this the President replied as follows:

WASHINGTON, *June* 26, 1862.

Your three dispatches of yesterday in relation, ending with the statement that you completely succeeded in making your point, are very gratifying. The later one, suggesting the probability of your being overwhelmed by 200,000 men, and talking of to whom the responsibility will belong, pains me very much. I give you all I can, and act on the presumption that you will do the best you can with what you have; while you continue, ungenerously I think, to assume that I could give you more if I would. I have omitted—I shall omit—no opportunity to send you re-enforcements whenever I can.

A. LINCOLN.

Gen. McClellan had foreseen the probhbility of being attacked, and had made arrangements for a defeat. "More than a week previous," he says in his report, "that is, on the 18th," he had prepared for a retreat to the James River, and had ordered supplies to that point. His extreme right was attacked at Mechanicsville on the afternoon of the 26th, but the enemy were repulsed. The movement, however, disclosed the purpose of the rebel army to crush his right wing and cut off his communications, if possible. Two plans were open to his adoption: he might have brought over his left wing, and so strengthened his right as to give it a victory, or he might have withdrawn his right across the Chickahominy—in itself a strong defensive line—and have pushed his whole force into

Richmond, and upon the rear of the attacking force. Concentration seemed to be absolutely essential to success in any event. But he did not attempt it. He left the right wing to contend next day with 30,000 men, without support, against the main body of the rebel army, and only withdrew it across the Chickahominy after it had been beaten with terrific slaughter on the 27th, in the battle of Gaines's Mill. On the evening of that day he informed his corps commanders of his purpose to fall back to the James River, and withdrew the remainder of his right wing across the Chickahominy. On the next day the whole army was put in motion on the retreat; and Gen. McClellan found time again to reproach the Government with neglect of his army. If he had 10,000 fresh men to use at once, he said, he could take Richmond; but as it was, all he could do would be to cover his retreat. He repeated that he was "not responsible" for the result, and that he must have instantly very large re-enforcements; and closed by saying to the Secretary of War—what we do not believe any subordinate was ever before permitted to say to his superior officer without instant dismissal—"If I save this army now, I tell you plainly that I *owe no thanks to you or to any persons in Washington: you have done your best to sacrifice this army.*"

To this dispatch the President replied as follows:

WASHINGTON, *June* 28, 1862.

Save your army at all events. Will send re-enforcements as fast as we can. Of course, they cannot reach you to-day, to-morrow, or next day. I have not said you were ungenerous for saying you needed re-enforcements; I thought you were ungenerous in assuming that I did not send them as fast as I could. I feel any misfortune to you and your army quite as keenly as you feel it yourself. If you have had a drawn battle or a repulse, it is the price we pay for the enemy not being in Washington. We protected Washington, and the enemy concentrated on you. Had we stripped Washington, he would have been upon us before the troops sent could have got to you. Less than a week ago you notified us that re-enforcements were leaving Richmond to come in front of us. It is the nature of the case, and neither you nor the Government is to blame. A. LINCOLN.

Under general orders from General McClellan, he and his staff proceeding in advance, and leaving word where the corps commanders were to make successive stands to resist pursuit, but taking no part personally in any one of the succeeding engagements, the army continued its march towards James River. They first resisted and repulsed the pursuing rebels on the 29th at Savage Station, in a bloody battle, fought under General Sumner, and on the 30th had another severe engagement at Glendale. On the 1st of July, our troops, strongly posted at Malvern Hill, were again attacked by the rebels, whom they repulsed and routed with terrible slaughter; and orders were at once issued for the further retreat of the army to Harrison's Landing, which General McClellan had personally examined and selected on the day before. Even before the battle of Malvern Hill, he had telegraphed to Washington for "fresh troops," saying he should fall back to the river if possible; to which dispatch he received the following reply:

WASHINGTON, *July* 1, 1862—3.30 P. M.

It is impossible to re-enforce you for your present emergency. If we had a million of men we could not get them to you in time. We have not the men to send. If you are not strong enough to face the enemy, you must find a place of security, and wait, rest, and repair. Maintain your ground if you can, but save the army at all events, even if you fall back to Fort Monroe. We still have strength enough in the country, and will bring it out. A. LINCOLN.

Major-General G. B. MCCLELLAN.

On the next day, in reply to a request from General McClellan for 50,000 more troops, the President thus addressed him:

WASHINGTON, *July* 2, 1862.

Your dispatch of yesterday induces me to hope that your army is having some rest. In this hope, allow me to reason with you for a moment. When you ask for 50,000 men to be promptly sent you, you surely labor under some gross mistake of fact. Recently you sent papers showing your disposal of forces made last spring for the defence of Washington, and advising a return to that plan. I find it included in and about Washington 75,000 men. Now, please be assured that I have not men enough to fill that very plan by 15,000. All of General Fremont's in the Valley, all of General Banks's, all of General McDowell's not with you, and all in Washington taken together, do not exceed, if they reach, 60,000. With General Wool and General Dix added to those mentioned, I have not, outside of your army, 75,000 men east of the mountains. Thus, the idea of sending you 50,000, or any other considerable forces promptly, is simply absurd. If in your frequent mention of responsibility you have the impression that I blame you for not doing more than you can, please be relieved of such impression. I only beg, that in like manner, you will not ask impossibilities of me. If you think you are not strong enough to take Richmond just now, I do not ask you to try just now. Save the army, material, and *personnel*, and I will strengthen it for the offensive again as fast as I can. The governors of eighteen States offer me a new levy of 300,000, which I accept.

A. LINCOLN.

On the next day, the 3d, General McClellan again wrote for 100,000 men—"more rather than less," in order to enable him to "accomplish the great task of capturing Richmond, and putting an end to the rebellion;" and at the same time he sent his chief of staff, General Marcy, to Washington, in order to secure a perfect understanding of the state of the army. The General said he hoped the enemy was as completely worn out as his own army, though he apprehended a new attack, from which, however, he trusted the bad condition of the roads might protect him. On the 4th, he repeated his call for "heavy re-enforcements," but said he held a very strong position, from which, with the aid of the gunboats, he could only be driven by overwhelming numbers. On the same day he received the following from the President:

WAR DEPARTMENT, WASHINGTON CITY, D. C., *July* 4, 1862.

I understand your position as stated in your letter, and by General Marcy. To re-enforce you so as to enable you to resume the offensive within a month, or even six weeks, is impossible. In addition to that arrived and now arriving from the Potomac (about ten thousand men, I suppose), and about ten thousand, I hope, you will have from Burnside very soon, and about five thousand from Hunter a little later, I do not see how I can send you another man within a month. Under these circumstances, the defensive, for the present, must be your only care. Save the army, first, where you are, if you *can;* and secondly, by removal, if you must. You, on the ground, must be the judge as to which you will attempt, and of the means for effecting it. I but give it as my opinion, that with the aid of the gunboats and the re-enforcements mentioned above, you can hold your present position; provided, and so long as you can keep the James River open below you. If you are not tolerably confident you can keep the James River open, you had better remove as soon as possible. I do not remember that you have expressed any apprehension as to the danger of having your communication cut on the river below you, yet I do not suppose it can have escaped your attention. A. LINCOLN.

P. S.—If at any time you feel able to take the offensive, you are not restrained from doing so.

A. L.

At this point on the 7th of July, General McClellan sent to the President a letter of advice on the general conduct of his Administration. He thought the time had come "when the Government should determine upon a civil and military policy covering the whole ground of our national trouble," and he proceeded to lay down the basis of such a policy as ought to be adopted. The war against the rebellion, he said, "should not be a war looking to the subjugation of the people of any State in any event. Neither confiscation of property, political execution of persons, territorial organization of States, nor forcible abolition of slavery, should be contemplated for a moment. He added:"

Military power should not be allowed to interfere with the relations of servitude, either by supporting or impairing the authority of the master, except for repressing disorder, as in other cases. Slaves, contraband, under the act of Congress, seeking military protection, should receive it. The right of the Government to appropriate permanently to its own service claims to slave labor, should be asserted, and the right of the owner to compensation therefor should be recognized. This principle might be extended, upon grounds of military necessity and security, to all the slaves of a particular State, thus working manumission in such State; and in Missouri, perhaps in Western Virginia also, and possibly even in Maryland, the expediency of such a measure is only a question of time. * *

Unless the principles governing the future conduct of our struggle shall be made known and approved, the effort to obtain requisite forces will be almost hopeless. A declaration of radical views, especially upon slavery, will rapidly disintegrate our present armies.

He closed this letter by saying that to carry out these views the President would require a Commander-in-Chief who possessed his confidence and could execute his orders: he did not ask that place for himself, but would serve in any position that might be assigned him. "I may be," he adds, "on the brink of eternity; and as I hope for forgiveness from my Maker, I have written this letter with sincerity towards you, and from love for my country."

The President, instead of entering upon a discussion as to the general policy of his Administration, continued to urge the general's attention to the state of his own army; and in order to inform himself more accurately as to its actual condition and prospects, visited the camp on the 8th of July, at Harrison's Landing. The actual strength of the army seems to have been at that time a matter of considerable difference of opinion; and in regard to it, on returning to Washington, the President thus addressed the general:

EXECUTIVE MANSION, WASHINGTON, *July* 13, 1862.

MY DEAR SIR: I am told that over 160,000 men have gone with your army on the Peninsula. When I was with you the other day, we made out 86,000 remaining, leaving 73,500 to be accounted for. I believe 3,500 will cover all the killed, wounded, and missing, in all your battles and skirmishes, leaving 50,000 who have left otherwise. Not more than 5,000 of these have died, leaving 45,000 of your army still alive, and not with it. I believe half or two-thirds of them are fit for duty to-day. Have you any more perfect knowledge of this than I have? If I am right, and you had these men with you, you could go into Richmond in the next three days. How can they be got to you, and how can they be prevented from getting away in such numbers for the future?

A. LINCOLN.

In reply to this letter, the general disclosed the fact that 38,250 men of his army were absent by authority—*i. e.*, on furloughs granted by permission of the Commanding General. The actual number of troops composing his army on the 20th of July, according to official returns, was 158,314, and the aggregate losses in the retreat to the James River was 15,249.

During the President's visit to the camp, the future movements of the army were a subject of anxious deliberation. It was understood that the rebels were gathering large forces for another advance upon Washington, which was comparatively unprotected—and as General McClellan did not consider himself strong enough to take the offensive, it was felt to be absolutely necessary to concentrate the army, either on the Peninsula or in front of Washington, for the protection of the capital. The former course, after the experience of the past season, was felt to be exceedingly hazardous, and the corps commanders of the Army of the Potomac were decidedly in favor of the latter. General McClellan at once addressed himself to the task of defeating the project. On the 11th, he telegraphed to the President that "the army was in fine spirits, and that he hoped he would soon make him strong enough to try again." On the 12th, he said he was "more and more convinced that the army ought not to be withdrawn, but promptly re-enforced and thrown *again* upon Richmond." He "dreaded the effects of any retreat on the *morale* of his men"—though his previous experience should have obviated any such apprehension in his mind. "If we have a little more than half a chance," he said, "we can take Richmond." On the 17th, he urged that General Burnside's whole command in North Carolina should be ordered to join him, to enable him to "assume the offensive as soon as possible." On the 18th, he repeated this request; and on the 28th, again urged that he should be "at once re-enforced by all available troops." On the 25th, General Halleck had visited the camp, and, after a careful inspection of the condition of the army, called an informal council of the officers, a majority of whom, upon learning the state of affairs, recommended its withdrawal from the Peninsula. On the 30th, he issued an order to General McClellan to make arrangements at once for a prompt removal of all the sick in his army, in order to enable him to move "in any direction." On the 2d of August, not having received any reply, General Halleck renewed his order to "remove them as rapidly as possible;" to which, on the 3d, General McClellan replied that it was "impossible to decide what cases to send off unless he knew what was to be done with the army"—and that if he was to be "kept longer in ignorance of what was to be effected, he could not be expected to accomplish the object in view." In reply, General Halleck informed him that his army was to be "withdrawn from the Peninsula to Acquia Creek," but that the withdrawal should be concealed even from his own officers. General McClellan, on the 4th, wrote a long protest against this movement—saying it mattered not what partial reverses might be sustained elsewhere—*there* was the "true defence of Washington," and he asked that the order might be rescinded. To this letter, after again urging General McClellan on the 4th to hasten the removal of the sick, which he was "expected to have done without waiting to know what were or would be the intentions of the Government respecting future movements," General Halleck on the 6th addressed him as follows:

HEAD-QUARTERS OF THE ARMY,
WASHINGTON, *August* 6, 1862.

GENERAL: Your telegram of yesterday was received this morning, and I immediately telegraphed a brief reply, promising to write you more fully by mail.

You, General, certainly could not have been more pained at receiving my order than I was at the necessity of issuing it. I was advised by high officers, in whose judgment I had great confidence, to make the order immediately on my arrival here, but I determined not to do so until I could learn your wishes from a personal interview. And even after that interview I tried every means in my power to avoid withdrawing your army, and delayed my decision as long as I dared to delay it.

I assure you, General, it was not a hasty and inconsiderate act, but one that caused me more anxious thoughts than any other of my life. But after full and mature consideration of all the *pros* and *cons*, I was reluctantly forced to the conclusion that the order must be issued—there was to my mind no alternative.

Allow me to allude to a few of the facts in the case.

You and your officers at our interview estimated the enemy's forces in and around Richmond at two hundred thousand men. Since then, you and others report that they have received and are receiving large re-enforcements from the South. General Pope's army, covering Washington, is only about forty thousand. Your effective force is only about ninety thousand. You are thirty miles from Richmond, and General Pope eighty or ninety, *with the enemy directly between you, ready to fall with his superior numbers upon one or the other as he may elect; neither can re-enforce the other in case of such an attack.*

If General Pope's army be diminished to re-enforce you, Washington, Maryland, and Pennsylvania, would be left uncovered and exposed. If your force be reduced to strengthen Pope, you would be too weak to even hold the position you now occupy, should the enemy turn round and attack you in full force. In other words, the old Army of the Potomac is split into two parts, with the entire force of the enemy directly between them. They cannot be united by land without exposing both to destruction, and yet they must be united. To send Pope's forces by water to the Peninsula is, under present circumstances, a military impossibility. The only alternative is to send the forces on the Peninsula to some point by water, say Fredericksburg, where the two armies can be united.

Let me now allude to some of the objections which you have urged: you say that the withdrawal from the present position will cause the certain demoralization of the army, "which is now in excellent discipline and condition."

I cannot understand why a simple change of position to a new and by no means distant base will demoralize an army in excellent discipline, unless the officers themselves assist in that demoralization, which I am satisfied they will not.

Your change of front from your extreme right at Hanover Court-House to your present condition was over thirty miles, but I have not heard that it demoralized your troops, notwithstanding the severe losses they sustained in effecting it.

A new base on the Rappahannock at Fredericksburg brings you within about sixty miles of Richmond, and secures a re-enforcement of forty or fifty thousand fresh and disciplined troops.

The change with such advantages will, I think, if properly represented to your army, encourage rather than demoralize your troops. Moreover, you yourself suggested that a junction might be effected at Yorktown, but that a flank march across the isthmus would be more hazardous than to retire to Fort Monroe.

You will remember that Yorktown is two or three miles further than Fredericksburg is. Besides, the latter is between Richmond and Washington, and covers Washington from any attack of the enemy.

The political effect of the withdrawal may at first be unfavorable; but I think the public are beginning to understand its necessity, and that they will have much more confidence in a united army than in its separated fragments.

But you will reply, why not re-enforce me here, so that I can strike Richmond from my present position? To do this, you said, at our interview, that you required thirty thousand additional troops. I told you that it was impossible to give you so many. You finally thought you would have "some chance" of success with twenty thousand. But you afterwards telegraphed me that you would require thirty-five thousand, as the enemy was being largely re-enforced.

If your estimate of the enemy's strength was correct, your requisition was perfectly reasonable; but it was utterly impossible to fill it until new troops could be enlisted and organized, which would require several weeks.

To keep your army in its present position until it could be so re-enforced would almost destroy it in that climate.

The months of August and September are almost fatal to whites who live on that part of James River; and even after you received the re-enforcement asked for, you admitted that you must reduce Fort Darling and the river batteries before you could advance on Richmond.

It is by no means certain that the reduction of these fortifications would not require considerable time—perhaps as much as those at Yorktown.

This delay might not only be fatal to the health of your army, but in the mean time General Pope's forces would be exposed to the heavy blows of the enemy without the slightest hope of assistance from you.

In regard to the demoralizing effect of a withdrawal from the Peninsula to the Rappahannock, I must remark that a large number of your highest officers, indeed a majority of those whose opinions have been reported to me, are decidedly in favor of the movement. Even several of those who originally advocated the line of the Peninsula now advise its abandonment.

I have not inquired, and do not wish to know, by whose advice or for what reasons the army of the Potomac was separated into two parts with the enemy between them. I must take things as I find them.

I find the forces divided, and I wish to unite them. Only one feasible plan has been presented for doing this. If you, or any one else, had presented a better plan, I certainly should have adopted it. But all of your plans require re-enforcements which it is impossible to give you. It is very easy to *ask* for re-enforcements, but it is not so easy to give them when you have no disposable troops at your command.

I have written very plainly as I understand the case, and I hope you will give me credit for having fully considered the matter, although I may have arrived at very different conclusions from your own.

Very respectfully, your obedient servant,

W. H. HALLECK, *General-in-Chief.*

Major-General G. B. McCLELLAN, *Commanding, etc., Berkeley, Virginia.*

The order for the removal of the sick was given to General McClellan on the 2d of August. On the 7th he reported that 3,740 had been sent, and 5,700 still remained. On the 9th, General Halleck telegraphed McClellan that the enemy was massing his forces in front of General Pope and Burnside to crush them and move upon Washington, and that re-enforcements must at once be sent to Aquia Creek; to which he replied that he would "move the whole army as soon as the sick were disposed of." On the 12th, in replyto the most pressing orders for immediate dispatch from General Halleck, who urged that Burnside had moved 13,000 troops in two days to Aquia Creek, General McClellan said if Washington was in danger, that army could scarcely arrive in time to save it. On the 14th, he announced that the movement had commenced; on the 17th, he said he "should not feel entirely secure until he had the whole army beyond the Chickahominy, but that he would *then* begin to forward troops by water as fast as transportation would permit." On the 23d, General Franklin's Corps started from Fortress Monroe; General McClellan followed the next day, and reached Aquia Creek on the 24th, and Alexandria on the evening of the 26th of August.

On the 27th of June the President had issued an order consolidating into one army, to be called the Army of Virginia, the forces under Major-Generals Fremont, Banks, and McDowell. The command of this army was assigned to Major-General John Pope; and the army was divided into three corps, of which the first was assigned to Fremont, the second to Banks, and the third to McDowell. Upon receiving this order Major-General Fremont applied to be relieved from the command which it assigned him, on the ground that by the appointment of General Pope to the chief command, his (Fremont's) position was "subordinate and inferior to that heretofore held by him, and to remain in the subordinate rank now assigned him, would largely reduce his rank and consideration in the service." In compliance with his request, General Fremont was at once relieved.

On the 27th of August, General McClellan was ordered by General Halleck to "*take entire direction of the sending out of the troops from Alexandria*" to re-enforce Pope, whom the enemy were pressing with a powerful army, and whose headquarters were then at Warrenton Junction. A portion of the

Army of the Potomac which arrived before General McClellan, had at once gone forward to the aid of Pope;—of those which arrived after him, or which were at Alexandria when he arrived, not one reached the field or took any part in the battles by which the army was saved from destruction, and the capital from capture.

The extent to which General McClellan, who had the "entire direction of the sending of these re-enforcements," was responsible for this result, is a matter of so much importance, not only to himself and the Government, but to the whole country, as to demand a somewhat detailed examination.

In his Report of August 4th, 1863, after giving a portion only of the correspondence between himself and the Government on this subject, General McClellan says:

It will be seen from what has preceded that I lost no time that could be avoided in moving the Army of the Potomac from the Peninsula to the support of the Army of Virginia; that I spared no effort to hasten the embarkation of the troops at Fort Monroe, Newport News, and Yorktown, remaining at Fort Monroe myself until the mass of the army had sailed; and that *after my arrival at Alexandria, I left nothing in my power undone to forward supplies and re-enforcements to General Pope.* I sent, with troops that moved, all the cavalry I could get hold of. Even my personal escort was sent out upon the line of the railway as a guard, with the provost and camp guards at head-quarters, retaining less than one hundred men, many of whom were orderlies, invalids, members of bands, &c. All the head-quarters teams that arrived were sent out with supplies and ammunition, none being retained even to move the head-quarters camp. The squadron that habitually served as my personal escort was left at Falmouth with General Burnside, as he was deficient in cavalry.

Before taking up more important matters, it may be well to remark, that as General McClellan was in the city of Alexandria, and not in any way exposed to personal danger, it is difficult to appreciate the merit he seems to make of yielding up his personal escort, provost and camp guards, and head-quarter baggage teams, when he had no use for them himself, and when they were needed for the purpose for which they are maintained—operating against the enemy, and that too in a pressing emergency. Even as it was, he seems to have retained nearly a hundred, many of whom he says were orderlies, etc., etc., around his person.

Leaving this personal matter, we come to the important question—Is it true that General McClellan left, as he avers, nothing undone in his power to forward supplies and re-enforcements to General Pope's Army? Did he, on this momentous occasion, honestly and faithfully do his whole duty in this respect, without any personal aims, or any jealousy, and with the single eye to the success of our arms, and the honor, welfare, and glory of the nation?

He had been repeatedly urged to hurry forward the troops from the Peninsula. On the 9th of August, he was informed by General Halleck that "the enemy is massing his forces in front of General Pope and Burnside to try and crush them and move forward to the Potomac;" and was further told: "considering the amount of transportation at your disposal, your delay is not satisfactory. *You must move with all celerity.*"

Again on the 10th, General Halleck informed him that "the enemy is crossing the Rapidan in large force. They are fighting General Pope to-day. *There must be no further delay in your movements:* that which has already occured was entirely unexpected, and must be satisfactorily explained. Let not a moment's time be lost, and telegraph me daily what progress you have made in executing the order to transfer your troops." Again on the 21st, he was told "the forces of Burnside and Pope are hard pushed and require aid as rapidly as you can. By all means see that the troops sent have plenty of ammunition. We have no time to supply them; moreover, they may have to fight as soon as they land."

Whether or not the delays of General McClellan were excusable, those telegrams must have shown him, if proof were necessary, the emergency in which Pope was placed, and that the concentration of the two armies was not being effected in the time expected, and as a consequence that Pope was in a critical position, needing immediate help to save his army from defeat. It was under these circumstances that General McClellan left the Peninsula.

When he reached Aquia on the 24th, under most positive and pressing orders from Washington, General Pope, who had been holding the line of the Rappahannock for nearly a week against the assaults of Lee's whole army, and keeping up communication with Fredericksburg, so as to receive the re-enforcements McClellan had been ordered to send up from the Peninsula—finding these re-enforcements not coming by water to join his left as fast as Lee marched by land around his right, and that his right, though stretched to Waterloo Bridge, had been turned and his rear threatened, had been obliged to throw back his right first to Warrenton, and then to Gainesville, and his left and centre from Rappahannock and Sulphur Springs, to Warrenton Junction, Bristol and Manassas. General McClellan knew on the 24th, when at Aquia, of the abandoning of Rappahannock Station, and of Pope's having broken his communication with Fredericksburg, and himself reported the facts to General Halleck.

August 26th, General Halleck ordered General McClellan from Aquia to Alexandria, and told him "General Franklin's Corps" which had arrived at Alexandria, "will march as soon as it receives transportation."

General Pope had, when his line was stretched from below Rappahannock Station to beyond Warrenton, asked that Franklin's Corps might be sent out to take post on his right at Gainesville, to which there was transportation by turnpike and railroad, to guard against what afterwards happened,—the movement of the enemy through that place, on his rear. The failure to have that corps at that place or in the action at all, was one of the chief causes of Pope's failure. Why was this?

August 27th, as already stated, General McClellan was directed "to take entire direction of the sending out of the troops from Alexandria." On the same day he was informed of the position of Pope's head-quarters; of that of most of Pope's forces; of where Pope wished re-enforcements sent him—Gainesville; and that Fitz John Porter, then under Pope, reported a battle imminent. At 10 A. M. on that day, he was told by Halleck, "that Franklin's Corps should march in that direction (Manassas) as soon as possible; and again at 12 P. M., he was further told by Halleck that "*Franklin's Corps should move out by forced marches, carrying three or four days' provisions, and to be supplied as far as possible by Railroad.*"

It is well to bear in mind these explicit orders, and the circumstances under which, and the object for which they were given, for General McClellan either seems to have forgotten them, or to have utterly failed to appreciate their importance. A battle reported by his favorite general, Fitz-John Porter, as imminent, within cannon sound of where he was,—the road to the battle-field, a wide, straight, Macadam turnpike, well-known to both General McClellan and General Franklin, as each had been over it more than once,—the whole of the enemy and army which had been pressing Pope since the 9th, now concentrating to overwhelm him,—here one would think, was every motive for him to do, as he claims to have done, every thing in his power to send re-enforcements forward, and to send them instantly.

Why was it then, that, at 7.15 P. M., on the 29th, more than two days after the order for it to go by *forced marches* to re-enforce an army engaged in battle, Franklin's Corps was still at Anandale, about seven miles from Alexandria, and Franklin himself in Alexandria? General Halleck says it was all contrary to his orders, and McClellan acknowledges himself "responsible for both these circumstances."

In the meantime, Pope's forces fought the battles of the 27th, 28th, and 29th, and were now to fight that of the 30th without Franklin's help. Why was this? Were the orders to send Franklin out countermanded? General Halleck says they were not. As it is never just to judge a person by the light obtained after the fact, let us see, so far as the correspondence enables us, what were the different phases of the case as they presented themselves at the time.

The intimation to McClellan on the 26th, that Franklin was to go to the front, was followed by the positive orders of the 27th, given at 10 A. M. and 12 M. On that day General McClellan reports that Generals Franklin, Smith, and Slocum are all in Washington; and that he had given orders to place the corps *in readiness to march* to the next in rank. At the same time, he reports heavy firing at Centreville.

On the 28th, Halleck, learning that McClellan, who it seems had also gone to Washington, had not returned to Alexandria, sent orders to Franklin direct, to move with his corps that day (the 28th) towards Manassas Junction. On the 28th, at 3.30 P. M., Halleck informs McClellan that "not a moment must be lost in pushing as large a force as possible towards Manassas so as to communicate with Pope before the enemy is re-enforced." On the same day, at 7.40 P. M., he again tells him:

> "There must be no further delay in moving Franklin's Corps towards Manassas. *They must go to-morrow morning ready or not ready.* If we delay too long to get ready, there will be no necessity to go at all, for Pope will either be defeated or victorious without our aid. If there is a want of wagons, the men must carry provisions with them till the wagons come to their relief."

There is no possible room for misunderstanding the intention of the General-in-Chief from these orders. He wished, and ordered, that communication should be at once re-established with Pope, and Pope re-enforced in time to be of service.

Why did not McClellan re-establish the communication, and re-enforce Pope in time to be of service? Why did he halt Franklin's Corps at Anandale?

He gives reasons for this in his telegram to Halleck of August 29th. "By referring to my telegrams," he says, "of 10.30 A. M., 12 M., and 1 P. M., together with your reply of 2.48 P. M., you will see why Franklin's Corps halted at Anandale." Let us examine these telegrams in connection with the circumstances then existing. The first is follows:

CAMP NEAR ALEXANDRIA,
August 29, 10.30 A. M.

"Franklin's Corps are in motion; started about six A. M. I can give him but two squadrons of cavalry. I propose moving General Cox to Upton's Hill to hold that important point with its works, and to push cavalry scouts to Vienna *via* Freeman Hill and Hunter's lane. Cox has two squadrons of cavalry. Please answer at once whether this meets your approval. I have directed Woodbury, with the Engineer Brigade, to hold Fort Lyon. Sumner detached last night two regiments to the vicinity of Forts Ethan Allen and Marcy. Meagher's Brigade is still at Aquia. *If Sumnermoves in support of Franklin,* it leaves us without any reliable troops in and near Washington; *yet Franklin is too weak alone.* What shall be done? No more cavalry arrived. Have but three squadrons belonging to the Army of the Potomac. Franklin has but forty rounds of ammunition, and no wagons to move more. I do not think Franklin is in a condition to accomplish much if he meets strong resistance. *I should not have moved him but for your pressing orders of last night.* What have you from Vienna and Drainsville?

GEO. B. MCCLELLAN, *Major-General.*

Major-General H. W. HALLECK, *General-in-Chief.*

To this Halleck replies:

WAR DEPARTMENT,
WASHINGTON, D. C., *August* 29, 1862.

Upton's Hill arrangement all right. We must send wagons and ammunition to Franklin as fast as they arrive. Meagher's Brigade ordered up yesterday. Fitzhugh Lee was, it is said on good authority, in Alexandria on Sunday last for three hours. I hear nothing from Drainsville.

H. W. HALLECK, *General-in-Chief.*

"Major-General McCLELLAN, Alexandria.

To this McClellan sends the *second* of the dispatches he refers to, as follows. There are two telegrams of the same date.

HEAD-QUARTERS ARMY POTOMAC,
August 29, 1862, 12 M.

Your telegram received. Do you wish the movement of Franklin's Corps *to continue?* He is without reserve ammunition, and without transportation.

GEO. B. McCLELLAN, *Major-General.*

Major-General H. W. HALLECK, *General-in-Chief.*

HEADQUARTERS ARMY POTOMAC,
ALEXANDRIA, VIRGINIA, *Aug.* 29, 1862, 12 M.

Have ordered most of the 12th Pennsylvania Cavalry to report to General Barnard for scouting duty toward Rockville, Poolesville, etc. If you apprehend a raid of cavalry on your side of river, I had better send a brigade or two of Sumner's to near Tennallytown. Would it meet your views to post rest of Sumner's Corps between Arlington and Fort Corcoran, where they can either support Cox, Franklin, Chain Bridge, and even Tennallytown?

Franklin has only 10,000 to 11,000 ready for duty. *How far do you wish the force to advance?*

GEORGE B. McCLELLAN, *Maj.-Gen. U. S. Army.*

Major-General HALLECK, *General-in-Chief.*

Then follows the telegram of 1 P. M.:

HEAD-QUARTERS NEAR ALEXANDRIA,
August 29, 1862, 1 P. M.

I anxiously await reply to my last dispatch in regard to Sumner. Wish to give order at once. Please authorize me to attach new regiments permanently to my old brigades. I can do much good to old and new troops in that way. I shall endeavor to hold a line in advance of Forts Allen and Marsh, at least with strong advanced guards. I wish to hold the line through Prospect Hill, Marshall's, Miner's, and Hall's Hills. This will give us timely warning. Shall I do *as seems best to me* with all the troops in this vicinity, *including Franklin,* who I really think *ought not,* under the present circumstances, to *proceed beyond Anandale?*

G. B. McCLELLAN, *Major-General.*

General HALLECK, *General-in-Chief.*

It certainly is not easy to discover in these dispatches any indications of a strong desire to re-enforce the Army of the Potomac, then fighting a battle in his front and within his hearing, but under another commander. They evince no special interest in the result of that battle, or the fate of that army—the army for which, while under his command, he had expressed so much affection, and whose defeat he afterwards declared, when he was again at its head, would be incomparably more disastrous to the nation than the capture of Washington itself. We find in these dispatches, which he cites in his own vindication, no evidence to sustain the declaration of his report, that from the moment of his arrival at Alexandria he "left nothing in his power undone to forward supplies and re-enforcements to Gen. Pope." On the contrary, they seem to show that he had decided to do, what in a telegram of the same date he had suggested to the President, "*leave Pope to get out of his scrape*," and devote himself exclusively to the safety of Washington.* He thinks any disposition of Franklin's and Sumner's troops wise, except sending them forward to re-enforce Pope. He is anxious to send them to Upton's Hill, to Chain Bridge, to Tennallytown, to Arlington, and Fort Corcoran—anywhere and everywhere except where they were wanted most, and where alone they could assist in getting

* On the 29th he had telegraphed to the President as follows:

I am clear that one of two courses should be adopted: First, to concentrate all our available forces to open communications with Pope; second, to *leave Pope to get out of his scrape, and at once use all our means to make the capital perfectly safe.* No middle ground will now answer. Tell me what you wish me to do, and I will do all in my power to accomplish it.

To this the President had thus replied:

WASHINGTON, *August* 29, 1862—4.10 P. M.

Yours of to-day just received. I think your first alternative, to wit, "to concentrate all our available forces to open communication with Pope" is the right one, but I wish not to control. That I now leave to General Halleck, aided by your counsels. A. LINCOLN.

Major-General McCLELLAN.

Pope "out of his scrape," and in saving the Army of the Potomac. It was natural and proper that he should give attention to the defence of Washington, for he had, as Gen. Halleck says, "general authority over all the troops" that were defending it. But his *special* duty was "sending out troops from Alexandria to re-enforce Pope." Why did he give so much attention to the former, and so little to the latter duty? Why was it that, from the time of his landing at Alexandria, not another man of his army joined Pope, or made a diversion in his favor, till after Pope had fallen back from Manassas and fought four battles without the aid he had a right to expect, and which Gen. McClellan was repeatedly and peremptorily ordered to give?

Those of McClellan's forces which had reached Alexandria before him, or were there before his arrival, Sturgis, Kearney, Hooker, and Heintzelman, had all gone forward and joined in these battles. Why could not Franklin—all of whose movements were controlled by McClellan—do as much with him as his brother commanders had done without him?

The first thing that McClellan did, on reaching Alexandria, in the discharge of his duties to send forward troops, was to stop those actually going! In his dispatch of August 27th, 9 o'clock P. M., he says to General Halleck—"I found part of Cox's command under orders to take the cars: *will halt it with Franklin until morning!*" And Cox never went out, though anxiously expected and under orders to move. What are the reasons given by McClellan for not sending, or not permitting Franklin to go? On the 27th, at 11.15 P. M., immediately after the positive order was issued for Franklin to move by forced marches and carry three or four days' provisions, McClellan says:

"Franklin's artillery has no horses except for four guns without caissons. I can pick up no cavalry. * * I do not see that we have force enough in hand to form a connection with Pope, whose exact position we do not know."

A part of the perplexity he seems to have been in was removed that day at 6 o'clock, P. M., when he received, as he says, a copy of a dispatch from Pope to Halleck, in which Pope says: "All forces now sent forward should be sent to my right at Gainesville."

The next day, at 1 P. M., he telegraphs,

"I have been doing all possible to hurry artillery and cavalry. The moment Franklin can be started with a *reasonable amount of artillery he shall go.*"

Again, at 4.40 of the 28th, he telegraphs,

General Franklin is *with me here.* I will know in a few moments the condition of artillery and cavalry. *We are not yet in a condition to move;* may be by to-morrow morning.

A few moments later, he says:

Your dispatch received. *Neither Franklin's nor Sumner's Corps is now in condition to move and fight a battle.* It would be a sacrifice to send them out now! I have sent aids to ascertain the condition of Colonel Tyler: but I still think that a premature movement in small force will accomplish nothing but the destruction of the troops sent out."

The small force (?) to which he refers consisted, as heretofore stated, of Sumner's Corps of 14,000 and Franklin's of 11,000, a total of 25,000—not going to fight a battle by itself, but to re-enforce an army already engaged, and constituting certainly a handsome re-enforcement on any field. On the 29th, he says:

Franklin has but forty rounds of ammunition and no wagons to move more. I do not think Franklin is in a condition to accomplish much if he meets strong resistance. I should not have moved him but for your pressing orders of last night.

On this same day—

Do you wish the movement of Franklin's Corps to continue? He is without reserve ammunition and without transportation.

It may be remarked here, that Franklin had not yet gone beyond Anandale—about seven miles—and had as yet, neither come upon the enemy or joined the army in front, nor gained any information about either. If, therefore, his movement was not to continue, it must be because it was too hazardous, or because he had no reserve ammunition or transportation.

So, it seems, it was Gen. McClellan's judgment that Franklin could not be sent, as soon as he landed, to re-enforce Pope—because, 1st, he had his artillery only partially mounted; 2d, he had no cavalry; 3d, he had but forty rounds of ammunition, and no transportation for more. The subsequent difficulties were, that he had no transportation for his reserve ammunition, and was too weak alone, and Sumner ought not to be sent to support him, as it would leave the Capital unprotected!

It is fortunate some of McClellan's corps preceded him from the Peninsula, and arrived and marched before he came up. For, if not, two of the corps who joined Pope and fought under him would have been halted for the reasons that stayed Franklin. Kearney joined without artillery, and Pope ordered two batteries to be given him; Porter had but forty rounds of ammunition—Heintzelman joined without cavalry.

Why, may it be asked, were "neither Sumner's nor Franklin's Corps in a condition to move and fight a battle?" McClellan had been told that in embarking his troops he must see they were supplied with ammunition, "as they might have to fight as soon as they landed." The men were not fatigued by hard marches, nor exhausted with fighting and lack of food, as were their companions in front. What was there to prevent their going to re-enforce them, but the orders and *pretexts* for delay of General McClellan?

It will have been noticed that lack of transportation was at the bottom of the alleged difficulties. Transportation was not required for supplies, for the men were ordered to carry their food with them. Is it not strange that, in view of the emergency of the case, some extraordinary means were not resorted to to impress horses and wagons—if none existed in the hands of the Government—in the cities of Alexandria, Georgetown, and Washington, where there was an abundance of both? Such things have been done even in this war, on much less important occasions than this one.

But will not this plea seem stranger still when it is found that there was no need of pressing any private property into service—that there was plenty of public transportation on hand? Let the following dispatch show:

WAR DEPARTMENT,
WASHINGTON, D. C., *August* 30th, 1862.

I am by no means satisfied with General Franklin's march of yesterday, considering the circumstances of the case. He was very wrong in stopping at Alexandria. Moreover, I learned *last night that the Quartermaster's Department would have given him plenty of transportation if he had applied for it any time since his arrival at Alexandria.* He knew the importance of opening communication with General Pope's army, and should have acted more promptly.

H. W. HALLECK, *General-in-Chief.*

Major-General MCCLELLAN, Alexandria.

But most strange of all is, that General McClellan *knew* of there being public transportation at hand, and yet did not use it, even when the fate of a campaign depended upon it, and afterwards assigned the want of it as the reason for not obeying his orders to send re-enforcements. He says, in his dispatch of August 30, to Gen. Pope:

The quartermasters here (Alexandria) said there was none *disposable. The difficulty seems to consist in the fact* (he adds), *that the greater part of the transportation on hand at Alexandria and Washington has been needed for current supplies of the garrisons.*"

The inference is irresistible that General McClellan, who had charge of every thing in and around Alexandria and

Washington, thought it was better that the Army of the Potomac, under Pope, should not be re-enforced, and be defeated, than that the *garrisons* should be subjected to the slightest inconvenience!

The answer of General Halleck to the telegrams of General McClellan, in which the latter made so many propositions about the movements of Sumner's Corps and the disposition of Cox's force and the other troops for the defence of Washington, is as follows:

WAR DEPARTMENT,
WASHINGTON, D. C., *August 29th*, 1862.

Your proposed disposition of Sumner's Corps seems to me judicious. Of course I have no time to examine into details. The present danger is a raid upon Washington in the night time. Dispose of all troops as you deem best. I want Franklin's Corps to go far enough to find out something about the enemy. Perhaps he may get such information at Anandale as to prevent his going further. *Otherwise, he will push on towards Fairfax.* Try to get something from direction of Manassas either by telegrams or through Franklin's scouts. Our people *must* move actively and find out where the enemy is. I am tired of guesses.

H. W. HALLECK, *General-in-Chief.*

Major-General MCCLELLAN, Alexandria.

It is in this dispatch that General McClellan finds his authority to halt Franklin at Anandale. Franklin had been repeatedly ordered to join Pope, but had been delayed by McClellan, who evidently did not intend he should get beyond his control if possible.

In his telegram to Halleck of 1 P. M. of the 29th, he asks if he may do as seems to him best with all the troops in the vicinity of Alexandria, including Franklin—Franklin being still in the vicinity of Alexandria. Halleck, in giving him authority to dispose of all troops in his vicinity evidently refers to the disposition to be made of those for the forts and defences, for he proceeds to say, I want "*Franklin's Corps* to go far enough to find out something about the enemy."

Franklin's Corps did not go out far enough to learn any thing about the enemy. What he learned he picked up at Anandale from citizens, and probably from Banks's wagon-train, which passed him as it came from the front, which it seems it was able to do with safety at the time McClellan considered it too hazardous for 40,000 men to move to the front to join the army.

It is unnecessary to pursue this matter any further, and show, as might easily be done, how similar delays were procured with respect to other troops which might have been sent to re-enforce Pope. It is sufficient to say that forty thousand men, exclusive of Burnside's force, were thus—as it seems to us intentionally—withheld from Pope at the time he was engaged in holding the army of Lee in check.

Having thus disposed of the question of *re-enforcements*, it now remains to say a word about *supplies* which General McClellan says he left nothing undone to forward to Pope.

When at Fort Monroe he telegraphed (August 21st, 10.52 P. M.):

> I have *ample supplies of ammunition* for infantry and artillery, and will have it up in time. *I can supply any deficiency that may exist in General Pope's army.*

August the 30th (1.45 P. M.), General Halleck telegraphed him:

> *Ammunition*, and particularly for artillery, must be immediately sent forward to Centreville for General Pope.

To which he replied:

> I know nothing of the calibres of Pope's artillery. All I can do is to direct my ordnance officer to load up all the wagons sent to him.

General McClellan might have very easily found out those calibres. His ordnance officer knew those of the corps of his own army, and he was in telegraphic communication with the ordnance officer in Washington, where a register is kept of all the batteries in service.

What was his course with respect to supplies of forage and subsistence, of which Pope's army was in such extreme need?

He directed Franklin to say to Pope he would send him out supplies if he, Pope, would send back cavalry to escort them out! "Such a request," (says Pope in his dispatch of 5 A. M., August 30), "when Alexandria is full of troops, and I fighting the enemy, needs no comment."

The Army of the Potomac, under General Pope, was defeated and driven back upon Washington. But it had contested every inch of the ground, and had fought every battle with a gallantry and tenacious courage that would have insured a decisive viciory if it had been properly and promptly supported. It was not broken, either in spirit or in organization; and it fell back upon the Capital prepared to renew the struggle for its salvation.

By this time, however, General McClellan had become the recognized head of a political party in the country, and a military clique in the army; and it suited the purposes of both to represent the defeat of the Army of the Potomac as due to the fact that General McClellan was no longer at its head. The progress of the rebel army, moreover, up the Potomac, with the evident intention of moving upon Baltimore or into Pennsylvania, had created a state of feeling throughout the country and in Washington eminently favorable to the designs of General McClellan's partisans; and upon the urgent but unjust representation of some of his officers that the army would not serve under any other commander, General Pope was relieved, and General McClellan again placed at the head of the Army of the Potomac, and on the 4th of September he commenced the movement into Maryland to repel the invading rebel forces.

On the 11th, he made urgent application for re-enforcements, asking that Colonel Miles be withdrawn from Harper's Ferry, and that one or two of the three army corps on the Potomac, opposite Washington, be at once sent to join him. "Even if Washington should be taken," he said, "while these armies are confronting each other, this would not in my judgment bear comparison with the ruin and disaster that would follow a single defeat of this army," although, as will be remembered, when that army was under Pope, and engaged in a battle which might destroy it, he had said (Aug. 27), "I think we should *first* provide for the defence of the Capital." General Halleck replied that "the capture of Washington would throw them back six months if not destroy them," and that Miles could not join him until communications were opened. On the 14th, the battle of South Mountain took place, the rebels falling back to the Potomac, and on the 17th, the battle of Antietam was fought, resulting in the defeat of the rebel forces, although no pursuit was made, and they were allowed, during the night and the whole of the next day, quietly to withdraw their shattered forces to the other side of the Potomac. The losses he had sustained and the disorganization of some of his commands were assigned by General McClellan as his reason for not renewing the attack, although the corps of General Fitz-John Porter had not been brought into action at all. Orders were issued, however, for a renewal of the battle on the 19th, but it was then suddenly discovered that the enemy was on the other side of the Potomac. General McClellan did not feel authorized on account of the condition of his army to cross in pursuit, and on the 23d, wrote to Washington, asking for re-enforcements, renewing the application on the 27th, and stating his purpose to be to hold the army where it was, and to attack the enemy *should he attempt to recross into Maryland.* He thought that only the troops necessary to garrison Washington should be retained there, and that every thing else available should be sent to him. If re-enforced and allowed to take his own course, he said, he would be responsible for the safety of the Capital.

On the 1st of October, President LINCOLN visited the army and made careful inquiry into its strength and condition. On the 6th, he issued the following order for an immediate advance:

WASHINGTON, D. C., *October* 6, 1862.

I am instructed to telegraph to you as follows: The President directs that you cross the Potomac and give battle to the enemy, or drive him south. Your army must move now, while the roads are good. If you cross the river between the enemy and Washington, and cover the latter by your operation, you can be re-enforced with thirty thousand men. If you move up the valley of the Shenandoah not more than twelve or fifteen thousand can be sent you. The President advises the interior line between Washington and the enemy, but does not order it. He is very desirous that your army move as soon as possible. You will immediately report what line you adopt, and when you intend to cross the river: also to what point the re-enforcements are to be sent. It is necessary that the plan of your operations be positively determined on, before orders are given for building bridges and repairing railroads. I am directed to add, that the Secretary of War and the General-in-Chief fully concur with the President in these instructions.

H. W. HALLECK, *General-in-Chief.*

Major-General MCCLELLAN.

On receiving this order, Gen. McClellan inquired as to the character of troops that would be sent him, and as to the number of tents at command of the army. He also called for very large quantities of shoes, clothing, and other supplies, and said that without these the army could not move. On the 11th, the rebel Gen. Stuart, with a force of about 2,500 men, made a raid into Pennsylvania, going completely round our army, and thwarting all the arrangements by which Gen. McClellan had reported that his capture was certain. On the 13th, in consequence of his protracted delays, the President addressed to General McClellan the following letter:

EXECUTIVE MANSION, WASHINGTON, *Oct.* 13, 1862.

MY DEAR SIR:—You remember my speaking to you of what I called your overcautiousness. Are you not overcautious when you assume that you cannot do what the enemy is constantly doing? Should you not claim to be at least his equal in prowess, and act upon the claim?

As I understand, you telegraphed Gen. Halleck that you cannot subsist your army at Winchester unless the railroad from Harper's Ferry to that point be put in working order. But the enemy does now subsist his army at Winchester, at a distance nearly twice as great from railroad transportation as you would have to do without the railroad last named. He now wagons from Culpepper Court-House, which is just about twice as far as you would have to do from Harper's Ferry. He is certainly not more than half as well provided with wagons as you are. I certainly should be pleased for you to have the advantage of the railroad from Harper's Ferry to Winchester; but it wastes all the remainder of autumn to give it to you, and, in fact, ignores the question of *time*, which cannot and must not be ignored.

Again, one of the standard maxims of war, as you know, is, "to operate upon the enemy's communications as much as possible, without exposing your own." You seem to act as if this applies *against* you, but can not apply in your *favor*. Change positions with the enemy, and think you not he would break your communication with Richmond within the next twenty-four hours? You dread his going into Pennsylvania. But if he does so in full force, he gives up his communications to you absolutely, and you have nothing to do but to follow and ruin him; if he does so with less than full force, fall upon and beat what is left behind all the easier.

Exclusive of the water line, you are now nearer Richmond than the enemy is by the route that you *can* and he *must* take. Why can you not reach there before him, unless you admit that he is more than your equal on a march? His route is the arc of a circle, while yours is the chord. The roads are as good on yours as on his.

You know I desired, but did not order, you to cross the Potomac below instead of above the Shenandoah and Blue Ridge. My idea was, that this would at once menace the enemy's communications, which I would seize if he would permit. If he should move northward, I would follow him closely, holding his communications. If he should prevent our seizing his communications, and move toward Richmond, I would press closely to him, fight him if a favorable opportunity should present, and at least try to beat him to Richmond on the inside track. I say "try;" if we never try, we shall never succeed. If he make a stand at Winchester, moving neither north nor south, I would fight him there, on the idea that if we cannot beat him when he bears the wastage of coming to us, we never can when we bear the wastage of going to him. This proposition is a simple truth, and is too important to be lost sight of for a moment. In coming to us, he tenders us an advantage which we should not waive. We should not so operate as to merely drive him away. As we must beat him somewhere, or fail finally, we can do it, if at all, easier near to us than far away. If we cannot beat the enemy where he now is, we never can, he again being within the intrenchments of Richmond. Recurring to the idea of going to Richmond on the inside track, the facility of supplying from the side away from the enemy is remarkable, as it were, by the different spokes of a wheel, extending from the hub toward the rim, and this whether you move directly by the chord, or on the inside arc, hugging the Blue Ridge more closely. The chord-line, as you see, carries you by Aldie, Haymarket, and Fredericksburg, and you see how turnpikes, railroads, and finally the Potomac by Aquia Creek, meet you at all points from Washington. The same, only the lines lengthened a little, if you press closer to the Blue Ridge part of the way. The gaps through the Blue Ridge I understand to be about the following distances from Harper's Ferry, to wit: Vestal's, five miles; Gregory's, thirteen; Snicker's, eighteen; Ashby's, twenty-eight; Manassas, thirty-eight; Chester, forty-five; and Thornton's, fifty-three. I should think it preferable to take the route nearest the enemy, disabling him to make an important move without your knowledge, and compelling him to keep his forces together for dread of you. The gaps would enable you to attack if you should wish. For a great part of the way you would be practically between the enemy and both Washington and Richmond, enabling us to spare you the greatest number of troops from here. When, at length, running to Richmond ahead of him enables him to move this way, if he does so, turn and attack him in the rear. But I think he should be engaged long before such point is reached. It is all easy if our troops march as well as the enemy, and it is unmanly to say they cannot do it. This letter is in no sense an order.

Yours, truly, A. LINCOLN.

Major-Gen. MCCLELLAN.

For over a fortnight longer Gen. McClellan delayed any attempt to move his army in obedience to the President's order. He spent this interval in complaints of inadequate supplies, and in incessant demands for re-enforcements; and on the 21st inquired whether it was still the President's wish that he should march upon the enemy at once, or await the arrival of fresh horses. He was told in reply that the order of the 6th was unchanged, and that while the President did not expect impossibilities, he was "very anxious that all this good weather should not be wasted in inactivity." Gen. McClellan states in his report that he inferred, from the tenor of this dispatch, that it was left to his own judgment whether it would be safe for the army to advance or not; and he accordingly fixed upon the first of November as the earliest date at which the forward movement could be commenced. On the 25th he complained to the Department of the condition of his cavalry, saying that the horses were fatigued and greatly troubled with sore tongue; whereupon the President addressed him the following inquiry:

WAR DEPARTMENT, WASHINGTON, *Oct.* 25, 1862.

I have just read your dispatch about sore-tongue and fatigued horses. Will you pardon me for asking what the horses of your army have done since the battle of Antietam that fatigues anything?

A. LINCOLN.

The General replied that they had been engaged in making reconnoissances, scouting, and picketing, to which the President thus rejoined:

EXECUTIVE MANSION,
WASHINGTON, *Oct. 26th*, 1862.

Yours in reply to mine about horses received. Of course you know the facts better than I. Still, two considerations remain: Stuart's cavalry outmarched ours, having certainly done more marked service on the Peninsula and everywhere since. Secondly: will not a movement of our army be a relief to the cavalry, compelling the enemy to concentrate instead of "foraging" in squads everywhere? But I am so rejoiced to learn from your dispatch to General Halleck that you began crossing the river this morning.

A. LINCOLN.

The General replied in a long dispatch, rehearsing in detail the labors performed by his cavalry, to which he thought the President had done injustice. This note elicited the following reply:

EXECUTIVE MANSION,
WASHINGTON, *Oct.* 26*th*, 1862.

Yours of yesterday received. Most certainly I intend no injustice to any, and if I have done any I deeply regret it. To be told, after more than five weeks total inaction of the army, and during which period we had sent to that army every fresh horse we possibly could, amounting in the whole to 7,918, that the cavalry horses were too much fatigued to move, presented a very cheerless, almost hopeless, prospect for the future, and it may have forced something of impatience into my dispatches. If not recruited and rested then, when could they ever be? I suppose the river is rising, and I am glad to believe you are crossing.

A. LINCOLN.

The General next started, as a new topic of discussion, the extent to which the line of the Potomac should be guarded after he left it, so as to cover Maryland and Pennsylvania from further invasions. He thought strong garrisons should be left at certain points, complained that his forces were inadequate, and made some suggestion concerning the position of the rebel army under Bragg, which led General Halleck in reply to remind him that Bragg was four hundred miles away, while Lee was but twenty. On the 27th the General telegraphed to the President that it was necessary to "fill up the old regiments of his command before taking them again into action," to which the President thus replied:

EXECUTIVE MANSION,
WASHINGTON, *Oct.* 27*th*, 1862.

Your dispatch of three P. M. to-day, in regard to filling up old regiments with drafted men, is received, and the request therein shall be complied with as far as practicable. And now I ask a distinct answer to the question, "Is it your purpose not to go into *action* again till the men now being drafted in the States are incorporated in the old regiments?"

A. LINCOLN

The General, in reply, explained that the language of the dispatch, which was prepared by one of his aids, had incorrectly expressed his meaning, and that he should not postpone the *advance* until the regiments were filled by drafted men. The army was gradually crossed over, and on the 5th of November the General announced to the President that it was all on the Virginia side. This was just a month after the order to cross had been given—the enemy meantime having taken possession of all the strong points, and falling back, at his leisure, towards his base of operations. These unaccountable delays in the movement of the army created the most intense dissatisfaction in the public mind, and completely exhausted the patience of the Government. Accordingly, on the 5th of November, an order was issued relieving General McClellan from the command of the Army of the Potomac, and directing General Burnside to take his place.

Thus closed a most remarkable chapter in the history of the war. For over fifteen months General McClellan had commanded the Army of the Potomac, the largest and most powerful army ever marshalled upon this continent—consisting of 160,000 men, and furnished, in lavish profusion, with every thing requisite for effective service. Throughout the whole of this long period that army had been restrained by its commander from attacking the enemy: except in the single instance of Antietam, where, moreover, there was no possibility of avoiding an engagement, every battle which it fought was on the defensive. According to the sworn testimony of his own commanders, General McClellan might have overwhelmed the rebel forces arrayed against him at Manassas, at Yorktown, after Williamsburgh, Fair Oaks, Malvern Hill, and Antietam; but on every one of these occasions he carefully forbore to avail himself of the superiority of his position, and gave the enemy ample time to prepare for more complete and effective resistance. It is no part of our present purpose to inquire into the causes of this most extraordinary conduct on the part of a commander to whom, more completely than to any other, were entrusted the destinies of the nation during the most critical period of its existence. Whether he acted from an innate disability, or upon a political theory—whether he intentionally avoided a decisive engagement in order to accomplish certain political results which he and his secret advisers deemed desirable, or whether he was, by the native constitution of his mind, unable to meet the gigantic responsibilities of his position when the critical moment of trial arrived, are points which the public and posterity will decide from an unbiased study of the evidence which his acts and his words afford. As the record we have given shows, President LINCOLN lost no opportunity of urging upon him more prompt and decisive action, while in no instance did he withhold from him any aid which it was in the power of the Government to give.

Nothing can show more clearly the disposition of the President to sustain him to the utmost, and to protect him from the rapidly rising tide of public censure and discontent with his ruinous and inexplicable delays, than the following remarks made by him at a war meeting held at Washington on the 6th of August, after the retreat to the James River, and just before the withdrawal of the army from the Peninsula:

FELLOW-CITIZENS; I believe there is no precedent for my appearing before you on this occasion, but it is also true that there is no precedent for your being here yourselves, and I offer, in justification of myself and of you, that, upon examination, I have found nothing in the Constitution against it. I, however, have an impression that there are younger gentlemen who will entertain you better, and better address your understanding than I will or could, and therefore I propose but to detain you a moment longer.

I am very little inclined on any occasion to say any thing unless I hope to produce some good by it. The only thing I think of just now not likely to be better said by some one else, is a matter in which we have heard some other persons blamed for what I did myself. There has been a very wide-spread attempt to have a quarrel between General McClellan and the Secretary of War. Now, I occupy a position that enables me to observe, that these two gentlemen are not nearly so deep in the quarrel as some pretending to be their friends. General McClellan's attitude is such that, in the very selfishness of his nature, he cannot but wish to be successful, and I hope he will—and the Secretary of War is in precisely the same situation. If the military commanders in the field cannot be successful, not only the Secretary of War, but myself, for the time being the master of them both, cannot but be failures. I know General McClellan wishes to be successful, and I know he does not wish it any more than the Secretary of War for him, and both of them together no more than I wish it. Sometimes we have a dispute about how many men General McClellan has had, and those who would disparage him say that he has had a very large number, and those who would disparage the Secretary of War insist that General McClellan has had a very small number. The basis for this is, there is always a wide difference, and on this occasion, perhaps a wider one than usual, between the grand total on McClellan's rolls and the men actually fit for duty; and those who would disparage him talk of the grand total on paper, and those who would disparage the Secretary of War talk of those at present fit for duty. General McClellan has sometimes asked for things that the Secretary of War did not give him. General McClellan is not to blame for asking what he wanted and needed, and the Secretary of War is not to blame for not giving when he had none to give. And I say here, as far as I know, the Secretary of War has withheld no one thing at any time in my power to give him. I have no accusation against him. I believe he is a brave and able man, and I stand here, as justice requires me to do, to take upon myself what has been charged on the Secretary of War, as withholding from him.

I have talked longer than I expected to do, and now I avail myself of my privilege of saying no more.

CHAPTER VII.

MILITARY OPERATIONS IN THE WEST AND SOUTH, AND THE GENERAL CONDUCT OF THE ADMINISTRATION IN 1862.

In every other section of the country, except in Eastern Virginia, the military operations of the year 1862 were marked by promptitude and vigor, and attended by success to the National arms. Early in February a lodgment had been effected by the expedition under General Burnside on the coast of North Carolina, and on the 19th of January the victory of Mill Springs had released Western Kentucky from rebel rule, and opened a path for the armies of the Union into East Tennessee. The President's order of January 27th, for an advance of all the forces of the Government on the 22d of February, had been promptly followed by the capture of Forts Henry and Donelson on the Cumberland River, which led to the evacuation of Bowling Green, the surrender of Nashville, and the fall of Columbus, the rebel stronghold on the Mississippi. Fort Pulaski, which guarded the entrance to Savannah, was taken, after eighteen hours bombardment, on the 12th of April, and the whole west coast of Florida had been occupied by our forces. By the skilful strategy of General Halleck, commanding the Western Department, seconded by the vigorous activity of General Curtis, the rebel commander in Missouri, General Price, had been forced to retreat, leaving the whole of that State in our hands; and he was badly beaten in a subsequent engagement at Sugar Creek in Arkansas. On the 14th, Island No. 10, commanding the passage of the Mississippi, was taken by General Pope, and on the 4th of June Forts Pillow and Randolph, still lower down, were occupied by our forces. On the 6th the city of Memphis was surrendered by the rebels. Soon after the fall of Nashville a formidable expedition had ascended the Tennessee River, and being joined by all the available Union forces in that vicinity, the whole under command of General Halleck, prepared to give battle to the rebel army which, swelled by large re-enforcements from every quarter, was posted in the vicinity of Corinth, ninety miles east of Memphis, intending by a sudden attack to break the force of the Union army, which was sweeping steadily down upon them from the field of its recent conquests. The rebels opened the attack with great fury and effect, on the morning of the 6th of April, at Pittsburg Landing, three miles in advance of Corinth. The fight lasted nearly all day, the rebels having decidedly the advantage; but in their final onset they were driven back, and the next day our army, strengthened by the opportune arrival of General Buell, completed what proved to be a signal and most important victory. When news of it reached Washington President Lincoln issued the following proclamation:

It has pleased Almighty God to vouchsafe signal victories to the land and naval forces engaged in suppressing an internal rebellion, and at the same time to avert from our country the dangers of foreign intervention and invasion.

It is therefore recommended to the people of the United States, that at their next weekly assemblages in their accustomed places of public worship, which shall occur after the notice of this Proclamation shall have been received, they especially acknowledge and render thanks to our Heavenly Father for these inestimable blessings; that they then and there implore spiritual consolation in behalf of all those who have been brought into affliction by the casualties and calamities of sedition and civil war; and that they reverently invoke the Divine guidance for our national counsels, to the end that they may speedily result in the restoration of peace, harmony, and unity throughout our borders, and hasten the establishment of fraternal relations among all the countries of the earth.

In witness whereof I have hereunto set my hand and caused the seal of the United States to be affixed.

Done at the city of Washington, this tenth day of April, in the year of [L. S.] our Lord one thousand eight hundred and sixty-two, and of the independence of the United States the eighty-sixth.

ABRAHAM LINCOLN.

By the President:

WM. H. SEWARD, *Secretary of State.*

On the 28th of May the rebels evacuated Corinth, and were pushed southward by our pursuing forces for some twenty-five or thirty miles. General Mitchell, by a daring and most gallant enterprise in the latter part of April, took possession of Huntsville in Alabama. In February a formidable naval expedition had been fitted out under Commodore Farragut for the capture of New Orleans; and on the 18th of April the attack commenced upon Forts Jackson and St. Philip, by which the passage of the Mississippi below the city is guarded. After six days' bombardment the whole fleet passed the forts on the night of the 23d, under a terrible fire from both; and on the 25th the rebel General Lovell, who had command of the military defences of the city, withdrew, and Commodore Farragut took possession of the town, which he retained until the arrival of General Butler on the 1st of May, who thereupon entered upon the discharge of his duties as commander of that Department.

During the summer a powerful rebel army, under General Bragg, invaded Kentucky for the double purpose of obtaining supplies and affording a rallying point for what they believed to be the secession sentiment of the State. In the accomplishment of the former object they were successful, but not in the latter. They lost more while in the State from desertions than they gained by recruits; and after a battle at Perryville on the 7th of October they began their retreat. On the 5th of October a severe battle was fought at Corinth, from which a powerful rebel army attempted to drive our troops under General Rosecrans, but they were repulsed with very heavy losses, and the campaign in Kentucky and Tennessee was virtually at an end. A final effort of the enemy in that region led to a severe engagement at Murfreesborough on the 31st of December, which resulted in the defeat of the rebel forces, and in relieving Tennessee from the presence of the rebel armies.

In all the military operations of this year especial care had been taken by the Generals in command of the several Departments, acting under the general direction of the Government, to cause it to be distinctly understood that the object of the war was the preservation of the Union and the restoration of the authority of the Constitution. The rebel authorities, both civil and military, lost no opportunity of exciting the fears and resentments of the people of the Southern States, by ascribing to the National Government designs of the most ruthless and implacable hostility to their institutions and their persons. It was strenuously represented that the object of the war was to rob the Southern people of their rights and their property, and especially to set free their slaves. The Government did every thing in its power to allay the apprehensions and hostilities which these statements were calculated to produce. General Garfield, while in Kentucky, just before the victory of Mill Springs, issued on the 16th of January an address to the citizens of that section of the State, exhorting them to return to their allegiance to the Federal Government, which had never made itself injuriously felt by any one among them, and promising them full protection for their persons and their property, and full reparation for any wrongs they might have sustained. After the battle of Mill Springs the Secretary of War, under the direction of the President, issued an order of thanks to the soldiers engaged in it, in which he again announced that the "purpose of the war was to attack, pursue and destroy a rebellious enemy, and to deliver the country from danger menaced by traitors." On the 20th of November, 1861, General Halleck, commanding the Department of the Missouri, on the eve of the advance into Tennessee, issued an order enjoining upon the troops the necessity of discipline and of order, and calling on them to prove by their acts that they came "to restore, not to violate the Constitution and the laws," and that the people of the South, under the flag of the Union, should "enjoy the same protection of life and property as in former days." "It does not belong to the military," said this order, "to decide upon the relation of master and slave. Such questions must be settled by the civil courts. No fugitive slave will, therefore, be admitted within our lines or camps except when specially ordered by the General commanding."* So also General Burnside, when about to land on the soil of North Carolina, issued an order, February 3d, 1262, calling upon the soldiers of his army to remember that they were there "to support the Constitution and the laws, to put down rebellion, and to protect the persons and property of the loyal and peaceable citizens of the State." And on the 18th of

* In regard to this order, which was afterwards severely criticised in Congress, General Halleck wrote the following letter of explanation:

HEAD-QUARTERS, DEPARTMENT OF THE MISSOURI,
ST. LOUIS, *December* 8, 1861.

MY DEAR COLONEL: Yours of the 4th instant is just received. Order No. 3 was, in my mind, clearly a military necessity. Unauthorized persons, black or white, free or slaves, must be kept out of our camps, unless we are willing to publish to the enemy every thing we do, or intend to do. It was a *military*, and not a *political* order.

I am ready to carry out any lawful instructions in regard to fugitive slaves, which my superiors may give me, and to enforce any law which Congress may pass. But I cannot make law, and will not violate it. You know my private opinion on the policy of confiscating the slave property of the rebels in arms. If Congress shall pass it, you may be certain that I shall enforce it. Perhaps my policy as to the treatment of rebels and their property is as well set out in Order No. 13, issued the day your letter was written, as I could now describe it.

Hon. F. F. BLAIR, Washington.

the same month, after Fort Henry and Roanoke Island had fallen into our hands, Commodore Goldsborough and General Burnside issued a joint proclamation, denouncing as false and slanderous the attempt of the rebel leaders to impose on the credulity of the Southern people by telling them of "our desire to destroy their freedom, demolish their property, and liberate their slaves," and declaring that the Government asked only that its authority might be recognized, and that "in no way or manner did it desire to interfere with their laws, constitutionally established, their institutions of any kind whatever, their property of any sort, or their usages in any respect." And on the 1st of March General Curtis in Arkansas had addressed a proclamation to the people of that State, denouncing as false and calumnious the statements widely circulated of the designs and sentiments of the Union armies, and declaring that they sought only "to put down rebellion by making war against those in arms, their aiders and abettors"—and that they came to "vindicate the Constitution, and to preserve and perpetuate civil and religious liberty under a flag that was embalmed in the blood of our revolutionary fathers." In all this the Government adhered, with just and rigorous fidelity, to the principles it had adopted for its conduct at the outset of the war; and in its anxiety to avoid all cause of complaint and all appearance of justification for those who were in arms against its authority, it incurred the distrust and even the denunciation of the more zealous and vehement among its own friends and supporters in the Northern States.

On the 22d of July, in order to secure unity of action among the commanders of the several military departments, upon the general use to be made of rebel property, the President directed the issue of the following order:

WAR DEPARTMENT, WASHINGTON, *July* 22, 1862.

First. Ordered that military commanders within the States of Virginia, North Carolina, Georgia, Florida, Alabama, Mississippi, Louisiana, Texas, and Arkansas, in an orderly manner seize and use any property, real or personal, which may be necessary or convenient for their several commands, for supplies, or for other military purposes; and that while property may be destroyed for proper military objects, none shall be destroyed in wantonness or malice.

Second. That military and naval commanders shall employ as laborers, within and from said States, so many persons of African descent as can be advantageously used for military or naval purposes, giving them reasonable wages for their labor.

Third. That, as to both property, and persons of African descent, accounts shall be kept sufficiently accurate and in detail to show quantities and amounts, and from whom both property and such persons shall have come, as a basis upon which compensation can be made in proper cases; and the several departments of this Government shall attend to and perform their appropriate parts towards the execution of these orders.

By order of the President:

EDWIN M. STANTON *Secretary of War.*

And on the 25th of July he issued the following proclamation, warning the people of the Southern States against persisting in their rebellion, under the penalties prescribed by the confiscation act passed by Congress at its preceding session:

By Order of the President of the United States.

A PROCLAMATION.

In pursuance of the sixth section of the Act of Congress, entitled "An Act to suppress insurrection, to punish treason and rebellion, to seize and confiscate the property of rebels, and for other purposes," approved July 17th, 1862, and which Act, and the joint resolution explanatory thereof, are herewith published, I, ABRAHAM LINCOLN, President of the United States, do hereby proclaim to and warn all persons within the contemplation of said sixth section to cease participating in, aiding, countenancing, or abetting the existing rebellion, or any rebellion, against the Government of the United States, and to return to their proper allegiance to the United States, on pain of the forfeiture and seizures as within and by said sixth section provided.

In testimony whereof I have hereunto set my hand and caused the seal of the United States to be affixed.

Done at the city of Washington, this twenty-fifth day of July, in the year of our Lord one thousand eight hundred and sixty-two, [L. S.] and of the independence of the United States the eighty-seventh.

ABRAHAM LINCOLN.

By the President:

WILLIAM H. SEWARD, *Secretary of State.*

Our relations with foreign nations during the year 1862 continued to be in the main satisfactory. The President held throughout, in all his intercourse with European powers, the same firm and decided language in regard to the rebellion which had characterized the correspondence of the previous year. Our Minister in London, with vigilance and ability, pressed upon the British Government the duty of preventing the rebel authorities from building and fitting out vessels of war in English ports to prey upon the commerce of the United States; but in every instance these remonstrances were without practical effect. The Government could never be convinced that the evidence in any specific case was sufficient to warrant its interference, and thus one vessel after another was allowed to leave British ports, go to some other equally neutral locality and take on board munitions of war, and enter upon its career of piracy in the rebel service. As early as the 18th of February, 1862, Mr. Adams had called the attention of Earl Russell to the fact that a steam gunboat, afterwards called the Oreto, was being built in a Liverpool ship-yard, under the supervision of well-known agents of the rebel Government, and evidently intended for the rebel service. The Foreign Secretary replied that the vessel was intended for the use of parties in Palermo, Sicily, and that there was no reason to suppose she was intended for any service hostile to the United States. Mr. Adams sent evidence to show that the claim of being designed for service in Sicily was a mere pretext; but he failed, by this dispatch, as in a subsequent personal conference with Earl Russell on the 15th of April, to induce him to take any steps for her detention. She sailed soon after, and was next heard of at the British "neutral" port of Nassau, where she was seized by the authorities at the instance of the American consul, but released by the same authorities on the arrival of Captain Semmes to take command of her as a Confederate privateer. In October an intercepted letter was sent to Earl Russell by Mr. Adams, written by the Secretary of the Navy of the Confederate Government, to a person in England, complaining that he had not followed the Oreto on her departure from England and taken command of her, in accordance with his original appointment. In June Mr. Adams called Earl Russell's attention to another powerful war-steamer, then in progress of construction in the ship-yard of a member of the House of Commons, evidently intended for the rebel service. This complaint went through the usual formalities, was referred to the "Lords Commissioners of her Majesty's Treasury," who reported in due time that they could discover no evidence sufficient to warrant the detention of the vessel. Soon afterwards, however, evidence was produced which was sufficient to warrant the collector of the port of Liverpool in ordering her detention; but before the necessary formalities could be gone through with, and through delays caused, as Earl Russell afterwards explained, by the "sudden development of a malady of the Queen's advocate, totally incapacitating him for the transaction of business," the vessel, whose managers were duly advertised of every thing that was going on, slipped out of port, took on board an armament in the Azores, and entered the rebel service as a privateer. Our Government subsequently notified the British Government that it would be held responsible for all the damage which this vessel, known first as "290," and afterwards as the Alabama, might inflict on American commerce.

Discussions were had upon the refusal of the British authorities to permit American vessels of war to take in coal at Nassau, upon the systematic attempts of British merchants to violate our blockade of Southern ports, and upon the recapture, by the crew, of the Emily St. Pierre, which had been seized in attempting to run the blockade at Charleston, and was on her way as a prize to the port of New York. The British Government vindicated her rescue as sanctioned by the principles of international law.

The only incident of special importance which occurred during the year in our foreign relations, grew out of an attempt on the part of the Emperor of the French to secure a joint effort at mediation between the Government of the United States and the rebel authorities, on the part of Great Britain and Russia in connection with his own Government. Rumors of such an intention on the part of the Emperor led Mr. Dayton to seek an interview with the Minister for Foreign Affairs on the 6th of November, at which indications of such a purpose were apparent. The attempt failed, as both the other powers consulted declined to join in any such action. The French Government thereupon determined to take action alone, and on the 9th of January, 1863, the Foreign Secretary wrote to the French Minister at Washington a dispatch, declaring the readiness of the French Emperor to do any thing in his power which might tend towards the termination of the war, and suggesting that "nothing would hinder the Government of the United States, without renouncing the advantages which it believes it can attain by a continuation of the war, from entering upon informal conferences with the Confederates of the South, in case they should show themselves disposed thereto." The specific advantages of such a conference, and the mode in which it was to be brought about, were thus set forth in this dispatch:

Representatives or commissioners of the two parties could assemble at such point as it should be deemed proper to designate, and which could, for this purpose, be declared neutral. Reciprocal complaints would be examined into at this meeting. In place of the accusations which North and South mutually cast upon each other at this time, would be substituted an argumentative discussion of the interests which divide them. They would seek out by means of well-ordered and profound deliberations whether these interests are definitively irreconcilable—whether separation is an extreme which can no longer be avoided, or whether the memories of a common existence, whether the ties of any kind which have made of the North and of the South one sole and whole Federative State, and have borne them on to so high a degree of prosperity, are not more powerful than the causes which have placed arms in the hands of the two populations. A negotiation, the object of which would be thus determinate, would not involve any of the objections raised against the diplomatic interventions of Europe, and, without giving birth to the same hopes as the immediate conclusion of an armistice, would exercise a happy influence on the march of events.

Why, therefore, should not a combination which respects all the relations of the United States obtain the approbation of the Federal Government? Persuaded on our part that it is in conformity with their true interests, we do not hesitate to recommend it to their attention; and, not having sought in the project of a mediation of the maritime powers of Europe any vain display of influence, we would applaud, with entire freedom from all susceptibility of self-esteem, the opening of a negotiation which would invite the two populations to discuss, without the co-operation of Europe, the solution of their difference.

The reply which the President directed to be made to this proposition embraces so many points of permanent interest and importance in connection with his Administration; that we give it in full. It was as follows:

DEPARTMENT OF STATE, WASHINGTON, *Feb.* 6, 1863.

SIR: The intimation given in your dispatch of January 15th, that I might expect a special visit from M. Mercier, has been realized. He called on the 3d instant, and gave me a copy of a dispatch which he had just then received from M. Drouyn de l'Huys under the date of the 9th of January.

I have taken the President's instructions, and I now proceed to give you his views upon the subject in question.

It has been considered with seriousness, resulting from the reflection that the people of France are known to be faultless sharers with the American nation in the misfortunes and calamities of our unhappy civil war; nor do we on this, any more than on other occasions, forget the traditional friendship of the two countries, which we unhesitatingly believe has inspired the counsels that M. Drouyn de l'Huys has imparted.

He says, "the Federal Government does not despair, we know, of giving more active impulse to hostilities;" and again he remarks, "the protraction of the struggle, in a word, has not shaken the confidence (of the Federal Government) in the definitive success of its efforts."

These passages seem to me to do unintentional injustice to the language, whether confidential or public, in which this Government has constantly spoken on the subject of the war. It certainly has had and avowed only one purpose—a determination to preserve the integrity of the country. So far from admitting any laxity of effort, or betraying any despondency, the Government has, on the contrary, borne itself cheerfully in all vicissitudes, with unwavering confidence in an early and complete triumph of the national cause. Now, when we are, in a manner, invited by a friendly power to review the twenty-one months' history of the conflict, we find no occasion to abate that confidence. Through such an alternation of victories and defeats as is the appointed incident of every war, the land and naval forces of the United States have steadily advanced, reclaiming from the insurgents the ports, forts, and posts which they had treacherously seized before the strife actually began, and even before it was seriously apprehended. So many of the States and districts which the insurgents included in the field of their projected exclusive slaveholding dominions have already been re-established under the flag of the Union, that they now retain only the States of Georgia, Alabama, and Texas, with half of Virginia, half of North Carolina, and two thirds of South Carolina, half of Mississippi, and one-third respectively of Arkansas and Louisiana. The national forces hold even this small territory in close blockade and siege.

This Government, if required, does not hesitate to submit its achievements to the test of comparison; and it maintains that in no part of the world, and in no times, ancient or modern, has a nation, when rendered all unready for combat by the enjoyment of eighty years of almost unbroken peace, so quickly awakened at the alarm of sedition, put forth energies so vigorous, and achieved successes so signal and effective as those which have marked the progress of this contest on the part of the Union.

M. Drouyn de l'Huys, I fear, has taken other light than the correspondence of this Government for his guidance in ascertaining its temper and firmness. He has probably read of divisions of sentiment among those who hold themselves forth as organs of public opinion here, and has given to them an undue importance. It is to be remembered that this is a nation of thirty millions, civilly divided into forty-one States and Territories, which cover an expanse hardly less than Europe; that the people are a pure democracy, exercising everywhere the utmost freedom of speech and suffrage; that a great crisis necessarily produces vehement as well as profound debate, with sharp collisions of individual, local, and sectional interests, sentiments, and ambitions; and that this heat of controversy is increased by the intervention of speculations, interests, prejudices, and passions from every other part of the civilized world. It is, however, through such debates that the agreement of the nation upon any subject is habitually attained, its resolutions formed, and its policy established. While there has been much difference of popular opinion and favor concerning the agents who shall carry on the war, the principles on which it shall be waged, and the means with which it shall be prosecuted, M. Drouyn de l'Huys has only to refer to the statute book of Congress and the Executive ordinances to learn that the national activity has hitherto been, and yet is, as efficient as that of any other nation, whatever its form of government, ever was, under circumstances of equally grave import to its peace, safety, and welfare. Not one voice has been raised anywhere, out of the immediate field of the insurrection, in favor of foreign intervention, of mediation, of arbitration, or of compromise, with the relinquishment of one acre of the national domain, or the surrender of even one constitutional franchise. At the same time, it is manifest to the world that our resources are yet abundant, and our credit adequate to the existing emergency.

What M. Drouyn de l'Huys suggests is that this Government shall appoint commissioners to meet, on neutral ground, commissioners of thy insurgents. He supposes that in the conferences to be thus held, reciprocal complaints could be discussed, and in place of the accusations which the North and South now mutually cast upon each other, the conferees would be engaged with discussions of the interests which divide them. He assumes, further, that the commissioners would seek by means of well-ordered and profound deliberation, whether these interests are definitively irreconcilable, whether separation is an extreme that can no longer be avoided, or whether the memories of a common existence, the ties of every kind which have made the North and the South one whole Federative State, and have borne them on to so high a degree of prosperity, are not more powerful than the causes which have placed arms in the hands of the two populations.

The suggestion is not an extraordinary one, and it may well have been thought by the Emperor of the French, in the earnestness of his benevolent desire for the restoration of peace, a feasible one. But when M. Drouyn de l'Huys shall come to review it in the light in which it must necessarily be examined in this country, I think he can hardly fail to perceive that it amounts to nothing less than a proposition that, while this Government is engaged in suppressing an armed insurrection, with the purpose of maintaining the constitutional national authority, and preserving the integrity of the country, it shall enter into diplomatic discussion with the insurgents upon the questions whether that authority shall not be renounced, and whether the country shall not be delivered over to disunion, to be quickly followed by ever-increasing anarchy.

If it were possible for the Government of the United States to compromise the national authority so far as to enter into such debates, it is not easy to perceive what good results could be obtained by them.

The commissioners must agree in recommending either that the Union shall stand or that it shall be voluntarily dissolved; or else they must leave the vital question unsettled, to abide at last the fortunes of the war. The Government has not shut out the knowledge of the present temper, any more than of the past purposes of the insurgents. There is not the least ground to suppose that the controlling actors would be persuaded at this moment, by any arguments which national commissioners could offer, to forego the ambition that has impelled them to the disloyal position they are occupying. Any commissioners who should be appointed by these actors, or through their dictation or influence, must enter the conference imbued with the spirit and pledged to the personal fortunes of the insurgent chiefs. The loyal people in the insurrectionary States would be unheard, and any offer of peace by this Government, on the condition of the maintenance of the Union, must necessarily be rejected.

On the other hand, as I have already intimated, this Government has not the least thought of relinquishing the trust which has been confided to it by the nation under the most solemn of all political sanctions; and if it had any such thought, it would still have abundant reason to know that peace proposed at the cost of dissolution would be immediately, unreservedly, and indignantly rejected by the American people. It is a great mistake that European statesmen make, if they suppose this people are demoralized. Whatever, in the case of an insurrection, the people of France, or of Great Britain, or of Switzerland, or of the Netherlands would do to save their national existence, no matter how the strife might be regarded by or might affect foreign nations, just so much, and certainly no less, the people of the United States will do, if necessary to save for the common benefit the region which is bounded by the Pacific and the Atlantic coasts, and by the shores of the Gulfs of St. Lawrence and Mexico, together with the free and common navigation of the Rio Grande, Missouri, Arkansas, Mississippi, Ohio, St. Lawrence, Hudson, Delaware, Potomac, and other natural highways by which this land, which to them is at once a land of inheritance and a land of promise, is opened and watered. Even if the agents of the American people now exercising their power should, through fear or faction, fall below this height of the national virtue, they would be speedily, yet constitutionally, replaced by others of sterner character and patriotism.

I must be allowed to say, also, that M. Drouyn de l'Huys errs in his description of the parties to the present conflict. We have here, in the political sense, no North and South, no Northern and Southern States. We have an insurrectionary party, which is located chiefly upon and adjacent to the shore of the Gulf of Mexico; and we have, on the other hand, a loyal people, who constitute not only Northern States, but also Eastern, Middle, Western, and Southern States.

I have on many occasions heretofore submitted to the French Government the President's views of the interests, and the ideas more effective for the time than even interests, which lie at the bottom of the determination of the American Government and people to maintain the Federal Union. The President has done the same thing in his Messages and other public declarations. I refrain, therefore, from reviewing that argument in connection with the existing question.

M. Drouyn de l'Huys draws to his aid the conferences which took place between the Colonies and Great Britain in our Revolutionary War. He will allow us to assume that action in the crisis of a nation must accord with its necessities, and therefore can seldom be conformed to precedents. Great Britain, when entering on the negotiations, had manifestly come to entertain doubts of her ultimate success; and it is certain that the councils of the Colonies could not fail to take new courage, if not to gain other advantage, when the parent State compromised so far as to treat of peace on the terms of conceding their independence.

It is true, indeed, that peace must come at some time, and that conferences must attend, if they are not allowed to precede the pacification. There is, however, a better form for such conferences than the one which M. Drouyn de l'Huys suggests. The latter would be palpably in derogation of the Constitution of the United States, and would carry no weight, because destitute of the sanction necessary to bind either the disloyal or the loyal portions of the people. On the other hand, the Congress of the United States furnishes a constitutional forum for debates between the alienated parties. Senators and representatives from the loyal portion of the people are there already, freely empowered to confer; and seats also are vacant, and inviting senators and representatives of this discontented party who may be constitutionally sent there from the States involved in the insurrection. Moreover, the conferences which can thus be held in Congress have this great advantage over any that could be organized upon the plan of M. Drouyn de l'Huys, namely, that the Congress, if it were thought wise, could call a national convention to adopt its recommendations, and give them all the solemnity and binding force of organic law. Such conferences between the alienated parties may be said to have already begun. Maryland, Virginia, Kentucky, Tennessee, and Missouri—States which are claimed by the insurgents—are already represented in Congress, and submitting with perfect freedom and in a proper spirit their advice upon the course best calculated to bring about, in the shortest time, a firm, lasting, and honorable peace. Representatives have been sent also from Louisiana, and others are understood to be coming from Arkansas.

There is a preponderating argument in favor of the Congressional form of conference over that which is suggested by M. Drouyn de l'Huys, namely, that while an accession to the latter would bring this Government into a concurrence with the insurgents in disregarding and setting aside an important part of the Constitution of the United States, and so would be of pernicious example, the Congressional conference, on the contrary, preserves and gives new strength to that sacred writing which must continue through future ages the sheet anchor of the Republic.

You will be at liberty to read this dispatch to M. Drouyn de l'Huys, and to give him a copy if he shall desire it.

To the end that you may be informed of the whole case, I transmit a copy of M. Drouyn de l'Huys's dispatch.

I am, sir, your obedient servant,

WILLIAM H. SEWARD.

The effect of this dispatch was very marked. It put an end to all talk of foreign intervention in any form, and met the cordial and even enthusiastic approbation of the people throughout the country. Its closing suggestions as to the mode in which the Southern States could resume their old relations to the Federal Government, were regarded as significant indications of the policy the Administration was inclined to pursue whenever the question of restoration should become practical; and while they were somewhat sharply assailed in some quarters, they commanded the general assent of the great body of the people.

The subject of appointing commissioners to confer with the authorities of the rebel Confederacy had been discussed, before the appearance of this correspondence, in the Northern States. It had emanated from the party most openly in hostility to the Administration, and those men in that party who had been most distinctly opposed to any measures of coercion, or any resort to force for the purpose of overcoming the rebellion. It was represented by these persons that the civil authorities of the Confederacy were restrained from abandoning the contest only by the refusal or neglect of the Government to give them an opportunity of doing so without undue humiliation and dishonor; and in December Hon. Fernando Wood, of New York, wrote to the President informing him that he had reason to believe the Southern States would "send representatives to the next Congress, provided a full and general amnesty should permit them to do so," and asking the appointment of commissioners to ascertain the truth of these assurances.

To this request the President made the following reply:

EXECUTIVE MANSION, WASHINGTON, *Dec.* 12, 1862.

HON. FERNANDO WOOD:

MY DEAR SIR:—Your letter of the 8th, with the accompanying note of same date, was received yesterday.

The most important paragraph in the letter, as I consider, is in these words: "On the 25th of November last I was advised by an authority which I deemed likely to be well informed as well as reliable and truthful, that the Southern States would send representatives to the next Congress, provided that a full and general amnesty should permit them to do so. No guarantee or terms were asked for other than the amnesty referred to."

I strongly suspect your information will prove to be groundless; nevertheless, I thank you for communicating it to me. Understanding the phrase in the paragraph above quoted—"the Southern States would send representatives to the next Congress"—to be substantially the same as that "the people of the Southern States would cease resistance, and would reinaugurate, submit to, and maintain the national authority within the limits of such States, under the Constitution of the United States," I say that in such case the war would cease on the part of the United States; and that if within a reasonable time "a full and general amnesty" were necessary to such end, it would not be withheld.

I do not think it would be proper now to communicate this, formally or informally, to the people of the Southern States. My belief is that they already know it; and when they choose, if ever, they can communicate with me unequivocally. Nor do I think it proper now to suspend military operations to try any experiment of negotiation.

I should nevertheless receive, with great pleasure, the exact information you now have, and also such other as you may in any way obtain. Such information might be more valuable before the 1st of January than afterward.

While there is nothing in this letter which I shall dread to see in history, it is, perhaps, better for the present that its existence should not become public. I therefore have to request that you will regard it as confidential. Your obedient servant,

A. LINCOLN.

The intimation in this letter that information concerning the alleged willingness of the rebels to resume their allegiance, "might be more valuable before the 1st of January than afterwards," had reference to the Emancipation Proclamation which he proposed to issue on that day, unless the offer of his preliminary proclamation should be accepted. That proclamation had been issued on the 22d of September, and the sense of responsibility under which this step was taken, was clearly indicated in the following remarks made by the President on the evening of the 24th of that month, in acknowledging the compliment of a serenade at the executive mansion:

FELLOW-CITIZENS: I appear before you to do little more than acknowledge the courtesy you pay me, and to thank you for it. I have not been distinctly informed why it is that on this occasion you appear to do me this honor, though I suppose it is because of the Proclamation. What I did, I did after a very full deliberation, and under a very heavy and solemn sense of responsibility. I can only trust in God I have made no mistake. I shall make no attempt on this occasion to sustain what I have done or said by any comment. It is now for the country and the world to pass judgment, and may be take action upon it. I will say no more upon this subject. In my position I am environed with difficulties. Yet they are scarcely so great as the difficulties of those who, upon the battle-field, are endeavoring to purchase with their blood and their lives, the future happiness and prosperity of this country. Let us never forget them. On the 14th and 17th days of this present month, there have been battles bravely, skilfully, and successfully fought. We do not yet know the particulars. Let us be sure that, in giving praise to certain individuals, we do no injustice to others. I only ask you at the conclusion of these few remarks, to give three hearty cheers to all good and brave officers and men who fought those successful battles.

In November the President published the following order regarding the observance of the day of rest, and the vice of profanity, in the army and navy:

EXECUTIVE MANSION, WASHINGTON, *Nov.* 16, 1862.

The President, commander-in-chief of the army and navy, desires and enjoins the orderly observance of the Sabbath by the officers and men in the military and naval service. The importance for man and beast of the prescribed weekly rest, the sacred rights of Christian soldiers and sailors, a becoming deference to the best sentiment of a Christian people, and a due regard for the Divine will, demand that Sunday labor in the army and navy be reduced to the measure of strict necessity.

The discipline and character of the national forces should not suffer, nor the cause they defend be imperilled, by the profanation of the day or name of the Most High. "At this time of public distress," adopting the words of Washington in 1776, "men may find enough to do in the service of God and their country, without abandoning themselves to vice and immorality." The first general order issued by the Father of his Country, after the Declaration of Independence, indicates the spirit in which our institutions were founded, and should ever be defended. "The general hopes and trusts that every officer and man will endeavor to live and act as becomes a Christian soldier defending the dearest rights and liberties of his country."

A. LINCOLN.

CHAPTER VII.

THE CONGRESSIONAL SESSION OF 1862–'63.—MESSAGE OF THE PRESIDENT, AND GENERAL ACTION OF THE SESSION.

The third session of the Thirty-seventh Congress opened on the first day of December, 1862—the supporters of the Administration having a large majority in both branches. The general condition of the country, and the progress made in quelling the rebellion, are clearly set forth in the following Message of President Lincoln, which was sent in to Congress at the beginning of the session:

Fellow-Citizens of the Senate and House of Representatives: Since your last annual assembling, another year of health and bountiful harvests has passed, and while it has not pleased the Almighty to bless us with a return of peace, we can but press on, guided by the best light He gives us, trusting that, in his own good time and wise way, all will be well.

The correspondence, touching foreign affairs, which has taken place during the last year, is herewith submitted, in virtual compliance with a request to that effect made by the House of Representatives near the close of the last session of Congress. If the condition of our relations with other nations is less gratifying than it has usually been at former periods, it is certainly more satisfactory than a nation so unhappily distracted as we are might reasonably have apprehended. In the month of June last there were some grounds to expect that the maritime Powers which, at the beginning of our domestic difficulties, so unwisely and unnecessarily, as we think, recognized the insurgents as a belligerent, would soon recede from that position, which has proved only less injurious to themselves than to our own country. But the temporary reverses which afterward befel the National arms, and which were exaggerated by our own disloyal citizens abroad, have hitherto delayed that act of simple justice.

The civil war which has so radically changed for the moment the occupations and habits of the American people, has necessarily disturbed the social condition, and affected very deeply the prosperity of the nations with which we have carried on a commerce that has been steadily increasing throughout a period of half a century. It has, at the same time, excited political ambitions and apprehensions which have produced a profound agitation throughout the civilized world. In this unusual agitation we have forborne from taking part in any controversy between foreign states, and between parties or factions in such states. We have attempted no propagandism, and acknowledged no revolution. But we have left to every nation the exclusive conduct and management of its own affairs. Our struggle has been, of course, contemplated by foreign nations with reference less to its own merits, than to its supposed and often exaggerated effects and consequences resulting to those nations themselves. Nevertheless, complaint on the part of this Government, even if it were just, would certainly be unwise.

The treaty with Great Britain for the suppression of the slave trade has been put into operation with a good prospect of complete success. It is an occasion of special pleasure to acknowledge that the execution of it on the part of Her Majesty's Government, has been marked with a jealous respect for the authority of the United States and the rights of their moral and loyal citizens.

The convention with Hanover for the abolition of the stade dues has been carried into full effect, under the act of Congress for that purpose.

A blockade of three thousand miles of seacoast could not be established and vigorously enforced, in a season of great commercial activity like the present, without committing occasional mistakes, and inflicting unintentional injuries upon foreign nations and their subjects.

A civil war occurring in a country where foreigners reside and carry on trade under treaty stipulations is necessarily fruitful of complaints of the violation of neutral rights. All such collisions tend to excite misapprehensions, and possibly to produce mutual reclamations between nations which have a common interest in preserving peace and friendship. In clear cases of these kinds I have, so far as possible, heard and redressed complaints which have been presented by friendly Powers. There is still, however, a large and an augmenting number of doubtful cases, upon which the Government is unable to agree with the Governments whose protection is demanded by the claimants. There are, moreover, many cases in which the United States, or their citizens, suffer wrongs from the naval or military authorities of foreign nations, which the Governments of these states are not at once prepared to redress. I have proposed to some of the foreign states thus interested, mutual conventions to examine and adjust such complaints. This proposition has been made especially to Great Britain, to France, to Spain, and to Prussia. In each case it has been kindly received, but has not yet been formally adopted.

I deem it my duty to recommend an appropriation in behalf of the owners of the Norwegian bark Admiral P. Tordenskiold, which vessel was in May, 1861, prevented by the commander of the blockading force off Charleston from leaving that port with cargo, notwithstanding a similar privilege had, shortly before, been granted to an English vessel. I have directed the Secretary of State to cause the papers in the case to be communicated to the proper committees.

Applications have been made to me by many free Americans of African descent to favor their emigration, with a view to such coloniza tion as was contemplated in recent acts of Congress. Other parties, at home and abroad—some from interested motives, others upon patriotic considerations, and still others influenced by philanthropic sentiments—have suggested similar measures; while, on the other hand, several of the Spanish-American Republics have protested against the sending of such colonies to their respective territories. Under these circumstances I have declined to move any such colony to any State without first obtaining the consent of its Government, with an agreement on its part to receive and protect such emigrants in all the rights of freemen; and I have at the same time offered to the several States situated within the tropics, or having colonies there, to negotiate with them, subject to the advice and consent of the Senate, to favor the voluntary emigration of persons of that class to their respective territories, upon conditions which shall be equal, just and humane. Liberia and Hayti are, as yet, the only countries to which colonists of African descent from here could go with certainty of being received and adopted as citizens; and I regret to say such persons, contemplating colonization do not seem so willing to migrate to those countries as to some others, nor so willing as I think their interest demands. I believe, however, opinion among them in this respect is improving; and that ere long there will be an augmented and considerable migration to both these countries from the United States.

The new commercial treaty between the United States and the Sultan of Turkey has been carried into execution.

A commercial and consular treaty has been negotiated, subject to the Senate's consent, with Liberia; and a similar negotiation is now pending with the Republic of Hayti. A considerable improvement of the national commerce is expected to result from these measures.

Our relations with Great Britain, France, Spain, Portugal, Russia, Prussia, Denmark, Sweden, Austria, the Netherlands, Italy, Rome, and the other European states remain undisturbed. Very favorable relations also continue to be maintained with Turkey, Morocco, China, and Japan.

During the last year there has not only been no change of our previous relations with the Independent States of our own continent, but more friendly sentiments than have heretofore existed are believed to be entertained by these neighbors, whose safety and progress are so intimately connected with our own. This statement especially applies to Mexico, Nicaragua, Costa Rica, Honduras, Peru, and Chili.

The commission under the convention with the Republic of New Granada closed its session without having audited and passed upon all the claims which were submitted to it. A proposition is pending to revive the convention, that it be able to do more complete justice. The joint commission between the United States and the Republic of Costa Rica has completed its labors and submitted its report.

I have favored the project for connecting the United States with Europe by an Atlantic telegraph, and a similar project to extend the telegraph from San Francisco to connect by a Pacific telegraph with the line which is being extended across the Russian Empire.

The Territories of the United States, with unimportant exceptions, have remained undisturbed by the civil war; and they are exhibiting such evidence of prosperity as justifies an expectation that some of them will soon be in a condition to be organized as States, and be constitutionally admitted into the Federal Union.

The immense mineral resources of some of those Territories ought to be developed as rapidly as possible. Every step in that direction would have a tendency to improve the revenues of the Government and diminish the burdens of the people. It is worthy of your serious consideration whether some extraordinary measures to promote that end cannot be adopted. The means which suggests itself as most likely to be effective, is a scientific exploration of the mineral regions in those Territories, with a view to the publication of its results at home and in foreign countries—results which cannot fail to be auspicious.

The condition of the finances will claim your most diligent consideration. The vast expenditures incident to the military and naval operations required for the suppression of the rebellion have been hitherto met with a promptitude and certainty unusual in similar circumstances: and the public credit has been fully maintained. The continuance of the war, however, and the increased disbursements made necessary by the augmented forces now in the field, demand your best reflections as to the best modes of providing the necessary revenue, without injury to business, and with the least possible burdens upon labor.

The suspension of specie payments by the Banks, soon after the commencement of your last session, made large issues of United States notes unavoidable. In no other way could the payment of the troops and the satisfaction of other just demands, be so economically or so well provided for. The judicious legislation of Congress, securing the receivability of these notes for loans and internal duties, and making them a legal tender for other debts, has made them a universal currency, and has satisfied, partially at least, and for the time, the long felt want of an uniform circulating medium, saving thereby to the people immense sums in discounts and exchanges.

A return to specie payments, however, at the earliest period compatible with due regard to all interests concerned, should ever be kept in view. Fluctuations in the value of currency are always injurious, and to reduce these fluctuations to the lowest possible point will always be a leading purpose in wise legislation. Convertibility, prompt and certain convertibility into coin, is generally acknowledged to be the best and surest safeguard against them; and it is extremely doubtful whether a circulation of United States notes, payable in coin, and sufficiently large for the wants of the people, can be permanently, usefully, and safely maintained.

Is there, then, any other mode in which the necessary provision for the public wants can be made, and the great advantages of a safe and uniform currency secured?

I know of none which promises so certain results, and is, at the same time, so unobjectionable as the organization of banking associations, under a general act of Congress, well guarded in its provisions. To such associations the Government might furnish circulating notes, on the security of United States bonds deposited in the Treasury. These notes, prepared under the supervision of proper officers, being uniform in appearance and security, and convertible always into coin, would at once protect labor against the evils of a vicious currency, and facilitate commerce by cheap and safe exchanges.

A moderate reservation from the interest on the bonds would compensate the United States for the preparation and distribution of the notes, and a general supervision of the system, and would lighten the burden of that part of the public debt employed as securities. The public credit, moreover, would be greatly improved, and the negotiation of new loans greatly facilitated by the steady market demand for Government bonds which the adoption of the proposed system would create.

It is an additional recommendation of the measure, of considerable weight, in my judgment, that it would reconcile as far as possible all existing interests, by the opportunity offered to existing institutions to reorganize under the act, substituting only the secured uniform national circulation for the local and various circulation, secured and unsecured, now issued by them.

The receipts into the Treasury, from all sources, including loans, and balance from the preceding year, for the fiscal year ending on the 30th of June, 1862, were $583,885,247 60, of which sum $49,056,397 62 were derived from customs; $1,795,331 73 from the direct tax; from public lands, $152,203 77; from miscellaneous sources, $931,787 64; from loans in all forms, $529,692,460 50. The remainder, $2,257,065 80, was the balance from last year.

The disbursements during the same period were for Congressional, Executive, and Judicial purposes, $5,939,009 29; for foreign intercourse, $1,339,710 35; for miscellaneous expenses, including the mints, loans, post-office deficiencies, collection of revenue, and other like charges, $14,129,771 50; for expenses under the Interior Department, $3,102,-985 52 under the War Department, $394,368,407 36; under the Navy Department, $42,674,569 69; for interest on public debt, $13,190,324 45; and for payment of public debt, including reimbursement of temporary loan, and redemptions, $96,096,922 09; making an aggregate of $570,841,700 25, and leaving a balance in the Treasury on the 1st day of July, 1862, of 13,043,546 81.

It should be observed that the sum of $96,096,922 09, expended for reimbursements and redemption of public debt, being included also in the loans made, may be properly deducted, both from receipts and expenditures, leaving the actual receipts for the year $487,788,324 97, and the expenditures, $474,744,778 16.

Other information on the subject of the finances will be found in the report of the Secretary of the Treasury, to whose statements and views I invite your most candid and considerate attention.

The reports of the Secretaries of War and of the Navy are herewith transmitted. These reports, though lengthy, are scarcely more than brief abstracts of the very numerous and extensive transactions and operations conducted through those Departments. Nor could I give a summary of them here, upon any principle which would admit of its being much shorter than the reports themselves. I therefore content myself with laying the reports before you, and asking your attention to them.

It gives me pleasure to report a decided improvement in the financial condition of the Post-Office Department, as compared with several preceding years. The receipts for the fiscal year 1861 amounted to $8,349,296, 40, which embraced the revenue from all the States of the Union for three quarters of that year. Notwithstanding the cessation of revenue from the so-called seceded States during the last fiscal year, the increase of the correspondence of the loyal States has been sufficient to produce a revenue during the same year of $8,299,820 90, being only $50,000 less than was derived from all the States of the Union during the previous year. The expenditures show a still more favorable result. The amount expended in 1861 was $13,606,759 11. For the last year the amount has been reduced to $11,125,364 13, showing a decrease of about $2,481,000 in the expenditures as compared with the preceding year, and about $3,750,000 as compared with the fiscal year 1860. The deficiency in the Department for the previous year was $4,551,966 98. For the last fiscal year it was reduced to $2,112,814 57. These favorable results are in part owing to the cessation of mail service in the insurrectionary States, and in part to a careful review of all expenditures in that department in the interest of economy. The efficiency of the postal service, it is believed, has also been much improved. The Postmaster-General has also opened a correspondence, through the Department of State, with foreign Governments, proposing a convention of postal representatives for the purpose of simplifying the rates of foreign postage, and to expedite the foreign mails. This proposition, equally important to our adopted citizens and to the commercial interests of this country, has been favorably entertained and agreed to by all the Governments from whom replies have been received.

I ask the attention of Congress to the suggestions of the Postmaster-General in his report respecting the further legislation required, in his opinion, for the benefit of the postal service.

The Secretary of the Interior reports as follows in regard to the public lands:

> The public lands have ceased to be a source of revenue. From the 1st July, 1861, to the 30th September, 1862, the entire cash receipts from the sale of lands were $137,476 26—a sum much less than the expenses of our land system during the same period. The homestead law, which will take effect on the 1st of January next, offers such inducements to settlers that sales for cash cannot be expected, to an extent sufficient to meet the expense of the General Land Office, and the cost of surveying and bringing the land into market.

The discrepancy between the sum here stated as arising from the sales of the public lands, and the sum derived from the same source as reported from the Treasury Department, arises, as I understand, from the fact that the periods of time, though apparently, were not really coincident at the beginning-point—the Treasury report including a considerable sum now which had previously been reported from the Interior—sufficiently large to greatly overreach the sum derived from the three months now reported upon by the Interior, and not by the Treasury.

The Indian tribes upon our frontiers have, during the past year, manifested a spirit of insubordination, and, at several points, have engaged in open hostilities against the white settlements in their vicinity. The tribes occupying the Indian country south of Kansas renounced their allegiance to the United States, and entered into treaties with the insurgents. Those who remained loyal to the United States were driven from the country. The chief of the Cherokees has visited this city for the purpose of restoring the former relations of the tribe with the United States. He alleges that they were constrained, by superior force, to enter into treaties with the insurgents, and that the United States neglected to furnish the protection which their treaty stipulations required.

In the month of August last, the Sioux Indians in Minnesota, attacked the settlement in their vicinity with extreme ferocity, killing, indiscriminately, men, women, and children. This attack was wholly unexpected, and therefore no means of defence had been provided. It is estimated that not less than eight hundred persons were killed by the Indians, and a large amount of property was destroyed. How this outbreak was induced is not definitely known, and suspicions, which may be unjust, need not to be stated. Information was received by the Indian Bureau, from different sources, about the time hostilities were commenced, that a simultaneous attack was to be made upon the white settlements by all the tribes between the Mississippi River and the Rocky Mountains. The State of Minnesota has suffered great injury from this Indian war. A large portion of her territory has been depopulated, and a severe loss has been sustained by the destruction of property. The people of that State manifest much anxiety for the removal of the tribes beyond the limits of the State as a guarantee against future hostilities. The Commissioner of Indian Affairs will furnish full details. I submit for your especial consideration whether our Indian system shall not be remodelled. Many wise and good men have impressed me with the belief that this can be profitably done.

I submit a statement of the proceedings of commissioners, which shows the progress that has been made in the enterprise of constructing the Pacific railroad. And this suggests the earliest completion of this road, and also the favorable action of Congress upon the projects now pending before them for enlarging the capacities of the great canals in New York and Illinois, as being of vital and rapidly increasing importance to the whole nation, and especially to the vast interior region hereinafter to be noticed at some greater length. I purpose having prepared and laid before you at an early day some interesting and valuable statistical information upon this subject. The military and commercial importance of enlarging the Illinois and Michigan canal, and improving the Illinois river, is presented in the report of Col. Webster to the Secretary of War, and now transmitted to Congress. I respectfully ask attention to it.

To carry out the provisions of the act of Congress of the 15th of May last, I have caused the Department of Agriculture of the United States to be organized.

The Commissioner informs me that within the period of a few months this department has established an extensive system of correspondence and exchanges, both at home and abroad, which promises to effect highly beneficial results in the development of a correct knowledge of recent improvements in agriculture, in the introduction of new products, and in the collection of the agricultural statistics of the different States. Also, that it will soon be prepared to distribute largely seeds, cereals, plants and cuttings, and has already published and liberally diffused much valuable information in anticipation of a more elaborate report, which will in due time be furnished, embracing some valuable tests in chemical science now in progress in the laboratory.

The creation of this department was for the more immediate benefit of a large class of our most valuable fellow-citizens; and I trust that the liberal basis upon which it has been organized will not only meet your approbation, but that it will realize, at no distant day, all the fondest anticipations of its most sanguine friends, and become the fruitful source of advantage to all our people.

On the 22d day of September last, a proclamation was issued by the Executive, a copy of which is herewith submitted.

In accordance with the purpose expressed in the second paragraph of that paper, I now respectfully call your attention to what may be called "compensated emancipation."

A nation may be said to consist of its territory, its people, and its laws. The territory is the only part which is of certain durability. "One generation passeth away, and another generation cometh, but the earth abideth forever." It is of the first importance to duly consider and estimate this ever-enduring part. That portion of the earth's surface which is owned and inhabited by the people of the United States, is well adapted to the home of one national family; and it is not well adapted for two or more. Its vast extent, and its variety of climate and productions, are of advantage in this age for one people, whatever they might have been in former ages. Steam, telegraphs, and intelligence have brought these to be an advantageous combination for one united people.

In the Inaugural Address I briefly pointed out the total inadequacy of disunion as a remedy for the differences between the people of the two sections. I did so in language which I cannot improve, and which, therefore, I beg to repeat:

"One section of our country believes slavery is right, and ought to be extended, while the other believes it is wrong, and ought not to be extended. This is the only substantial dispute. The fugitive slave clause of the Constitution, and the law for the suppression of the foreign slave-trade, are each as well enforced, perhaps, as any law can ever be in a community where the moral sense of the people imperfectly supports the law itself. The great body of the people abide by the dry legal obligation in both cases, and a few break over in each. This, I think, cannot be perfectly cured; and it would be worse, in both cases, after the separation of the sections than before. The foreign slave-trade, now imperfectly suppressed, would be ultimately revived without restriction in one section; while fugitive slaves, now only partially surrendered, would not be surrendered at all by the other.

"Physically speaking, we cannot separate. We cannot remove our respective sections from each other, nor build an impassable wall between them. A husband and wife may be divorced, and go out of the presence and beyond the reach of each other; but the different parts of our country cannot do this. They cannot but remain face to face;

and intercourse, either amicable or hostile, must continue between them. Is it possible, then, to make that intercourse more advantageous or more satisfactory after separation than before? Can aliens make treaties easier than friends can make laws? Can treaties be more faithfully enforced between aliens than laws can among friends? Suppose you go to war, you cannot fight always; and when, after much loss on both sides, and no gain on either, you cease fighting, the identical old questions, as to terms of intercourse, are again upon you."

There is no line, straight or crooked, suitable for a national boundary, upon which to divide. Trace through, from east to west, upon the line between the free and slave country, and we shall find a little more than one-third of its length are rivers, easy to be crossed, and populated, or soon to be populated, thickly upon both sides; while nearly all its remaining length are merely surveyors' lines, over which people may walk back and forth without any consciousness of their presence. No part of this line can be made any more difficult to pass by writing it down on paper or parchment as a national boundary. The fact of separation, if it comes, gives up, on the part of the seceding section, the fugitive slave clause, along with all other constitutional obligations upon the section seceded from, while I should expect no treaty stipulation would ever be made to take its place.

But there is another difficulty. The great interior region, bounded east by the Alleghanies, north by the British dominions, west by the Rocky Mountains, and south by the line along which the culture of corn and cotton meets, and which includes part of Virginia, part of Tennessee, all of Kentucky, Ohio, Indiana, Michigan, Wisconsin, Illinois, Missouri, Kansas, Iowa, Minnesota, and the Territories of Dakota, Nebraska, and part of Colorado, already has above ten millions of people, and will have fifty millions within fifty years if not prevented by any political folly or mistake. It contains more than one-third of the country owned by the United States—certainly more than one million of square miles. Once half as populous as Massachusetts already is, it would have more than seventy-five millions of people. A glance at the map shows that, territorially speaking, it is the great body of the Republic. The other parts are but marginal borders to it, the magnificent region sloping west from the Rocky Mountains to the Pacific being the deepest, and also the richest in undeveloped resources. In the production of provisions, grains, grasses, and all which proceed from them, this great interior region is naturally one of the most important of the world. Ascertain from the statistics the small proportion of the region which has as yet been brought into cultivation, and also the large and rapidly increasing amount of its products, and we shall be overwhelmed with the magnitude of the prospect presented. And yet this region has no seacoast—touches no ocean anywhere. As part of one nation, its people now find, and may forever find, their way to Europe by New York, to South America and Africa by New Orleans, and to Asia by San Francisco. But separate our common country into two nations, as designed by the present rebellion, and every man of this great interior region is thereby cut off from some one or more of these outlets, not perhaps by a physical barrier, but by embarrassing and onerous trade regulations.

And this is true, wherever a dividing or boundary line may be fixed. Place it between the now free and slave country, or place it south of Kentucky, or north of Ohio, and still the truth remains that none south of it can trade to any port or place north of it, and none north of it can trade to any port or place south of it, except upon terms dictated by a Government foreign to them. These outlets, east, west, and south, are indispensable to the well-being of the people inhabiting and to inhabit this vast interior region. Which of the three may be the best is no proper question. All are better than either, and all of right belong to that people and to their successors forever. True to themselves, they will not ask where a line of separation shall be, but will vow rather that there shall be no such line. Nor are the marginal regions less interested in these communications to and through them to the great outside world. They too, and each of them, must have access to this Egypt of the West, without paying toll at the crossing of any national boundary.

Our national strife springs not from our permanent part; not from the land we inhabit; not from our national homestead. There is no possible severing of this but would multiply and not mitigate evils among us. In all its adaptations and aptitudes it demands union and abhors separation. In fact, it would ere long force reunion, however much of blood and treasure the separation might have cost.

Our strife pertains to ourselves—to the passing generations of men; and it can, without convulsion, be hushed forever with the passing of one generation.

In this view, I recommend the adoption of the following resolution and articles amendatory to the Constitution of the United States:

Resolved by the Senate and House of Representatives of the United States of America in Congress assembled (two-thirds of both Houses concurring), That the following articles be proposed to the Legislatures (or Conventions) of the several States as amendments to the Constitution of the

United States, all or any of which articles, when ratified by three-fourths of the said Legislatures (or Conventions), to be valid as part or parts of the said Constitution, viz:

ARTICLE. — Every State, wherein Slavery now exists, which shall abolish the same therein at any time or times before the first day of January, in the year of our Lord one thousand and nine hundred, shall receive compensation from the United States as follows, to wit:

The President of the United States shall deliver to every such State bonds of the United States, bearing interest at the rate of —— per cent. per annum, to an amount equal to the aggregate sum of —— for each slave shown to have been therein by the eighth census of the United States, said bonds to be delivered to such State by installments, or in one parcel, at the completion of the abolishment, accordingly as the same shall have been gradual, or at one time, within such State; and interest shall begin to run upon any such bond only from the proper time of its delivery as aforesaid. Any State having received bonds as aforesaid, and afterwards reintroducing or tolerating slavery therein, shall refund to the United States the bonds so received, or the value thereof, and all interest paid thereon.

ARTICLE. — All slaves who shall have enjoyed actual freedom by the chances of the war, at any time before the end of the rebellion, shall be forever free; but all owners of such who shall not have been disloyal shall be compensated for them at the same rates as is provided for States adopting abolishment of slavery, but in such way that no slave shall be twice accounted for.

ARTICLE. — Congress may appropriate money, and otherwise provide for colonizing free colored persons, with their own consent, at any place or places without the United States.

I beg indulgence to discuss these proposed articles at some length. Without slavery the rebellion could never have existed; without slavery it could not continue.

Among the friends of the Union there is great diversity of sentiment and of policy in regard to slavery, and the African race amongst us. Some would perpetuate slavery; some would abolish it suddenly, and without compensation; some would abolish it gradually, and with compensation; some would remove the freed people from us, and some would retain them with us: and there are yet other minor diversities. Because of these diversities we waste much strength among ourselves. By mutual concession we should harmonize and act together. This would be compromise; but it would be compromise among the friends, and not with the enemies of the Union. These articles are intended to embody a plan of such mutual concessions. If the plan shall be adopted, it is assumed that emancipation will follow in at least several of the States.

As to the first article, the main points are: first, the emancipation; secondly, the length of time for consummating it- -thirty-seven years; and, thirdly, the compensation.

The emancipation will be unsatisfactory to the advocates of perpetual slavery; but the length of time should greatly mitigate their dissatisfaction. The time spares both races from the evils of sudden derangement—in fact, from the necessity of any derangement; while most of those whose habitual course of thought will be disturbed by the measure will have passed away before its consummation. They will never see it. Another class will hail the prospect of emancipation, but will deprecate the length of time. They will feel that it gives too little to the now living slaves. But it really gives them much. It saves them from the vagrant destitution which must largely attend immediate emancipation in localities where their numbers are very great; and it gives the inspiring assurance that their posterity shall be free forever. The plan leaves to each State choosing to act under it, to abolish slavery now, or at the end of the century, or at any intermediate time, or by degrees, extending over the whole or any part of the period; and it obliges no two States to proceed alike. It also provides for compensation, and generally the mode of making it. This, it would seem, must further mitigate the dissatisfaction of those who favor perpetual slavery, and especially of those who are to receive the compensation. Doubtless some of those who are to pay and not receive will object. Yet the measure is both just and economical. In a certain sense the liberation of slaves is the destruction of property—property acquired by descent or by purchase, the same as any other property. It is no less true for having been often said, that the people of the South are not more responsible for the original introduction of this property than are the people of the North; and when it is remembered how unhesitatingly we all use cotton and sugar, and share the profits of dealing in them, it may not be quite safe to say that the South has been more responsible than the North for its continuance. If, then, for a common object this property is to be sacrificed, is it not just that it be done at a common charge?

And if with less money, or money more easily paid, we can preserve the benefits of the Union by this means than we can by the war alone, is it not also economical to do it? Let us consider it, then. Let us ascertain the sum we have expended in the war since compensated emancipation was proposed last March, and consider whether, if that measure had been promptly accepted by even some of the Slave States, the same sum would not have done more to close the war than has been otherwise done. If so, the measure would save money, and, in that view, would be a prudent and economical measure. Certainly it is not so easy to pay something as it is to pay nothing; but it is easier pay a large sum than it is to pay a larger one. And it is easier to to pay any sum when we are able than it is to pay it before we are able. The war requires large sums, and requires them at once. The aggregate sum necessary for compensated emancipation of course would be large. But it would require no ready cash, nor the bonds even, any faster than the emancipation progresses. This might not, and probably would not, close before the end of the thirty-seven years. At that time we shall probably have a hundred millions of people to share the burden, instead of thirty-one millions, as now. And not only so, but the increase of our population may be expected to continue for a long time after that period as rapidly as before; because our territory will not have become full. I do not state this inconsiderately.

At the same ratio of increase which we have maintained, on an average, from our first national census, in 1790, until that of 1860, we should, in 1900, have a population of 103,208,415. And why may we not continue that ratio—far beyond that period? Our abundant room—our broad national homestead—is our ample resource. Were our territory as limited as are the British Isles, very certainly our population could not expand as stated. Instead of receiving the foreign born as now, we should be compelled to send part of the native born away. But such is not our condition. We have two millions nine hundred and sixty-three thousand square miles. Europe has three millions and eight hundred thousand, with a population averaging seventy-three and one-third persons to the square mile. Why may not our country at some time average as many? Is it less fertile? Has it more waste surface, by mountains, rivers, lakes, deserts, or other causes? Is it inferior to Europe in any natural advantage? If then we are, at some time, to be as populous as Europe, how soon? As to when this may be, we can judge by the past and the present; as to when it will be, if ever, depends much on whether we maintain the Union. Several of our States are already above the average of Europe—seventy-three and a third to the square mile. Massachusetts 157; Rhode Island 133; Connecticut 99; New York and New Jersey, each 80. Also two other great States, Pennsylvania and Ohio, are not far below, the former having 63 and the latter 59. The States already above the European average, except New York, have increased in as rapid a ratio, since passing that point, as ever before; while no one of them is equal to some other parts of our country in natural capacity for sustaining a dense population.

Taking the nation in the aggregate, and we find its population and ratio of increase, for the several decennial periods, to be as follows:

1799....	3,929,827	
1800....	5,305,937	35.02 per cent. ratio of increase.
1810....	7,239,814	36.45 " " "
1820....	9,638,131	33.13 " " "
1830....	12,866,020	33.49 " " "
1840....	17,069,453	32.67 " " "
1850....	23,191,876	35.87 " " "
1860....	31,443,790	35.58 " " "

This shows an average decennial increase of 34.60 per cent. in population through the seventy years, from our first to our last census yet taken. It is seen that the ratio of increase, at no one of these two periods, is either two per cent. below or two per cent. above the average; thus showing how inflexible, and consequently how reliable, the law of increase in our case is. Assuming that it will continue, it gives the following results:

1870..............................	42,323,341
1880..............................	56,967,216
1890..............................	76,677,872
1900..............................	103,208,415
1910..............................	138,918,526
1920..............................	186,984,335
1930..............................	251,680,914

These figures show that our country may be as populous as Europe now is at some point between 1920 and 1930—say about 1925—our territory, at seventy-three and a third persons to the square mile, being of capacity to contain 217,186,000.

And we will reach this, too, if we do not ourselves relinquish the chance, by the folly and evils of disunion, or by long and exhausting wars springing from the only great element of national discord among us. While it cannot be foreseen exactly how much one huge example of secession, breeding lesser ones indefinitely, would retard population, civilization, and prosperity, no one can doubt that the extent of it would be very great and injurious.

Tho proposed emancipation would shorten the war, perpetuate peace, insure this increase of population, and proportionately the wealth of the country. With these we should pay all the emancipation would cost, together with our other debt, easier than we should pay our other debt without it. If we had allowed our old national debt to run at six per cent. per annum, simple interest, from the end of our Revolutionary struggle until to-day, without paying anything on either principal or interest, each man of us would owe less upon that debt now than each man owed upon it then; and this because our increase of men, through the whole period, has been greater than six per cent.; has run faster than the interest upon the debt. Thus, time alone relieves a debtor nation, so long as its population increases faster than unpaid interest accumulates on its debt.

This fact would be no excuse for delaying payment of what is justly due; but it shows the great importance of time in this connection—the great advantage of a policy by which we shall not have to pay until we number a hundred millions, what, by a different policy, we would have to pay now, when we number but thirty-one millions. In a word, it shows that a dollar will be much harder to pay for the war than will be a dollar for the emancipation on the proposed plan. And then the latter will cost no blood, no precious life. It will be a saving of both.

As to the second article, I think it would be impracticable to return to bondage the class of persons therein contemplated. Some of them, doubtless, in the property sense, belong to loyal owners; and hence provision is made in this article for compensating such.

The third article relates to the future of the freed people. It does not oblige, but merely authorizes Congress to aid in colonizing such as may consent. This ought not to be regarded as objectionable on the one hand or on the other, in so much as it comes to nothing unless by the mutual consent of the people to be deported, and the American voters, through their representatives in Congress.

I cannot make it better known than it already is that I strongly favor colonization. And yet I wish to say there is an objection urged against free colored persons remaining in the country which is largely imaginary, if not sometimes malicious.

It is insisted that their presence would injure and displace white labor and white laborers. If there ever could be a proper time for mere catch arguments, that time surely is not now. In times like the present men should utter nothing for which they would not willingly be responsible through time and in eternity. Is it true, then, that colored people can displace any more white labor by being free than by remaining slaves? If they stay in their old places they jostle no white laborers; if they leave their old places they leave them open to white laborers. Logically there is neither more nor less of it. Emancipation even without deportation, would probably enhance the wages of white labor, and, very surely, would not reduce them. Thus the customary amount of labor would still have to be performed—the freed people would surely not do more than their old proportion of it, and very probably for a time would do less, leaving an increased part to white laborers, bringing their labor into greater demand, and consequently enhancing the wages of it. With deportation, even to a limited extent, enhanced wages to white labor is mathematically certain. Labor is like any other commodity in the market—increase the demand for it and you increase the price of it. Reduce the supply of black labor, by colonizing the black laborer out of the country, and by precisely so much you increase the demand for and wages of white labor.

But it is dreaded that the freed prople will swarm forth and cover the whole land! Are they not already in the land? Will liberation make them any more numerous? Equally distributed among the whites of the whole country, and there would be but one colored to seven whites. Could the one, in any way, greatly disturb the seven? There are many communities now having more than one free colored person to seven whites; and this, without any apparent consciousness of evil from it. The District of Columbia and the States of Maryland and Delaware are all in this condition. The District has more than one free colored to six whites; and yet, in its frequent petitions to Congress, I believe it has never presented the presence of free colored persons as one of its grievances. But why should emancipation South send the freed people North? People of any color seldom run unless there be something to run from. Heretofore colored people to some extent have fled North from bondage; and now, perhaps, from bondage and destitution. But if gradual emancipation and deportation be adopted they will have neither to flee from. Their old masters will give them wages at least until new laborers can be procured, and the freed men in turn will gladly give their labor for the wages till new homes can be found for them in congenial climes and with people of their own blood and race. This proposition can be trusted on the mutual interests involved. And in any event, cannot the North decide for itself whether to receive them?

Again, as practice proves more than theory, in any case, has there been any irruption of colored people northward because of the abolishment of slavery in this District last spring?

What I have said of the proportion of free colored persons to the whites in the District is from the census of 1860, having no reference to persons called contrabands, nor to those made free by the act of Congress, abolishing slavery here.

The plan consisting of these articles is recommended, not but that a restoration of national authority would be accepted without its adoption.

Nor will the war, nor proceedings under the proclamation of September 22, 1862, be stayed because of the recommendation of this plan. Its timely adoption, I doubt not, would bring restoration, and thereby stay both.

And, notwithstanding this plan, the recommendation that Congress provide by law for compensating any State which may adopt emancipation before this plan shall have been acted upon, is hereby earnestly renewed. Such would be only an advanced part of the plan, and the same arguments apply to both.

This plan is recommended as a means, not in exclusion of, but additional to, all others for restoring and preserving the national authority throughout the Union. The subject is presented exclusively in its economical aspect. The plan would, I am confident, secure peace more speedily, and maintain it more permanently, than can be done by force alone; while all it would cost, considering amounts, and manner of payment, and times of payment, would be easier paid than will be the additional cost of the war, if we solely rely upon force. It is much—very much—that it would cost no blood at all.

The plan is proposed as permanent constitutional law. It cannot become such, without the concurrence of, first, two-thirds of Congress, and afterward three-fourths of the States. The requisite three-fourths of the States will necessarily include seven of the Slave States. Their concurrence, if obtained, will give assurance of their severally adopting emancipation, at no very distant day, upon the new constitutional terms. This assurance would end the struggle now, and save the Union forever.

I do not forget the gravity which should characterize a paper addressed to the Congress of the nation by the Chief Magistrate of the nation. Nor do I forget that some of you are my seniors; nor that many of you have more experience than I in the conduct of public affairs. Yet I trust that, in view of the great responsibility resting upon me, you will perceive no want of respect to yourselves in any undue earnestness I may seem to display.

Is it doubted, then, that the plan I propose, if adopted, would shorten the war, and thus lessen its expenditure of money and of blood? Is it doubted that it would restore the national authority and national prosperity, and perpetuate both indefinitely? Is it doubted that we here—Congress and Executive—can secure its adoption? Will not the good people respond to a united and earnest appeal from us? Can we, can they, by any other means, so certainly or so speedily assure these vital objects? We can succeed only by concert. It is not "can any of us imagine better?" but "can we all do better?" Object whatsoever is possible, still the question recurs, "can we do better?" The dogmas of the quiet past are inadequate to the stormy present. The occasion is piled high with difficulty, and we must rise with the occasion. As our case is new, so we must think anew, and act anew. We must disenthral ourselves, and then we shall save our country.

Fellow-citizens, we cannot escape history. We of this Congress and this Administration will be remembered in spite of ourselves. No personal significance or insignificance can spare one or another of us. The fiery trial through which we pass will light us down in honor or dishonor to the latest generation. We say that we are for the Union. The world will not forget that we say this. We know how to save the Union. The world knows we do know how to save it. We—even we here—hold the power and bear the responsibility. In giving freedom to the slave we assure freedom to the free—honorable alike in what we give and what we preserve. We shall nobly save or meanly lose the last best hope of earth. Other means may succeed; this could not, cannot fail. The way is plain, peaceful, generous, just—a way which, if followed, the world will forever applaud and God must forever bless.

ABRAHAM LINCOLN.

December 1, 1862.

At the very outset of the session, resolutions were introduced by the opponents of the Administration, censuring, in strong terms, its arrest of individuals, in the loyal States, suspected of giving, or intending to give aid and comfort to the rebellion. These arrests were denounced as utterly unwarranted by the Constitution and laws of the United States, and as involving the subversion of the public liberties. In the Senate, the general subject was discussed in a debate, commencing on the 8th of December, the opponents of the Administration setting forth very fully and very strongly their opinion of the unjustifiable nature of this action, and its friends vindicating it as made absolutely necessary by the emergencies of the case. Every department of the Government, and every section of the country, were filled at the outset of the war with men actively engaged in doing the work of spies and informers for the rebel authorities; and it was known that, in repeated instances, the plans and purposes of the Government had been betrayed and defeated by these aiders and abettors of treason. It became absolutely necessary, not for purposes of punishment but of prevention, to arrest these men in the injurious and perhaps fatal action they were preparing to take; and on this ground the action of the Government was vindicated and justified by the Senate. On the 8th of December, in the House of Representatives, a bill was introduced, declaring the suspension of the writ of *habeas corpus* to have been required by the public safety, confirming and declaring valid all arrests and imprisonments, by whomsoever made or caused to be made, under the authority of the President, and indemnifying the President, secretaries, heads of departments, and all persons who have been concerned in making such arrests, or in doing or advising any such acts, and making void all prosecutions and proceedings whatever against them in relation to the matters in question. It also authorized the President, during the existence of the war, to declare the suspension of the writ of *habeas corpus*, "at such times, and in such places, and with regard to such persons, as in his judgment the public safety may require." This bill was passed, receiving ninety votes in its favor, and forty-five against it. It was taken up in the Senate on the 22d of December, and after a discussion of several days, a new bill was substituted and passed; ayes 33, noes 7. This was taken up in the House on the 18th of February, and the substitute of the Senate was rejected. This led to the appointment of a committee of conference, which recommended that the Senate recede from its amendments, and that the bill, substantially as it came from the House, be passed. This report was agreed to, after long debate, and the bill thus became a law.

The relations in which the Rebel States are placed by their acts of secession towards the General Government, became a topic of discussion in the House of Representatives, in a debate which arose on the 8th of January, upon an item in the appropriation bill, limiting the amount to be paid to certain commissioners to the amount that might be collected from taxes in the insurrectionary States. Mr. Stevens, of Pennsylvania, pronounced the opinion that the Constitution did not embrace a State that was in arms against the Government of the United States. He maintained that those States held towards us the position of alien enemies—that every obligation existing between them and us had been annulled, and that with regard to all the Southern States in rebellion, the Constitution has no binding force and no application. This position was very strongly controverted by men of both parties. Those who were not in full sympathy with the Administration opposed it, because it denied to the Southern people the protection of the Constitution; while many Republicans regarded it as a virtual acknowledgment of the validity and actual force of the ordinances of secession passed by the Rebel States. Mr. Thomas, of Massachusetts, expressed the sentiment of the latter class very clearly when he said that one object of the bill under discussion was to impose a tax upon States in rebellion,—that our only authority for so doing was the Constitution of the United States,—and that we could only do it on the ground that the authority of the Government over those States is just as valid now as it was before the acts of secession were passed, and that every one of those acts is utterly null and void. No vote was taken which declared directly the opinion of the House on the theoretical question thus involved.

The employment of negroes as soldiers was subjected to a vigorous discussion, started on the 27th of January, by an amendment offered to a pending bill by Mr. Stevens, directing the President to raise, arm, and equip as many volunteers of African descent as he might deem useful, for such term of service as he might think proper, not exceeding five years,—to be officered by white or black persons in the President's discretion—slaves to be accepted as well as freemen. The members from the Border States opposed this proposition with great earnestness, as certain to do great harm to the Union cause among their constituents, by arousing prejudices which, whether reasonable or not, were very strong, and against which argument would be found utterly unavailing. Mr. Crittenden, of Kentucky, objected to it mainly because it would convert the war against the rebellion into a servile war, and establish abolition as the main end for which the war was carried on. Mr. Sedgwick, of New York, vindicated the policy suggested as having been dictated rather by necessity than choice. He pointed out the various steps by which the President, as the responsible head of the Government, had endeavored to prosecute the war successfully without interfering with slavery, and showed also how the refusal of the Rebel States to return to their allegiance had compelled him to advance, step by step, to the more rigorous and effective policy which had now become inevitable. After considerable further discussion, the bill, embodying substantially the amendment of Mr. Stevens, was passed; ayes 83, noes 54. On reaching the Senate it was referred to the Committee on Military Affairs, which, on the 12th of February, reported against its passage, on the ground that the authority which it was intended to confer upon the President was already sufficiently granted in the act of the previous session, approved July 17, 1862, which authorized the President to employ, in any military or naval service for which they might be found competent, persons of African descent.

One of the most important acts of the session was that which provided for the creation of a national force by enrolling and drafting the militia of the whole country,—each State being required to contribute its quota in the ratio of its population, and the whole force, when raised, to be under the control of the President. Some measure of the kind seemed to have been rendered absolutely necessary by the revival of party spirit throughout the loyal States, and by the active and effective efforts made by the Democratic party, emboldened by the results of the fall elections of 1862, to discourage and prevent volunteering. So successful had they been in this work, that the Government seemed likely to fail in its efforts to raise men for another campaign; and it was to avert this threatening evil that the bill in question was brought forward for the action of Congress. It encountered a violent resistance from the opposition party, and especially from those members whose sympathies with the secessionists were the most distinctly marked. But after the rejection of numerous amendments, more or less affecting its character and force, it was passed in the Senate, and taken up on the 23d of February in the House, where it encountered a similar ordeal. It contained various provisions for exempting from service persons upon whom others were most directly and entirely dependent for support,—such as the only son of a widow, the only son of aged and infirm parents who relied upon him for a maintenance, etc. It allowed drafted persons to procure substitutes; and, to cover the cases in which the prices of substitutes might become exorbitant, it also provided that upon payment of $300 the Government itself would procure a substitute, and release the person drafted from service. The bill was passed in the House with some amendments, by a vote of 115 to 49,—and the amendments being concurred in by the Senate, the bill became a law.

The finances of the country enlisted a good deal of attention during this session. It was necessary to provide in some way for the expenses of the war, and also for a currency; and two bills were accordingly introduced at an early stage of the session relating to these two subjects. The Financial bill, as finally passed by both houses, authorized the Secretary of the Treasury to borrow and issue bonds for $900,000,000, at not more than six per cent. interest, and payable at a time not less than ten nor more than forty years. It also authorized the Secretary to issue Treasury notes to the amount of $400,000,000, bearing interest, and also notes not bearing interest to the amount of $150,000,000. While this bill was pending, a joint resolution was passed by both houses, authorizing the issue of Treasury notes to the amount of $100,000,000 to meet the immediate wants of the soldiers and sailors in the service.

The President announced that he had signed this resolution in the following

MESSAGE.

To the Senate and House of Representatives:

I have signed the joint resolution to provide for the immediate payment of the army and navy of the United States, passed by the House of Representatives on the 14th, and by the Senate on the 15th inst. The joint resolution is a simple authority, amounting, however, under the existing circumstances, to a direction to the Secretary of the Treasury to make an additional issue of $100,000,000 in United States notes, if so much money is needed, for the payment of the army and navy. My approval is given in order that every possible facility may be afforded for the prompt discharge of all arrears of pay due to our soldiers and our sailors.

While giving this approval, however, I think it my duty to express my sincere regret that it has been found necessary to authorize so large an additional issue of United States notes, when this circulation, and that of the suspended banks together, have become already so redundant as to increase prices beyond real values, thereby augmenting the cost of living, to the injury of labor, and the cost of supplies—to the injury of the whole country. It seems very plain that continued issues of United States notes, without any check to the issues of suspended banks, and without adequate provision for the raising of money by loans, and for funding the issues, so as to keep them within due limits, must soon produce disastrous consequences; and this matter appears to me so important that I feel bound to avail myself of this occasion to ask the special attention of Congress to it.

That Congress has power to regulate the currency of the country can hardly admit of doubt, and that a judicious measure to prevent the deterioration of this currency, by a reasonable taxation of bank circulation, or otherwise, is needed, seems equally clear. Independently of this general consideration, it would be unjust to the people at large to exempt banks enjoying the special privilege of circulation, from their just proportion of the public burdens.

In order to raise money by way of loans most easily and cheaply, it is clearly necessary to give every possible support to the public credit. To that end, a uniform currency, in which taxes, subscriptions, loans, and all other ordinary public dues may be paid, is almost if not quite indispensable. Such a currency can be furnished by banking associations authorized under a general act of Congress, as suggested in my message at the beginning of the present session. The securing of this circulation by the pledge of the United States bonds, as herein suggested, would still further facilitate loans, by increasing the present and causing a future demand for such bonds.

In view of the actual financial embarrassments of the Government, and of the greater embarrassment sure to come if the necessary means of relief be not afforded, I feel that I should not perform my duty by a simple announcement of my approval of the joint resolution, which proposes relief only by increasing the circulation, without expressing my earnest desire that measures, such in substance as that I have just referred to, may receive the early sanction of Congress. By such measures, in my opinion, will payment be most certainly secured, not only to the army and navy, but to all honest creditors of the Government, and satisfactory provision made for future demands on the Treasury.

ABRAHAM LINCOLN.

The second bill—that to provide a national currency, secured by a pledge of United States stocks, and to provide for the circulation and redemption thereof, was passed in the Senate,—ayes 23, noes 21, and in the House, ayes 78, noes 64,—under the two-fold conviction that so long as the war continued the country must have a large supply of paper-money, and that it was also highly desirable that this money should be national in its character, and rest on the faith of the Government as its security.

Another act of importance, passed by Congress at this session, was the admission of Western Virginia into the Union. The Constitution of the United States declares that no new State shall be formed within the jurisdiction of any State without the consent of the Legislature of the State concerned, as well as of the Congress. The main question on which the admission of the new State turned, therefore, was whether that State had been formed with the consent of the Legislature of Virginia. The facts of the case were these: In the winter of 1860–61, the Legislature of Virginia, convened in extra session, had called a convention, to be held on the 14th of February, 1861, at Richmond, to decide on the question of secession. A vote was also to be taken, when the delegates to this convention should be elected, to decide whether an ordinance of secession, if passed by the convention, should be referred back to the people; and this was decided in the affirmative by a majority of nearly 60,000. The convention met, and an ordinance of secession was passed, and referred to the people at an election to be held on the fourth Tuesday of May. Without waiting for this vote, the authorities of the State levied war against the United States, joined the Rebel Confederacy, and invited the Confederate armies to occupy portions of their territory. A convention of nearly five hundred delegates, chosen in Western Virginia under a popular call, met early in May, declared the ordinance of secession null and void, and called another convention of delegates from all the counties of Virginia, to be held at Wheeling, on the 11th of June, in case the secession ordinance should be ratified by the popular vote. It was so ratified and the convention met. It proceeded on the assumption that the officers of the old government of the State had vacated their offices by joining the rebellion: and it accordingly proceeded to fill them, and to reorganize the gov ernment of the whole State. On the 20th of August the convention passed an ordinance to "provide for the formation of a new State out of a portion of the territory of this State." Under that ordinance, delegates were elected to a convention which met at Wheeling, November 26, and proceeded to draft a Constitution for the State of Western Virginia, as the new State was named, which was submitted to the people of Western Virginia in April, 1862, and by them ratified,—18,862 voting in favor of it, and 514 against it. The Legislature of Virginia, the members of which were elected by authority of the Wheeling convention of June 11th, met in extra session, called by the Governor appointed by that convention, on the 6th of May, 1862, and passed an act giving its consent to the formation of the new State, and making application to Congress for its admission into the Union. The question to be decided by Congress, therefore, was whether the legislature which met at Wheeling on the 11th of June was "the Legislature of Virginia," and thus competent to give its consent to the formation of a new State within the State of Virginia. The bill for admitting it, notwithstanding the opposition of several leading and influential Republicans, was passed in the House, ayes 96, noes 55. It passed in the Senate without debate, and was approved by the President on the 31st of December, 1862.

A bill was brought forward in the Senate for discussion on the 29th of January, proposing a grant of money to aid in the abolition of slavery in the State of Missouri. It gave rise to a good deal of debate, some Senators doubting whether Congress had any constitutional right to make such an appropriation, and a marked difference of opinion, moreover, growing up as to the propriety of gradual or immediate emancipation in that State. Mr. Sumner, Mr. Wilson, and several others, insisted that the aid proposed should be granted only on condition that emancipation should be immediate; while the Senators from Missouri thought that the State would be much more certain to provide for getting rid of slavery if the time were extended to twenty-three years, as the bill proposed, than if she were required to set free all her slaves at once. The Senators from the Slave States generally opposed the measure, on the ground that Congress had no authority under the Constitution to appropriate any portion of the public money for such a purpose. The bill was finally passed in the Senate, but it failed to pass the House.

Two members of Congress from the State of Louisiana were admitted to seats in the House of Representatives under circumstances which made that action of considerable importance. Immediately after the occupation of New Orleans by the national forces under General Butler, the President had appointed General Shepley military governor of the State of Louisiana. The rebel forces were driven out from the city of New Orleans, and some of the adjoining parishes; and when, during the ensuing summer, the people were invited to resume their allegiance to the Government of the United States, over 60,000 came forward, took the oath of allegiance, and were admitted to their rights as citizens. On the 3d of December General Shepley, acting as military governor of the State, ordered an election for members of Congress in the two districts into which the city of New Orleans is divided—each district embracing also some of the adjoining parishes. In one of these districts B. F. Flanders was elected, receiving 2,370 votes, and all others 273, and in the other Michael Hahn was elected, receiving 2,799 votes out of 5,117, the whole number cast. A committee of the House, to which the application of these gentlemen for admission to their seats had been referred, reported, on the 9th of February, in favor of their claim. It was represented in this report that the requirements of the Constitution of the State of Louisiana had in all respects been complied with, the only question being, whether a military governor, appointed by the President of the United

States, could properly and rightfully perform the functions of the civil governor of the State. The committee held that he could, and cited a decision of the Supreme Court of the United States, not only recognizing the power of the President to appoint a military governor, but also recognizing both his civil and military functions as of full validity and binding obligation. On the other hand, it was maintained that representatives can be elected to the Federal Legislature only in pursuance of an act of the State Legislature, or of an act of the Federal Congress. In this case neither of these requirements had been fulfilled. The House, however, admitted both these gentlemen to their seats, by a vote of 92 to 44.

Before adjourning, Congress passed an act, approved on the 3d of March, authorizing the President, "in all domestic and foreign wars," to issue to private armed vessels of the United States, letters of marque and reprisal,—said authority to terminate at the end of three years from the date of the act. Resolutions were also adopted, in both Houses, protesting against every proposition of foreign interference, by proffers of mediation or otherwise, as "unreasonable and inadmissible," and declaring the "unalterable purpose of the United States to prosecute the war until the rebellion shall be overcome." These resolutions, offered by Mr. Sumner, received in the Senate 31 votes in their favor, while but 5 were cast against them, and in the House 103 were given for their passage, and 28 against it.

The session closed on the 4th of March, 1863. Its proceedings had been marked by the same thorough and fixed determination to carry on the war, by the use of the most vigorous and effective measures for the suppression of the rebellion, and by the same full and prompt support of the President, which had characterized the preceding Congress.

While some members of the Administration party, becoming impatient of the delays which seemed to mark the progress of the war, were inclined to censure the caution of the President, and to insist upon bolder and more sweeping assaults upon the persons and property of the people of the Rebel States, and especially upon the institution of slavery—and while, on the other hand, its more open opponents denounced every thing like severity, as calculated to exasperate the South and prolong the war, the great body of the members, like the great body of the people, manifested a steady and firm reliance on the patriotic purpose and the calm sagacity evinced by the President in his conduct of public affairs.

CHAPTER VIII.

ARBITRARY ARRESTS.—THE SUSPENSION OF THE WRIT OF HABEAS CORPUS.—THE DRAFT.

At the very outbreak of the rebellion, the Administration was compelled to face one of the most formidable of the many difficulties which have embarrassed its action. Long before the issue had been distinctly made by the rebels in the Southern States, while under the protecting toleration of Mr. Buchanan's administration the conspirators were making preparations for armed resistance to the Government of the United States, evidences were not wanting that they relied upon the active co-operation of men and parties in the Northern States, whose political sympathies had always been in harmony with their principles and their action. As early as in January, 1861, while the rebels were diligently and actively collecting arms and other munitions of war, by purchase in the Northern States, for the contest on which they had resolved, Fernando Wood, then Mayor of New York, had apologized to Senator Toombs, of Georgia, for the seizure by the police of New York of "arms intended for and consigned to the State of Georgia," and had assured him that "if he had the power he should summarily punish the authors of this illegal and unjustifiable seizure of private property." The departments at Washington, the army and the navy, all places of responsibility and trust under the Government, and all departments of civil and political activity in the Northern States, were found to be largely filled by persons in active sympathy with the secession movement, and ready at all times to give it all the aid and comfort in their power. Upon the advent of the new Administration, and when active measures began to be taken for the suppression of the rebellion, the Government found its plans betrayed and its movements thwarted at every turn. Prominent presses and politicians, moreover, throughout the country, began, by active hostility, to indicate their sympathy with those who sought, under cover of opposition to the Administration, to overthrow the Government, and it became speedily manifest that there was sufficient of treasonable sentiment throughout the North to paralyze the authorities in their efforts, aided only by the ordinary machinery of the law, to crush the secession movement.

Under these circumstances it was deemed necessary to resort to the exercise of the extraordinary powers with which, in extraordinary emergencies, the Constitution had clothed the Government. That instrument had provided that "the privilege of the writ of *habeas corpus* should not be suspended; unless when, in cases of rebellion or invasion, the public safety might require it." By necessary implication, whenever, in such cases either of rebellion or invasion, the public safety *did* require it, the privilege of that writ might be suspended; and, from the very necessity of the case, the Government which was charged with the care of the public safety, was empowered to judge when the contingency should occur. The only question that remained was, *which department* of the Government was to meet this responsibility. If the act was one of legislation, it could only be performed by Congress and the President; if it was in its nature executive, then it might be performed, the emergency requiring it, by the President alone. The pressing emergency of the case, moreover, went far towards dictating the decision. Congress had adjourned on the 4th of March, and could not be again assembled for some months; and infinite, and perhaps fatal mischief might be done during the interval, if the Northern allies of the rebellion were allowed with impunity to prosecute their plans.

Under the influence of these considerations the President, in his proclamation of the 3d of May, 1861, directing the commander of the forces of the United States on the Florida coast to permit no person to exercise any authority upon the islands of Key West, the Tortugas, and Santa Rosa, which might be inconsistent with the authority of the United States, also authorized him, "if he should find it necessary, to suspend the writ of *habeas corpus*, and to remove from the vicinity of the United States fortresses all dangerous or suspected persons." This was the first act of the Administration in that direction; but it was very soon found necessary to resort to the exercise of the same powers in other sections of the country. On the 25th of May, John Merryman, a resident of Hayfield, in Baltimore County, Maryland, known by the Government to be in communication with the rebels, and to be giving them aid and comfort, was arrested and imprisoned in Fort McHenry, then commanded by General Cadwallader. On the same day he forwarded a petition to Roger B. Taney, Chief-Justice of the United States, reciting the circumstances of his arrest, and praying for the issue of the writ of *habeas corpus*. The writ was forthwith issued, and General Cadwallader was ordered to bring the body of Merryman before the Chief-Justice on the 27th. On that day Colonel Lee presented a written communication from General Cadwallader, stating that Merryman had been arrested and committed to his custody by officers acting under the authority of the United States, charged with various acts of treason, with holding a commission as lieutenant in a company avowing its purpose of armed hostility against the Government, and with having made often and unreserved declarations of his association with this armed force, and of his readiness to co-operate with those engaged in the present rebellion against the Government of the United States. The General added that he was "duly authorized by the President of the United States to suspend the writ of *habeas corpus* for the public safety;" and that, while he fully appreciated the delicacy of the trust, he was also instructed "that, in times of civil strife, errors, if any, should be on the side of safety to the country." The commanding General accordingly declined to obey the writ, whereupon an attachment was forthwith issued against him for contempt of court, made returnable at noon on the next day. On that day, the marshal charged with serving the attachment made return that he was not admitted within the fortress, and had consequently been unable to serve the writ. The Chief-Justice, thereupon, read an opinion that the President could not suspend the writ of *habeas corpus*, nor authorize any military officer to do so, and that a military officer had no right to arrest any person, not subject to the rules and articles of war, for an offence against the laws of the United States, except in aid of the judicial authority, and subject to its control. The Chief-Justice stated further, that the marshal had the power to summon out the *posse comitatus* to enforce the service of the writ, but as it was apparent that it would be resisted by a force notoriously superior, the Court could do nothing further in the premises.

On the 12th of May, another writ was issued by Judge Giles, of Baltimore, to Major Morris, of the United States Artillery, at Fort McHenry, who, in a letter dated the 14th, refused to obey the writ, because at the time it was issued, and for two weeks previous, the city of Baltimore had been completely under the control of the rebel authorities—United States soldiers had been murdered in the streets—the intention to capture that fort had been openly proclaimed, and the Legislature of the State was at that moment debating the question of making war upon the Government of the United States. All this, in his judgment, constituted a case of rebellion, and afforded sufficient legal cause for suspending the writ of *habeas corpus*. Similar cases arose, and were disposed of in a similar manner, in other sections of the country.

The Governor of Virginia had proposed to Mr. G. Heincken, of New York, the agent of the New York and Virginia Steamship Company, payment for two steamers of that line, the Yorktown and Jamestown, which he had seized for the rebel service, an acceptance of which proffer, Mr. Heincken was informed, would be treated as an act of treason to the Government; and on his application, Mr. Seward, the Secretary of State, gave him the following reasons for this decision:

An insurrection has broken out in several of the States of this Union, including Virginia, designed to overthrow the Government of the United States. The executive authorities of that State are parties to that insurrection, and so are public enemies. Their action in seizing or buying vessels to be employed in executing that design, is not merely without authority of law, but is treason. It is treason for any person to give aid and comfort to public enemies. To sell vessels to them which it is their purpose to use as ships of war, is to give them aid and comfort. To receive money from them in payment for vessels which they have seized for those purposes, would be to attempt to convert the unlawful seizure into a sale, and would subject the party so offending to the pains and penalties of treason, and the Government would not hesitate to bring the offender to punishment.

These acts and decisions of the Government were vehemently assailed by the party opponents of the Administration, and led to the most violent and intemperate assaults upon the Government in many of the public prints. Some of these journals were refused the privilege of the public mails, the Government not holding itself under any obligation to aid in circulating assaults upon its own authority, and stringent restrictions were placed upon the transmission of intelligence by telegraph. On the 5th of July, 1862, Attorney-General Bates transmitted to the President an elaborate opinion, prepared at his request, upon his power to make arrests of persons known to have criminal intercourse with the insurgents, or against whom there is probable cause for suspicion of such criminal complicity,—and also upon his right to refuse to obey a writ of *habeas corpus* in case of such arrests. The Attorney-General discussed the subject at considerable length, and reached a conclusion favorable to the action of the Government. From that time forward the Government exerted, with vigor and energy, all the power thus placed in its hands to prevent the rebellion from receiving aid from those in sympathy with its objects in the Northern States. A large number of persons, believed to be in complicity with the insurgents, were placed in arrest, but were released upon taking an oath of allegiance to the United States. Baltimore continued for some time to be the head-quarters of conspiracies and movements of various kinds in aid of the rebellion, and the arrests were consequently more numerous there than elsewhere. Indeed, very strenuous efforts were made throughout the summer to induce some action on the part of the Legislature which should place the State in alliance with the rebel Confederacy, and it was confidently believed that an ordinance looking to this end would be passed at the extra session which was convened for the 17th of September; but on the 16th nine secession members of the House of Delegates, with the officers of both houses, were arrested by General McClellan, then in command of the army, who expressed his full approbation of the proceedings, and the session was not held.

The President at the time gave the following statement of his views in regard to these arrests:

The public safety renders it necessary that the grounds of these arrests should at present be withheld, but at the proper time they will be made public. Of one thing the people of Maryland may rest assured, that no arrest has been made, or will be made, not based on substantial and unmistakable complicity with those in armed rebellion against the Government of the United States. In no case has an arrest been made on mere suspicion, or through personal or partisan animosities, but in all cases the Government is in possession of tangible and unmistakable evidence, which will, when made public, be satisfactory to every loyal citizen.

Arrests continued to be made under authority of the State Department, not without complaint, certainly, from large numbers of the people, but with the general acquiescence of the whole community, and beyond all question greatly to the advantage of the Government and the country. On the 14th of February, 1862, an order was issued on the subject, which transferred control of the whole matter to the War Department. The circumstances which had made these arrests necessary are stated with so much clearness and force in that order, that we insert it at length as follows:

EXECUTIVE ORDERS IN RELATION TO STATE PRISONERS.

WAR DEPARTMENT, WASHINGTON, *Feb.* 14.

The breaking out of a formidable insurrection, based on a conflict of political ideas, being an event without precedent in the United States, was necessarily attended by great confusion and perplexity of the public mind. Disloyalty, before unsuspected, suddenly became bold, and treason astonished the world by bringing at once into the field military forces superior in numbers to the standing army of the United States.

Every department of the Government was paralyzed by treason. Defection appeared in the Senate, in the House of Representatives, in the Cabinet, in the Federal Courts; Ministers and Consuls returned from foreign countries to enter the insurrectionary councils, or land or naval forces; commanding and other officers of the army and in the navy betrayed the councils or deserted their posts for commands in the insurgent forces. Treason was flagrant in the revenue and in the post-office service, as well as in the territorial governments and in the Indian reserves.

Not only Governors, Judges, Legislators, and ministerial officers in the States, but even whole States, rushed, one after another, with apparent unanimity, into rebellion. The capital was besieged and its connection with all the States cut off.

Even in the portions of the country which were most loyal, political combinations and secret societies were formed furthering the work of disunion, while, from motives of disloyalty or cupidity, or from excited passions or perverted sympathies, individuals were found furnishing men, money, and materials of war and supplies to the insurgents' military and naval forces. Armies, ships, fortifications, navy yards, arsenals, military posts and garrisons, one after another, were betrayed or abandoned to the insurgents.

Congress had not anticipated and so had not provided for the emergency. The municipal authorities were powerless and inactive. The judicial machinery seemed as if it had been designed not to sustain the Government, but to embarrass and betray it.

Foreign intervention, openly invited and industriously instigated by the abetters of the insurrection, became imminent, and has only been prevented by the practice of strict and impartial justice with the most perfect moderation in our intercourse with nations.

The public mind was alarmed and apprehensive, though fortunately not distracted or disheartened. It seemed to be doubtful whether the Federal Government, which one year before had been thought a model worthy of universal acceptance, had indeed the ability to defend and maintain itself.

Some reverses, which perhaps were unavoidable, suffered by newly levied and inefficient forces, discouraged the loyal, and gave new hopes to the insurgents. Voluntary enlistments seemed about to cease, and desertions commenced. Parties speculated upon the question whether conscription had not become necessary to fill up the armies of the United States.

In this emergency the President felt it his duty to employ with energy the extraordinary powers which the Constitution confides to him in cases of insurrection. He called into the field such military and naval forces, unauthorized by the existing laws, as seemed necessary. He directed measures to prevent the use of the post-office for treasonable correspondence. He subjected passengers to and from foreign countries to new passport regulations, and he instituted a blockade, suspended the writ of *habeas corpus* in various places, and caused persons who were represented to him as being or about to engage in disloyal and treasonable practices to be arrested by special civil as well as military agencies, and detained in military custody, when necessary, to prevent them and deter others from such practices. Examinations of such cases were instituted, and some of the persons so arrested have been discharged from time to time, under circumstances or upon conditions compatible, as was thought, with the public safety.

Meantime a favorable change of public opinion has occurred. The line between loyalty and disloyalty is plainly defined; the whole structure of the Government is firm and stable; apprehensions of public danger and facilities for treasonable practices have diminished with the passions which prompted heedless persons to adopt them. The insurrection is believed to have culminated and to be declining.

The President, in view of these facts, and anxious to favor a return to the normal course of the Administration, as far as regard for the public welfare will allow, directs that all political prisoners or State prisoners now held in military custody, be released on their subscribing to a parole engaging them to render no aid or comfort to the enemies in hostility to the United States.

The Secretary of War will, however, at his discretion, except from the effect of this order any persons detained as spies in the service of the insurgents, or others whose release at the present moment may be deemed incompatible with the public safety.

To all persons who shall be so released, and who shall keep their parole, the President grants an amnesty for any past offences of treason or disloyalty which they may have committed.

Extraordinary arrests will hereafter be made under the direction of the military authorities alone.

By order of the President:

EDWIN M. STANTON, *Secretary of War.*

On the 27th of the same month, a Commission was appointed by the War Department, consisting of Major-General Dix and Hon. Edwards Pierrepont, of New York, to examine into the cases of the State prisoners then remaining in custody, and to determine whether, in view of the public safety and the existing rebellion, they should be discharged, or remain in arrest, or be remitted to the civil tribunals for trial. These gentlemen entered at once upon the discharge of their duties, and a large number of prisoners were released from custody on taking the oath of allegiance. Wherever the public safety seemed to require it, however, arrests continued to be made—the President, in every instance, assuming all the responsibility of these acts, and throwing himself upon the Courts and the judgment of the country for his vindication. But the President himself had not up to this time directed any general suspension of the writ of *habeas corpus*, or given any public notice of the rules by which the Government would be guided in its action upon cases that might arise. It was left to the Secretary of War to decide in what instances and for what causes arrests should be made, and the privilege of the writ should be suspended. In some of the Courts into which these cases were brought, the ground was accordingly taken that, although the President might have authority under the Constitution, when, in cases of rebellion or invasion, the public safety should require it, to suspend the writ, he could not delegate that authority to any subordinate. To meet this case, therefore, the President, on the 24th of September, 1862, issued the following

PROCLAMATION.

Whereas, it has been necessary to call into service, not only volunteers, but also portions of the militia of the States by draft, in order to suppress the insurrection existing in the United States, and disloyal persons are not adequately restrained by the ordinary processes of law from hindering this measure, and from giving aid and comfort in various ways to the insurrection,

Now, therefore, be it ordered—

First, That during the existing insurrection, and as a necessary measure for suppressing the same, all rebels and insurgents, their aiders and abettors, within the United States, and all persons discouraging volunteer enlistments, resisting military drafts, or guilty of any disloyal practice affording aid and comfort to the rebels against the authority of the United States, shall be subject to martial law, and liable to trial and punishment by courts-martial or military commission.

Second, That the writ of *habeas corpus* is suspended in respect to all persons arrested, or who are now, or hereafter during the rebellion shall be, imprisoned in any fort, camp, arsenal, military prison, or other place of confinement, by any military authority, or by the sentence of any court-martial or military commission.

action in the public mind, and had so far relieved the Administration from apprehension as to warrant the promulgation of the following order:

WAR DEPARTMENT, WASHINGTON, *Nov.* 22, 1862.

Ordered—1. That all persons now in military custody, who have been arrested for discouraging volunteer enlistments, opposing the draft, or for otherwise giving aid and comfort to the enemy, in States where the draft has been made, or the quota of volunteers and militia has been furnished, shall be discharged from further military restraint.

2. The persons who, by the authority of the military commander or governor in rebel States, have been arrested and sent from such State for disloyalty or hostility to the Government of the United States, and are now in military custody, may also be discharged upon giving their parole to do no act of hostility against the Government of the United States, nor render aid to its enemies. But all such persons shall remain subject to military surveillance and liable to arrest on breach of their parole. And if any such persons shall prefer to leave the loyal States on condition of their not returning again during the war, or until special leave for that purpose be obtained from the President, then such person shall, at his option, be released and depart from the United States, or be conveyed beyond the military lines of the United States forces.

3. This order shall not operate to discharge any person who has been in arms against the Government, or by force and arms has resisted or attempted to resist the draft, nor relieve any person from liability to trial and punishment by civil tribunals, or by court-martial or military commission, who may be amenable to such tribunals for offences committed.

By order of the Secretary of War:

E. D. TOWNSEND, *Assistant Adjutant-General.*

During the succeeding winter, while Congress was in session, public sentiment was comparatively at rest on this subject. Congress had enacted a law, sanctioning the action of the President in suspending the writ of *habeas corpus*, and clothing him with full authority to check and punish all attempts to defeat the efforts of the Government in the prosecution of the war. After the adjournment, however, when the political activity of the country was transferred from the action in the public mind, and had so far relieved the Administration from apprehension as to warrant the promulgation of the following order:

WAR DEPARTMENT, WASHINGTON, *Nov.* 22, 1862.

Ordered—1. That all persons now in military custody, who have been arrested for discouraging volunteer enlistments, opposing the draft, or for otherwise giving aid and comfort to the enemy, in States where the draft has been made, or the quota of volunteers and militia has been furnished, shall be discharged from further military restraint.

2. The persons who, by the authority of the military commander or governor in rebel States, have been arrested and sent from such State for disloyalty or hostility to the Government of the United States, and are now in military custody, may also be discharged upon giving their parole to do no act of hostility against the Government of the United States, nor render aid to its enemies. But all such persons shall remain subject to military surveillance and liable to arrest on breach of their parole. And if any such persons shall prefer to leave the loyal States on condition of their not returning again during the war, or until special leave for that purpose be obtained from the President, then such person shall, at his option, be released and depart from the United States, or be conveyed beyond the military lines of the United States forces.

3. This order shall not operate to discharge any person who has been in arms against the Government, or by force and arms has resisted or attempted to resist the draft, nor relieve any person from liability to trial and punishment by civil tribunals, or by court-martial or military commission, who may be amenable to such tribunals for offences committed.

By order of the Secretary of War:

E. D. TOWNSEND, *Assistant Adjutant-General.*

During the succeeding winter, while Congress was in session, public sentiment was comparatively at rest on this subject. Congress had enacted a law, sanctioning the action of the President in suspending the writ of *habeas corpus*, and clothing him with full authority to check and punish all attempts to defeat the efforts of the Government in the prosecution of the war. After the adjournment, however, when the political activity of the country was transferred from the

Capital to the people in their respective localities, the party agitation was revived, and public meetings were again held to denounce the conduct of the Government, and to protest against the further prosecution of the war. One of the most active of these advocates of peace with the rebel Confederacy was Hon. C. L. Vallandigham, a member of Congress from Ohio, who had steadily opposed all measures for the prosecution of the war throughout the session. After the adjournment he made a political canvass of his district, and in a speech at Mount Vernon, on the 1st of May, he denounced the Government at Washington as aiming, in the conduct of the war, not to restore the Union, but to crush out liberty and establish a despotism. He declared that the war was waged for the freedom of the blacks and the enslaving of the whites—that the Government could have had peace long before if it had desired it—that the mediation of France ought to have been accepted, and that the Government had deliberately rejected propositions by which the Southern States could have been brought back to the Union. He also denounced an order, No. 38, issued by General Burnside, in command of the Department, forbidding certain disloyal practices, and giving notice that persons declaring sympathy for the enemy would be arrested for trial, proclaimed his intention to disobey it, and called on the people who heard him to resist and defeat its execution.

For this speech Mr. Vallandigham was arrested, by order of General Burnside, on the 4th of May, and ordered for trial before a court-martial at Cincinnati. On the 5th, he applied, through his counsel, Senator Pugh, to the Circuit Court of the United States for a writ of *habeas corpus*. In reply to this application, a letter was read from General Burnside, setting forth the considerations which had led him to make the arrest, and Vallandigham's counsel was then heard in a very long argument on the case. Judge Stewart pronounced his decision, *refusing* the writ, on the ground that the action of General Burnside was necessary for the public safety. "The legality of the arrest," said the judge, "depends upon the extent of the necessity for making it, and that was to be determined by the military commander." And he adds:

Men should know and lay the truth to heart, that there is a course of conduct not involving overt treason, and not therefore subject to punishment as such, which, nevertheless, implies moral guilt, and a gross offence against the country. Those who live under the protection and enjoy the blessings of our benignant Government, must learn that they cannot stab its vitals with impunity. If they cherish hatred and hostility to it, and desire its subversion, let them withdraw from its jurisdiction, and seek the fellowship and protection of those with whom they are in sympathy. If they remain with us, while they are not of us, they must be subject to such a course of dealing as the great law of self-preservation prescribes and will enforce. And let them not complain if the stringent doctrine of military necessity should find them to be the legitimate subjects of its action. I have no fear that the recognition of this doctrine will lead to an arbitrary invasion of the personal security, or personal liberty, of the citizen. It is rare indeed that a charge of disloyalty will be made on insufficient grounds. But if there should be an occasional mistake, such an occurrence is not to be put in competition with the preservation of the nation; and I confess I am but little moved by the eloquent appeals of those who, while they indignantly denounce violation of personal liberty, look with no horror upon a despotism as unmitigated as the world has ever witnessed.

The military commission, before which Vallandigham was ordered for trial, met on the 6th, found him guilty of the principal offences charged, and sentenced him to be placed in close confinement in some fortress of the United States, to be designated by the commanding officer of that Department. Major-General Burnside approved the sentence, and designated Fort Warren, in Boston harbor, as the place of confinement. The President modified this sentence by directing that, instead of being imprisoned, Mr. Vallandigham should be sent within the rebel lines, and should not return to the United

States until after the termination of the war. This sentence was at once carried into execution.

The arrest, trial, and sentence of Mr. Vallandigham created a good deal of excitement throughout the country. The opponents of the Administration treated it as a case of martyrdom, and held public meetings for the purpose of denouncing the action of the Government as tyrannical and highly dangerous to the public liberties. One of the earliest of these demonstrations was held at Albany, on the 16th of May, at which Hon. Erastus Corning presided, and to which Governor Seymour addressed a letter, expressing in the strongest terms his condemnation of the course pursued by the Government. "If this proceeding," said he, speaking of the arrest of Vallandigham, "is approved by the Government, and sanctioned by the people, it is not merely a step towards revolution,—it is revolution. It will not only lead to military despotism,—it establishes military despotism. In this aspect it must be accepted, or in this aspect rejected. * * The people of this country now wait with the deepest anxiety the decision of the Administration upon these acts. Having given it a generous support in the conduct of the war, we pause to see what kind of a government it is for which we are asked to pour out our blood and our treasure. The action of the Administration will determine, in the minds of more than one-half of the people of the loyal States, whether this war is waged to put down rebellion at the South, or destroy free institutions at the North." The resolutions which were adopted at this meeting pledged the Democratic party of the State to the preservation of the Union, but condemned in strong terms the whole system of arbitrary arrests, and the suspension of the writ of *habeas corpus*.

A copy of these resolutions was forwarded by the presiding officer to President LINCOLN, who sent the following letter in reply:

EXECUTIVE MANSION, WASHINGTON, *June* 13, 1863.

HON. ERASTUS CORNING AND OTHERS:

Gentlemen: Your letter of May 19, inclosing the resolutions of a public meeting held at Albany, N. Y., on the 16th of the same month, was received several days ago.

The resolutions, as I understand them, are resolvable into two propositions—first, the expression of a purpose to sustain the cause of the Union, to secure peace through victory, and to support the Administration in every constitutional and lawful measure to suppress the rebellion; and, secondly, a declaration of censure upon the Administration for supposed unconstitutional action, such as the making of military arrests. And from the two propositions a third is deduced, which is, that the gentlemen composing the meeting are resolved on doing their part to maintain our common Government and country, despite the folly or wickedness, as they may conceive, of any Administration. This position is eminently patriotic, and as such I thank the meeting and congratulate the nation for it. My own purpose is the same, so that the meeting and myself have a common object, and can have no difference, except in the choice of means or measures for effecting that object.

And here I ought to close this paper, and would close it, if there were no apprehension that more injurious consequences than any merely personal to myself might follow the censures systematically cast upon me for doing what, in my view of duty, I could not forbear. The resolutions promise to support me in every constitutional and lawful measure to suppress the rebellion, and I have not knowingly employed, nor shall knowingly employ, any other. But the meeting, by their resolutions, assert and argue that certain military arrests, and proceedings following them, for which I am ultimately responsible, are unconstitutional. I think they are not. The resolutions quote from the Constitution the definition of treason, and also the limiting safeguards and guarantees therein provided for the citizen on trial for treason, and on his being held to answer for capital, or otherwise infamous crimes, and, in criminal prosecutions, his right to a speedy and public trial by an impartial jury. They proceed to resolve, "that these safeguards of the rights of the citizen against the pretensions of arbitrary power were intended more *especially* for his protection in times of civil commotion."

And, apparently to demonstrate the proposition, the resolutions proceed: "They were secured substantially to the English people *after* years of protracted civil war, and were adopted into our Constitution at the *close* of the Revolution." Would not the demonstration have been better if it could have been truly said that these safeguards had been adopted and applied *during* the civil wars and *during* our Revolution, instead of *after* the one and at the *close* of the other? I, too, am devotedly for them *after* civil war, and *before* civil war, and at all times, "except when, in cases of rebellion or invasion, the public safety may require" their suspension. The resolutions proceed to tell us that these safeguards "have stood the test of seventy-six years of trial, under our republican system, under circumstances which show that, while they constitute the foundation of all free government, they are the elements of the enduring stability of the Republic." No one denies that they have so stood the test up to the beginning of the present rebellion, if we except a certain occurrence at New Orleans; nor does any one question that they will stand the same test much longer after the rebellion closes. But these provisions of the Constitution have no application to the case we have in hand, because the arrests complained of were not made for treason—that is, not for *the* treason defined in the Constitution, and upon conviction of which the punishment is death—nor yet were they made to hold persons to answer for any capital or otherwise infamous crimes; nor were the proceedings following, in any constitutional or legal sense, "criminal prosecutions." The arrests were made on totally different grounds, and the proceedings following accorded with the grounds of the arrest. Let us consider the real case with which we are dealing, and apply to it the parts of the Constitution plainly made for such cases.

Prior to my installation here, it had been inculcated that any State had a lawful right to secede from the national Union, and that it would be expedient to exercise the right whenever the devotees of the doctrine should fail to elect a President to their own liking. I was elected contrary to their liking, and accordingly, so far as it was legally possible, they had taken seven States out of the Union, had seized many of the United States forts, and had fired upon the United States flag, all before I was inaugurated, and, of course, before I had done any official act whatever. The rebellion thus began soon ran into the present civil war; and, in certain respects, it began on very unequal terms between the parties. The insurgents had been preparing for it more than thirty years, while the Government had taken no steps to resist them. The former had carefully considered all the means which could be turned to their account. It undoubtedly was a well-pondered reliance with them that, in their own unrestricted efforts to destroy Union, Constitution, and law altogether, the Government would, in great degree, be restrained by the same Constitution and law from arresting their progress. Their sympathizers pervaded all departments of the Government, and nearly all communities of the people. From this material, under cover of "liberty of speech," "liberty of the press," and "habeas corpus," they hoped to keep on foot among us a most efficient corps of spies, informers, suppliers, and aiders and abettors of their cause in a thousand ways. They knew that in times such as they were inaugurating, by the Constitution itself, the "habeas corpus" might be suspended; but they also knew they had friends who would make a question as to *who* was to suspend it: meanwhile, their spies and others might remain at large to help on their cause. Or if, as has happened, the Executive should suspend the writ, without ruinous waste of time, instances of arresting innocent persons might occur, as are always likely to occur in such cases, and then a clamor could be raised in regard to this which might be, at least, of some service to the insurgent cause. It needed no very keen perception to discover this part of the enemy's programme, so soon as, by open hostilities, their machinery was put fairly in motion. Yet, thoroughly imbued with a reverence for the guaranteed rights of individuals, I was slow to adopt the strong measures which by degrees I have been forced to regard as being within the exceptions of the Constitution, and as indispensable to the public safety. Nothing is better known to history than that courts of justice are utterly incompetent to such cases. Civil courts are organized chiefly for trials of individuals, or, at most, a few individuals acting in concert, and this in quiet times, and on charges of crimes well defined in the law. Even in times of peace, bands of horse-thieves and robbers frequently grow too numerous and powerful for the ordinary courts of justice. But what comparison, in numbers, have such bands ever borne to the insurgent sympathizers even in many of the loyal States? Again, a jury too frequently has at least one member more ready to hang the panel than to hang the traitor. And yet, again, he who dissuades one man from volunteering, or induces one soldier to desert, weakens the Union cause as much as he who kills a Union soldier in battle. Yet this dissuasion or inducement may be so conducted as to be no defined crime of which any civil court would take cognizance.

Ours is a case of rebellion—so called by the resolution before me—in fact, a clear, flagrant, and gigantic case of rebellion; and the provision of the Constitution that "the privilege of the writ of *habeas corpus* shall not be suspended unless when, in cases of rebellion or invasion, the public safety may require it," is *the* provision which specially applies to our present case. This provision plainly attests the understanding of those who made the Constitution, that ordinary courts of justice are inadequate to "cases of rebellion"—attests their purpose that, in such cases, men may be held in custody whom the courts, acting on ordinary rules, would discharge. *Habeas corpus* does not discharge men who are proved to be guilty of defined crime; and its suspension is allowed by the Constitution on purpose that men may be arrested and held who cannot be proved to be guilty of defined crime, "when, in cases of rebellion or invasion, the public safety may require it." This is precisely our present case—a case of rebellion, wherein the public safety *does* require the suspension. Indeed, arrests by process of courts, and arrests in cases of rebellion, do not proceed altogether upon the same basis. The former is directed at the small percentage of ordinary and continuous perpetration of crime; while the latter is directed at sudden and extensive uprisings against the Government, which at most will succeed or fail in no great length of time. In the latter case arrests are made, not so much for what has been done as for what probably would be done. The latter is more for the preventive and less for the vindictive than the former. In such cases the purposes of men are much more easily understood than in cases of ordinary crime. The man who stands by and says nothing when the peril of his Government is discussed, cannot be misunderstood. If not hindered, he is sure to help the enemy; much more, if he talks ambiguously—talks for his country with "buts," and "ifs" and "ands." Of how little value the constitutional provisions I have quoted will be rendered, if arrests shall never be made until defined crimes shall have been committed, may be illustrated by a few notable examples. Gen. John C. Breckinridge, Gen. Robert E. Lee, Gen. Joseph E. Johnston, Gen. John B. Magruder, Gen. William B. Preston, Gen. Simon D. Buckner, and Commodore Franklin Buchanan, now occupying the very highest places in the rebel war service, were all within the power of the Government since the rebellion began, and were nearly as well known to be traitors then as now. Unquestionably, if we had seized and held them, the insurgent cause would be much weaker. But no one of them had then committed any crime defined in the law. Every one of them, if arrested, would have been discharged on *habeas corpus*, were the writ allowed to operate. In view of these and similar cases, I think the time not unlikely to come when I shall be blamed for having made too few arrests rather than too many.

By the third resolution, the meeting indicate their opinion that military arrests may be constitutional in localities where rebellion actually exists, but that such arrests are unconstitutional in localities where rebellion or insurrection does *not* actually exist. They insist that such arrests shall not be made "outside of the lines of necessary military occupation and the scenes of insurrection." Inasmuch, however, as the Constitution itself makes no such distinction, I am unable to believe that there *is* any such constitutional distinction. I concede that the class of arrests complained of can be constitutional only when, in cases of rebellion or invasion, the public safety may require them; and I insist that in such cases they are constitutional *wherever* the public safety does require them; as well in places to which they may prevent the rebellion extending as in those where it may be already prevailing; as well where they may restrain mischievous interference with the raising and supplying of armies to suppress the rebellion, as where the rebellion may actually be; as well where they may restrain the enticing men out of the army, as where they would prevent mutiny in the army; equally constitutional at all places where they will conduce to the public safety, as against the dangers of rebellion or invasion. Take the particular case mentioned by the meeting. It is asserted, in substance, that Mr. Vallandigham was, by a military commander, seized and tried "for no other reason than words addressed to a public meeting, in criticism of the course of the Administration, and in condemnation of the military orders of the general." Now, if there be no mistake about this; if this assertion is the truth and the whole truth; if there was no other reason for the arrest, then I concede that the arrest was wrong. But the arrest, as I understand, was made for a very different reason. Mr. Vallandigham avows his hostility to the war on the part of the Union; and his arrest was made because he was laboring, with some effect, to prevent the raising of troops; to encourage desertions from the army; and to leave the rebellion without an adequate military force to suppress it. He was not arrested because he was damaging the political prospects of the Administration, or the personal interests of the commanding general, but because he was damaging the army, upon the existence and vigor of which the life of the nation depends. He was warring upon the military, and this gave the military constitutional jurisdiction to lay hands upon him. If Mr. Vallandigham was not damaging the military power of the country, then this arrest was made on mistake of fact, which I would be glad to correct on reasonably satisfactory evidence.

I understand the meeting, whose resolutions I am considering, to be in favor of suppressing the rebellion by military force—by armies. Long experience has shown that armies cannot be maintained unless desertions shall be punished by the severe penalty of death. The case requires, and the law and the Constitution sanction, this punishment. Must I shoot a simple-minded soldier boy who deserts, while I must not touch a hair of a wily agitator who induces him to desert? This is none the less injurious when effected by getting a father, or brother, or friend, into a public meeting, and there working upon his feelings till he is persuaded to write the soldier boy that he is fighting in a bad cause, for a wicked Administration of a contemptible Government, too weak to arrest and punish him if he shall desert. I think that in such a case to silence the agitator and save the boy is not only constitutional, but withal a great mercy.

If I be wrong on this question of constitutional power, my error lies in believing that certain proceedings are constitutional when, in cases of rebellion or invasion, the public safety requires them, which would not be constitutional when, in the absence of rebellion or invasion, the public safety does *not* require them; in other words, that the Constitution is not, in its application, in all respects the same, in cases of rebellion or invasion involving the public safety, as it is in time of profound peace and public security. The Constitution itself makes the distinction; and I can no more be persuaded that the Government can constitutionally take no strong measures in time of rebellion, because it can be shown that the same could not be lawfully taken in time of peace, than I can be persuaded that a particular drug is not good medicine for a sick man, because it can be shown not to be good food for a well one. Nor am I able to appreciate the danger apprehended by the meeting that the American people will, by means of military arrests during the rebellion, lose the right of public discussion, the liberty of speech and the press, the law of evidence, trial by jury, and *habeas corpus*, throughout the indefinite peaceful future, which I trust lies before them, any more than I am able to believe that a man could contract so strong an appetite for emetics during temporary illness as to persist in feeding upon them during the remainder of his healthful life.

In giving the resolutions that earnest consideration which you request of me, I cannot overlook the fact that the meeting speak as "Democrats." Nor can I, with full respect for their known intelligence, and the fairly presumed deliberation with which they prepared their resolutions, be permitted to suppose that this occurred by accident, or in any way other than that they preferred to designate themselves

"Democrats" rather than "American citizens." In this time of national peril, I would have preferred to meet you on a level one step higher than any party platform; because I am sure that, from such more elevated position, we could do better battle for the country we all love than we possibly can from those lower ones where, from the force of habit, the prejudices of the past, and selfish hopes of the future, we are sure to expend much of our ingenuity and strength in finding fault with and aiming blows at each other. But, since you have denied me this, I will yet be thankful, for the country's sake, that not all Democrats have done so. He on whose discretionary judgment Mr. Vallandigham was arrested and tried is a Democrat, having no old party affinity with me; and the judge who rejected the constitutional view expressed in these resolutions, by refusing to discharge Mr. Vallandigham on *habeas corpus*, is a Democrat of better days than these, having received his judicial mantle at the hands of President Jackson. And still more, of all those Democrats who are nobly exposing their lives and shedding their blood on the battle field, I have learned that many approve the course taken with Mr. Vallandigham, while I have not heard of a single one condemning it. I cannot assert that there are none such. And the name of Jackson recalls an incident of pertinent history: After the battle of New Orleans, and while the fact that the treaty of peace had been concluded was well known in the city, but before official knowledge of it had arrived, General Jackson still maintained martial or military law. Now that it could be said the war was over, the clamor against martial law, which had existed from the first, grew more furious. Among other things, a Mr. Louiallier published a denunciatory newspaper article. General Jackson arrested him. A lawyer by the name of Morrel procured the United States Judge Hall to issue a writ of *habeas corpus* to relieve Mr. Louiallier. General Jackson arrested both the lawyer and the judge. A Mr. Hollander ventured to say of some part of the matter that "it was a dirty trick." General Jackson arrested him. When the officer undertook to serve the writ of *habeas corpus*, General Jackson took it from him, and sent him away with a copy. Holding the judge in custody a few days, the General sent him beyond the limits of his encampment, and set him at liberty, with an order to remain till the ratification of peace should be regularly announced, or until the British should have left the Southern coast. A day or two more elapsed, the ratification of a treaty of peace was regularly announced, and the judge and others were fully liberated. A few days more, and the judge called General Jackson into court and fined him $1,000 for having arrested him and the others named. The General paid the fine, and there the matter rested for nearly thirty years, when Congress refunded principal and interest. The late Senator Douglas, then in the House of Representatives, took a leading part in the debates, in which the constitutional question was much discussed. I am not prepared to say whom the journals would show to have voted for the measure.

It may be remarked: First, that we had the same Constitution then as now; secondly, that we then had a case of invasion, and now we have a case of rebellion; and, thirdly, that the permanent right of the people to public discussion, the liberty of speech and of the press, the trial by jury, the law of evidence, and the *habeas corpus*, suffered no detriment whatever by that conduct of General Jackson, or its subsequent approval by the American Congress.

And yet, let me say that, in my own discretion, I do not know whether I would have ordered the arrest of Mr. Vallandigham. While I cannot shift the responsibility from myself, I hold that, as a general rule, the commander in the field is the better judge of the necessity in any particular case. Of course, I must practise a general directory and revisory power in the matter.

One of the resolutions expresses the opinion of the meeting that arbitrary arrests will have the effect to divide and distract those who should be united in suppressing the rebellion, and I am specifically called on to discharge Mr. Vallandigham. I regard this as, at least, a fair appeal to me on the expediency of exercising a constitutional power which I think exists. In response to such appeal, I have to say, it gave me pain when I learned that Mr. Vallandigham had been arrested—that is, I was pained that there should have seemed to be a necessity for arresting him—and that it will afford me great pleasure to discharge him so soon as I can, by any means, believe the public safety will not suffer by it. I further say that, as the war progresses, it appears to me, opinion and action which were in great confusion at first, take shape and fall into more regular channels, so that the necessity for strong dealing with them gradually decreases. I have every reason to desire that it should cease altogether; and far from the least is my regard for the opinions and wishes of those who, like the meeting at Albany, declare their purpose to sustain the Government in every constitutional and lawful measure to suppress the rebellion. Still, I must continue to do so much as may seem to be required by the public safety.

A. LINCOLN.

Similar meetings were held in New York, Philadelphia, and other cities and towns of the North, and, on the 11th of June, a State Convention of the Democratic party was held at Columbus, Ohio, for the nomination of State officers. Mr. Vallandigham was, at that Convention, made the Democratic candidate for Governor, receiving, on the first ballot, 448 votes out of 461, the whole number cast. Senator Pugh was nominated for Lieutenant-Governor, and resolutions were adopted protesting against President LINCOLN'S emancipation proclamation; condemning martial law in loyal States, where war does not exist; denouncing the suspension of the writ of *habeas corpus*; protesting very strongly against the banishment of Vallandigham, and calling on the President to restore him to his rights; declaring that they would hail with delight the desire of the seceded States to return to their allegiance, and that they would co-operate with the citizens of those States in measures for the restoration of peace.

A committee of the Convention visited Washington, and on the 26th of June presented to the President the resolutions adopted by the Convention, and urged the immediate recall and restoration of Mr. Vallandigham, their candidate for Governor. To this President LINCOLN made the following reply:

WASHINGTON, *June* 29, 1863.

GENTLEMEN: The resolutions of the Ohio Democratic State Convention, which you present me, together with your introductory and closing remarks, being in position and argument mainly the same as the resolutions of the Democratic meeting at Albany, New York, I refer you to my response to the latter as meeting most of the points in the former.

This response you evidently used in preparing your remarks, and I desire no more than that it be used with accuracy. In a single reading of your remarks, I only discovered one inaccuracy in matter which I suppose you took from that paper. It is where you say, "The undersigned are unable to agree with you in the opinion you have expressed that the Constitution is different in time of insurrection or invasion from what it is in time of peace and public security."

A recurrence to the paper will show you that I have not expressed the opinion you suppose. I expressed the opinion that the Constitution is different *in its application* in cases of rebellion or invasion, involving the public safety, from what it is in times of profound peace and public security; and this opinion I adhere to, simply because by the Constitution itself things may be done in the one case which may not be done in the other.

I dislike to waste a word on a merely personal point, but I must respectfully assure you that you will find yourselves at fault should you ever seek for evidence to prove your assumption that I "opposed in discussions before the people the policy of the Mexican war."

You say: "Expunge from the Constitution this limitation upon the power of Congress to suspend the writ of *habeas corpus*, and yet the other guarantees of personal liberty would remain unchanged." Doubtless, if this clause of the Constitution, improperly called, as I think, a limitation upon the power of Congress, were expunged, the other guarantees would remain the same; but the question is, not how those guarantees would stand with that clause *out* of the Constitution, but how they stand with that clause remaining in it, in case of rebellion or invasion, involving the public safety. If the liberty could be indulged in expunging that clause, letter and spirit, I really think the constitutional argument would be with you.

My general view on this question was stated in the Albany response, and hence I do not state it now. I only add that, as seems to me, the benefit of the writ of *habeas corpus* is the great means through which the guarantees of personal liberty are conserved and made available in the last resort; and corroborative of this view is the fact that Mr. Vallandigham, in the very case in question, under the advice of able lawyers, saw not where else to go but to the *habeas corpus*. But by the Constitution the benefit of the writ of *habeas corpus* itself may be suspended, when, in case of rebellion or invasion, the public safety may require it.

You ask, in substance, whether I really claim that I may override all the guaranteed rights of individuals, on the plea of conserving the public safety—when I may choose to say the public safety requires it. This question, divested of the phraseology calculated to represent me as struggling for an arbitrary personal preroragtive, is either simply a question *who* shall decide, or an affirmation that *nobody* shall decide, what the public safety does require in cases of rebellion or invasion. The Constitution contemplates the question as likely to occur for decision, but it does not expressly declare who is to decide it. By necessary implication, when rebellion or invasion comes, the decision is to be made from time to time; and I think the man whom, for the time, the people have, under the Constitution, made the commander-in-chief of their army and navy, is the man who holds the power and bears the responsibility of making it. If he uses the power justly, the same people will probably justify him; if he abuses it, he is in their hands to be dealt with by all the modes they have reserved to themselves in the Constitution.

The earnestness with which you insist that persons can only, in times of rebellion, be lawfully dealt with in accordance with the rules for criminal trials and prnishments in times of peace, induces me to add a word to what I said on that point in the Albany response. You claim that men may, if they choose, embarrass those whose duty it is to combat a giant rebellion, and then be dealt with only in turn as if there were no rebellion. The Constitution itself rejects this view. The military arrests and detentions which have been made, including those of Mr. Vallandigham, which are not different in principle from the other, have been for *prevention*, and not for *punishment*—as injunctions to stay injury, as proceedings to keep the peace—and hence, like proceedings in such cases and for like reasons, they have not been accompanied with indictments, or trial by juries, nor in a single case by any punishment whatever beyond what is purely incidental to the prevention. The original sentence of imprisonment in Mr. Vallandigham's case was to prevent injury to the military service only, and the modification of it was made as a less disagreeable mode to him of securing the same prevention.

I am unable to perceive an insult to Ohio in the case of Mr. Vallandigham. Quite surely nothing of this sort was or is intended. I was wholly unaware that Mr. Vallandigham was, at the time of his arrest, a candidate for the Democratic nomination of governor, until so informed by your reading to me the resolutions of the convention. I am grateful to the State of Ohio for many things, especially for the brave soldiers and officers she has given in the present national trial to the armies of the Union.

You claim, as I understand, that according to my own position in the Albany response, Mr. Vallandigham should be released; and this because, as you claim, he has not damaged the military service by discouraging enlistments, encouraging desertions, or otherwise; and that if he had, he should have been turned over to the civil authorities under the recent acts of Congress. I certainly do not *know* that Mr. Vallandigham has specifically and by direct language advised against enlistments and in favor of desertions and resistance to drafting. We all know that combinations, armed in some instances, to resist the arrest of deserters, began several months ago; that more recently the like has appeared in resistance to the enrolment preparatory to a draft; and that quite a number of assassinations have occurred from the same animus. These had to be met by military force, and this again has led to bloodshed and death. And now, under a sense of responsibility more weighty and enduring than any which is merely official, I solemnly declare my belief that this hindrance of the military, including maiming and murder, is due to the cause in which Mr. Vallandigham has been engaged, in a greater degree than to any other cause; and it is due to him personally in a greater degree than to any other man.

These things have been notorious, known to all, and of course known to Mr. Vallandigham. Perhaps I would not be wrong to say they originated with his especial friends and adherents. With perfect knowledge of them he has frequently, if not constantly, made speeches in Congress and before popular assemblies; and if it can be shown that, with these things staring him in the face, he has ever uttered a word of rebuke or counsel against them, it will be a fact greatly in his favor with me, and of which, as yet, I am totally ignorant. When it is known that the whole burden of his speeches has been to stir up men against the prosecution of the war, and that in the midst of resistance to it he has not been known in any instance to counsel against such resistance, it is next to impossible to repel the inference that he has counselled directly in favor of it.

With all this before their eyes, the convention you represent have nominated Mr. Vallandigham for governor of Ohio, and both they and you have declared the purpose to sustain the national Union by all constitutional means, but, of course, they and you, in common, reserve to yourselves to decide what are constitutional means, and, unlike the Albany meeting, you omit to state or intimate that, in your opinion, an army is a constitutional means of saving the Union against a rebellion, or even to intimate that you are conscious of an existing rebellion being in progress with the avowed object of destroying that very Union. At the same time, your nominee for governor, in whose behalf you appeal, is known to you, and to the world, to declare against the use of an army to suppress the rebellion. Your own attitude, therefore, encourages desertion, resistance to the draft, and the like, because it teaches those who incline to desert and to escape the draft to believe it is your purpose to protect them, and to hope that you will become strong enough to do so.

After a short personal intercourse with you, gentlemen of the committee, I cannot say I think you desire this effect to follow your attitude; but I assure you that both friends and enemies of the Union look upon it in this light. It is a substantial hope, and by consequence, a real strength to the enemy. If it is a false hope, and one which you would willingly dispel, I will make the way exceedingly easy. I send you duplicates of this letter, in order that you, or a majority, may, if you choose, indorse your names upon one of them, and return it thus indorsed to me, with the understanding that those signing are thereby committed to the following propositions, and to nothing else:

1. That there is now rebellion in the United States, the object and tendency of which is to destroy the national Union; and that, in your opinion, an army and navy are constitutional means for suppressing that rebellion.

2. That no one of you will do any thing which, in his own judgment, will tend to hinder the increase, or favor the decrease, or lessen the efficiency of the army and navy, while engaged in the effort to suppress that rebellion; and—

3. That each of you will, in his sphere, do all he can to have the officers, soldiers, and seamen of the army and navy, while engaged in the effort to suppress the rebellion, paid, fed, clad, and otherwise well provided for and supported.

And with the further understanding that upon receiving the letter and names thus indorsed, I will cause them to be published, which publication shall be, within itself, a revocation of the order in relation to Mr. Vallandigham.

It will not escape observation that I consent to the release of Mr. Vallandigham upon terms not embracing any pledge from him or from others as to what he will or will not do. I do this because he is not present to speak for himself, or to authorize others to speak for him; and hence I shall expect that on returning he would not put himself practically in antagonism with the position of his friends. But I do it chiefly because I thereby prevail on other influential gentlemen of Ohio to so define their position as to be of immense value to the army—thus more than compensating for the consequences of any mistake in allowing Mr. Vallandigham to return, so that, on the whole, the public safety will not have suffered by it. Still, in regard to Mr. Vallandigham and all others, I must hereafter, as heretofore, do so much as the public service may seem to require.

I have the honor to be respectfully, yours, &c.,

A. LINCOLN.

The canvass throughout the summer was very animated. As a matter of course, the opponents of the Administration in Ohio, as elsewhere throughout the country, made this matter of arbitrary arrests a very prominent point of attack. Special stress was laid upon the fact that instead of acting directly and upon his own responsibility in these cases, the President left them to the discretion of military commanders in the several departments. This was held to be in violation of the law of Congress which authorized the President to suspend the writ of *habeas corpus*, but not to delegate that high prerogative. To meet this objection, therefore, and also in order to establish a uniform mode of action on the subject, the President issued the following

PROCLAMATION:

Whereas, The Constitution of the United States has ordained that "The privilege of the writ of *habeas corpus* shall not be suspended, unless, when in cases of rebellion or invasion, the public safety may require it; and, whereas, a rebellion was existing on the 3d day of March, 1863, which rebellion is still existing; and, whereas, by a statute which was approved on that day, it was enacted by the Senate and House of Representatives of the United States, in Congress assembled, that during the present insurrection the President of the United States, whenever, in his judgment, the public safety may require, is authorized to suspend the privilege of the writ of *habeas corpus* in any case throughout the United States, or any part thereof; and, whereas, in the judgment of the President the public safety does require that the privilege of the said writ shall now be suspended throughout the United States in cases where, by the authority of the President of the United States, military, naval and civil officers of the United States, or any of them, hold persons under their command or in their custody, either as prisoners of war, spies, or aiders or abettors of the enemy, or officers, soldiers, or seamen enrolled, drafted, or mustered, or enlisted in, or belonging to the land or naval forces of the United States, or as deserters therefrom, or otherwise amenable to military law, or to the rules and articles of war, or the rules and regulations prescribed for the military or naval services by the authority of the President of the United States, or for resisting the draft, or for any other offence against the military or naval service; now, therefore, I, ABRAHAM LINCOLN, President of the United States, do hereby proclaim and make known to all whom it may concern, that the privilege of the writ of *habeas corpus* is suspended throughout the United States, in the several cases before-mentioned, and that this suspension will continue throughout the duration of the said rebellion, or until this Proclamation shall, by a subsequent one, to be issued by the President of the United States, be modified and revoked. And I do hereby require all magistrates, attorneys, and other civil officers within the United States, and all officers and others in the military and naval services of the United States, to take distinct notice of this suspension and give it full effect, and all citizens of the United States to conduct and govern themselves accordingly, and in conformity with the Constitution of the United States, and the laws of Congress in such cases made and provided.

In testimony whereof, I have hereunto set my hand and caused the seal of the United States to be affixed, this fifteenth day of September, in the year of our Lord one thousand eight hundred and sixty-three, and of the independence of the United States of America the eighty-eighth.

ABRAHAM LINCOLN.

By the President:
WM. H. SEWARD, *Secretary of State.*

The act passed by Congress "for enrolling and calling out the national forces," commonly called the Conscription Act, provided that all able-bodied male citizens, and persons of foreign birth who had declared their intention to become citizens, between the ages of twenty and forty-five, were liable to be called into service. The strenuous efforts made by the enemies of the Administration to arouse the hostility of the people against its general policy, had proved so far successful as greatly to discourage volunteer enlistments; and the Government was thus compelled to resort to the extraordinary powers conferred upon it by this act. Questions had been raised as to the liability of foreigners to be drafted under this law; and in order to settle this point the President, on the 8th of May, issued the following

PROCLAMATION:

WASHINGTON, *May* 8, 1863.

By the President of the United States of America, a Proclamation.

Whereas, The Congress of the United States, at its last session, enacted a law, entitled "An act for enrolling and calling out the national forces, and for other purposes," which was approved on the 3d day of March last; and

Whereas, It is recited in the said act that there now exists in the United States an insurrection and rebellion against the authority thereof, and it is, under the Constitution of the United States, the duty of the Government to suppress insubordination and rebellion, to guarantee to each State a republican form of government, and to preserve the public tranquillity; and

Whereas, For these high purposes, a military force is indispensable, to raise and support which all persons ought willingly to contribute; and

Whereas, No service can be more praiseworthy and honorable than that which is rendered for the maintenance of the Constitution and the Union, and the consequent preservation of free government; and

Whereas, For the reasons thus recited it was enacted by the said statute that all able-bodied male citizens of the United States, and persons of foreign birth who shall have declared on oath their intentions to become citizens under and in pursuance of the laws thereof, between the ages of twenty and forty-five years, with certain exemptions not necessary to be here mentioned, are declared to constitute the national forces, and shall be liable to perform military duty in the service of the United States, when called out by the President for that purpose; and

Whereas, It is claimed, on and in behalf of persons of foreign birth, within the ages specified in said act, who have heretofore declared on oath their intentions to become citizens under and in pursuance to the laws of the United States, and who have not exercised the right of suffrage, or any other political franchise under the laws of the United States, or of any of the States thereof, that they are not absolutely precluded by their aforesaid declaration of intention from renouncing their purpose to become citizens; and that, on the contrary, such persons, under treaties and the law of nations, retain a right to renounce that purpose, and to forego the privilege of citizenship and residence within the United States, under the obligations imposed by the aforesaid act of Congress:

Now, therefore, to avoid all misapprehensions concerning the liability of persons concerned to perform the service required by such enactment, and to give it full effect, I do hereby order and proclaim that no plea of alienage will be received, or allowed to exempt from the obligations imposed by the aforesaid act of Congress any person of foreign birth who shall have declared on oath his intention to become a citizen of the United States, under the laws thereof, and who shall be found within the United States at any time during the continuance of the present insurrection and rebellion, at or after the expiration of the period of sixty-five days from the date of this proclamation; nor shall any such plea of alienage be allowed in favor of any such person who has so, as aforesaid, declared his intention to become a citizen of the United States, and shall have exercised at any time the right of suffrage, or any other political franchise within the United States, under the laws thereof, or under the laws of any of the several States.

In witness whereof, I have hereunto set my hand, and caused the seal of the United States to be affixed.

Done at the city of Washington this 8th day of May, in the year
[L. S.] of our Lord 1863, and of the independence of the United
States the eighty-seventh.

By the President: ABRAHAM LINCOLN.

WILLIAM H. SEWARD, *Secretary of State.*

It was subsequently ordered that the draft should take place in July, and public proclamation was made of the number which each State would be required to furnish. Enrolling officers had been appointed for the several districts of all the States, and, all the names being placed in a wheel, the number required were to be publicly drawn, under such regulations as were considered necessary to insure equal and exact justice. Very great pains had been taken by the opponents of the Administration to excite odium against that clause of the law which fixed the price of exemption from service under the draft at $300. It was represented that this clause was for the special benefit of the rich, who could easily pay the sum required; while poor men who could not pay it would be compelled, at whatever hardships to themselves and their families, to enter the army. The draft was commenced in the city of New York on Saturday, July 11th, and was conducted quietly and successfully during that day. On Sunday plots were formed and combinations entered into to resist it; and no sooner was it resumed on Monday morning, July 13, than a sudden and formidable attack was made by an armed mob upon the office in one of the districts; the wheel was destroyed, the lists scattered, and the building set on fire. The excitement spread through the city. Crowds gathered everywhere, with no apparent common object; but during the day the movement seemed to be controlled by leaders in two general directions. The first was an attack upon the negroes; the second an assault upon every one who was supposed to be in any way concerned in the draft, or prominently identified, officially or otherwise, with the Administration or the Republican party. Unfortunately, the militia regiments of the city had been sent to Pennsylvania to withstand the rebel invasion; and the only guardians left for the public peace were the regular police and a few hundred soldiers who garrisoned the forts. Both behaved with the greatest vigor and fidelity, but they were too few to protect the dozen miles between the extremities of the city. The mob, dispersed in one quarter, would reassemble at another, and for four days the city seemed given up to their control. The outrages committed during this time were numerous and aggravated. Negroes were assaulted, beaten to death, mutilated, and hung; building after building was sacked and burned; gangs of desperadoes patrolled the streets, levying contributions, and ordering places of business to be closed. A Colored Orphan Asylum, sheltering some hundreds of children, was sacked and burned. After the first day the riot, which was at first directed against the draft, took a new turn. The entire mass of scoundrelism in the city seemed to have been let loose for indiscriminate plunder. Women, half-grown boys, and children, were foremost in the work of robbery, and no man felt safe from attack. The police force did their duty manfully, aided at first by the few troops at the disposal of the authorities, and subsequently by the regiments who began to return from Pennsylvania. In the street fights which occurred many of the defenders of law and order lost their lives, while a far larger number of the rioters were killed. The bands of rioters were finally dispersed, and the peace of the city was restored.

During these occurrences the draft was necessarily suspended; and on the 3d of August, Governor Seymour addressed a long letter to the President, asking that further proceedings under the draft might be postponed until it should be seen whether the number required from the State of New York could not be raised by volunteering, and also until the constitutionality of the law could be tested in the judicial tribunals of the country. The Governor pointed out an alleged injustice in the application of the law, by which, in four districts of the State of New York a far higher quota in proportion to the population was required than in the other districts of the State; and this was urged as an additional reason for postponing the further execution of the law.

To this appeal the President, on the 7th of August, made the following reply:

EXECUTIVE MANSION, WASHINGTON, *August* 7, 1863.

His Excellency, HORATIO SEYMOUR,
Governor of New York, Albany, N. Y.:

Your communication of the 3d inst., has been received and attentively considered. I cannot consent to suspend the draft in New York, as you request, because, among other reasons, TIME is too important. By the figures you send, which I presume are correct, the twelve districts represented fall in two classes of eight and four respectively.

The disparity of the quotas for the draft in these two classes is certainly very striking, being the difference between an average of 2,200 in one class, and 4,864 in the other. Assuming that the districts are equal, one to another, in entire population, as required by the plan on which they were made, this disparity is such as to require attention. Much of it, however, I suppose will be accounted for by the fact that so many more persons fit for soldiers are in the city than are in the country, who have too recently arrived from other parts of the United States and from Europe to be either included in the census of 1860, or to have voted in 1862. Still, making due allowance for this, I am yet unwilling to stand upon it as an entirely sufficient explanation of the great disparity. I shall direct the draft to proceed in all the districts, drawing, however, at first from each of the four districts—to wit, the Second, Fourth, Sixth, and Eighth —only, 2,200, being the average quota of the other class. After this drawing, these four districts, and also the Seventeenth and Twenty-ninth, shall be carefully re-enrolled; and, if you please, agents of yours may witness every step of the process. Any deficiency which may appear by the new enrolment will be supplied by a special draft for that object, allowing due credit for volunteers who may be obtained from these districts respectively during the interval; and at all points, so far as consistent with practical convenience, due credits shall be given for volunteers, and your Excellency shall be notified of the time fixed for commencing a draft in each district.

I do not object to abide a decision of the United States Supreme Court, or of the Judges thereof, on the constitutionality of the draft law. In fact, I should be willing to facilitate the obtaining of it. But I cannot consent to lose the time while it is being obtained. We are contending with an enemy who, as I understand, drives every able-bodied man he can reach into his ranks, very much as a butcher drives bullocks into a slaughter-pen. No time is wasted, no argument is used. This produces an army which will soon turn upon our now victorious soldiers already in the field, if they shall not be sustained by recruits as they should be. It produces an army with a rapidity not to be matched on our side, if we first waste time to re-experiment with the volunteer system, already deemed by Congress, and palpably, in fact, so far exhausted as to be inadequate; and then more time to obtain a Court decision as to whether a law is constitutional which requires a part of those not now in the service to go to the aid of those who are already in it; and still more time to determine with absolute certainty that we get those who are to go in the precisely legal proportion to those who are not to go. My purpose is to be in my action just and constitutional, and yet practical, in performing the important duty with which I am charged, of maintaining the unity and the free principles of our common country. Your obedient servant,

A. LINCOLN.

On the 8th Governor Seymour replied, reasserting the unfairness and injustice of the enrolments, and expressing his regret at the President's refusal to postpone the draft. He also sent a voluminous statement prepared by Judge-Advocate Waterbury, designed to sustain the position he had previously assumed. To this the President thus replied :—

EXECUTIVE MANSION,
WASHINGTON, *August* 11, 1863.

His Excellency HORATIO SEYMOUR,
Governor of New York:

Yours of the 8th, with Judge-Advocate General Waterbury's report, was received to-day.

Asking you to remember that I consider time as being very important, both to the general cause of the country and to the soldiers in the field, I beg to remind you that I waited, at your request, from the 1st until the 6th inst. to receive your communication dated the 3d. In view of its great length, and the known time and apparent care taken in its preparation, I did not doubt that it contained your full case as you desired to present it. It contained the figures for twelve districts, omitting the other nineteen, as I supposed, because you found nothing to complain of as to them. I answered accordingly. In doing so I laid down the principle to which I purpose adhering, which is to proceed with the draft, at the same time employing infallible means to avoid any great wrong. With the communication received to-day you send figures for twenty-eight districts, including the twelve sent before, and still omitting three, for which I suppose the enrolments are not yet received. In looking over the fuller list of twenty-eight districts, I find that the quotas for sixteen of them are above 2,000 and below 2,700, while of the rest, six are above 2,700 and six are below 2,000. Applying the principle to these new facts, the Fifth and Seventh Districts must be added to the four in which the quotas have already been reduced to 2,200 for the first draft; and with these four others must be added to those to be re-enrolled. The correct case will then stand: the quotas of the Second, Fourth, Fifth, Sixth, Seventh, and Eighth Districts fixed at 2,200 for the first draft. The Provost-Marshal General informs me that the drawing is already completed in the Sixteenth, Seventeenth, Eighteenth, Twenty-Second, Twenty-Fourth, Twenty-Sixth, Twenty-Seventh, Twenty-Eighth, Twenty-Ninth, and Thirtieth Districts. In the others, except the three outstanding, the drawing will be made upon the quotas as now fixed. After the first draft, the

Second, Fourth, Fifth, Sixth, Seventh, Eighth, Sixteenth, Seventeenth, Twenty-First, Twenty-Fifth, Twenty-Ninth, and Thirty-First will be enrolled for the purpose, and in the manner stated in my letter of the 7th inst. The same principle will be applied to the now outstanding districts when they shall come in. No part of my former letter is repudiated by reason of not being restated in this, or for any other cause.

Your obedient servant,

A. LINCOLN.

The draft in New York was resumed on the 19th of August, and as ample preparations had been made for the preservation of the public peace, it encountered no further opposition. In every other part of the country the proceedings were conducted and completed without resistance.

Some difficulty was experienced in Chicago, and the Mayor and Comptroller of that city addressed the President on the subject of alleged frauds in the enrolment, and received the following dispatch in reply:

WASHINGTON, *August* 27, 1863.

F. C. SHERMAN, Mayor; J. S. HAYS, Comptroller:

Yours of the 24th, in relation to the draft, is received. It seems to me the government here will be overwhelmed if it undertakes to conduct these matters with the authorities of cities and counties. They must be conducted with the Governors of States, who will, of course, represent their cities and counties. Meanwhile, you need not be uneasy until you again hear from here.

A. LINCOLN.

Subsequently, in reply to further representations on the subject, the same gentlemen received the following:

WASHINGTON, *August* 7, 1863.

Yours of August 29th just received. I suppose it was intended by Congress that this Court should execute the act in question without dependence upon any other Government, State, City, or County. It is, however, within the range of practical convenience to confer with the Governments of States, while it is quite beyond that range to have correspondence on the subject with counties and cities. They are too numerous. As instances, I have corresponded with Gov. Seymour, but not with Mayor Opdyke; with Gov. Curtin, but not with Mayor Henry.

A. LINCOLN.

CHAPTER IX.

MILITARY EVENTS OF 1863—THE REBEL DEFEAT AT GETTYSBURG—FALL OF VICKSBURG AND PORT HUDSON.

The military events of 1863, though of very great importance, are much less closely connected with the direct action of the President than those which occurred in 1862; we shall not attempt, therefore, to narrate them as much in detail. When General Burnside succeeded General McClellan in command of the Army of the Potomac, on the 7th of November, 1862, that army was at Warrenton, the rebel forces falling back before it towards Richmond. Deeming it impossible to force the enemy to a decisive battle, and unsafe to follow him to Richmond on a line which must make it very difficult to keep up his communications, General Burnside, on the 15th, turned his army towards Fredericksburg—marching on the north bank of the Rappahannock, intending to cross the river, take possession of Fredericksburg, and march upon Richmond from that point. The advance division, under General Sumner, arrived opposite Fredericksburg on the 19th; but a pontoon train, which had been ordered and was expected to be there at the same time, had not come—so that crossing at the moment was impossible. The delay that thus became unavoidable, enabled General Lee to bring up a strong force from the rebel army, and possess himself of the heights of Fredericksburg. On the night of the 10th of December, General Burnside threw a bridge of pontoons across the river, and the next day constructed four bridges, under cover of a terrific bombardment of the town. On the 11th and 12th his army was crossed over, and on the 13th attacked the enemy—General Sumner commanding in front, and General Franklin having command of a powerful flanking movement against the rebel right. The rebels, however, were too strongly posted to be dislodged. Our forces suffered severely, and were unable to advance. On the night of the 15th, they were therefore withdrawn to the opposite bank of the river. Our losses in this engagement were 1,138 killed, 9,105 wounded, 2,078 missing; total, 12,321.

The army remained quiet until the 20th of January, when General Burnside again issued orders for an advance, intending to cross the river some six or eight miles above Fredericksburg, and make a flank attack upon the left wing of the rebel army. The whole army was moved to the place of crossing early in the morning, but a heavy storm on the preceding night had so damaged the roads as to make it impossible to bring up artillery and pontoons with the promptness essential to success. On the 24th, General Burnside was relieved from command of the Army of the Potomac, and General Hooker appointed in his place. Three months were passed in inaction, the season forbidding any movement; but on the 27th of April, General Hooker pushed three divisions of his army to Kelley's Ford, twenty-five miles above Fredericksburg, and by the 30th had crossed the river, and turning south had reached Chancellorsville—five or six miles southwest of that town. A strong cavalry force, under General Stoneman, had been sent to cut the railroad in the rear of the rebel army, so as to prevent their receiving re-enforcements from Richmond,—General Hooker's design being to attack the enemy in flank and rear. The other divisions of his army had crossed and joined his main force at Chancellorsville, General Sedgwick, with one division only, being left opposite Fredericksburg. On the 2d of May, the left wing of the rebel army, under General Jackson, attacked our right, and gained a decided advantage of position, which was recovered, however, before the day closed. The action was renewed next day, and the advantage remained with the enemy. General Sedgwick, meantime, had crossed the river and occupied the heights of Fredericksburg, but was driven from them and compelled to retreat on the night of the 4th. On the morning of the 5th a heavy rainstorm set in, and in the night of that day General Hooker withdrew his army to the north bank of the Rappahannock, having lost not far from 18,000 in the movement.

Both armies remained inactive until the 9th of June, when it was discovered that the rebel forces under Lee were leaving their position near Fredericksburg and moving northwest, through the valley of the Shenandoah. On the 13th the rebel General Ewell, with a heavy force, attacked our advance post of seven thousand men at Winchester under General Milroy, and not only compelled him to retreat but pursued him so closely as to convert his retreat into a rout: and on the 14th of June the rebel army began to cross the Potomac and advanced upon Hagerstown, Maryland, with the evident purpose of invading Pennsylvania. The movement created the most intense excitement throughout the country. President Lincoln issued a proclamation calling for 100,000 militia from the States most directly menaced, to serve for six months, and New York was summoned to send 20,000 also. On the 27th the main body of the rebel army crossed the Potomac at Williamsport, and General Lee took up his head-quarters at Hagerstown.

Meantime, as soon as the movement of the rebel forces from Fredericksburg was discovered, our army had broken up its encampment and marched northward, on a line nearly parallel with that of the enemy, and on the 27th, the same day that the rebels reached Hagerstown, the head-quarters of our army were at Frederick City—our whole force being thus interposed between the rebels and both Baltimore and

Washington, and prepared to follow them into Pennsylvania. On that day General Hooker was relieved from command of the army, which was conferred upon General Meade, who at once ordered an advance into Pennsylvania in the general direction of Harrisburg—towards which the enemy was rapidly advancing in force. On the 1st of July our advanced corps, the First and Eleventh, under Generals Reynolds and Howard, came in contact with the enemy, strongly posted near the town of Gettysburg, and attacking at once, fought an indecisive battle; the enemy being so far superior in numbers as to compel General Howard, who was in command at the time, to fall back to Cemetery Hill and wait for re-enforcements. During the night all the corps of our army were concentrated and the next day posted around that point. The Eleventh Corps retained its position on the Cemetery ridge: the First Corps was on the right of the Eleventh, on a knoll, connecting with the ridge extending to the south and east, on which the Second Corps was placed. The right of the Twelfth Corps rested on a small stream. The Second and Third Corps were posted on the left of the Eleventh, on the prolongation of Cemetery ridge. The Fifth was held in reserve until the arrival of the Sixth, at 2 P. M. on the 2d, after a march of thirty-two miles in seventeen hours, when the Fifth was ordered to the extreme left and the Sixth placed in reserve.

At about 3 o'clock the battle was opened by a tremendous onset of the enemy, whose troops were massed along a ridge a mile or so in our front, upon the Third Corps, which formed our extreme left and which met the shock with heroic firmness, until it was supported by the Third and Fifth. General Sickles, who commanded the Third Corps, was severely wounded early in the action, and General Birney, who succeeded to the command, though urged to fall back, was enabled, by the help of the First and Sixth Corps, to hold his ground, and at about sunset the enemy retired in confusion. Another assault was made on our left during the evening, which was also repulsed. On the morning of the 3d a spirited assault was made upon the right of our line, but without success; and at 1 P. M. the enemy opened an artillery fire upon our centre and left from one hundred and twenty-five guns, which continued for over two hours, without reply from our side, when it was followed by a heavy assault of infantry, directed mainly against the Second Corps, and repelled with firmness and success by that Corps, supported by Doubleday's Division and Stannard's Brigade of the First Corps. This terminated the battle. On the morning of the 4th a reconnoissance showed that the enemy had withdrawn his left flank, maintaining his position in front of our left, with the apparent purpose of forming a new line of attack; but the next morning it was ascertained that he was in full retreat. The Sixth Corps, with all disposable cavalry, were at once sent in pursuit; but ascertaining that the enemy had availed himself of very strong passes which could be held by a small force, General Meade determined to pursue by a flank movement, and after burying the dead and succoring the wounded, the whole army was put in motion for the Potomac. On the 12th it arrived in front of the enemy strongly posted on the heights, in advance of Williamsport. The next day was devoted to an examination of the position; but on advancing for an attack on the 14th, it was discovered that the enemy had succeeded in crossing by the bridge at Falling Waters and the ford at Williamsport. The pursuit was continued still further, but the enemy, though greatly harassed and subjected to severe losses, succeeding in gaining the line of the Rapidan, and our forces again occupied their old position on the Rappahannock.

On the morning of the 4th of July, the day celebrated throughout the country as the anniversary of the Declaration of Independence, the President issued the following :—

WASHINGTON, *July* 4, 10.30 A. M.

The President announces to the country that news from the Army of the Potomac, up to 10 P. M. of the 3d, is such as to cover that army with the highest honor; to promise a great success to the cause of the Union, and to claim the condolence of all for the many gallant fallen; and that for this he especially desires that on this day, He, whose will, not ours, should ever be done, be everywhere remembered and reverenced with profoundest gratitude. A. LINCOLN.

The result of this battle—one of the severest and most sanguinary of the war—was of the utmost importance. It drove the rebels back from their intended invasion of Pennsylvania and Maryland, and compelled them to evacuate the upper part of the Valley of the Shenandoah, leaving in our hands nearly 14,000 prisoners, and 25,000 small arms collected on the battle-field. Our own losses were very severe, amounting to 2,834 killed, 13,709 wounded, and 6,643 missing—in all, 23,186.

During the ensuing season, a piece of ground, seventeen and a half acres in extent, adjoining the town cemetery, and forming an important part of the battle-field, was purchased by the State of Pennsylvania to be used as a national burying-ground for the loyal soldiers who fell in that great engagement. It was dedicated, with solemn and impressive ceremonies, on the 19th of November, 1863, the President and members of his Cabinet being in attendance, and a very large and imposing military display adding grace and dignity to the occasion. Hon. Edward Everett delivered the formal address, and President Lincoln made the following remarks:

Fourscore and seven years ago our fathers brought forth upon this continent a new nation, conceived in liberty, and dedicated to the proposition that all men are created equal. Now we are engaged in a great civil war, testing whether that nation, or any nation so conceived and so dedicated can long endure. We are met on a great battle-field of that war. We have come to dedicate a portion of that field as a final resting-place for those who here gave their lives that that nation might live. It is altogether fitting and proper that we should do this. But in a larger sense we cannot dedicate, we cannot consecrate, we cannot hallow this ground. The brave men, living and dead, who struggled here, have consecrated it far above our power to add or detract. The world will little note, nor long remember, what we say here, but it can never forget what they did here. It is for us, the living, rather to be dedicated here to the unfinished work which they who fought here have thus far so nobly advanced. It is rather for us to be here dedicated to the great task remaining before us, that from these honored dead we take increased devotion to that cause for which they gave the last full measure of devotion; that we here highly resolve that these dead shall not have died in vain; that this nation under God, shall have a new birth of freedom, and that government of the people, by the people, and for the people, shall not perish from the earth.

The other great military achievement of the year, was the capture of Port Hudson and Vicksburg, and the opening of the Mississippi river throughout its entire length to the commerce of the United States. General N. P. Banks, who succeeded General Butler in command of the military department of Louisiana, reached New-Orleans, sustained by a formidable expedition from New-York, and assumed command on the 15th of December, 1862, and at once took possession of Baton Rouge. On the 21st, an expedition under General W. T. Sherman started from Memphis, passed down the Mississippi to the mouth of the Yazoo, some ten miles above Vicksburg, and on the 26th ascended that river, landed and commenced an attack upon the town from the rear. Severe fighting continued for three days, during which time our army pushed within two miles of the city; but on the 30th they were repulsed with heavy loss. On the 2d of January, General McClernand arrived and took command, and the attack upon Vicksburg was for the time abandoned as hopeless. Several forts on the Arkansas and White Rivers were taken, and an effort was subsequently made to cut a channel across the neck of land on the extremity of which Vicksburg is situated, so as to divert the channel of the Mississippi, and make Vicksburg substantially an inland town. Various attempts upon the place were made during the succeeding month, but without success. On the 30th of April, General Grant landed his forces at Bruinsburg, sixty-five miles below Vicksburg, and immediately advanced upon Port Gibson, where he was opposed by the rebel General Bowen, who was defeated, with a loss in killed, wounded, and prisoners, of 1,500 men. At Grand Gulf, ten miles above Bruinsburg, the enemy had begun to erect strong fortifications. These had been fired upon by our gunboats a few days before, under cover of which the fleet had run past. Grant having now gained the rear of this strong post, Admiral Porter, two days after the fight at Port Gibson, returned to Grand Gulf and found it abandoned. Grant's Army then marched upward toward Vicksburg, and on the 12th of May encountered the enemy again at Raymond, not far from Jackson, the capital of the State of Mississippi, and again defeated them with a loss of 800. Two days after, May 14, they were opposed by a corps of the enemy under General Joseph E. Johnston, formerly the Commander-in-chief of the Confederate army, who had been assigned to the command of the Department of the Mississippi. Johnston was defeated, and the city of Jackson fell into our hands, with seventeen pieces of artillery and large stores of supplies. Grant then turned to the west, directly upon the rear of Vicksburg. General Pemberton, the commander at that point, advanced with the hope of checking him, but was defeated, on the 16th, at Baker's Creek, losing 4,000 men and twenty-nine pieces of artillery. On the next day the same force was encountered and defeated at Big Black River Bridge, ten miles from Vicksburg, with a loss of 2,600 men, and seventeen pieces of artillery. On the 18th, Vicksburg was closely invested, and the enemy were shut up within their works, which were found to be very strong. An attempt to carry them by storm was unsuccessful, and regular siege was at once laid to the city by the land forces, the gunboats in the river co-operating. Our approaches were pushed forward with vigorous perseverance; our works, in spite of the most strenuous opposition of the garrison under General Pemberton, drawing nearer every day, and the gunboats in the river keeping up an almost constant bombardment. The enemy, it was known, were greatly straitened by want of supplies and ammunition, and their only hope of relief was that General Johnston would be able to collect an army sufficient to raise the siege by attacking Grant in his rear. This had been so strongly defended that a force of 50,000 men would have been required to make the attempt with any hope of success, and Johnston was not able to concentrate half of that number. On the morning of the 4th of July, therefore, General Pemberton proposed to surrender Vicksburg, on condition that his troops should be permitted to march out. Grant refused, demanding an absolute surrender of the garrison as prisoners of war. Upon consultation with his officers, Pemberton acceded to these terms. By this surrender about 31,000 prisoners, 220 cannon, and 70,000 stand of small arms fell into our hands. The prisoners were at once released on parole. The entire loss of the enemy during the campaign which was thus closed by the surrender of Vicksburg, was nearly 40,000; ours was not far from 7,000.

The capture of Vicksburg was immediately followed by that of Port Hudson, which was surrendered on the 8th of July to General Banks, together with about 7,000 prisoners, fifty cannon, and a considerable number of small arms. The whole course of the Mississippi, from its source to its mouth, was thus opened, and the Confederacy virtually separated into two parts, neither capable of rendering any effective assistance to the other.

The great victories, by which the Fourth of July had been so signally, and so gloriously commemorated, called forth the most enthusiastic rejoicings in every section of the country. Public meetings were held in nearly all the cities and principal towns, at which eloquent speeches and earnest resolutions expressed the joy of the people, and testified their unflinching purpose to prosecute the war until the rebellion should be extinguished. A large concourse of the citizens of Washington preceded by a band of music, visited the residence of the President, and the members of his cabinet—giving them, in succession, the honors of a serenade—which the President acknowledged, in the following remarks:

FELLOW-CITIZENS: I am very glad indeed to see you to-night, and yet I will not say I thank you, for this call; but I do most sincerely thank Almighty God for the occasion on which you have called. How long ago is it,—eighty odd years since on the Fourth of July, for the first time, in the history of the world, a nation, by its representatives, assembled and declared as a self-evident truth, "that all men are created equal." That was the birthday of the United States of America. Since then the Fourth of July has had several very peculiar recognitions. The two men most distinguished in the framing and support of the Declaration were THOMAS JEFFERSON and JOHN ADAMS—the one having penned it, and the other sustained it the most forcibly in debate—the only two of the fifty-five who signed it, and were elected Presidents of the United States. Precisely fifty years after they put their hands to the paper, it pleased Almighty God to take both from this stage of action. This was indeed an extraordinary and remarkable event in our history. Another President, five years after, was called from this stage of existence on the same day and month of the year; and now on this last Fourth of July, just passed, when we have a gigantic rebellion, at the bottom of which is an effort to overthrow the principle that all men were created equal, we have the surrender of a most powerful position and army on that very day. And not only so, but in a succession of battles in Pennsylvania, near to us, through three days, so rapidly fought that they might be called one great battle, on the first, second, and third of the month of July; and on the fourth the cohorts of those who opposed the Declaration that all men are created equal, "turned tail" and run. [Long continued cheers.] Gentlemen, this is a glorious theme, and the occasion for a speech, but I am not prepared to make one worthy of the occasion. I would like to speak in terms of praise due to the many brave officers and soldiers who have fought in the cause of the Union and liberties of their country from the beginning of the war. These are trying occasions, not only in success, but for the want of success. I dislike to mention the name of one single officer, lest I might do wrong to those I might forget. Recent events bring up glorious names, and particularly prominent ones; but these I will not mention. Having said this much, I will now take the music.

The President, a few days afterwards, wrote to General Grant the following letter:

EXECUTIVE MANSION, WASHINGTON, *July* 13, 1863.

Major-General GRANT:

MY DEAR GENERAL:—I do not remember that you and I ever met personally. I write this now as a grateful acknowledgment for the almost inestimable service you have done the country. I write to say a word further. When you first reached the vicinity of Vicksburg, I thought you should do what you finally did—march the troops across the neck, run the batteries with the transports, and thus go below; and I never had any faith, except a general hope that you knew better than I, that the Yazoo Pass expedition, and the like, could succeed. When you got below, and took Port Gibson, Grand Gulf, and vicinity, I thought you should go down the river, and join General Banks, and when you turned northward, east of the Big Black, I feared it was a mistake. I now wish to make the personal acknowledgment, that you were right and I was wrong. Yours, truly,

A. LINCOLN.

These victories, together with others, both numerous and important, which were achieved in other sections of the country, gave such strong grounds of encouragement and hope for the speedy overthrow of the rebellion, that, on the 15th of July, the President issued the following proclamation for a day of National Thanksgiving:

By the President of the United States of America.

A PROCLAMATION.

It has pleased Almighty God to hearken to the supplications and prayers of an afflicted people, and to vouchsafe to the Army and the Navy of the United States, on the land and on the sea, victories so signal and so effective as to furnish reasonable grounds for augmented confidence that the Union of these States will be maintained, their Constitution preserved, and their peace and prosperity permanently secured; but these victories have been accorded, not without sacrifice of life, limb, and liberty, incurred by brave, patriotic, and loyal citizens. Domestic affliction, in every part of the country, follows in the train of these fearful bereavements. It is meet and right to recognize and confess the presence of the Almighty Father, and the power of His hand equally in these triumphs and these sorrows.

Now, therefore, be it known, that I do set apart Thursday, the sixth day of August next, to be observed as a day for National Thanksgiving, praise, and prayer; and I invite the people of the United States to assemble on that occasion in their customary places of worship, and in the form approved by their own conscience, render the homage due to the Divine Majesty, for the wonderful things He has done in the Nation's behalf, and invoke the influence of His Holy Spirit, to subdue the anger which has produced, and so long sustained a needless and cruel rebellion; to change the hearts of the insurgents; to guide the counsels of the Government with wisdom adequate to so great a National emergency, and to visit with tender care, and consolation, throughout the length and breadth of our land, all those who, through the vicissitudes of marches, voyages, battles, and sieges, have been brought to suffer in mind, body, or estate, and finally, to lead the whole nation through paths of repentance and submission to the Divine will, back to the perfect enjoyment of union and fraternal peace.

In witness whereof, I have hereunto set my hand, and caused the seal of the United States to be affixed.

Done at the City of Washington, this 15th day of July, in the year of our Lord one thousand eight hundred and sixty-three, and of [L. S.] the independence of the United States of America the eighty-eighth.

ABRAHAM LINCOLN.

By the President:

WM. H. SEWARD, *Secretary of State.*

In other portions of the field of war, our arms, during the year 1863, had achieved other victories of marked importance which deserve mention, though their relation to the special object of this work is not such as to require them to be described in detail.

After the retreat of the rebel General Lee to the south side of the Rapidan, a considerable portion of his army was detached and sent to re-enforce Bragg, threatened by Rosecrans, at Chattanooga; but, with his numbers thus diminished, Lee assumed a threatening attitude against Meade, and turning his left flank forced him to fall back to the line of Bull Run. Several sharp skirmishes occurred during these operations, in which both sides sustained considerable losses, but no substantial advantage was gained by the rebels, and by the 1st of November they had resumed their original position on the south side of the Rapidan.

After the battle of Murfreesboro, and the occupation of that place by our troops, on the 5th of January, 1863, the enemy took position at Shelbyville and Tullahoma, and the winter and spring were passed in raids and unimportant skirmishes. In June, while General Grant was besieging Vicksburg, information reached the government which led to the belief that a portion of Bragg's army had been sent to the relief of that place; and General Rosecrans was urged to take advantage of this division of the rebel forces and drive them back into Georgia, so as completely to deliver East Tennessee from the rebel armies. He was told that General Burnside would move from Kentucky in aid of this movement. General Rosecrans, however, deemed his forces unequal to such an enterprise; but, receiving re-enforcements, he commenced on the 25th of June a forward movement upon the enemy, strongly intrenched at Tullahoma, with his main force near Shelbyville. Deceiving the rebel General by a movement upon his left flank, Rosecrans threw the main body of his army upon the enemy's right, which he turned so completely that Bragg abandoned his position, and fell back rapidly, and in confusion, to Bridgeport, Alabama, being pursued as far as practicable by our forces. General Burnside had been ordered to connect himself with Rosecrans, but had failed to do so. Bragg continued his retreat across the Cumberland Mountain and the Tennessee River, and took post at Chattanooga, whither he was pursued by Rosecrans, who reached the Tennessee on the 20th of August, and on the 21st commenced shelling Chattanooga and making preparation for throwing his army across the river. A reconnoisance, made by General Crittenden on the 9th of September, disclosed the fact, that the rebels had abandoned the position, which was immediately occupied by our forces, who pushed forward towards the South. Indications that the rebel General was receiving heavy re-enforcements and manœuvring to turn the right of our army, led to a concentration of all our available forces, and, subsequently, to the appointment of General Grant to command the whole army thus brought together. On the 19th of September, General Rosecrans was attacked by the rebel forces—their main force being directed against his left wing under General Thomas, endeavoring to turn it so as to gain the road to Chattanooga. The attack was renewed the next morning, and with temporary success—Longstreet's Corps having reached the field and poured its massive columns through a gap left in the centre of our line by an unfortunate misapprehension of an order; but the opportune arrival and swift energy of General Granger checked his advance, and the desperate valor of Thomas and his troops repulsed every subsequent attempt of the enemy to carry the position. Our losses, in this series of engagements, were 1,644 killed, 9,262 wounded, and 4,845 missing—a total swelled by the estimated losses of our cavalry to about 16,351. The rebel General immediately sent Longstreet against Burnside, who was at Knoxville, while he established his main force again in the neighborhood of Chattanooga. On the 23d of November, General Grant moved his army to attack him, and on the 25th the whole of the range of heights known as Missionary Ridge, held by Bragg, was carried by our troops after a desperate struggle, and the enemy completely routed. This was a very severe engagement, and our loss was estimated at about 4,000. Generals Thomas and Hooker pushed the rebel forces back into Georgia, and Granger and Sherman were sent into East Tennessee to relieve Burnside and raise the siege of Knoxville, which was pressed by Longstreet, who, failing in this attempt, soon after retreated towards Virginia.

Upon receiving intelligence of these movements the President issued the following recommendation:

EXECUTIVE MANSION, WASHINGTON, D. C., *December* 7, 1863.

Reliable information being received that the insurgent force is retreat ing from East Tennessee, under circumstances rendering it probable that the Union forces cannot hereafter be dislodged from that important position; and esteeming this to be of high national consequence, I recommend that all loyal people do, on receipt of this information, assemble at their places of worship, and render special homage and gratitude to Almighty God for this great advancement of the National cause.

A. LINCOLN.

On the 3d of October, the President had issued the following proclamation, recommending the observance of the last Thursday of November as a day of Thanksgiving:

PROCLAMATION

By the President of the United States of America.

The year that is drawing towards its close has been filled with the blessings of fruitful fields and healthful skies. To these bounties, which are so constantly enjoyed that we are prone to forget the source from which they come, others have been added which are of so extraordinary a nature that they cannot fail to penetrate and soften even the heart which is habitually insensible to the ever watchful providence of Almighty God. In the midst of a civil war of unequalled magnitude and severity, which has sometimes seemed to invite and provoke the aggressions of foreign States, peace has been preserved with all nations, order has been maintained, the laws have been respected and obeyed, and harmony has prevailed everywhere except in the theatre of military conflict, while that theatre has been greatly contracted by the advancing armies and navies of the Union. The needful diversion of wealth and strength from the fields of peaceful industry to the national defence, have not arrested the plough, the shuttle, or the ship. The axe has enlarged the borders of our settlements, and the mines, as well of iron and coal as of the precious metals, have yielded even more abundantly than heretofore. Population has steadily increased, notwithstanding the waste that has been made in the camp, the siege, and the battle-field; and the country, rejoicing in the consciousness of augmented strength and vigor, is permitted to expect a continuance of years, with large increase of freedom.

No human counsel hath devised, nor hath any mortal hand worked out these great things. They are the gracious gifts of the Most High God, who, while dealing with us in anger for our sins, hath nevertheless remembered mercy.

It has seemed to me fit and proper that they should be solemnly, reverently, and gratefully acknowledged, as with one heart and voice, by the whole American people. I do, therefore, invite my fellow-citizens in every part of the United States, and also those who are at sea, and those who are sojourning in foreign lands, to set apart and observe the last Thursday of November next as a day of thanksgiving and prayer to our beneficent Father, who dwelleth in the heavens. And I recommend to them that, while offering up the ascriptions justly due to Him for such singular deliverances and blessings, they do also, with humble penitence for our national perverseness and disobedience, commend to his tender care all those who have become widows, orphans, mourners, or sufferers in the lamentable civil strife in which we are unavoidably engaged, and fervently implore the interposition of the Almighty hand to heal the wounds of the nation, and to restore it, as soon as may be consistent with the divine purposes, to the full enjoyment of peace, harmony, tranquillity, and union.

In testimony whereof, I have hereunto set my hand, and caused the seal of the United States to be affixed.

Done at the city of Washington, this third day of October, in the
[L. S.] year of our Lord 1863, and of the independence of the
United States the eighty-eighth.

ABRAHAM LINCOLN.

By the President:

WILLIAM H. SEWARD, *Secretary of State.*

CHAPTER X.

POLITICAL MOVEMENTS IN MISSOURI.—THE STATE ELECTIONS OF 1863.

THE condition of affairs in Missouri has been somewhat peculiar, from the very outbreak of the rebellion. At the outset the Executive Department of the State government was in the hands of men in full sympathy with the secession cause, who, under pretence of protecting the State from domestic violence, were organizing its forces for active co-operation with the rebel movement. On the 30th of July, 1861, the State Convention, originally called by Governor Jackson, for the purpose of taking Missouri out of the Union, but to which the people had elected a large majority of Union men, declared all the Executive offices of the State vacant, by reason of the treasonable conduct of the incumbents, and appointed a Provisional Government, of which the Hon. H. R. Gamble was at the head. He at once took measures to maintain the National authority within the State. He ordered the troops belonging to the rebel confederacy to withdraw from it, and called upon all the citizens of the State to organize for its defence, and for the preservation of peace within its borders. He also issued a proclamation, framed in accordance with the following suggestions from Washington:

WASHINGTON, *August* 3, 1861.

To His Excellency Gov. GAMBLE, Governor of Missouri:

In reply to your Message, addressed to the President, I am directed to say, that if, by a Proclamation, you promise security to citizens in arms, who voluntarily return to their allegiance, and behave as peaceable and loyal men, this Government will cause the promise to be respected.

SIMON CAMERON, *Secretary of War.*

Two days after this, Governor Jackson, returning from Richmond, declared the State to be no longer one of the United States; and on the 2d of November, the Legislature, summoned by him as Governor, ratified a compact, by which certain commissioners, on both sides, had agreed that Missouri should join the rebel confederacy. The State authority was thus divided—two persons claiming to wield the Executive authority, and two bodies, also, claiming to represent the popular will,—one adhering to the Union, and the other to the Confederacy in organized rebellion against it. This state of things naturally led to wide-spread disorder, and carried all the evils of civil war into every section and neighborhood of the State.

To these evils were gradually added others, growing out of a division of sentiment, which afterwards ripened into sharp hostility, among the friends of the Union within the State. One of the earliest causes of this dissension was the action and removal of General Fremont, who arrived at St. Louis, to take command of the Western Department, on the 26th of July, 1861. On the 31st of August he issued a Proclamation, declaring that circumstances, in his judgment, of sufficient urgency, rendered it necessary that "*the commanding general of the Department should assume the administrative power of the State*," thus superseding entirely the authority of the civil rulers. He also proclaimed the whole State to be under martial law, declared that all persons taken with arms in their hands, within the designated lines of the Department, should be tried by court-martial, and if found guilty, shot; and confiscating the property and emancipating the slaves of "all persons who should be proved to have taken an active part with the enemies of the United States." This latter clause, transcending the authority conferred by the confiscation act of Congress, was subsequently modified by order of the President of the United States.*

* See page 161.

On the 14th of October, after a personal inspection of affairs in that department by the Secretary of War, an order was issued from the War Department, in effect censuring General Fremont for having expended very large sums of the public money, through agents of his own appointment, and not responsible to the government;—requiring all contracts and disbursements to be made by the proper officers of the army;—directing the discontinuance of the extensive field-works, which the General was erecting around St. Louis and Jefferson City; and also the barracks in construction around his head-quarters, and also notifying him that the officers, to whom he had issued commissions, would not be paid until those commissions should have been approved by the President. On the 1st of November, General Fremont entered into an agreement with General Sterling Price, commanding the rebel forces in Missouri, by which each party stipulated that no further arrests of citizens should be made on either side for the expression of political opinions, and releasing all who were then in custody on such charges.

On the 2d of November, General Fremont was relieved from his command in the Western Department, in consequence of his action in the matters above referred to, his command devolving on General Hunter, to whom, as soon as a change in the command of the Department had been decided on, the President had addressed the following letter:

WASHINGTON, *October* 24, 1861.

SIR:—The command of the Department of the West having devolved upon you, I propose to offer you a few *suggestions*, knowing how hazardous it is to bind down a distant commander in the field to specific lines of operation, as so much always depends on the knowledge of localities and passing events. It is intended, therefore, to leave considerable margin for the exercise of your judgment and discretion.

The main rebel army (Price's) west of the Mississippi is believed to have passed Dade county in full retreat upon Northwestern Arkansas, leaving Missouri almost free from the enemy, excepting in the southeast part of the State. Assuming this basis of fact, it seems desirable—as you are not likely to overtake Price, and are in danger of making too long a line from your own base of supplies and re-enforcements—that you should give up the pursuit, halt your main army, divide it into two corps of observation, one occupying Sedalia and the other Rolla, the present termini of railroads, then recruit the condition of both corps by re-establishing and improving their discipline and instruction, perfecting their clothing and equipments, and providing less uncomfortable quarters. Of course, both railroads must be guarded and kept open, judiciously employing just so much force as is necessary for this. From these two points, Sedalia and Rolla, and especially in judicious co-operation with Lane on the Kansas border, it would be very easy to concentrate, and repel any army of the enemy returning on Missouri on the Southwest. As it is not probable any such attempt to return will be made before or during the approaching cold weather, before spring the people of Missouri will be in no favorable mood for renewing for next year the troubles which have so much afflicted and impoverished them during this.

If you take this line of policy, and if, as I anticipate, you will see no enemy in great force approaching, you will have a surplus force which you can withdraw from those points, and direct to others, as may be needed—the railroads furnishing ready means of re-enforcing those main points, if occasion requires.

Doubtless local uprisings for a time will continue to occur, but those can be met by detachments of local forces of our own, and will ere long tire out of themselves.

While, as stated at the beginning of this letter, a large discretion must be and is left with yourself, I feel sure that an indefinite pursuit of Price, or an attempt by this long and circuitous route to reach Memphis, will be exhaustive beyond endurance, and will end in the loss of the whole force engaged in it. Your obedient servant,

A. LINCOLN.

The Commander of the Department of the West.

General Hunter's first act was to repudiate the agreement of Gen. Fremont with General Price, and, on the 18th of November, General Halleck arrived as his successor.

The action of General Fremont had given rise to very serious complaints on the part of the people of Missouri; and these in turn had led to strong demonstrations on his behalf.

His removal was made the occasion for public manifestations of sympathy for him, and of censure for the government. An address was presented to him, signed by large numbers of the citizens of St. Louis, those of German birth largely predominating, in which his removal was ascribed to jealousy of his popularity, and to the fact that his policy in regard to emancipation was in advance of the government at Washington. "You have risen," said this address, "too fast in popular favor. The policy announced in your proclamation, although hailed as a political and military necessity, furnished your ambitious rivals and enemies with a cruel weapon for your intended destruction. The harbingers of truth will ever be crucified by the Pharisees. We cannot be deceived by shallow and flimsy pretexts, by unfounded and slanderous reports. We entertain no doubt of your ability to speedily confound and silence your traducers. The day of reckoning is not far distant, and the people will take care that the schemes of your opponents shall, in the end be signally defeated." The General accepted these tributes to his merits, and these denunciations of the government, with grateful acknowledgments, saying that the kind and affectionate demonstrations which greeted him, cheered and strengthened his confidence—"my confidence," he said, "already somewhat wavering, in our republican institutions."

The sharp personal discussions to which this incident gave rise, were made still more bitter, by denunciations of General Halleck's course in excluding, for military reasons, which have been already noticed,* fugitive slaves from our lines, and by the contest that soon came up in the State Convention, on the general subject of emancipation. On the 7th of June, 1862, a bill was introduced into the Convention by Judge Breckinridge, of St. Louis, for gradual emancipation, framed in accordance with the recommendation of the President's Mes-

* See page 292.

sage. By the combined votes of those who were opposed to emancipation in any form, and those who were opposed to the President's plan of gradual emancipation, this bill was summarily laid on the table. But on the 13th, the subject was again brought up by a Message from Governor Gamble, calling attention to the fact, that Congress had passed a resolution, in accordance with the President's recommendation, declaring that "the United States ought to co-operate with any State which might adopt a gradual emancipation of slavery, giving to such State, at its discretion, compensation for the inconvenience, public and private, caused by such a change of system." This message was referred to a special committee, which reported resolutions, recognizing the generous spirit of this proposal, but declining to take any action upon it. These resolutions were adopted, and on the 16th a Mass Convention of Emancipationists, consisting of 195 delegates from 25 counties, met at Jefferson City, and passed resolutions, declaring it to be the duty of the next General Assembly to pass laws, giving effect to a gradual system of emancipation on the basis proposed.

At the State election, in the following November, the question of emancipation was the leading theme of controversy. Throughout the State the canvass turned upon this issue, and resulted in the choice of a decided majority of the Assembly favorable to emancipation. But the division in the ranks of this party still continued, and gave rise to very heated and bitter contests, especially in St. Louis. During the summer, the main rebel army having been driven from the State, and the Union army being of necessity in the main withdrawn to other fields, the State was overrun by reckless bands of rebel guerrillas, who robbed and plundered Union citizens, and created very great alarm among the people. In consequence of these outrages, Governor Gamble ordered the organization of the entire militia of the State, and authorized General

Schofield to call into active service such portions of it as might be needed to put down marauders, and defend peaceable and loyal citizens. The organization was effected with great promptness, and the State militia became a powerful auxiliary of the national forces, and cleared all sections of the State of the lawless bands which had inflicted so much injury and committed so many outrages.

On the 19th of September, the States of Missouri, Kansas, and Arkansas, were formed into a military district, of which the command was assigned to General Curtis, who was thoroughly in sympathy with the friends of immediate emancipation and the supporters of General Fremont in his differences with the government. He had control of the national forces in his district, but Governor Gamble did not give him command of the State militia.

The differences of political sentiment between the two sections of the Union men of the State came thus to be represented, to some extent, by two organized military forces; and the contest between their respective partisans continued to be waged with increasing bitterness, greatly to the embarrassment of the government at Washington, and to the weakening of the Union cause. This continued until the spring of 1863, when the President removed General Curtis from his command, and appointed General Schofield in his place. This gave rise to very vehement remonstrances and protests, to one of which, sent by telegraph, the President made the following reply:

> Your dispatch of to-day is just received. It is very painful to me that you, in Missouri, cannot, or will not, settle your factional quarrel among yourselves. I have been tormented with it beyond endurance, for months, by both sides. Neither side pays the least respect to my appeals to your reason. I am now compelled to take hold of the case.
>
> A. LINCOLN.

To General Schofield himself, the President soon after addressed the following letter:

EXECUTIVE MANSION,
WASHINGTON, *May* 27, 1863.

General J. M. SCHOFIELD:

DEAR SIR:—Having removed General Curtis and assigned you to the command of the Department of the Missouri, I think it may be of some advantage to me to state to you why I did it. I did not remove General Curtis because of my full conviction that he had done wrong by commission or omission. I did it because of a conviction in my mind that the Union men of Missouri, constituting, when united, a vast majority of the people, have entered into a pestilent, factious quarrel, among themselves, General Curtis, perhaps not of choice, being the head of one faction, and Governor Gamble that of the other. After months of labor to reconcile the difficulty, it seemed to grow worse and worse, until I felt it my duty to break it up somehow, and as I could not remove Governor Gamble, I had to remove General Curtis. Now that you are in the position, I wish you to undo nothing merely because General Curtis or Governor Gamble did it, but to exercise your own judgment, and do right for the public interest. Let your military measures be strong enough to repel the invaders and keep the peace, and not so strong as to unnecessarily harass and persecute the people. It is a difficult *rôle*, and so much greater will be the honor if you perform it well. If both factions, or neither, shall abuse you, you will probably be about right. Beware of being assailed by one and praised by the other.

Yours truly, A. LINCOLN.

This action gave special dissatisfaction to the more radical Unionists of the State. They had been anxious to have the Provisional Government, of which Governor Gamble was the Executive head, set aside by the national authority, and the control of the State vested in a Military Governor clothed with the authority which General Fremont had assumed to exercise by his proclamation of August 31st, 1861;—and the Germans enlisted in the movement had made very urgent demands for the restoration of General Fremont himself. Several deputations visited Washington, for the purpose of representing these views and wishes to the President,—though they by no means restricted their efforts at reform to matters within their own State, but insisted upon sundry changes in the

Cabinet, upon the dismissal of General Halleck from the position of Commander of the Armies of the United States and upon other matters of equal magnitude and importance.

The following report of President LINCOLN's reply to these various requests, was made by a member of a Committee appointed at a mass meeting, composed mainly of Germans, and held at St. Louis on the 10th of May: although made by a person opposed to the President's action, it probably gives a substantially correct statement of his remarks:

Messrs. EMILE PRETORIOUS, THEODORE OLSHAUSEN, R. E. ROMBAUR, etc.:

GENTLEMEN:—During a professional visit to Washington city, I presented to the President of the United States, in compliance with your instructions, a copy of the resolutions adopted in mass meeting at St. Louis on the 10th of May, 1863, and I requested a reply to the suggestions therein contained. The President, after a careful and loud reading of the whole report of proceedings, saw proper to enter into a conversation of two hours' duration, in the course of which most of the topics embraced in the resolutions and other subjects were discussed.

As my share in the conversation is of secondary importance, I propose to omit it entirely in this report, and, avoiding details, to communicate to you the substance of noteworthy remarks made by the President.

1. The President said that it may be a misfortune for the nation that he was elected President. But, having been elected by the people, he meant to be President, and perform his duty according to *his* best understanding, if he had to die for it. No General will be removed, nor will any change in the Cabinet be made, to suit the views or wishes of any particular party, faction or set of men. General Halleck is not guilty of the charges made against him, most of which arise from misapprehension or ignorance of those who prefer them.

2. The President said that it was a mistake to suppose that Generals John C. Fremont, B. F. Butler, and F. Sigel are "systematically kept out of command," as stated in the fourth resolution; that, on the contrary, he fully appreciated the merits of the gentlemen named; that by their own actions they had placed themselves in the positions which they occupied; that he was not only willing, but anxious to place them again in command as soon as he could find spheres of action for them, without doing injustice to others, but that at present he "had more pegs than holes to put them in."

3. As to the want of unity, the President, without admitting such to be the case, intimated that each member of the Cabinet was responsible

mainly for the manner of conducting the affairs of his particular department; that there was no centralization of responsibility for the action of the Cabinet anywhere, except in the President himself.

4. The dissensions between Union men in Missouri are due solely to a factious spirit which is exceedingly reprehensible. The two parties "ought to have their heads knocked together." "Either would rather see the defeat of their adversary than that of Jefferson Davis." To this spirit of faction is to be ascribed the failure of the Legislature to elect senators and the defeat of the Missouri Aid Bill in Congress, the passage of which the President strongly desired.

The President said that the Union men in Missouri who are in favor of *gradual emancipation* represented his views better than those who are in favor of *immediate emancipation*. In explanation of his views on this subject, the President said that in his speeches he had frequently used as an illustration, the case of a man who had an excrescence on the back of his neck, the removal of which, *in one operation*, would result in the death of the patient, while "tinkering it off by degrees" would preserve life. Although sorely tempted, I did not reply with the illustration of the dog whose tail was amputated by inches, but confined myself to arguments. *The President announced clearly that, as far as he was at present advised, the Radicals in Missouri had no right to consider themselves the exponents of his views on the subject of emancipation in that State.*

5. General Curtis was not relieved on account of any wrong act or great mistake committed by him. The System of Provost-Marshals, established by him throughout the State, gave rise to violent complaint. That the President had thought at one time to appoint General Fremont in his place; that at another time he had thought of appointing General McDowell, whom he characterized as a good and loyal though very unfortunate soldier; and that, at last, General Schofield was appointed, with a view, if possible, to reconcile and satisfy the two factions in Missouri. He has instructions not to interfere with either party, but to confine himself to his military duties. I assure you, gentlemen, that our side was as fully presented as the occasion permitted. At the close of the conversation, the President remarked that there was evidently a "serious misunderstanding" springing up between him and the Germans of St. Louis, which he would like to see removed. Observing to him that the difference of opinion related to facts, men, and measures, I withdrew.

I am, very respectfully, etc.

JAMES TAUSSIG.

On the 1st of July the State Convention, in session at Jefferson City, passed an amendment to the Constitution declaring that slavery should cease to exist in Missouri on the

4th of July, 1870, with certain specified exceptions. This, however, was by no means accepted as a final disposition of the matter. The demand was made for immediate emancipation, and Gov. Gamble and the members of the Provisional Government who had favored the policy adopted by the State Convention, were denounced as the advocates of slavery and allies of the rebellion. In the early part of August a band of rebel guerrillas made a raid into the town of Lawrence, Kansas, and butchered in cold blood over two hundred unarmed citizens of the place. This brutal act aroused the most intense excitement in the adjoining State of Missouri, of which the opponents of the Provisional Government took advantage to throw upon it and General Schofield, who had command of the State militia as well as of the national forces, the responsibility in having permitted this massacre to take place.

A Mass Convention was held at Jefferson City on the 2d of September, at which resolutions were adopted denouncing the military policy pursued in the State and the delegation of military powers to the provisional government. A Committee of one from each county was appointed to visit Washington and lay their grievances before the President; and arrangements were also made for the appointment of a Committee of Public Safety, to organize and arm the loyal men of the State, and, in the event of not obtaining relief, to call on the people in their sovereign capacity to "take such measures of redress as the emergency might require." In the latter part of September the Committee appointed by this Convention visited Washington and had an interview with the President on the 30th, in which they represented Governor Gamble and General Schofield as in virtual alliance with the rebels, and demanded the removal of the latter as an act of justice to the loyal and anti-slavery men of the State. The Committee visited several of the northern cities, and held public meetings for the purpose of enlisting public sentiment in their support.

At these meetings it was claimed that the radical emancipation party was the only one which represented the loyalty of Missouri, and President LINCOLN was very strongly censured for "closing his ears to just, loyal, and patriotic demands of the radical party, while he indorsed the disloyal and oppressive demands of Governor Gamble, General Schofield, and their adherents."

On the 5th of October President LINCOLN made to the representations and requests of the Committee the following reply:

EXECUTIVE MANSION, WASHINGTON, *Oct.* 5, 1863.

Hon. CHARLES DRAKE and others, Committee:

GENTLEMEN:—Your original address, presented on the 30th ult., and the four supplementary ones presented on the 3d inst., have been carefully considered. I hope you will regard the other duties claiming my attention, together with the great length and importance of these documents, as constituting a sufficient apology for my not having responded sooner.

These papers, framed for a common object, consist of the things demanded, and the reasons for demanding them.

The things demanded are:

First—That General Schofield shall be relieved, and General Butler be appointed as Commander of the Military Department of Missouri;

Second—That the system of enrolled militia in Missouri may be broken up, and National forces be substituted for it; and

Third—That at elections, persons may not be allowed to vote who are not entitled by law to do so.

Among the reasons given, enough of suffering and wrong to Union men, is certainly, and I suppose truly, stated. Yet the whole case, as presented, fails to convince me that General Schofield, or the enrolled militia, is responsible for that suffering and wrong. The whole can be explained on a more charitable, and, as I think, a more rational hypothesis.

We are in civil war. In such cases there always is a main question; but in this case that question is a perplexing compound—Union and Slavery. It thus becomes a question not of two sides merely, but of at least four sides, even among those who are for the Union, saying nothing of those who are against it. Thus, those who are for the Union *with*, but not *without Slavery*—those for it *without* but not *with*—those for it *with* or *without*, but prefer it *with*, and those for it *with* or *without*, but prefer it *without*.

Among these, again, is a subdivision of those who are for *gradual*, but not for *immediate*, and those who are for *immediate*, but not for *gradual* extinction of slavery.

It is easy to conceive that all these shades of opinion and even more, may be sincerely entertained by honest and truthful men. Yet, all being for the Union, by reason of these differences, each will prefer a different way of sustaining the Union. At once, sincerity is questioned, and motives are assailed. Actual war coming, blood grows hot, and blood is spilled. Thought is forced from old channels into confusion. Deception breeds and thrives. Confidence dies, and universal suspicion reigns. Each man feels an impulse to kill his neighbor, lest he be killed by him. Revenge and retaliation follow. And all this, as before said, may be among honest men only. But this is not all. Every foul bird comes abroad, and every dirty reptile rises up. These add crime to confusion. Strong measures deemed indispensable but harsh at best, such men make worse by maladministration. Murders for old grudges, and murders for pelf proceed under any cloak that will best serve for the occasion.

These causes amply account for what has occurred in Missouri, without ascribing it to the weakness or wickedness of any general. The newspaper files, those chroniclers of current events, will show that the evils now complained of, were quite as prevalent under Fremont, Hunter, Halleck, and Curtis, as under Schofield. If the former had greater force opposed to them, they also had greater force with which to meet it. When the organized rebel army left the State, the main Federal force had to go also, leaving the Department Commander at home, relatively no stronger than before. Without disparaging any, I affirm with confidence, that no Commander of that Department has, in proportion to his means, done better than General Schofield.

The first specific charge against General Schofield is, that the enrolled militia was placed under his command, whereas it had not been placed under the command of General Curtis. The fact is, I believe, true; but you do not point out, nor can I conceive how that did, or could, injure loyal men or the Union cause.

You charge that General Curtis being superseded by General Schofield, Franklin A. Dick was superseded by James O. Broadhead as Provost-Marshal General. No very specific showing is made as to how this did or could injure the Union cause. It recalls, however, the condition of things, as presented to me, which led to a change of commander of that department.

To restrain contraband intelligence and trade, a system of searches, seizures, permits and passes, had been introduced, I think, by General Fremont. When General Halleck came, he found and continued the system, and added an order, applicable to some parts of the State, to levy and collect contributions from noted rebels, to compensate losses, and relieve destitution caused by the rebellion. The action of General Fremont and General Halleck, as stated, constituted a sort of system which General Curtis found in full operation when he took command of the department. That there was a necessity for something of the sort was clear; but that it could only be justified by stern necessity, and that it was liable to great abuse in administration, was equally clear. Agents to execute it, contrary to the great prayer, were led into temptation. Some might, while others would not resist that temptation. It was not possible to hold any to a very strict accountability; and those yielding to the temptation, would sell permits and passes to those who would pay most, and most readily for them; and would seize property and collect levies in the aptest way to fill their own pockets. Money being the object, the man having money, whether loyal or disloyal, would be a victim. This practice doubtless existed to some extent, and it was a real additional evil, that it could be, and was plausibly charged to exist in greater extent than it did.

When General Curtis took command of the department, Mr. Dick, against whom I never knew anything to allege, had general charge of this system. A controversy in regard to it rapidly grew into almost unmanageable proportions. One side ignored the *necessity* and magnified the evils of the system, while the other ignored the evils and magnified the necessity; and each bitterly assailed the other. I could not fail to see that the controversy enlarged in the same proportion as the professed Union men there distinctly took sides in two opposing political parties. I exhausted my wits, and very nearly my patience also, in efforts to convince both that the evils they charged on each other were inherent in the case, and could not be cured by giving either party a victory over the other.

Plainly, the irritating system was not to be perpetual; and it was plausibly urged that it could be modified at once with advantage. The case could scarcely be worse, and whether it could be made better could only be determined by a trial. In this view, and not to ban, or brand General Curtis, or to give a victory to any party, I made the change of commander for the department. I now learn that soon after this change Mr. Dick was removed, and that Mr. Broadhead, a gentleman of no less good character, was put in the place. The mere fact of this change is more distinctly complained of than is any conduct of the new officer, or other consequence of the change.

I gave the new commander no instructions as to the administration of the system mentioned, beyond what is contained in the private letter afterward surreptitiously published, in which I directed him to act solely for the public good, and independently of both parties. Neither anything you have presented me, nor anything I have otherwise learned, has convinced me that he has been unfaithful to this charge.

Imbecility is urged as one cause for removing General Schofield, and the late massacre at Lawrence, Kansas, is pressed as evidence of that imbecility. To my mind that fact scarcely tends to prove the proposition. That massacre is only an example of what Grierson, John Morgan, and many others, might have repeatedly done on their respective raids, had they chosen to incur the personal hazard, and possessed the fiendish hearts to do it.

The charge is made that General Schofield, on purpose to protect the Lawrence murderers, would not allow them to be pursued into Missouri. While no punishment could be too sudden or too severe for those murderers, I am well satisfied that the preventing of the threatened remedial raid into Missouri was the only way to avoid an indiscrimate massacre there, including probably more innocent than guilty. Instead of condemning, I therefore approve what I understand General Schofield did in that respect.

The charge that General Schofield has purposely withheld protection from loyal people, and purposely facilitated the objects of the disloyal, are altogether beyond my power of belief. I do not arraign the veracity of gentlemen as to the facts complained of; but I do more than question the judgment which would infer that these facts occurred in accordance with the purposes of General Schofield.

With my present views, I must decline to remove General Schofield. In this I decide nothing against General Butler. I sincerely wish it were convenient to assign him a suitable command.

In order to meet some existing evils, I have addressed a letter of instruction to General Schofield, a copy of which I inclose to you. As to the "Enrolled Militia," I shall endeavor to ascertain, better than I now know, what is its exact value. Let me say now, however, that your proposal to substitute national force for the "Enrolled Militia," implies that, in your judgment, the latter is doing something which needs to be done; and if so, the proposition to throw that force away, and to supply its place by bringing other forces from the field where they are urgently needed, seems to me very extraordinary. Whence shall they come? Shall they be withdrawn from Banks, or Grant, or Steele, or Rosecrans?

Few things have been so grateful to my anxious feelings, as when, in June last, the local force in Missouri aided General Schofield to so promptly send a large general force to the relief of General Grant, then investing Vicksburg, and menaced from without by General Johnston. Was this all wrong? Should the Enrolled Militia then have been broken up, and General Heron kept from Grant, to police Missouri? So far from finding cause to object, I confess to a sympathy for whatever relieves our general force in Missouri, and allows it to serve elsewhere.

I therefore, as at present advised, cannot attempt the destruction of the Enrolled Militia of Missouri. I may add, that the force being under the national military control, it is also within the proclamation with regard to the *habeas corpus*.

I concur in the propriety of your request in regard to elections, and have, as you see, directed General Schofield accordingly. I do not feel justified to enter upon the broad field you present in regard to the political differences between Radicals and Conservatives. From time to time I have done and said what appeared to me proper to do and say. The public knows it well. It obliges nobody to follow me, and I trust it obliges me to follow nobody. The Radicals and Conservatives each agree with me in some things and disagree in others. I could wish both to agree with me in all things; for then they would agree with each other, and would be too strong for any foe from any quarter. They, however, choose to do otherwise, and I do not question their right. I, too, shall do what seems to be my duty. I hold whoever commands in Missouri or elsewhere responsible to me, and not to either Radicals or Conservatives. It is my duty to hear all; but, at last, I must, within my sphere, judge what to do and what to forbear.

Your obedient servant, A. LINCOLN.

INSTRUCTIONS TO GENERAL SCHOFIELD.

EXECUTIVE MANSION, WASHINGTON, D. C., *Oct.* 1, 1863.

General JOHN M. SCHOFIELD:

There is no organized military force in avowed opposition to the General Government now in Missouri, and if any shall reappear, your duty in regard to it will be too plain to require any special instruction. Still, the condition of things, both there and elsewhere, is such as to render it indispensable to maintain, for a time, the United States military establishment in that State, as well as to rely upon it for a fair contribution of support to that establishment generally. Your immediate duty in regard to Missouri now is to advance the efficiency of that establishment, and to so use it, as far as practicable, to compel the excited people there to let one another alone.

Under your recent order, which I have approved, you will only arrest individuals, and suppress assemblies or newspapers, when they may be working *palpable* injury to the military in your charge; and in no other case will you interfere with the expression of opinion in any form, or allow it to be interfered with violently by others. In this you have a discretion to exercise with great caution, calmness, and forbearance.

With the matter of removing the inhabitants of certain counties *en masse*, and of removing certain individuals from time to time, who are supposed to be mischievous, I am not now interfering, but am leaving to your own discretion.

Nor am I interfering with what may still seem to you to be necessary restrictions upon trade and intercourse. I think proper, however, to enjoin upon you the following: Allow no part of the military under your command to be engaged in either returning fugitive slaves, or in forcing or enticing slaves from their homes; and, so far as practicable, enforce the same forbearance upon the people.

Report to me your opinion upon the availability for good of the enrolled militia of the State. Allow no one to enlist colored troops, except upon orders from you, or from here through you.

Allow no one to assume the functions of confiscating property, under the law of Congress, or otherwise, except upon orders from here.

At elections see that those and only those, are allowed to vote, who are entitled to do so by the laws of Missouri, including as of those laws the restrictions laid by the Missouri Convention upon those who may have participated in the rebellion.

So far as practicable, you will, by means of your military force, expel guerrillas, marauders, and murderers, and all who are known to harbor, aid, or abet them. But in like manner you will repress assumptions of unauthorized individuals to perform the same service, because under pretence of doing this they become marauders and murderers themselves.

To now restore peace, let the military obey orders; and those not of the military leave each other alone, thus not breaking the peace themselves.

In giving the above directions, it is not intended to restrain you in other expedient and necessary matters not falling within their range.

Your obedient servant, A. LINCOLN.

The condition of affairs in this department continued to be greatly disturbed by political agitations, and the personal controversies to which they gave rise; and after a lapse of some months the President deemed it wise to relieve General Schofield from further command in this department. This was done by an order from the War Department, dated January 24th, 1864, by which, also, General Rosecrans was appointed in his place. In his order assuming command, dated January 30th, General Rosecrans paid a very high compliment to his predecessor, for the admirable order in which he found the business of the Department, and expressed the hope that he might receive "the honest, firm, and united support of all true national and Union men of the Department, without regard to politics, creed, or party, in his endeavors to maintain law and re-establish peace, and secure prosperity throughout its limits."

Before closing this notice of the perplexities and annoyances to which the President was subjected by the domestic contentions of Missouri, we may mention, as an illustration of the extent to which they were carried, the case of Rev. Dr. McPheeters, who had been silenced by General Curtis for preaching disloyalty to his congregation in St. Louis. The incident gave rise to a good deal of excitement, which was continued throughout the year. Toward the close of it the President wrote the following letter in reply to an appeal for his interference:

EXECUTIVE MANSION, WASHINGTON, *Dec.* 23, 1863.

I have just looked over a petition signed by some three dozen citizens of St. Louis, and their accompanying letters, one by yourself, one by a Mr. Nathan Ranney, and one by a Mr. John D. Coalter, the whole relating to the Rev. Dr. McPheeters. The petition prays, in the name of justice and mercy, that I will restore Dr. McPheeters to all his ecclesiastical rights.

This gives no intimation as to what ecclesiastical rights are withdrawn. Your letter states that Provost-Marshal Dick, about a year ago, ordered the arrest of Dr. McPheeters, Pastor of the Vine Street Church, prohibited him from officiating, and placed the management of affairs of the church out of the control of the chosen trustees; and near the close you state that a certain course "would insure his release." Mr. Ranney's letter says: "Dr. Samuel McPheeters is enjoying all the rights of a civilian, but cannot preach the gospel!" Mr. Coalter, in his letter, asks: "Is it not a strange illustration of the condition of things, that the question who shall be allowed to preach in a church in St. Louis shall be decided by the President of the United States?"

Now, all this sounds very strangely; and, withal, a little as if you gentlemen, making the application, do not understand the case alike; one affirming that his doctor is enjoying all the rights of a civilian, and another pointing out to me what will secure his *release!* On the 2d of January last, I wrote to General Curtis in relation to Mr. Dick's order upon Doctor McPheeters; and, as I suppose the doctor is enjoying all the rights of a civilian, I only quote that part of my letter which relates to the church. It was as follows: "But I must add that the United States Government must not, as by this order, undertake to run the churches. When an individual, in a church or out of it, becomes dangerous to the public interest, he must be checked; but the churches, as such, must take care of themselves. It will not do for the United States to appoint trustees, supervisors, or other agents for the churches."

This letter going to General Curtis, then in command, I supposed, of course, it was obeyed, especially as I heard no further complaint from Doctor Mc. or his friends for nearly an entire year. I have never interfered, nor thought of interfering, as to who shall or shall not preach in any church; nor have I knowingly or believingly tolerated any one else to interfere by my authority. If any one is so interfering by color of my authority, I would like to have it specifically made known to me.

If, after all, what is now sought, is to have me put Doctor Mc. back over the heads of a majority of his own congregation, that, too, will be declined. I will not have control of any church or any side.

A. LINCOLN.

The Presbytery, the regular church authority in the matter, subsequently decided that Dr. McPheeters could not return to his pastoral charge.

The victories of the Union arms during the summer of 1863—the repulse of the rebels at Gettysburg, the capture of Vicksburg and Port Hudson, and the consequent restoration of the Mississippi to the commerce of the nation, produced the most salutary effect upon the public sentiment of the country. There was a good deal of partisan opposition to specific measures of the Administration, and in some quarters this took the form of open hostility to the further prosecution of the war. But the spirit and determination of the people were at their height, and the Union party entered upon the political contests of the Autumn of 1863, in the several States, with confidence and courage.

The President had been invited by the Republican State

Committee of Illinois to attend the State Convention, to be held at Springfield on the 3d of September. Finding it impossible to accept the invitation, he wrote in reply the following letter, in which several of the most conspicuous features of his policy are defended against the censures by which they had been assailed :

EXECUTIVE MANSION, WASHINGTON, *August* 26, 1863.

Hon. JAMES C. CONKLING :

MY DEAR SIR :—Your letter inviting me to attend a mass meeting of unconditional Union men, to be held at the capital of Illinois, on the 3d day of September, has been received. It would be very agreeable for me thus to meet my old friends at my own home; but I cannot just now be absent from here so long as a visit there would require.

The meeting is to be of all those who maintain unconditional devotion to the Union; and I am sure that my old political friends will thank me for tendering, as I do, the nation's gratitude to those other noble men whom no partisan malice or partisan hope can make false to the nation's life.

There are those who are dissatisfied with me. To such I would say: you desire peace, and you blame me that we do not have it. But how can we attain it? There are but three conceivable ways: First—to suppress the Rebellion by force of arms. This I am trying to do. Are you for it? If you are, so far we are agreed. If you are not for it, a *second* way is to give up the Union. I am against this. Are you for it? If you are, you should say so plainly. If you are not for *force*, nor yet for *dissolution*, there only remains some imaginable *compromise*.

I do not believe that any compromise embracing the maintenance of the Union is now possible. All that I learn leads to a directly opposite belief. The strength of the Rebellion is its military, its army. That army dominates all the country, and all the people within its range. Any offer of terms made by any man or men within that range, in opposition to that army, is simply nothing for the present; because such man or men have no power whatever to enforce their side of a compromise, if one were made with them.

To illustrate: Suppose refugees from the South and peace men of the North get together in convention, and frame and proclaim a compromise embracing a restoration of the Union. In what way can that compromise be used to keep Lee's army out of Pennsylvania? Meade's army can keep Lee's army out of Pennsylvania, and, I think, can ultimately drive it out of existence. But no paper compromise to which the controllers of Lee's army are not agreed can at all affect that army. In an effort at such compromise we would waste time, which the enemy would improve to our disadvantage; and that would be all.

A compromise, to be effective, must be made either with those who control the rebel army, or with the people, first liberated from the domination of that army by the success of our own army. Now, allow me to assure you that no word or intimation from that rebel army, or from any of the men controlling it, in relation to any peace compromise, has ever come to my knowledge or belief. All charges and insinuations to the contrary are deceptive and groundless. And I promise you that if any such proposition shall hereafter come, it shall not be rejected and kept a secret from you. I freely acknowledge myself to be the servant of the people, according to the bond of service, the United States Constitution; and that, as such, I am responsible to them.

But, to be plain. You are dissatisfied with me about the negro. Quite likely there is a difference of opinion between you and myself upon that subject. I certainly wish that all men could be free, while you, I suppose, do not. Yet, I have neither adopted nor proposed any measure which is not consistent with even your view, provided that you are for the Union. I suggested compensated emancipation; to which you replied you wished not be taxed to buy negroes. But I had not asked you to be taxed to buy negroes, except in such way as to save you from greater taxation to save the Union exclusively by other means.

You dislike the Emancipation Proclamation, and perhaps would have it retracted. You say it is unconstitutional. I think differently. I think the Constitution invests its Commander-in-Chief with the law of war in time of war. The most that can be said, if so much, is, that slaves are property. Is there, has there ever been, any question that by the law of war, property, both of enemies and friends, may be taken when needed? And is it not needed whenever it helps us and hurts the enemy? Armies, the world over, destroy enemies' property when they cannot use it; and even destroy their own to keep it from the enemy. Civilized belligerents do all in their power to help themselves or hurt the enemy, except a few things regarded as barbarous or cruel. Among the exceptions are the massacre of vanquished foes and non-combatants, male and female.

But the Proclamation, as law, either is valid or is not valid. If it is not valid it needs no retraction. If it is valid it cannot be retracted, any more than the dead can be brought to life. Some of you profess to think its retraction would operate favorably for the Union. Why better *after* the retraction than *before* the issue? There was more than a year and a half of trial to suppress the Rebellion before the Proclamation was issued, the last one hundred days of which passed under an explicit notice that it was coming, unless averted by those in revolt returning to their allegiance. The war has certainly progressed as favorably for us since the issue of the Proclamation as before.

I know as fully as one can know the opinions of others that some of the commanders of our armies in the field, who have given us our most important victories, believe the Emancipation policy and the use of colored troops constitute the heaviest blows yet dealt to the Rebellion, and that at least one of those important successes could not have been achieved when it was but for the aid of black soldiers.

Among the commanders who hold these views are some who have never had any affinity with what is called "Abolitionism," or with "Republican party politics," but who hold them purely as military opinions. I submit their opinions as entitled to some weight against the objections often urged that emancipation and arming the blacks are unwise as military measures, and were not adopted as such in good faith.

You say that you will not fight to free negroes. Some of them seem willing to fight for you; but no matter. Fight you, then, exclusively, to save the Union. I issued the Proclamation on purpose to aid you in saving the Union. Whenever you shall have conquered all resistance to the Union, if I shall urge you to continue fighting, it will be an apt time then for you to declare you will not fight to free negroes. I thought that in your struggle for the Union, to whatever extent the negroes should cease helping the enemy, to that extent it weakened the enemy in his resistance to you. Do you think differently? I thought that whatever negroes can be got to do as soldiers, leaves just so much less for white soldiers to do in saving the Union. Does it appear otherwise to you? But negroes, like other people, act upon motives. Why should they do any thing for us if we will do nothing for them? If they stake their lives for us they must be prompted by the strongest motive, even the promise of freedom. And the promise, being made, must be kept.

The signs look better. The Father of Waters again goes unvexed to the sea. Thanks to the great Northwest for it; nor yet wholly to them. Three hundred miles up they met New England, Empire, Keystone, and Jersey, hewing their way right and left. The sunny South, too, in more colors than one, also lent a helping hand. On the spot, their part of the history was jotted down in black and white. The job was a great national one, and let none be slighted who bore an honorable part in it. And while those who have cleared the great river may well be proud, even that is not all. It is hard to say that any thing has been more bravely and well done than at Antietam, Murfreesboro, Gettysburg, and on many fields of less note. Nor must Uncle Sam's web feet be forgotten. At all the watery margins they have been present, not only on the deep sea, the broad bay, and the rapid river, but also up the narrow, muddy bayou, and wherever the ground was a little damp they have been and made their tracks. Thanks to all. For the great Republic—for the principle it lives by and keeps alive—for man's vast future—thanks to all.

Peace does not appear so distant as it did. I hope it will come soon and come to stay; and so come as to be worth the keeping in all future time. It will then have been proved that among freemen there can be no successful appeal from the ballot to the bullet, and that they who take such appeal are sure to lose their case and pay the cost. And there will be some black men who can remember that with silent tongue, and clinched teeth, and steady eye, and well-poised bayonet, they have helped mankind on to this great consummation, while I fear there will be some white ones unable to forget that with malignant heart and deceitful speech they have striven to hinder it.

Still, let us not be over-sanguine of a speedy, final triumph. Let us be quite sober. Let us diligently apply the means, never doubting that a just God, in His own good time, will give us the rightful result.

Yours, very truly, A. LINCOLN.

The result of the canvass justified the confidence of the friends of the Administration. Every State in which elections were held, with the single exception of New Jersey, voted to sustain the Government; and in all the largest and most important States the majorities were so large as to make the result of more than ordinary significance. In Ohio, Vallandigham, who had been put in nomination mainly on account of the issue he had made with the Government in the matter of his arrest, was defeated by a majority of nearly 100,000. New York, which had elected Governor Seymour the year before, and had been still further distinguished and disgraced by the anti-draft riots of July, gave a majority of not far from 30,000 for the Administration; and Pennsylvania, in spite of the personal participation of General McClellan in the canvass against him, re-elected Gov. Curtin by about the same majority. These results followed a very active and earnest canvass, in which the opponents of the Administration put forth their most vigorous efforts for its defeat. The ground taken by its friends in every State was that which had been held by the President from the beginning—that the rebellion must be suppressed and the Union preserved at whatever cost —that this could only be done by force, and that it was not only the right but the duty of the Government to use all the means at its command, not incompatible with the laws of war and the usages of civilized nations, for the accomplishment of this result. They vindicated the action of the Government in the matter of arbitrary arrests, and sustained throughout the canvass, in every State, the policy of the President in regard to slavery and in issuing the Proclamation of Emancipation as a military measure, against the vehement and earnest efforts of the Opposition. The result was, therefore, justly claimed as a decided verdict of the people in support of the Government. It was so regarded by all parties throughout the country, and its effect upon their action was of marked importance. While it gave renewed vigor and courage to the friends of the Administration everywhere, it developed the division of sentiment in the ranks of the Opposition, which, in its incipient stages, had largely contributed to their defeat. The majority of that party were inclined to acquiesce in the deliberate judgment of the country, that the rebellion could be subdued only by successful war, and to sustain the Government in whatever measures might be deemed necessary for its effectual prosecution:—but the resolute resistance of some of its more conspicuous leaders has thus far withheld them from open action in this direction.

CHAPTER XI.

THE CONGRESS OF 1863–4.—MESSAGE OF THE PRESIDENT.—ACTION OF THE SESSION.

CONGRESS met on Monday, December 7, 1863. The House of Representatives was promptly organized by the election of Hon. Schuyler Colfax, a Republican from Indiana, to be Speaker—he receiving 101 votes out of 181, the whole number cast. Mr. Cox, of Ohio, was the leading candidate of the Democratic opposition, but he received only 51 votes, the remaining 29 being divided among several Democratic members. In the Senate, the Senators from Western Virginia were admitted to their seats by a vote of 36 to 5.

On the 9th, the President transmitted to both Houses the following MESSAGE:

Fellow-Citizens of the Senate and House of Representatives:

Another year of health and of sufficiently abundant harvests has passed. For these, and especially for the improved condition of our national affairs, our renewed and profoundest gratitude to God is due. We remain in peace and friendship with foreign Powers. The efforts of disloyal citizens of the United States to involve us in foreign wars to aid an inexcusable insurrection have been unavailing. Her Britannic Majesty's Government, as was justly expected, have exercised their authority to prevent the departure of new hostile expeditions from British ports.

The Emperor of France has, by a like proceeding, promptly vindicated the neutrality which he proclaimed at the beginning of the contest.

Questions of great intricacy and importance have arisen out of the blockade, and other belligerent operations between the Government and several of the maritime Powers, but they have been discussed, and, as far as was possible, accommodated in a spirit of frankness, justice, and mutual good-will.

It is especially gratifying that our prize Courts, by the impartiality of their adjudications, have commanded the respect and confidence of maritime Powers.

The supplemental treaty between the United States and Great Britain for the suppression of the African Slave trade, made on the 17th day of February last, has been duly ratified and carried into execution. It is believed that so far as American ports and American citizens are concerned, that inhuman and odious traffic has been brought to an end.

I have thought it proper, subject to the approval of the Senate, to concur with the interested commercial Powers, in an arrangement for the liquidation of the Scheldt dues, upon the principles which have been heretofore adopted in regard to the imposts upon navigation in the waters of Denmark.

The long-pending controversy between this Government and that of Chili, touching the seizure at Sitana, in Peru, by Chilian officers, of a large amount in treasure, belonging to citizens of the United States, has been brought to a close by the award of His Majesty the King of the Belgians, to whose arbitration the question was referred by the parties.

The subject was thoroughly and patiently examined by that justly respected magistrate; and although the sum awarded to the claimants may not have been as large as they expected, there is no reason to distrust the wisdom of His Majesty's decision. That decision was promptly complied with by Chili when intelligence in regard to it reached that country.

The Joint Commission under the act of the last session for carrying into effect the Convention with Peru on the subject of claims, has been organized at Lima, and is engaged in the business intrusted to it.

Difficulties concerning interoceanic transit through Nicaragua, are in course of amicable adjustment.

In conformity with principles set forth in my last Annual Message, I have received a representative from the United States of Colombia, and have accredited a Minister to that Republic.

Incidents occurring in the progress of our civil war have forced upon my attention the uncertain state of international questions touching the rights of foreigners in this country and of United States citizens abroad.

In regard to some Governments, these rights are at least partially defined by treaties. In no instance, however, is it expressly stipulated that in the event of civil war a foreigner residing in this country, within the lines of the insurgents, is to be exempted from the rule which classes him as a belligerent, in whose behalf the Government of his country cannot expect any privileges or immunities distinct from that character. I regret to say, however, that such claims have been put forward, and, in some instances, in behalf of foreigners who have lived in the United States the greater part of their lives.

There is reason to believe that many persons born in foreign countries, who have declared their intention to become citizens, or who have been fully naturalized, have evaded the military duty required of them by denying the fact, and thereby throwing upon the Government the burden of proof. It has been found difficult or impracticable to obtain this proof, from the want of guides to the proper sources of information. These might be supplied by requiring Clerks of Courts, where declarations of intention may be made, or naturalizations effected, to send periodically lists of the names of the persons naturalized or declaring their intention to become citizens, to the Secretary of the Interior, in whose Department those names might be arranged and printed for general information. There is also reason to believe that foreigners frequently become citizens of the United States for the sole purpose of evading duties imposed by the laws of their native countries, to which, on becoming naturalized here, they at once repair, and though never returning to the United States, they still claim the interposition of this Government as citizens. Many altercations and great prejudices have heretofore arisen out of this abuse. It is, therefore, submitted to your serious consideration. It might be advisable to fix a limit beyond which no citizen of the United States residing abroad may claim the interposition of his Government.

The right of suffrage has often been assumed and exercised by aliens under pretences of naturalization, which they have disavowed when drafted into the military service.

Satisfactory arrangements have been made with the Emperor of Russia, which, it is believed, will result in effecting a continuous line of telegraph through that Empire from our Pacific coast.

I recommend to your favorable consideration the subject of an international telegraph across the Atlantic Ocean, and also of a telegraph between this Capital and the national forts along the Atlantic seaboard and the Gulf of Mexico. Such communications, established with any reasonable outlay, would be economical as well as effective aids to the diplomatic, military, and naval service.

The Consular system of the United States, under the enactments of the last Congress, begins to be self-sustaining, and there is reason to hope that it may become entirely so with the increase of trade, which will ensue whenever peace is restored.

Our Ministers abroad have been faithful in defending American rights. In protecting commercial interests, our Consuls have necessarily had to encounter increased labors and responsibilities growing out of the war. These they have, for the most part, met and discharged with zeal and efficiency. This acknowledgment justly includes those Consuls who, residing in Morocco, Egypt, Turkey, Japan, China, and other Oriental countries, are charged with complex functions and extraordinary powers.

The condition of the several organized territories is generally satisfactory, although Indian disturbances in New Mexico have not been entirely suppressed.

The mineral resources of Colorado, Nevada, Idaho, New Mexico, and Arizona, are proving far richer than has been heretofore understood. I lay before you a communication on this subject from the Governor of New Mexico. I again submit to your consideration the expediency of establishing a system for the encouragement of emigration. Although this source of national wealth and strength is again flowing with greater freedom than for several years before the insurrection occurred, there is still a great deficiency of laborers in every field of industry, especially in agriculture and in our mines, as well of iron and coal as of the precious metals. While the demand for labor is thus increased here, tens of thousands of persons, destitute of remunerative occupation, are thronging our foreign consulates, and offering to emigrate to the United States, if essential, but very cheap, assistance can be afforded them. It is easy to see that under the sharp discipline of civil war the nation is beginning a new life. This noble effort demands the aid, and ought to receive the attention and support of the Government.

Injuries unforeseen by the Government, and unintended, may in some cases have been inflicted on the subjects or citizens of foreign countries, both at sea and on land, by persons in the service of the United States. As this Government expects redress from other Powers when similar injuries are inflicted by persons in their service upon citizens of the United States, we must be prepared to do justice to foreigners. If the existing judicial tribunals are inadequate to this purpose, a special Court may be authorized, with power to hear and decide such claims of the character referred to as may have arisen under treaties and the public law. Conventions for adjusting the claims by joint commission have been proposed to some Governments, but no definite answer to the proposition has yet been received from any.

In the course of the session I shall probably have occasion to request you to provide indemnification to claimants where decrees of restitution have been rendered, and damages awarded by Admiralty Courts, and in other cases, where this Government may be acknowledged to be liable in principle, and where the amount of that liability has been ascertained by an informal arbitration, the proper officers of the Treasury have deemed themselves required by the law of the United States upon the subject, to demand a tax upon the incomes of foreign Consuls in this country. While such a demand may not, in strictness, be in derogation of public law, or perhaps of any existing treaty between the United States and a foreign country, the expediency of so far modifying the act as to exempt from tax the income of such consuls as are not citizens of the United States, derived from the emoluments of their office, or from property not situate in the United States, is submitted to your serious consideration. I make this suggestion upon the ground that a comity which ought to be reciprocated exempts our Consuls in all other countries from taxation to the extent thus indicated. The United States, I think, ought not to be exceptionably illiberal to international trade and commerce.

The operations of the Treasury during the last year have been successfully conducted. The enactment by Congress of a National Banking Law has proved a valuable support of the public credit, and the general legislation in relation to loans has fully answered the expectation of its favorers. Some amendments may be required to perfect existing laws, but no change in their principles or general scope is believed to be needed. Since these measures have been in operation, all demands on the Treasury, including the pay of the Army and Navy, have been promptly met and fully satisfied. No considerable body of troops, it is believed, were ever more amply provided and more liberally and punctually paid; and, it may be added, that by no people were the burdens incident to a great war more cheerfully borne.

The receipts during the year, from all sources, including loans and the balance in the Treasury at its commencement, were $901,125,-674 86, and the aggregate disbursements $895,796,630 65, leaving a balance on the 1st of July, 1863, of $5,329,044 21. Of the receipts, there were derived from Customs $69,059,642 40; from Internal Revenue, $37,640,787 95; from direct tax, $1,485,103 61; from lands, $167,617 17; from miscellaneous sources, $3,046,615 35; and from loans, $776,682,361 57, making the aggregate $901,125,674 86. Of the disbursements there were for the civil service $23,253,922 08; for pensions and Indians, $4,216,520 79; for interest on public debt, $24,729,846 51; for the War Department, $599,298,600 83; for the

Navy Department, $63,211,105 27; for payment of funded and temporary debt, $181,086,635 07, making the aggregate $895,796,630 65, and leaving the balance of $5,329,044 21.

But the payment of the funded and temporary debt, having been made from moneys borrowed during the year, must be regarded as merely nominal payments, and the moneys borrowed to make them as merely nominal receipts; and their amount, $181,086,535 07, should therefore be deducted both from receipts and disbursements. This being done, there remains, as actual receipts, $720,039,039 79, and the actual disbursements $714,709,995 58, leaving the balance as already stated.

The actual receipts and disbursements for the first quarter, and the estimated receipts and disbursements for the remaining three quarters of the current fiscal year, 1864, will be shown in detail by the report of the Secretary of the Treasury, to which I invite your attention.

It is sufficient to say here, that it is not believed that actual results will exhibit a state of the finances less favorable to the country than the estimates of that officer heretofore submitted, while it is confidently expected that, at the close of the year, both disbursements and debt will be found very considerably less than has been anticipated.

The report of the Secretary of War is a document of great interest. It consists of:

First.—The military operations of the year detailed in the report of the General-in-Chief.

Second.—The organization of colored persons into the war service.

Third.—The exchange of prisoners fully set forth in the letter of General Hitchcock.

Fourth.—The operations under the act for enrolling and calling out the National forces, detailed in the report of the Provost-Marshal General.

Fifth.—The organization of the Invalid Corps. And

Sixth.—The operations of the several departments of the Quartermaster-General, Commissary-General, Paymaster-General, Chief of Engineers, Chief of Ordnance, and Surgeon-General. It has appeared impossible to make a valuable summary of this report, except such as would be too extended for this place, and hence I content myself by asking your careful attention to the report itself. The duties devolving on the naval branch of the service during the year, and throughout the whole of this unhappy contest, have been discharged with fidelity and eminent success. The extensive blockade has been constantly increasing in efficiency, as the navy has expanded, yet on so long a line it has, so far, been impossible entirely to suppress illicit trade. From returns received at the Navy Department, it appears that more than one thousand vessels have been captured since the blockade was instituted, and that the value of prizes already sent in for adjudication, amount to over thirteen millions of dollars.

The naval force of the United States consists at this time of five hundred and eighty-eight vessels completed and in the course of completion, and of these seventy-five are iron-clad or armored steamers. The events of the war give an increased interest and importance to the navy, which will probably extend beyond the war itself. The armored vessels in our navy, completed and in service, or which are under contract and approaching completion, are believed to exceed in number those of any other Power; but while these may be relied upon for harbor defence and coast service, others of greater strength and capacity will be necessary for cruising purposes, and to maintain our rightful position on the ocean.

The change that has taken place in naval vessels and naval warfare since the introduction of steam as a motive power for ships of war, demands either a corresponding change in some of our existing Navy-yards, or the establishment of new ones, for the construction and necessary repair of modern naval vessels. No inconsiderable embarrassment, delay, and public injury, have been experienced from the want of such governmental establishments.

The necessity of such a Navy-yard, so furnished, at some suitable place upon the Atlantic seaboard, has, on repeated occasions, been brought to the attention of Congress by the Navy Department, and is again presented in the report of the Secretary, which accompanies this communication. I think it my duty to invite your special attention to this subject, and also to that of establishing a yard and dépôt for naval purposes upon one of the Western rivers. A naval force has been created on these interior waters, and under many disadvantages, within a little more than two years, exceeding in number the whole naval force of the country at the commencement of the present Administration. Satisfactory and important as have been the performances of the heroic men of the navy at this interesting period, they are scarcely more wonderful than the success of our mechanics and artisans in the production of war-vessels, which has created a new form of naval power.

Our country has advantages superior to any other nation in our resources of iron and timber, with inexhaustible quantities of fuel in the immediate vicinity of both, and all available and in close proximity to navigable waters. Without the advantage of public works, the resources of the nation have been developed, and its power displayed, in the construction of a navy of such magnitude, which has at the very period of its creation rendered signal service to the Union.

The increase of the number of seamen in the public service from 7,500 men in the Spring of 1861, to about 34,000 at the present time, has been accomplished without special legislation or extraordinary bounties to promote that increase. It has been found, however, that the operation of the draft, with the high bounties paid for army recruits, is beginning to affect injuriously the naval service, and will, if not corrected, be likely to impair its efficiency by detaching seamen from their proper vocation, and inducing them to enter the army. I therefore respectfully suggest that Congress might aid both the army and naval service by a definite provision on this subject, which would at the same time be equitable to the communities more especially interested.

I commend to your consideration the suggestions of the Secretary of the Navy, in regard to the policy of fostering and training seamen, and also the education of officers and engineers for the naval service. The Naval Academy is rendering signal service in preparing Midshipmen for the highly responsible duties which in after life they will be required to perform. In order that the country should not be deprived of the proper quota of educated officers, for which legal provision has been made at the naval school, the vacancies caused by the neglect or omission to make nominations from the States in insurrection, have been filled by the Secretary of the Navy. The school is now more full and complete than at any former period, and in every respect entitled to the favorable consideration of Congress.

During the last fiscal year the financial condition of the Post-office Department has been one of increasing prosperity, and I am gratified in being able to state that the actual postal revenue has nearly equalled the entire expenditures, the latter amounting to $11,314,206 84, and the former to $11,163,789 59, leaving a deficiency of but $150,417 25. In 1860, the year immediately preceding the rebellion, the deficiency amounted to $5,656,705 49, the postal receipts for that year being $2,647,225 19 less than those of 1863. The decrease since 1860 in the annual amount of transportation has been only about 25 per cent.; but the annual expenditure on account of the same has been reduced 35 per cent. It is manifest, therefore, that the Post-office Department may become self-sustaining in a few years, even with the restoration of the whole service.

The international conference of postal delegates from the principal countries of Europe and America, which was called at the suggestion of the Postmaster-General, met at Paris on the 11th of May last, and concluded its deliberations on the 8th of June. The principles established by the conference as best adapted to facilitate postal intercourse between nations, and as the basis of future postal conventions, inaugurates a general system of uniform international charges at reduced rates of postage, and cannot fail to produce beneficial results. I refer you to the Report of the Secretary of the Interior, which is herewith laid before you, for useful and varied information in relation to Public Lands, Indian Affairs, Patents, Pensions, and other matters of the public concern pertaining to his department.

The quantity of land disposed of during the last and the first quarter of the present fiscal years, was three millions, eight hundred and forty-one thousand, five hundred and forty-nine acres, of which one hundred and sixty-one thousand, nine hundred and eleven acres were sold for cash. One million, four hundred and fifty-six thousand, five hundred and fourteen acres, were taken up under the Homestead Law, and the residue disposed of under laws granting lands for military bounties, for railroad and other purposes. It also appears that the sale of public lands is largely on the increase.

It has long been a cherished opinion of some of our wisest statesmen that the people of the United States had a higher and more enduring interest in the early settlement and substantial cultivation of the public lands than in the amount of direct revenue to be derived from the sale of them. This opinion has had a controlling influence in shaping legislation upon the subject of our national domain. I may cite, as evidence of this, the liberal measures adopted in reference to actual settlers, the grant to the States of the overflowed lands within their limits, in order to their being reclaimed and rendered fit for cultivation, the grants to railway companies of alternate sections of land upon the contemplated lines of their roads, which, when completed, will so largely multiply the facilities for reaching our distant possessions. This policy has received its most signal and beneficent illustration in the recent enactment granting homesteads to actual settlers. Since the first day of January last the before mentioned quantity of one million four hundred and fifty-six thousand five hundred and fourteen acres of land have been taken up under its provisions. This fact, and the amount of sales, furnish gratifying evidence of increasing settlement upon the public lands, notwithstanding the great struggle in which the energies of the nation have been engaged, and which has required so large a withdrawal of our citizens from their accustomed pursuits. I cordially concur in the recommendation of the Secretary of the Interior, suggesting a modification of the act in favor of those engaged in the military and naval service of the United States.

I doubt not that Congress will cheerfully adopt such measures as will, without essentially changing the general features of the system, secure to the greatest practical extent its benefits to those who have left their homes in defence of the country in this arduous crisis.

I invite your attention to the views of the Secretary as to the propriety of raising, by appropriate legislation, a revenue from the mineral lands of the United States. The measures provided at your last session for the removal of certain Indian tribes have been carried into effect. Sundry treaties have been negotiated, which will, in due time, be submitted for the constitutional action of the Senate. They contain stipulations for extinguishing the possessory rights of the Indians to large and valuable tracts of lands. It is hoped that the effect of these treaties will result in the establishment of permanent friendly relations with such of these tribes as have been brought into frequent and bloody collision with our outlying settlements and emigrants. Sound policy, and our imperative duty to these wards of the Government, demand our anxious and constant attention to their material well-being, to their progress in the arts of civilization, and, above all, to that moral training which, under the blessing of Divine Providence, will confer upon them the elevated and sanctifying influences, the hopes and consolations of the Christian faith. I suggested in my last Annual Message the propriety of remodelling our Indian system. Subsequent events have satisfied me of its necessity. The details set forth in the report of the Secretary evince the urgent need for immediate legislative action.

I commend the benevolent institutions, established or patronized by the government in this District, to your generous and fostering care.

The attention of Congress, during the last session, was engaged to some extent with a proposition for enlarging the water communication between the Mississippi River and the northeastern seaboard, which proposition, however, failed for the time. Since then, upon a call of the greatest respectability, a Convention has been held at Chicago upon the same subject, a summary of whose views is contained in a Memorial Address to the President and Congress, and which I now have the honor to lay before you. That the interest is one which will ere long force its own way I do not entertain a doubt, while it is submitted entirely to your wisdom as to what can be done now. Augmented interest is given to this subject by the actual commencement of work upon the Pacific railroad, under auspices so favorable to rapid progress and completion. The enlarged navigation becomes a palpable need to the great road.

I transmit the second annual report of the Commissioners of the Department of Agriculture, asking your attenntion to the developments in that vital interest of the nation.

When Congress assembled a year ago, the war had already lasted nearly twenty months, and there had been many conflicts on both land and sea, with varying results; the rebellion had been pressed back into reduced limits; yet the tone of public feeling and opinion, at home and abroad, was not satisfactory. With other signs, the popular elections then just past indicated uneasiness among ourselves, while, amid much that was cold and menacing, the kindest words coming from Europe were uttered in accents of pity that we were too blind to surrender a hopeless cause. Our commerce was suffering greatly by a few vessels built upon and furnished from foreign shores, and we were threatened with such additions from the same quarters as would sweep our trade from the seas and raise our blockade. We had failed to elicit from European governments any thing hopeful upon this subject.

The preliminary Emancipation Proclamation issued in September, was running its assigned period to the beginning of the new year. A month later, the final proclamation came, including the announcement that colored men of suitable condition would be received in the war service. The policy of emancipation and of employing black soldiers gave to the future a new aspect, about which hope and fear and doubt contended in uncertain conflict. According to our political system, as a matter of civil administration the Government had no lawful power to effect emancipation in any State, and for a long time it had been hoped that the rebellion could be suppressed without resorting to it as a military measure. It was all the while deemed possible that the necessity for it might come, and that if it should, the crisis of the contest would then be presented. It came, and, as was anticipated, was followed by dark and doubtful days.

Eleven months having now passed, we are permitted to take another review. The rebel borders are pressed still further back, and by the complete opening of the Mississippi, the country dominated by the rebellion is divided into distinct parts with no practical communication between them. Tennessee and Arkansas have been substantially cleared of insurgent control, and influential citizens in each—owners of slaves and advocates of slavery at the beginning of the rebellion—now declare openly for emancipation in their respective States. Of those States not included in the Emancipation Proclamation, Maryland and Missouri, neither of which three years ago would tolerate any restraint upon the extension of slavery into new Territories, only dispute now as to the best mode of removing it within their own limits.

Of those who were slaves at the beginning of the rebellion, full one hundred thousand are now in the United States military service, about one-half of which number actually bear arms in the ranks—thus giving the double advantage of taking so much labor from the insurgent cause and supplying the places which otherwise must be filled with so many white men. So far as tested, it is difficult to say they are not as good soldiers as any. No servile insurrection or tendency to violence or cruelty has marked the measures of emancipation and arming the blacks. These measures have been much discussed in foreign countries, and, cotemporary with such discussion, the tone of public sentiment there is much improved. At home the same measures have been fully discussed, supported, criticised and denounced, and the annual elections following are highly encouraging to those whose official duty it is to bear the country through this great trial. Thus we have the new reckoning. The crisis which threatened to divide the friends of the Union is past.

Looking now to the present and future, and with a reference to a resumption of the National authority, in the States wherein that authority has been suspended, I have thought fit to issue a proclamation—a copy of which is herewith transmitted. On examination of this proclamation, it will appear, as is believed, that nothing is attempted beyond what is amply justified by the Constitution. True, the form of an oath is given, but no man is coerced to take it. The man is only promised a pardon in case he voluntarily takes the oath. The Constitution authorizes the Executive to grant or withdraw the pardon at his own absolute discretion, and this includes the power to grant on terms, as is fully established by judicial and other authorities. It is also proffered that if in any of the States named a State Government shall be in the mode prescribed set up, such government shall be recognized and guaranteed by the United States, and that under it the State shall, on the constitutional conditions, be protected against invasion and domestic violence.

The constitutional obligation of the United States to guarantee to every State in the Union a Republican form of Government, and to protect the State in the cases stated, is explicit and full. But why tender the benefits of this provision only to a State Government set up in this particular way? This section of the Constitution contemplates a case wherein the element within a State favorable to Republican government in the Union may be too feeble for an opposite and hostile element external to or even within the State, and such are precisely the cases with which we are now dealing.

An attempt to guarantee and protect a revived State Government, constructed in whole or in preponderating part from the very element against whose hostility and violence it is to be protected, is simply absurd. There must be a test by which to separate the opposing elements, so as to build only from the sound; and that test is a sufficiently liberal one which accepts as sound whoever will make a sworn recantation of his former unsoundness.

But if it be proper to require, as a test of admission to the political body, an oath of allegiance to the Constitution of the United States and to the Union under it, why also to the laws and proclamations in regard to slavery?

Those laws and proclamations were enacted and put forth for the purpose of aiding in the suppression of the rebellion. To give them their fullest effect there had to be a pledge for their maintenance. In my judgment they have aided and will further aid the cause for which they were intended.

To now abandon them would be not only to relinquish a lever of power, but would also be a cruel and an astounding breach of faith.

I may add, at this point, that while I remain in my present position, I shall not attempt to retract or modify the Emancipation Proclamation, nor shall I return to slavery any person who is free by the terms of that proclamation, or by any of the acts of Congress.

For these and other reasons, it is thought best that support of these measures shall be included in the oath, and it is believed that the Executive may lawfully claim it in return for pardon and restoration of forfeited rights, which he has a clear constitutional power to withhold altogether or grant upon the terms which he shall deem wisest for the public interest. It should be observed, also, that this part of the oath is subject to the modifying and abrogating power of legislation and supreme judicial decision.

The proposed acquiescence of the National Executive in any reasonable temporary State arrangement for the freed people, is made with the view of possibly modifying the confusion and destitution which must at best attend all classes by a total revolution of labor throughout whole States. It is hoped that the already deeply afflicted people in those States may be somewhat more ready to give up the cause of their affliction, if, to this extent, this vital matter be left to themselves, while no power of the National Executive to prevent an abuse is abridged by the proposition.

The suggestion in the proclamation as to maintaining the political frame work of the States on what is called reconstruction, is made in the hope that it may do good, without danger of harm. It will save labor, and avoid great confusion. But why any proclamation now upon this subject? This question is beset with the conflicting views that the step might be delayed too long, or be taken too soon. In some States the elements for resumption seem ready for action but remain inactive, apparently for want of a rallying point—a plan of action. Why shall A adopt the plan of B, rather than B that of A? And if A and B should agree, how can they know but that the General Government here will reject their plan? By the proclamation a plan is presented which may be accepted by them as a rallying point—and which they are assured in advance will not be rejected here. This may bring them to act sooner than they otherwise would.

The objection to a premature presentation of a plan by the National Executive consists in the danger of committals on points which could be more safely left to further developments. Care has been taken to so shape the document as to avoid embarrassments from this source. Saying that on certain terms certain classes will be pardoned with rights restored, it is not said that other classes or other terms will never be included. Saying that reconstruction will be accepted if presented in a specified way, it is not said it will never be accepted in any other way. The movements by State action for emancipation in several of the States not included in the Emancipation Proclamation are matters of profound gratulation. And while I do not repeat in detail what I have heretofore so earnestly urged upon this subject, my general views and feelings remain unchanged; and I trust that Congress will omit no fair opportunity of aiding these important steps to the great consummation.

In the midst of other cares, however important, we must not lose sight of the fact that the war power is still our main reliance. To that power alone can we look for a time, to give confidence to the people in the contested regions, that the insurgent power will not again overrun them. Until that confidence shall be established, little can be done anywhere for what is called reconstruction. Hence our chiefest care must still be directed to the army and navy, who have thus far borne their harder part so nobly and well. And it may be esteemed fortunate that in giving the greatest efficiency to these indispensable arms, we do also honorably recognize the gallant men, from commander to sentinel, who compose them, and to whom, more than to others, the world must stand indebted for the home of freedom, disenthralled, regenerated, enlarged and perpetuated.

(Signed) ABRAHAM LINCOLN.

December 8, 1863.

The following proclamation is appended to the message:

PROCLAMATION

Whereas, In and by the Constitution of the United States, it is provided that the President shall have power to grant reprieves and pardons for offences against the United States, except in cases of impeachment—and, whereas, a rebellion now exists, whereby the loyal State Governments of several States have for a long time been subverted, and many persons have committed and are now guilty of treason against the United States; and

Whereas, With reference to said rebellion and treason, laws have been enacted by Congress, declaring forfeitures and confiscation of property and liberation of slaves, all upon terms and conditions therein stated, and also declaring that the President was thereby authorized at any time thereafter, by proclamation, to extend to persons who may have participated in the existing rebellion in any State or part thereof, pardon and amnesty, with such exceptions and at such times and on such conditions as he may deem expedient for the public welfare; and

Whereas, The Congressional declaration for limited and conditional pardon accords with the well-established judicial exposition of the pardoning power; and

Whereas, With reference to the said rebellion, the President of the United States has issued several proclamations with provisions in regard to the liberation of slaves; and

Whereas, It is now desired by some persons heretofore engaged in said rebellion to resume their allegiance to the United States, and to reinaugurate loyal State Governments within and for their respective States; therefore

I, ABRAHAM LINCOLN, President of the United States, do proclaim, declare and make known to all persons who have directly or by implication participated in the existing rebellion, except as hereinafter excepted, that a full pardon is hereby granted to them and each of them, with restoration of all rights of property, except as to slaves, and in property cases where rights of third parties shall have intervened, and upon the condition that every such person shall take and subscribe an oath and thenceforward keep and maintain said oath inviolate, an oath which shall be registered for permanent preservation, and shall be of the tenor and effect following, to wit:

"I, ——— ———, do solemnly swear, in presence of Almighty God, that I will henceforth faithfully support, protect and defend the Constitution of the United States and the Union of the States thereunder; and that I will in like manner abide by and faithfully support all acts of Congress passed during the existing rebellion with reference to slaves, so long and so far as not repealed, modified, or held void by Congress or by decision of the Supreme Court; and that I will in like manner abide by and faithfully support all proclamations of the President made during the existing rebellion having reference to slaves, so long and so far as not modified or declared void by decision of the Supreme Court. So help me God."

The persons excepted from the benefits of the foregoing provisions are: All who are, or shall have been civil or diplomatic officers or agents of the so-called Confederate Government; all who have left judicial stations under the United States to aid the rebellion; all who are, or shall have been military or naval officers of said so-called Confederate Government, above the rank of Colonel in the army, or of Lieutenant in the navy; all who left seats in the United States Congress to aid the rebellion; all who resigned commissions in the army or navy of the United States, and afterward aided the rebellion; and all who have engaged in any way in treating colored persons, or white persons in charge of such, otherwise than lawfully as prisoners of war, and which persons may have been found in the United States service as soldiers, seamen, or any other capacity; and I do further proclaim, declare and make known that, whenever, in any of the States of Arkansas, Texas, Louisiana, Mississippi, Tennessee, Alabama, Georgia, Florida, South Carolina, and North Carolina, a number of persons not less than one-tenth in number of the votes cast in such States at the Presidential election of the year of our Lord one thousand eight hundred and sixty, each having taken the oath aforesaid, and not having since violated it, and being a qualified voter by the election law of the State existing immediately before the so-called act of Secession, and excluding all others, shall re-establish a State Government which shall be Republican, and in no wise contravening said oath, such shall be recognized as the true government of the State, and the State shall receive thereunder the benefits of the constitutional provision, which declares that

"The United States shall guarantee to every State in this Union a Republican form of government, and shall protect each of them against invasion, and on application of the Legislature, or the Executive, when the Legislature cannot be convened, against domestic violence."

And I do further proclaim, declare, and make known, that any provision which may be adopted by such State Government in relation to the freed people of such State, which shall recognize and declare their permanent freedom, provide for their education, and which may yet be consistent, as a temporary arrangement, with their present condition as a laboring, landless, and homeless class, will not be objected to by the National Executive.

And it is suggested as not improper that, in constructing a loyal State Government in any State, the name of the State, the boundary, the subdivisions, the Constitution, and the general code of laws, as before the rebellion, be maintained, subject only to the modifications made necessary by the conditions herein before stated, and such others, if any, not contravening said conditions, and which may be deemed expedient by those framing the new State Government. To avoid misunderstanding, it may be proper to say that this proclamation, so far as it relates to State Governments, has no reference to States wherein loyal State Governments have all the while been maintained; and for the same reason it may be proper to further say, that whether members sent to Congress from any State shall be admitted to seats, constitutionally rests exclusively with the respective Houses, and not to any extent with the Executive. And still further, that this proclamation is intended to present the people of the States wherein the national authority has been suspended, and loyal State Governments have been subverted, a mode in and by which the national authority and loyal State Governments may be re-established within said States, or in any of them. And, while the mode presented is the best the Executive can suggest with his present impressions, it must not be understood that no other possible mode would be acceptable.

Given under my hand at the city of Washington, the eighth day of December, A. D. one thousand eight hundred and sixty-three, and of the independence of the United States of America the Eighty-eighth.

By the President: ABRAHAM LINCOLN.

WM. H. SEWARD, *Secretary of State.*

In further prosecution of the object sought by this measure of amnesty, the President subsequently issued the following additional explanatory PROCLAMATION:

By the President of the United States of America:

Whereas, it has become necessary to define the cases in which insurgent enemies are entitled to the benefits of the Proclamation of the President of the United States, which was made on the 8th day of December, 1863, and the manner in which they shall proceed to avail themselves of these benefits; and whereas the objects of that proclamation were to suppress the insurrection and to restore the authority of the United States; and whereas the amnesty therein proposed by the President was offered with reference to these objects alone;

Now, therefore, I, ABRAHAM LINCOLN, President of the United States, do hereby proclaim and declare that the said proclamation does not apply to the cases of persons who, at the time when they seek to obtain the benefits thereof by taking the oath thereby prescribed, are in military, naval or civil confinement or custody, or under bonds, or on parole of the civil, military or naval authorities, or agents of the United States, as prisoners of war, or persons detained for offences of any kind, either before or after conviction; and that on the contrary it does apply only to those persons who, being yet at large, and free from any arrest, confinement, or duress, shall voluntarily come forward and take the said oath, with the purpose of restoring peace and establishing the national authority.

Persons excluded from the amnesty offered in the said proclamation may apply to the President for clemency, like all other offenders, and their application will receive due consideration.

I do further declare and proclaim that the oath presented in the aforesaid proclamation of the 8th of December, 1863, may be taken and subscribed before any commissioned officer, civil, military, or naval, in the service of the United States, or any civil or military officer of a State or Territory not in insurrection, who, by the laws thereof, may be qualified for administering oaths.

All officers who receive such oaths are hereby authorized to give certificates thereof to the persons respectively by whom they are made, and such officers are hereby required to transmit the original records of such oaths at as early a day as may be convenient, to the Department of State, where they will be deposited, and remain in the archives of the Government.

The Secretary of State will keep a registry thereof, and will, on application, in proper cases, issue certificates of such records in the customary form of official certificates.

In testimony whereof I have hereunto set my hand and caused the seal of the United States to be affixed. Done at the city of Washington, the 26th day of March, in the year of our Lord 1864, and of the independence of the United States the Eighty-eighth.

[L. S.]

By the President: ABRAHAM LINCOLN.

WILLIAM H. SEWARD, *Secretary of State.*

The action of Congress at this session has not been of special interest or importance. Public attention continued to be absorbed by military operations, and Congress, at its previous session, had so fully provided for the emergencies, present and prospective, of the war, that little in this direction remained to be done. Resolutions were introduced by members of the opposing parties, some approving and others condemning the policy of the Administration. Attempts were made to amend the conscription bill, but the two houses failing to agree on some of the more important changes proposed, the bill, as finally passed, did not vary essentially from the original law. The leading topic of discussion in this connection was the employment of colored men, free and slave, as soldiers. The policy of thus employing them had been previously established by the action of the Government in all departments; and all that remained was to regulate the mode of their enlistment. A proviso was finally adopted by both houses that colored troops, "while they shall be credited in the quotas of the several States or subdivisions of States wherein they are respectively drafted, enlisted, or shall volunteer, shall not be assigned as State troops, but shall be mustered into regiments or companies as 'United States Colored Volunteers.'"

The general tone of the debates in Congress indicates the growing conviction on the part of the people of the whole country, without regard to party distinctions, that the destruction of slavery is inseparable from the victorious prosecution of the war. Men of all parties have acquiesced in the position that the days of slavery are numbered,—that the rebellion, organized for the purpose of strengthening it, has placed it at the mercy of the national force, and compelled the Government to assail its existence as the only means of subduing the rebellion and preserving the Union. The certainty that the prosecution of the war must result in the emancipation of the slaves, has led to the proposal of measures suited to this emergency. On the 6th of February, a bill was reported in the House for the establishment of a Bureau of Freedmen's Affairs, which should determine all questions relating to persons of African descent, and make regulations for their employment and proper treatment on abandoned plantations; and after a sharp and discursive debate, it was passed by a vote of 69 to 67. A resolution has also been adopted to submit to the action of the several States, an amendment to the Constitution of the United States, prohibiting the existence of slavery within the States and Territories of the Union forever. This proposition has encountered but little opposition. The experience of the last three years has left but little inclination in any quarter to prolong the existence of slavery, and the political necessities which formerly gave it strength and protection, have ceased to exist. At the commencement of the session resolutions were offered by several members in both Houses, aiming at its prohibition by such an amendment of the Constitution. This mode of accomplishing the object sought was held to be free from the objections to which every other is exposed, as it is unquestionably competent for the people to amend the Constitution, in accordance with the forms prescribed by its own provisions. One or two Southern senators, Mr. Saulsbury, of Delaware, and Mr. Powell, of Kentucky, being prominent, have urged that it is a palpable violation of State rights for the people thus to interfere with any thing which State laws declare to be property; but they were answered by Reverdy Johnson, of Maryland, who urged that when the Constitution was originally framed this prohibition of slavery might unquestionably have been embodied in it, and that it was competent for the people to do now whatever they might have done then.

A bill was passed in both Houses restoring the grade of Lieutenant-General, and, on the nomination of the President, General Grant was appointed by the Senate to that office, and invested with the command of the armies of the United States.

Toward the close of the year, as the terms of service of many of the volunteer forces were about to expire, the President issued a proclamation for 300,000 volunteers. The military successes of the season had raised the public courage and inspired new confidence in the final issue of the contest for the preservation of the Union; it was believed, therefore, that an appeal for volunteers would be responded to with alacrity, and save the necessity for a resort to another draft. The proclamation was as follows:

A PROCLAMATION

By the President of the United States.

Whereas, the term of service of part of the volunteer forces of the United States will expire during the coming year; and, whereas, in addition to the men raised by the present draft, it is deemed expedient to call out three hundred thousand volunteers to serve for three years or during the war, not, however, exceeding three years; Now, therefore, I, ABRAHAM LINCOLN, President of the United States and Commander-in-Chief of the army and navy thereof, and of the militia of the several States when called into actual service, do issue this my proclamation, calling upon the Governors of the different States to raise, and have enlisted into the United States service, for the various companies and regiments in the field from their respective States, the quotas of three hundred thousand men.

I further proclaim that all the volunteers thus called out and duly enlisted shall receive advance pay, premium, and bounty, as heretofore communicated to the Governors of States by the War Department through the Provost-Marshal General's office, by special letters.

I further proclaim that all volunteers received under this call, as well as all others not heretofore credited, shall be duly credited and deducted from the quotas established for the next draft.

I further proclaim that if any State shall fail to raise the quota assigned to it by the War Department under this call, then a draft for the deficiency in said quota shall be made in said State, or on the districts of said State for their due proportion of said quota, and the said draft shall commence on the 5th day of January, 1864.

And I further proclaim that nothing in this proclamation shall interfere with existing orders, or with those which may be issued for the present draft in the States where it is now in progress, or where it has not yet been commenced.

The quotas of the States and districts will be assigned by the War Department through the Provost-Marshal General's office, due regard being had for the men heretofore furnished, whether by volunteering or drafting; and the recruiting will be conducted in accordance with such instructions as have been or may be issued by that Department.

In issuing this proclamation, I address myself not only to the Governors of the several States, but also to the good and loyal people thereof, invoking them to lend their cheerful, willing, and effective aid to the measures thus adopted, with a view to re-enforce our victorious army now in the field, and bring our needful military operations to a prosperous end, thus closing forever the fountains of sedition and civil war.

In witness whereof, I have hereunto set my hand, and caused the seal of the United States to be affixed.

[L. S.] Done at the city of Washington, this 17th day of October, 1863, and of the independence of the United States the eighty-eighth.

By the President: ABRAHAM LINCOLN.

WM. H. SEWARD, *Secretary of State.*

By the act of 1861 for raising troops, a government bounty of one hundred dollars was paid to each volunteer; and this amount had been increased from time to time until each soldier who had already filled his term of service was entitled to receive four hundred dollars on re-enlisting, and each new volunteer three hundred. After the President's proclamation was issued, enlistments, especially of men already in the service, proceeded with great rapidity, and the amount to be paid for bounties threatened to be very large. Under these circumstances, Congress adopted an amendment to the enrolment act, by which the payment of all bounties except those authorized by the act of 1861, was to cease after the 5th day of January. Both the Secretary of War and the Provost-Marshal General feared that the effect of this, when it came to be generally understood, would be to check the volunteering which was then proceeding in a very satisfactory manner; and on the 5th of January, the day when the prohibition was to take effect, the President sent to Congress the following communication:

WASHINGTON, *January* 5, 1864.

Gentlemen of the Senate and House of Representatives:

By a joint resolution of your honorable bodies, approved December 23, 1863, the paying of bounties to veteran volunteers, as now practised by the War Department, is, to the extent of three hundred dollars in each case, prohibited after the fifth day of the present month. I transmit for your consideration a communication from the Secretary of War, accompanied by one from the Provost-Marshal General to him, both relating to the subject above mentioned. I earnestly recommend that this law be so modified as to allow bounties to be paid as they now are, at least to the ensuing 1st day of February. I am not without anxiety lest I appear to be importunate in thus recalling your attention to a subject upon which you have so recently acted, and nothing but a deep conviction that the public interest demands it could induce me to incur the hazard of being misunderstood on this point. The executive approval was given by me to the resolution mentioned, and it is now by a closer attention and a fuller knowledge of facts that I feel constrained to recommend a reconsideration of the subject.

A. LINCOLN.

A resolution extending the payment of bounties, in accordance with this recommendation, to the 1st of April, was at once reported by the Military Committee of the Senate, and passed by both Houses of Congress.

The action of Congress thus far during the session has related mainly to questions connected with taxation and the currency, and does not call for detailed mention in this connection. Considerable time has been consumed, and a good deal of ill-feeling created, by a controversy between General F. P. Blair, junior, of Missouri, whose seat in Congress is contested, and other members of the Missouri delegation. General Blair was accused by one of his colleagues of very discreditable transactions in granting permits to trade within the limits of his department, from which he was, however, completely exonerated by the investigations of a Committee of the House. After this matter was closed, General Blair resigned his seat in the House and returned to his post in the army. The House, by resolution, called upon the President for information as to the circumstances of his restoration to command, and received on the 28th of April the following in reply:

To the House of Representatives:—

In obedience to the resolution of your honorable body, a copy of which is herewith returned, I have the honor to make the following brief statement, which is believed to contain the information sought.

Prior to and at the meeting of the present Congress, Robert C. Schenck, of Ohio, and Frank P. Blair, Jr., of Missouri, members elect thereto, by and with the consent of the Senate, held commissions from the Executive as Major-Generals in the volunteer army. General Schenck tendered the resignation of his said commission, and took his seat in the House of Representatives, at the assembling thereof, upon the distinct verbal understanding with the Secretary of War and the Executive that he might at any time during the session, at his own pleasure, withdraw said resignation and return to the field.

General Blair was, by temporary agreement of General Sherman, in command of a corps through the battles in front of Chattanooga, and in marching to the relief of Knoxville, which occurred in the latter days of December last, and of course was not present at the assembling of Congress. When he subsequently arrived here he sought and was allowed by the Secretary of War and the Executive the same conditions and promise as was allowed and made to General Schenck.

General Schenck has not applied to withdraw his resignation; but when General Grant was made Lieutenant-General, producing some changes of commanders, General Blair sought to be assigned to the command of a corps. This was made known to General Grant and General Sherman, and assented to by them, and the particular corps for him was designated. This was all arranged and understood, as now remembered, so much as a month ago; but the formal withdrawal of General Blair's resignation, and the reissuing of the order assigning him to the command of a corps, were not consummated at the War Department until last week, perhaps on the 23d of April instant. As a summary of the whole it may be stated that General Blair holds no military commission or appointment other than as herein stated, and that it is believed he is now acting as Major-General upon the assumed validity of the commission herein stated and not otherwise.

There are some letters, notes, telegrams, orders, entries, and perhaps other documents, in connection with this subject, which it is believed would throw no additional light upon it, but which will be cheerfully furnished if desired.

ABRAHAM LINCOLN.

April 28, 1864.

On the same day the President sent to Congress the following Message, which sufficiently explains itself:

To the Honorable Senate and House of Representatives:—

I have the honor to transmit herewith an address to the President of the United States, and through him to both Houses of Congress, on the condition of the people of East Tennessee, and asking their attention to the necessity for some action on the part of the government for their relief, and which address is presented by the Committee or Organization, called "The East Tennessee Relief Association." Deeply commiserating the condition of those most loyal people, I am unprepared to make any specific recommendation for their relief. The military is doing, and will continue to do, the best for them within its power. Their address represents that the construction of a direct railroad communication between Knoxville and Cincinnati, by way of Central Kentucky, would be of great consequence in the present emergency. It may be remembered that in my annual Message of December, 1861, such railroad construction was recommended. I now add that, with the hearty concurrence of Congress, I would yet be pleased to construct the road, both for the relief of those people and for its continuing military importance.

ABRAHAM LINCOLN.

The diplomatic correspondence of the year 1863, which was transmitted to Congress with the President's Message, was voluminous and interesting. But it touched few points of general interest, relating mainly to matters of detail in the relations between the United States and foreign powers. One point of importance was gained in the course of our correspondence with Great Britain,—the issuing of an order by that Government forbidding the departure of formidable rams which were building in English ports unquestionably for the Rebel service. Our minister in London had been unwearied in collecting evidence of the purpose and destination of these vessels and in pressing upon the British Government the absolute necessity, if they wished to preserve peaceful relations with the United States, of not permitting their professedly neutral ports to be used as naval dépots and dock-yards for the service of the rebels. On the 5th of September, 1863, Mr. Adams had written to Lord Russell, acknowledging the receipt of a letter from him in which the deliberate purpose of the British Government to take no action in regard to these rams was announced. Mr. Adams had expressed his regret at such a decision, which he said he could regard as no otherwise than as practically opening to the insurgents free liberty in Great Britain to prepare for entering and destroying any of the Atlantic seaports of the United States. "It would be superfluous in me," added Mr. Adams, "to point out to your lordship that this is war. No matter what may be the theory adopted of neutrality in a struggle, when this process is carried on in the manner indicated, from a territory and with the aid of the subjects of a third party, that third party to all intents and purposes ceases to be neutral. Neither is it necessary to show, that any Government which suffers it to be done, fails in enforcing the essential conditions of international amity towards the country against whom the hostility is directed. In my belief it is impossible that any nation, retaining a proper degree of self-respect, could tamely submit to a continuance of relations so utterly deficient in reciprocity. I have no idea that Great Britain would do so for a moment." On the 8th of September Earl Russell wrote to Mr. Adams, to inform him that "instructions had been issued which would prevent the departure of the two iron-clad vessels from Liverpool." The Earl afterwards explained in Parliament, however, when charged with having taken this action under an implied menace of war conveyed in the letter of Mr. Adams, that it was taken in pursuance of a decision which had been made previous to the receipt of that letter and in ignorance of its existence.

On the 11th of July Mr. Seward forwarded a dispatch to Mr. Adams, elicited by the decision of the British Court in the case of the Alexandra, which had been seized on suspicion of having been fitted out in violation of the laws of Great Britain against the enlistment of troops to serve against nations with which that government was at peace. The decision was a virtual repeal of the enlistment act as a penal measure of prevention, and actually left the agents of the Rebels at full liberty to prepare ships of war in English ports to cruise against the commerce of the United States. Mr. Seward conveyed to Mr. Adams the President's views on the extraordinary state of affairs which this decision revealed. Assuming that the British Government had acted throughout in perfect good faith and that the action of its judicial tribunals was not to be impeached, this dispatch stated that "if the rulings of the Chief Baron of the Exchequer in the case of the Alexandra should be affirmed by the Court of last resort, so as to regulate the action of Her Majesty's Government, the President would be left to understand that there is no law in Great

Britain which will be effective to preserve mutual relations of forbearance between the subjects of her Majesty and the Government and people of the United States in the only point where they are exposed to infraction. And the United States will be without any guarantee whatever against the indiscriminate and unlawful employment of capital, industry and skill by British subjects, in building, arming, equipping, and sending forth ships-of-war from British ports to make war against the United States." The suggestion was made whether it would not be wise for Parliament to amend a law thus proved to be inadequate to the purpose for which it was intended. If the law must be left without amendment and be construed by the Government in conformity with the rulings in this case then, said Mr. Seward, "there will be left for the United States no alternative but to protect themselves and their commerce against armed cruisers proceeding from British ports as against the naval forces of a public enemy; and also to claim and insist upon indemnities for the injuries which all such expeditions have hitherto committed or shall hereafter commit against this Government and the citizens of the United States." "Can it be an occasion for either surprise or complaint," asked Mr. Seward, "that if this condition of things is to remain and receive the deliberate sanction of the British Government, the navy of the United States will receive instructions to pursue these enemies into the ports which thus, in violation of the law of nations and the obligations of neutrality, become harbors for the pirates?" Before the receipt of this dispatch, Mr. Adams had so clearly presented the same views, of the inevitable results of the policy the British Government seemed to be pursuing, to Lord Russell, as to render its transmission to him unnecessary,—Mr. Seward, on the 13th of August, informing Mr. Adams that he regarded his "previous communications to Earl Russell on the subject as an execution of his instructions by way of anticipation."

Our relations with France continued to be friendly; but the proceedings of the French in Mexico gave rise to representations on both sides which may have permanent importance for the welfare of both countries. Rumors were circulated from time to time in France that the government of the United States had protested, or was about to protest, against the introduction into Mexico of a monarchical form of government, under a European prince, to be established and supported by French arms; and these reports derived a good deal of plausibility from the language of the American press, representing the undoubted sentiment of a very large portion of the American people. Various incidental conversations were had on this subject during the summer of 1863 between Mr. Dayton, our Minister in Paris, and the French Minister of Foreign Affairs, in which the latter uniformly assured Mr. Dayton that France had no thought of conquering Mexico or establishing there a dominant and permanent power. She desired simply to enforce the payment of just claims and to vindicate her honor. In a conversation reported by Mr. Dayton in a letter dated August 21, M. Drouyn de l'Huys "took occasion again to say that France had no purpose in Mexico other than heretofore stated,—that she did not mean to appropriate permanently any part of that country, and that she should leave it as soon as her griefs were satisfied, and she could do so with honor." "In the *abandon* of a conversation somewhat familiar," adds Mr. Dayton, "I took occasion to say that in quitting Mexico she might leave a *puppet* behind her. He said no; the *strings would be too long to work.* He added that they had had enough of colonial experience in Algeria: that the strength of France was in her compact body and well-defined boundary. In that condition she had her resources always at command."

In a dispatch dated September 14, Mr. Dayton reports a conversation in which the French Minister referred to the "almost universal report that our government only awaits the termination of our domestic troubles to drive the French out of Mexico." He said that the French naturally conclude that, if they are to have trouble with us, it would be safest to take their own time; and he assured M. Drouyn de l'Huys that "relying on the constant assurances of France as to its purposes in Mexico, and its determination to leave the people free as to their form of government, and not to hold or colonize any portion of their territories," our government had indicated no purpose to interfere in the quarrel, not concealing at the same time our earnest solicitude for the well-being of that country, and an especial sensitiveness as to any forcible interference in the form of its government.

On the 21st of September Mr. Seward instructed Mr. Dayton to call the attention of the French Minister to the apparent deviations of the French in Mexico from the tenor of the assurances uniformly given by the French government that they did not intend permanent occupation of that country, or any violence to the sovereignty of its people. And on the 26th of the same month Mr. Seward set forth at some length the position of our government upon this question, which is mainly embodied in the following extract:—

The United States hold, in regard to Mexico, the same principles that they hold in regard to all other nations. They have neither a right nor a disposition to intervene by force in the internal affairs of Mexico, whether to establish and maintain a republic or even a domestic government there, or to overthrow an imperial or a foreign one, if Mexico chooses to establish or accept it. The United States have neither the right nor the disposition to intervene by force on either side in the lamentable war which is going on between France and Mexico. On the contrary, they practise in regard to Mexico, in every phase of that war, the non-intervention which they require all foreign powers to observe in regard to the United States. But notwithstanding this self-restraint, this government knows full well that the inherent normal opinion of Mexico favors a government there republican in form and domestic in its organization in preference to any monarchical institutions to be imposed from abroad. This government knows also that this normal opinion of the people of Mexico resulted largely from the influence of popular opinion in this country, and is continually invigorated by it. The President believes, moreover, that this popular opinion of the United States is just in itself and eminently essential to the progress of civilization on the American continent, which civilization, it believes, can and will, if left free from European resistance, work harmoniously together with advancing refinement on the other continents. This government believes that foreign resistance, or attempts to control American civilization, must and will fail before the ceaseless and ever increasing activity of material, moral, and political forces, which peculiarly belong to the American continent. Nor do the United States deny that, in their opinion, their own safety and the cheerful destiny to which they aspire are intimately dependent on the continuance of free republican institutions throughout America. They have submitted these opinions to the Emperor of France, on proper occasions, as worthy of his serious consideration, in determining how he would conduct and close what might prove a successful war in Mexico. Nor is it necessary to practise reserve upon the point that if France should, upon due consideration, determine to adopt a policy in Mexico adverse to the American opinion and sentiments which I have described, that policy would probably scatter seeds which would be fruitful of jealousies which might ultimately ripen into collision between France and the United States and other American republics. . . . The statements made to you by M. Drouyn de l'Huys concerning the Emperor's intentions are entirely satisfactory, if we are permitted to assume them as having been authorized to be made by the Emperor in view of the present condition of affairs in Mexico.

The French Minister, in a conversation on the 8th of October, stated to Mr. Dayton that the vote of the entire population of Mexico, Spanish and Indian, would be taken as to the form of government to be established, and he had no doubt a large majority of that vote would be in favor of the Archduke Maximilian. He also expressed a desire that the United States would express its acquiescence in such a result, and its readiness to enter into peaceful relations with such a government, by acknowledging it as speedily as possible,—inasmuch as such a course would enable France the sooner to leave Mexico and the new government to take care of itself. In replying to this request, on the 23d of October Mr. Seward repeated the determination of our government to maintain a position of complete neutrality in the war between France and Mexico, and declared that while they could not anticipate the action of the people of Mexico, they had not "the least purpose or desire to interfere with their proceedings, or control or interfere with their free choice, or disturb them in the exercise of whatever institutions of government they may, in the exercise of an absolute freedom, establish." As we did not consider the war yet closed, however, we were not at liberty to consider the question of recognizing the government which, in the further chances of that war, might take the place of the one now existing in Mexico, with which our relations were those of peace and friendship.

The policy of the President, therefore, in regard to the war in Mexico has been that of neutrality; and, although this policy has in some respects contravened the traditional purposes and principles of the government and people of the United States, it is not easy to see what other could have been adopted without inviting hazards which no responsible statesman has a right to incur. The war against Mexico was undertaken ostensibly for objects and purposes which we were compelled to regard as legitimate, and we could not ourselves depart from a strict neutrality without virtually conceding the right, not only of France but of every other nation interested in our downfall, to become party to the war against us. While we have to a certain extent pledged ourselves to hold the whole continent open to republican institutions, our first duty is clearly to preserve the existence of our own Republic, not only for ourselves, but as the only condition on which republicanism anywhere is possible. The President, therefore, in holding this country wholly aloof from the war with France, has consulted the ultimate and permanent interests of Democratic institutions not less than the safety and welfare of the United States, and has pursued the only policy at all compatible with the preservation of our Union and the final establishment of the Monroe doctrine. Neither the President nor the people, however, have indicated any purpose to acquiesce in the imposition of a foreign prince upon the Mexican people by foreign armies; and on the 3d of April, 1864, the House of Representatives adopted the following resolution upon the subject, which embodies, beyond all doubt, the settled sentiment of the people of this country.

THE MEXICAN MONARCHY.

Resolved, That the Congress of the United States are unwilling by silence to leave the nations of the world under the impression that they are indifferent spectators of the deplorable events now transpiring in the Republic of Mexico; therefore, they think it fit to declare that it does not accord with the sentiment of the people of the United States to acknowledge a monarchical government erected on the ruins of any republican government in America, under the auspices of any European Power.

No action up to the present time (May 5) has been taken upon this resolution in the Senate.

CHAPTER XII.

MOVEMENTS TOWARDS RECONSTRUCTION.—THE REBELLION AND LABOR.—THE PRESIDENT ON BENEVOLENT ASSOCIATIONS.—ADVANCING ACTION CONCERNING THE NEGRO RACE.

THE Proclamation, which accompanied the Annual Message of the President, embodied the first suggestions of the administration on the important subject of reconstructing the governments of those States, which had joined in the secession movement. The matter had been canvassed somewhat extensively by the public press, and by prominent politicians, in anticipation of the overthrow of the rebellion, and the view taken of the subject had been determined, to a very considerable extent, by the sentiments and opinions of the different parties as to the object and purpose of the war. The supporters of the administration did not all hold precisely the same ground on this subject. As has already been seen, in the debates of the Congress of 1862–3, a considerable number of the friends of the government, in both houses, maintained that, by the act of secession, the revolted States had put themselves outside the pale of the Constitution, and were henceforth to be regarded and treated, not as members of the Union, but as alien enemies:*—that their State organizations and

* President Lincoln's view of this position is stated in the following note addressed by him to the publishers of the *North American Review*, which contained an article upon his policy of administration:

"EXECUTIVE MANSION, WASHINGTON, *January* 16, 1864.

"Messrs. CROSBY & NICHOLS:

"Gentlemen:—The number for this month and year of the *North American Review* was duly received, and for which please accept my thanks. Of course I am not the most impartial judge; yet, with due

State boundaries had been expunged by their own act; and that they were to be re-admitted to the jurisdiction of the Constitution, and to the privileges of the Union, only upon such terms and conditions as the Federal government of the loyal States might prescribe. On the other hand it was held that the acts of secession, passed by the several State governments, were absolutely null and void, and that while the persons who passed them, and those who aided in giving them effect, by taking up arms against the United States, had rendered themselves liable individually to the penalties of treason, they had not, in any respect, changed the relations of their States,

allowance for this, I venture to hope that the article entitled 'The President's Policy' will be of value to the country. I fear I am not worthy of all which is therein kindly said of me personally.

"The sentence of twelve lines, commencing at the top of page 252, I could wish to be not exactly what it is. In what is there expressed, the writer has not correctly understood me. I have never had a theory that secession could absolve States or people from their obligations. Precisely the contrary is asserted in the inaugural address; and it was because of my belief in the continuation of those *obligations* that I was puzzled, for a time, as to denying the legal *rights* of those citizens who remained individually innocent of treason or rebellion. But I mean no more now than to merely call attention to this point.

"Yours respectfully,

"A. LINCOLN."

The sentence referred to by Mr. Lincoln is as follows:

"Even so long ago as when Mr. Lincoln, not yet convinced of the danger and magnitude of the crisis, was endeavoring to persuade himself of Union majorities at the South, and carry on a war that was half peace, in the hope of a peace that would have been all war, while he was still enforcing the Fugitive Slave law, under some theory that secession, however it might absolve States from their obligations, could not escheat them of their claims under the Constitution, and that slaveholders in rebellion had alone among mortals, the privilege of having their cake and eating it at the same time,—the enemies of free government were striving to persuade the people that the war was an abolition crusade. To rebel without reason was proclaimed as one of the rights of man, while it was carefully kept out of sight that to suppress rebellion is the first duty of government."

as such, to the federal government. The governments of those States had been for a time subverted :—but they might at any time be re-established upon a republican basis, under the authority and protection of the United States. The Proclamation proceeded, in the main, upon the latter theory. The President had the power, under the Constitution, and by specific legislation of Congress, to grant pardons upon such conditions as he might deem expedient. In the exercise of this power, President LINCOLN released from legal penalties, and restored to the rights of citizenship all, in each State, with certain specified exceptions, who should take and abide by a prescribed oath; and then he proclaimed his purpose to recognize *them* as the citizens of such State, and as alone competent to organize and carry on the local government; and he pledged the power of the general government to protect such republican State governments as they might establish, "against invasion, and against domestic violence." By way of precaution against a usurpation of power by strangers, he insisted on the same qualifications for voting as had been required by the Constitution and laws of the State previous to secession :—and to provide against usurpation of power by an insignificant minority, he also required that the new government should be elected by at least one tenth as many voters as had voted in the State at the Presidential election of 1860. In the oath, which he imposed as essential to citizenship, the President required a pledge to sustain the Constitution of the United States, the laws of Congress and the Executive Proclamations and acts on the subject of slavery, so long and so far as the same should not be declared invalid and of no binding obligation, by the Supreme Court of the United States. These were the foundations of the broad and substantial basis laid by the President for the restoration of the Union, and the re-establishment of loyal republican governments in the several seceded States.

Various indications in the Southern States, had satisfied the President that the time had come when the work of reconstruction might safely and wisely be thus commenced. In Tennessee, where the rebels had never maintained any permanent foothold, but where the government at Washington had found it necessary to commit the local authority to Andrew Johnson, as Provisional Governor, there had been a very strong party in favor of restoring the State to its former position as a member of the Federal Union. But in Louisiana, the movements in the same direction had been earlier and more decided than in any other Southern State. The occupation of New Orleans by the national forces, and the advent of General Butler as Commander of that Military Department, on the 1st of May, 1862, speedily satisfied a very considerable portion of the inhabitants, who had property at stake in the City and State, that the rebel authority could never be restored; and preparations were accordingly made to hold an election in the fall of that year for Members of the Congress of the United States. General Shepley had been appointed Military Governor of the State, and to him the President, in November, addressed the following letter on that subject:

EXECUTIVE MANSION, WASHINGTON, *November* 21, 1862.

DEAR SIR:—Dr. Kennedy, bearer of this, has some apprehension that Federal officers, not citizens of Louisiana, may be set up as candidates for Congress in that State. In my view there could be no possible object in such an election. We do not particularly need members of Congress from those States to enable us to get along with legislation here. What we do want is the conclusive evidence that respectable citizens of Louisiana are willing to be members of Congress and to swear support to the Constitution, and that other respectable citizens there are willing to vote for them and send them. To send a parcel of Northern men here as representatives, elected as would be understood (and perhaps really so), at the point of the bayonet, would be disgraceful and outrageous; and were I a member of Congress here, I would vote against admitting any such man to a seat.

Yours, very truly,

A. LINCOLN.

Hon. G. F. SHEPLEY.

The election was held, and Messrs. Flanders and Hahn were chosen and admitted to their seats at the ensuing session, as has been already seen.

On the 23d of May, 1863, the various Union associations of New Orleans applied to the Military Governor of the State for authority to call a Convention of the loyal citizens of Louisiana, for the purpose of framing a new State Constitution, and of re-establishing civil government under the Constitution of the United States. What they especially desired of him was that he should order a registration of the loyal voters of the State, and appoint commissioners of registration in each parish to register the names of all citizens who should take the oath of allegiance to the Constitution of the United States, and repudiate allegiance to the Rebel Confederacy. General Shepley, in reply, recognized fully the great importance of the proposed movement, but thought it of the utmost consequence that it should proceed as the spontaneous act of the people of the State, without the slightest appearance or suspicion of having been in any degree the result of military dictation. He consented to provide for the registration of such voters as might voluntarily come forward for the purpose of being enrolled, but deferred action upon the other points submitted to him until he could receive definite instructions on the subject from the Government at Washington.

In June, a Committee of Planters, recognizing the propriety of some movement for the re-establishment of civil authority in the State, and not concurring in the policy of those who proposed to form a new Constitution, applied to the President, asking him to grant a full recognition of the rights of the State as they existed before the act of secession, so that they might return to their allegiance under the old Constitution of the State, and that he would order an election for State officers, to be held on the 1st Monday of November.

To this application the President made the following reply:

EXECUTIVE MANSION, WASHINGTON, *June* 19, 1863.

GENTLEMEN:—Since receiving your letter, reliable information has reached me that a respectable portion of the Louisiana people desire to amend their State Constitution, and contemplate holding a Convention for that object. This fact alone, it seems to me, is a sufficient reason why the General Government should not give the committee the authority you seek to act under the existing State Constitution. I may add, that while I do not perceive how such a committee could facilitate our military operations in Louisiana, I really apprehend it might be so used as to embarrass them.

As to an election to be held in November, there is abundant time without any order or proclamation from me just now. The people of Louisiana shall not lack an opportunity for a fair election for both Federal and State officers by want of any thing within my power to give them.

Your obedient servant, A. LINCOLN.

After the appearance of the President's proclamation, the movement towards reconstruction in Louisiana assumed greater consistency, and was carried forward with greater steadiness and strength. On the 8th of January a very large Free State convention was held at New Orleans, at which resolutions were adopted indorsing all the acts and proclamations of the President, and urging the immediate adoption of measures for the restoration of the State to its old place in the Union. On the 11th, General Banks issued a proclamation, appointing an election for State officers on the 22d of February, who were to be installed on the 4th of March, and another election for delegates to a convention to revise the Constitution of the State on the first Monday in April. The old Constitution and laws of Louisiana were to be observed, except so far as they relate to Slavery, "which," said General Banks, "being inconsistent with the present condition of public affairs, and plainly inapplicable to any class of persons within the limits of the State, must be suspended, and they are now declared inoperative and void." The oath of allegiance required by the President in his proclamation, with the condition affixed to the elective franchise by the Constitution of Louisiana, was prescribed as constituting the qualification of voters.

Under this order, parties were organized for the election of State officers. The friends of the national government were divided, and two candidates were put in nomination for governer, Hon. Michael Hahn being the regular nominee, and representing the supporters of the policy of the President, and Hon. B. F. Flanders being put in nomination by those who desired a more radical policy than the President had proposed. Both took very decided ground against the continued existence of slavery within the State. Hon. C. Roselius was nominated by that portion of the people who concurred in the wish for the return of Louisiana to the Union, and were willing to take the oath of allegiance prescribed by the President, but who nevertheless disapproved of the general policy of the Administration, especially on the subject of slavery. The election resulted in the election of Mr. Hahn.

In Arkansas, where a decided Union feeling has existed from the outbreak of the rebellion, the appearance of the proclamation was the signal for a movement to bring the State back into the Union. On the 20th of January, a delegation of citizens from that State had an interview with the President, in which they urged the adoption of certain measures for the re-establishment of a legal State government, and especially the ordering of an election for governor. In consequence of this application, and in substantial compliance with their request, the President wrote the following letter to General Steele, who commanded in that Department:

EXECUTIVE MANSION, WASHINGTON, *Jan.* 20, 1864.

Major-General STEELE:

Sundry citizens of the State of Arkansas petition me that an election may be held in that State, at which to elect a governor; that it be assumed at that election and thenceforward, that the Constitution and laws of the State, as before the rebellion, are in full force, except that the Constitution is so modified as to declare that there shall be neither slavery nor involuntary servitude, except in the punishment of crimes whereof the party shall have been duly convicted; that the General Assembly may make such provisions for the freed people as shall recognize and declare their permanent freedom, and provide for their education, and which may yet be construed as a temporary arrangement suitable to their condition as a laboring, landless, and homeless class; that said election shall be held on the 28th of March, 1864, at all the usual places of the State, or all such as voters may attend for that purpose; that the voters attending at 8 o'clock in the morning of said day may choose judges and clerks of election for such purpose; that all persons qualified by said Constitution and laws, and taking the oath presented in the President's proclamation of December 8, 1863, either before or at the election, and none others, may be voters; that each set of judges and clerks may make returns directly to you on or before the —th day of ——— next; that in all other respects said election may be conducted according to said Constitution and laws; that on receipt of said returns, when 5,406 votes shall have been cast, you can receive said votes and ascertain all who shall thereby appear to have been elected; that on the —th day of ——— next, all persons so appearing to have been elected, who shall appear before you at Little Rock, and take the oath, to be by you severally administered, to support the Constitution of the United States, and said modified Constitution of the State of Arkansas, may be declared by you qualified and empowered to immediately enter upon the duties of the offices to which they shall have been respectively elected.

You will please order an election to take place on the 28th of March, 1864, and returns to be made in fifteen days thereafter.

A. LINCOLN.

Upon the return of the delegation to Arkansas, they issued an address to the people of the State, urging them to avail themselves of the opportunity thus afforded for restoring their State to its old prosperity, and assuring them, from personal observation, that the people of the Northern States would most cordially welcome their return to the Union. Meantime a convention had assembled at Little Rock, composed of delegates elected without any formality, and not under the authority of the General Government, and proceeded to form a new State Constitution. Upon learning this fact, the President wrote the following letter to one of the most prominent members:

To WILLIAM FISHBACK:

When I fixed a plan for an election in Arkansas, I did it in ignorance that your convention was at the same work. Since I learned the latter fact, I have been constantly trying to yield my plan to theirs. I have sent two letters to General Steele, and three or four dispatches to you and others, saying that he (General Steele) must be master, but that it will probably be best for him to keep the convention on its own plan. Some single mind must be master, else there will be no agreement on any thing; and General Steele, commanding the military and being on the ground, is the best man to be that master. Even now citizens are telegraphing me to postpone the election to a later day than either fixed by the convention or me. This discord must be silenced. A. LINCOLN.

The Convention framed a Constitution abolishing Slavery, which was subsequently adopted by a large majority of the people.

The military movements of the year 1864 thus far call for no special notice in this place. Three enterprises of considerable magnitude have been undertaken, but neither of them was attended with results of any great importance.

As early as the 15th of December, 1863, Gen. Gillmore, commanding the Department of the South, applied to the Government for permission to send an expedition into Florida, for the purpose of cutting off supplies of the enemy; and in January, in urging the matter still further upon the attention of Gen. Halleck, he suggested that measures might be also inaugurated for restoring the State of Florida to her allegiance under the terms of the President's Proclamation. Gen. Gillmore was authorized to take such action in the matter as he should deem proper,—and he accordingly organized an expedition, which left Port Royal on the 5th of February, under General Seymour, and was followed soon afterwards by General Gillmore himself—to whom, on the 13th of January, the President had addressed the following letter:

EXECUTIVE MANSION, WASHINGTON, *Jan.* 13, 1864.

Major-General GILLMORE:

I understand an effort is being made by some worthy gentlemen to reconstruct a legal State government in Florida. Florida is in your department, and it is not unlikely you may be there in person. I have given Mr. Hay a commission of Major, and sent him to you, with some blank books and other blanks, to aid in the reconstruction. He will explain as to the manner of using the blanks, and also my general views on the subject. It is desirable for all to co-operate, but if irreconcilable differences of opinion shall arise, you are master. I wish the thing done in the most speedy way, so that when done it be within the range of the late proclamation on the subject. The detail labor will, of course, have to be done by others; but I will be greatly obliged if you will give it such general supervision as you can find consistent with your more strictly military duties.

ABRAHAM LINCOLN.

The advance portion of the expedition reached Jacksonville on the 8th of February. Gen. Gillmore returned to Port Royal on the 16th, leaving the command of the expedition to Gen. Seymour. The first operations were successful. Near Jacksonville one hundred prisoners, with eight pieces of serviceable artillery, fell into our hands, and expeditions were pushed forward into the interior, by which large amounts of stores and supplies were destroyed. On the 17th General Seymour, with 5,000 men, was on the Florida Central Railroad, about forty-five miles from Jacksonville. Here they remained until the 20th, when the preparations for a movement toward Lake City were completed. The enemy was found in force, a little before reaching Lake City, at Olustee, a small station on the railroad. The engagement was commenced between the enemy's skirmishers and our advance. The fire directed against our men was so hot that they were compelled to fall back; then we brought two batteries to bear on the enemy, and our whole force became engaged with more than twice their number of the enemy, who occupied a strong position, flanked by a marsh. Again we retreated, taking another position; but it was impossible to contend with a force so greatly superior, and, after a battle of three hours and a half, General Seymour retreated, leaving his dead and severely wounded on the field. Five guns were lost, and about a thousand men killed, wounded, and missing.

On the 3d of February, General Sherman, with a strong force, set out from Vicksburg, in light marching order, and moved eastward. Shortly after, a cavalry expedition, under General Smith, set out from Memphis, to work its way south-eastward, and join Sherman somewhere on the borders of Mississippi and Alabama. By the 18th Smith had accomplished nearly one-half of his proposed march, but soon after found the enemy concentrated in superior force in his way. Finding it impossible to proceed, he fell back, destroying the bridges on the Memphis and Ohio Railroad in his retreat. There was continual skirmishing, but no decisive battle during the retreat, which lasted until the 25th, when the expedition accomplished its return to Memphis. Much damage was done to the enemy by the destruction of property, but the main object of making a junction with Sherman failed. Sherman went as far east as Meridian, almost on the borders of Mississippi and Alabama, and after destroying large quantities of the rebel stores, and breaking their means of communication, he returned to Vicksburg.

The other enterprise to which reference is made above, was a raid upon Richmond, made by a large cavalry force under General Kilpatrick. Leaving his camp on the 28th of February, he crossed the Rapidan, gained the rear of Lee's army without being discovered, and pushed rapidly on in the direction of Richmond. A detachment under Colonel Dahlgren was sent from the main body to Frederick's Hall, on the Virginia Central Railroad. The road was torn up for some distance, and then the James River Canal was struck, and six grist-mills destroyed, which formed one of the main sources of supply for the Confederate army. Several locks on the canal were destroyed, and other damage done. Dahlgren's main body then pressed onward toward Richmond, and came within three miles of the city, when, encountering a Confederate force, it was compelled to withdraw, Dahlgren himself being killed, and a large part of his force captured. Kilpatrick, meanwhile, pressed onward to Spottsylvania Court-House, and thence to Beaver Dam, near where the two lines of railway from Richmond, those running to Gordonsville and Fredericksburg, cross. Here the railway was torn up, and the telegraphic line cut, and the cavalry pushed straight on toward Richmond. They reached the outer line of fortifications at a little past ten on the morning of the 1st of March, about three and a half miles from the city. These were fairly passed, and the second line, a mile nearer, was reached, and a desultory fire was kept up for some hours. Toward evening Kilpatrick withdrew, and encamped six miles from the city. In the night an artillery attack was made upon the camp, and our troops retired still farther, and on the following morning took up their line of march down the Peninsula toward Williamsburg. Several miles of railway connection of great importance to the enemy were interrupted, stores to the value of several millions of dollars were destroyed, and some hundreds of prisoners were captured, as the result of this expedition.

The relations of the war which is carried on to maintain the Republican Government of the United States, against the efforts of the slave-holding oligarchy for its overthrow, to the general interests of labor, have from time to time enlisted a good deal of the thoughts of the President, and elicited from him expressions of his own sentiments on the subject. On the 31st of December, 1863, a very large meeting of working-men was held at Manchester, England, to express their opinion in regard to the war in the United States. At that meeting an address to President LINCOLN was adopted, expressing the kindest sentiments towards this country, and declaring that, since it had become evident that the destruction of Slavery was involved in the overthrow of the rebellion, their sympathies had been thoroughly and heartily with the Government of the United States in the prosecution of the war. This address was forwarded to the President through the American Minister in London, and elicited the following reply:

EXECUTIVE MANSION, WASHINGTON, *January* 19, 1863.

To the Workingmen of Manchester:

I have the honor to acknowledge the receipt of the address and resolutions which you sent me on the eve of the new year. When I came on the 4th of March, 1861, through a free and constitutional election, to preside in the Government of the United States, the country was found at the verge of civil war. Whatever might have been the cause, or whosesoever the fault, one duty, paramount to all others, was before me, namely, to maintain and preserve at once the Constitution and the integrity of the Federal Republic. A conscientious purpose to perform this duty, is the key to all the measures of administration which have been, and to all which will hereafter be pursued. Under our frame of government and my official oath, I could not depart from this purpose if I would. It is not always in the power of governments to enlarge or restrict the scope of moral results which follow the policies that they may deem it necessary, for the public safety, from time to time to adopt.

I have understood well that the duty of self-preservation rests solely with the American people. But I have at the same time been aware that favor or disfavor of foreign nations might have a material influence in enlarging or prolonging the struggle with disloyal men in which the country is engaged. A fair examination of history has served to authorize a belief that the past actions and influences of the United States, were generally regarded as having been beneficial toward mankind. I have, therefore, reckoned upon the forbearance of nations. Circumstances—to some of which you kindly allude—induced me especially to expect that if justice and good faith should be practised by the United States, they would encounter no hostile influence on the part of Great Britain. It is now a pleasant duty to acknowledge the demonstration you have given of your desire that a spirit of amity and peace toward this country may prevail in the councils of your Queen, who is respected and esteemed in your own country only more than she is by the kindred nation which has its home on this side of the Atlantic.

I know, and deeply deplore the sufferings which the workingmen at Manchester, and in all Europe, are called to endure in this crisis. It has been often and studiously represented that the attempt to overthrow this Government, which was built upon the foundation of human rights, and to substitute for it one which should rest exclusively on the basis of human slavery, was likely to obtain the favor of Europe. Through the action of our disloyal citizens, the workingmen of Europe have been subjected to severe trials, for the purpose of forcing their sanction to that attempt. Under the circumstances, I cannot but regard your decisive utterances upon the question as an instance of sublime Christian heroism, which has not been surpassed in any age or in any country. It is indeed an energetic and reinspiring assurance of the inherent power of truth, and of the ultimate and universal triumph of justice, humanity, and freedom. I do not doubt that the sentiments you have expressed will be sustained by your great nation, and on the other hand, I have no hesitation in assuring you that they will excite admiration, esteem, and the most reciprocal feelings of friendship among the American people. I hail this interchange of sentiment, therefore, as an augury that whatever else may happen, whatever misfortune may befall your country or my own, the peace and friendship which now exist between the two nations will be, as it shall be my desire to make them, perpetual.

ABRAHAM LINCOLN.

The workingmen of London held a similar meeting at about the same time, and took substantially the same action. The President made the following response to their address:

EXECUTIVE MANSION, *Feb.* 2, 1863.

To the Workingmen of London:

I have received the New Year's Address which you have sent me, with a sincere appreciation of the exalted and humane sentiments by which it was inspired.

As these sentiments are manifestly the enduring support of the free institutions of England, so I am sure also that they constitute the only reliable basis for free institutions throughout the world.

The resources, advantages, and powers of the American people are very great, and they have consequently succeeded to equally great responsibilities. It seems to have devolved upon them to test whether a government established on the principles of human freedom, can be maintained against an effort to build one upon the exclusive foundation of human bondage. They will rejoice with me in the new evidences which your proceedings furnish, that the magnanimity they are exhibiting is justly estimated by the true friends of freedom and humanity in foreign countries.

Accept my best wishes for your individual welfare, and for the welfare and happiness of the whole British people.

ABRAHAM LINCOLN.

On the 21st of March, 1864, a committee from the Workingmen's Association of the city of New York waited upon the

President and delivered an address, stating the general objects and purposes of the Association, and requesting that he would allow his name to be enrolled among its honorary members. To this address the President made the following reply:

GENTLEMEN OF THE COMMITTEE:—The honorary membership in your association, as generously tendered, is gratefully accepted.

You comprehend, as your address shows, that the existing rebellion means more and tends to do more than the perpetuation of African slavery—that it is, in fact, a war upon the rights of all working people. Partly to show that this view has not escaped my attention, and partly that I cannot better express myself, I read a passage from the message to Congress in December, 1861:

"It continues to develop that the insurrection is largely, if not exclusively, a war upon the first principle of popular government, the rights of the people. Conclusive evidence of this is found in the most grave and maturely considered public documents, as well as in the general tone of the insurgents. In those documents we find the abridgement of the existing right of suffrage, and the denial to the people of all right to participate in the selection of public officers, except the legislative, boldly advocated, with labored argument to prove that large control of the people in government is the source of all political evil. Monarchy itself is sometimes hinted at as a possible refuge from the power of the people.

"In my present position I could scarcely be justified were I to omit raising a warning voice against this approach of returning despotism.

"It is not needed, nor fitting here, that a general argument should be made in favor of popular institutions; but there is one point with its connections, not so hackneyed as most others, to which I ask a brief attention. It is the effort to place *capital* on an equal footing, if not above *labor*, in the structure of government. It is assumed that labor is available only in connection with capital; that nobody labors unless somebody else, owning capital, somehow by the use of it induces him to labor. This assumed, it is next considered whether it is best that capital shall *hire* laborers, and thus induce them to work by their own consent, or *buy* them, and drive them to it without their consent. Having proceeded so far, it is naturally concluded that all laborers are either *hired* laborers, or what we call slaves. And, further, it is assumed that whoever is once a hired laborer, is fixed in that condition for life. Now there is no such relation between capital and labor as assumed, nor is there any such thing as a free man being fixed for life in the condition of a hired laborer. Both these assumptions are false, and all inferences from them are groundless.

"Labor is prior to, and independent of, capital. Capital is only the fruit of labor, and could never have existed if labor had not first existed. Labor is the superior of capital, and deserves much the higher consideration. Capital has its rights, which are as worthy of protection as any other rights. Nor is it denied that there is, and probably always will be, a relation between capital and labor, producing mutual benefits. The error is in assuming that the whole labor of a community exists within that relation. A few men own capital, and that few avoid labor themselves, and, with their capital, hire or buy another few to labor for them. A large majority belong to neither class—neither work for others, nor have others working for them. In most of the Southern States a majority of the whole people of all colors, are neither slaves nor masters; while in the Northern, a large majority are neither hirers nor hired. Men with their families—wives, sons, and daughters—work for themselves, on their farms, in their houses, and in their shops, taking the whole product to themselves, and asking no favors of capital on the one hand nor of hired laborers or slaves on the other. It is not forgotten that a considerable number of persons mingle their own labor with capital; that is, they labor with their own hands, and also buy or hire others to labor for them, but this is only a mixed and not a distinct class. No principle stated is disturbed by the existence of this mixed class.

"Again, as has already been said, there is not, of necessity, any such thing as the free hired laborer being fixed to that condition for life. Many independent men everywhere in these States, a few years back in their lives were hired laborers. The prudent penniless beginner in the world labors for wages a while, saves a surplus with which to buy tools or land for himself, then labors on his own account another while, and at length hires another new beginner to help him. This is the just and generous and prosperous system which opens the way to all—gives hope to all, and consequent energy and progress, and improvement of condition to all. No men living are more worthy to be trusted than those who toil up from poverty—none less inclined to touch or take aught which they have not honestly earned. Let them beware of surrendering a political power they already possess, and which, if surrendered, will surely be used to close the door of advancement against such as they, and to fix new disabilities and burdens upon them, till all of liberty shall be lost."

The views then expressed remain unchanged, nor have I much to add. None are so deeply interested to resist the present rebellion as the working people. Let them beware of prejudices, working division and hostility among themselves. The most notable feature of a disturbance in your city last summer was the hanging of some working people by other working people. It should never be so. The strongest bond of human sympathy, outside of the family relation, should be one uniting all working people, of all nations, and tongues, and kindreds. Nor should this lead to a war upon property or the owners of property. Property is the fruit of labor; property is desirable; is a positive good in the world. That some should be rich shows that others may become rich, and, hence, is just encouragement to industry and enterprise. Let not him who is houseless pull down the house of another, but let him labor diligently and build one for himself, thus by example assuring that his own shall be safe from violence when built.

The President had always taken a deep interest in the volunteer movements of benevolent people throughout the country, for relieving the sufferings of the sick and wounded among our soldiers. A meeting of one of these organizations, the Christian Commission, was held at Washington, on the 22d of February, 1863, to which President LINCOLN, unable to attend and preside, addressed the following letter:

EXECUTIVE MANSION, *February* 22, 1863.

REV. ALEXANDER REED:

MY DEAR SIR:—Your note, by which you, as General Superintendent of the U. S. Christian Commission, invite me to preside at a meeting to be held this day, at the hall of the House of Representatives in this city, is received.

While, for reasons which I deem sufficient, I must decline to preside, I cannot withhold my approval of the meeting, and its worthy objects. Whatever shall be, sincerely and in God's name, devised for the good of the soldiers and seamen in their hard spheres of duty, can scarcely fail to be blessed. And whatever shall tend to turn our thoughts from the unreasoning and uncharitable passions, prejudices, and jealousies incident to a great national trouble such as ours, and to fix them on the vast and long-enduring consequences, for weal or for woe, which are to result from the struggle, and especially to strengthen our reliance on the Supreme Being for the final triumph of the right, cannot but be well for us all.

The birthday of Washington and the Christian Sabbath coinciding this year, and suggesting together the highest interests of this life and of that to come, is most propitious for the meeting proposed.

Your obedient servant, A. LINCOLN.

On the 16th of March, 1864, at the close of a fair in Washington, given at the Patent Office, for the benefit of the sick and wounded soldiers of the army, President LINCOLN happening to be present, in response to loud and continuous calls, made the following remarks:

LADIES AND GENTLEMEN:—I appear to say but a word. This extraordinary war in which we are engaged falls heavily upon all classes of people, but the most heavily upon the soldier. For it has been said, all that a man hath will he give for his life; and while all contribute of their substance, the soldier puts his life at stake, and often yields it up in his country's cause. The highest merit, then, is due to the soldier.

In this extraordinary war, extraordinary developments have manifested themselves, such as have not been seen in former wars; and among these manifestations nothing has been more remarkable than these fairs for the relief of suffering soldiers and their families. And the chief agents in these fairs are the women of America.

I am not accustomed to the use of language of eulogy; I have never studied the art of paying compliments to women; but I must say, that if all that has been said by orators and poets since the creation of the world in praise of women were applied to the women of America, it would not do them justice for their conduct during this war. I will close by saying, God bless the women of America!

Still another occasion of a similar character occurred at Baltimore on the 18th of April, at the opening of a Fair for the benefit of the Sanitary Commission. The President accepted an invitation to attend the opening exercises, and made the following remarks:

LADIES AND GENTLEMEN:—Calling to mind that we are in Baltimore, we cannot fail to note that the world moves. Looking upon these many people assembled here to serve, as they best may, the soldiers of the Union, it occurs at once that three years ago the same soldiers could not so much as pass through Baltimore. The change from then till now is both great and gratifying. Blessings on the brave men who have wrought the change, and the fair women who strive to reward them for it.

But Baltimore suggests more than could happen within Baltimore. The change within Baltimore is part only of a far wider change. When the war began, three years ago, neither party, nor any man, expected it would last till now. Each looked for the end, in some way, long ere to-day. Neither did any anticipate that domestic slavery would be much affected by the war. But here we are; the war has not ended, and slavery has been much affected—how much needs not now to be recounted. So true is it that man proposes and God disposes.

But we can see the past, though we may not claim to have directed it; and seeing it, in this case, we feel more hopeful and confident for the future.

The world has never had a good definition of the word liberty, and the American people, just now, are much in want of one. We all declare for liberty; but in using the same *word* we do not all mean the same *thing*. With some the word liberty may mean for each man to do as he pleases with himself, and the product of his labor; while with others the same word may mean for some men to do as they please with other men, and the product of other men's labor. Here are two, not only different, but incompatible things, called by the same name, liberty. And it follows that each of the things is, by the respective parties, called by two different and incompatible names—liberty and tyranny.

The shepherd drives the wolf from the sheep's throat, for which the sheep thanks the shepherd as a *liberator*, while the wolf denounces him for the same act, as the destroyer of liberty, especially as the sheep was a black one. Plainly, the sheep and the wolf are not agreed upon a definition of the word liberty; and precisely the same difference prevails to-day among us human creatures, even in the North, and all professing to love liberty. Hence we behold the process by which thousands are daily passing from under the yoke of bondage hailed by some as the advance of liberty, and bewailed by others as the destruction of all liberty. Recently, as it seems, the people of Maryland have been doing something to define liberty· and thanks to them that, in what they have done, the wolf's dictionary has been repudiated.

It is not very becoming for one in my position to make speeches at great length; but there is another subject upon which I feel that I ought to say a word. A painful rumor, true I fear, has reached us of the massacre, by the rebel forces at Fort Pillow, in the west end of Tennessee, on the Mississippi River, of some three hundred colored soldiers and white officers, who had just been overpowered by their assailants. There seems to be some anxiety in the public mind whether the Government is doing its duty to the colored soldier, and to the service, at this point. At the beginning of the war, and for some time, the use of colored troops was not contemplated; and how the change of purpose was wrought, I will not now take time to explain. Upon a clear conviction of duty, I resolved to turn that element of strength to account; and I am responsible for it to the American people, to the Christian world, to history, and on my final account to God. Having determined to use the negro as a soldier, there is no way but to give him all the protection given to any other soldier. The difficulty is not in stating the principle, but in practically applying it. It is a mistake to suppose the Government is indifferent to this matter, or is not doing the best it can in regard to it. We do not to-day *know* that a colored soldier, or white officer commanding colored soldiers, has been massacred by the rebels when made a prisoner. We fear it, believe it, I may say, but we do not *know* it. To take the life of one of their prisoners on the assumption that they murder ours, when it is short of certainty that they do murder ours, might be too serious, too cruel a mistake. We are having the Fort Pillow affair thoroughly investigated; and such investigation will probably show conclusively how the truth is. If, after all that has been said, it shall turn out that, there has been no massacre at Fort Pillow, it will be almost safe to say there has been none, and will be none elsewhere. If there has been the massacre of three hundred there, or even the tenth part of three hundred, it will be conclusively proven; and being so proven, the retribution shall as surely come. It will be matter of grave consideration in what exact course to apply the retribution; but in the supposed case, it must come.

It became manifest, soon after the commencement of the war, that its progress would inevitably have the effect of freeing very many, if not all, the slaves of the Southern States. The President's attention was therefore directed at an early day to the proper disposition of those who should thus be freed. As his Messages show, he was strongly in favor of colonizing them, with their own consent, in some country where they could be relieved from the embarrassments occasioned by the hostile prejudices of the whites, and enter upon a career of their own. In consequence of his urgent representations upon this subject, Congress at its session of 1862 passed an act placing at his disposal the sum of $600,000 to be expended, in his discretion, in removing, with their own consent, free persons of African descent to some country which they might select as adapted to their condition and necessities.

On the 14th of August, 1862, the President received a deputation of colored persons, with whom he had an interview on the subject, of which one of the parties interested has made the following record:

WASHINGTON, *Thursday, August* 14, 1862.

This afternoon the President of the United States gave an audience to a Committee of colored men at the White House. They were introduced by Rev. J. Mitchell, Commissioner of Emigration. E. M. Thomas, the Chairman, remarked that they were there by invitation to hear what the Executive had to say to them.

Having all been seated, the President, after a few preliminary observations, informed them that a sum of money had been appropriated by Congress, and placed at his disposition, for the purpose of aiding the colonization in some country of the people, or a portion of them, of African descent, thereby making it his duty, as it had for a long time been his inclination, to favor that cause; and why, he asked, should the people of your race be colonized, and where? Why should they leave this country? This is, perhaps, the first question for proper consideration. You and we are different races. We have between us a broader difference than exists between almost any other two races. Whether it is right or wrong I need not discuss; but this physical difference is a great disadvantage to us both, as I think. Your race suffer very greatly, many of them by living among us, while ours suffer from your presence. In a word we suffer on each side. If this is admitted, it affords a reason, at least, why we should be separated. You here are freemen, I suppose.

A voice—Yes, Sir.

The President—Perhaps you have long been free, or all your lives. Your race are suffering, in my judgment, the greatest wrong inflicted on any people. But even when you cease to be slaves, you are yet far removed from being placed on an equality with the white race. You are cut off from many of the advantages which the other race enjoys. The aspiration of men is to enjoy equality with the best when free, but on this broad continent not a single man of your race is made the equal of a single man of ours. Go where you are treated the best, and the ban is still upon you. I do not propose to discuss this, but to present it as a fact, with which we have to deal. I cannot alter it if I would. It is a fact about which we all think and feel alike, I and you. We look to our condition. Owing to the existence of the two races on this continent, I need not recount to you the effects upon white men, growing out of the institution of Slavery. I believe in its general evil effects on the white race. See our present condition—the country engaged in war! our white men cutting one another's throats—none knowing how far it will extend—and then consider what we know to be the truth. But for your race among us there could not be war, although many men engaged on either side do not care for you one way or the other. Nevertheless, I repeat, without the institution of Slavery, and the colored race as a basis, the war could not have an existence. It is better for us both, therefore, to be separated. I know that there are free men among you who, even if they could better their condition, are not as much inclined to go out of the country as those who, being slaves, could obtain their freedom on this condition. I suppose one of the principal difficulties in the way of colonization is that the free colored man cannot see that his comfort would be advanced by it. You may believe that you can live in Washington, or elsewhere in the United States, the remainder of your life; perhaps more so than you can in any foreign country, and hence you may come to the conclusion that you have nothing to do with the idea of going to a foreign country. This is (I speak in no unkind sense) an extremely selfish view of the case. But you ought to do something to help those who are not so fortunate as yourselves. There is an unwillingness on the part of our people, harsh as it may be, for you free colored people to remain with us. Now if you could give a start to the white people you would open a wide door for many to be made free. If we deal with those who are not free at the beginning, and whose intellects are clouded by Slavery, we have very poor material to start with. If intelligent colored men, such as are before me, would move in this matter, much might be accomplished. It is exceedingly important that we have men at the beginning capable of thinking as white men, and not those who have been systematically oppressed. There is much to encourage you. For the sake of your race you should sacrifice something of your present comfort for the purpose of being as grand in that respect as the white people. It is a cheering thought throughout life, that something can be done to ameliorate the condition of those who have been subject to the hard usages of the world. It is difficult to make a man miserable while he feels he is worthy of himself and claims kindred to the great God who made him. In the American Revolutionary War sacrifices were made by men engaged in it, but they were cheered by the future. General Washington himself endured greater physical hardships than if he had remained a British subject, yet he was a happy man, because he was engaged in benefiting his race; in doing something for the children of his neighbors, having none of his own.

The colony of Liberia has been in existence a long time. In a certain sense, it is a success. The old President of Liberia, Roberts, has just been with me the first time I ever saw him. He says they have within the bounds of that colony between three and four hundred thousand people, or more than in some of our old States, such as Rhode Island or Delaware, or in some of our newer States, and less than in some of our larger ones. They are not all American colonists or their descendants. Something less than 12,000 have been sent thither from this country. Many of the original settlers have died, yet, like people elsewhere, their offspring outnumber those deceased. The question is, if the colored people are persuaded to go anywhere, why not there? One reason for unwillingness to do so is, that some of you would rather remain within reach of the country of your nativity. I do not know how much attachment you may have toward our race. It does not strike me that you have the greatest reason to love them. But still you are attached to them at all events. The place I am thinking about having for a colony, is in Central America. It is nearer to us than Liberia—not much more than one-fourth as far as Liberia, and within seven days' run by steamers. Unlike Liberia, it is a great line of travel—it is a highway. The country is a very excellent one for any people, and with great natural resources and advantages, and especially because of the similarity of climate with your native soil, thus being suited to your physical condition. The particular place I have in view, is to be a great highway from the Atlantic or Caribbean Sea to the Pacific Ocean, and this particular place has all the advantages for a colony. On both sides there are harbors among the finest in the world. Again, there is evidence of very rich coal mines. A certain amount of coal is valuable in any country, and there may be more than enough for the wants of any country. Why I attach so much importance to coal is, it will afford an opportunity to the inhabitants for immediate employment till they get ready to settle permanently in their homes. If you take colonists where there is no good landing, there is a bad show; and so where there is nothing to cultivate, and of which to make a farm. But if something is started so that you can get your daily bread as soon as you reach there, it is a great advantage. Coal land is the best thing I know of with which to commence an enterprise. To return—you have been talked to upon this subject, and told that a speculation is intended by gentlemen who have an interest in the country, including the coal mines. We have been mistaken all our lives if we do not know whites, as well as blacks, look to their self-interest. Unless among those deficient of intellect, everybody you trade with makes something. You meet with these things here and everywhere. If such persons have what will be an advantage to them, the question is, whether it cannot be made of advantage to you? You are intelligent and know that success does not as much depend on external help as on self-reliance. Much, therefore, depends upon yourselves. As to the coal mines, I think I see the means available for your self-reliance. I shall, if I get a sufficient number of you engaged, have provision made that you shall not be wronged. If you will engage in the enterprise, I will spend some of the money intrusted to me. I am not sure you will succeed. The Government may lose the money, but we cannot succeed unless we try; but we think with care we can succeed. The political affairs in Central America are not in quite as satisfactory condition as I wish. There are contending factions in that quarter; but it is true, all the factions are agreed alike on the subject of colonization, and want it, and are more generous than we are here. To your colored race they have no objection. Besides, I would endeavor to have you made equals, and have the best assurance that you should be the equals of the best. The practical thing I want to ascertain is, whether I can get a number of able-bodied men, with their wives and children, who are willing to go, when I present evidence of encouragement and protection. Could I get a hundred tolerably intelligent men, with their wives and children, and able to "cut their own fodder," so to speak? Can I have fifty? If I could find twenty-five able-bodied men, with a mixture of women and children—good things in the family relation, I think—I could make a successful commencement. I want you to let me know whether this can be done or not. This is the practical part of my wish to see you. These are subjects of very great importance—worthy of a month's study, of a speech delivered in an hour. I ask you, then, to consider seriously, not pertaining to yourselves merely, nor for your race and ours for the present time, but as one of the things, if successfully managed, for the good of mankind—not confined to the present generation, but as

"From age to age descends the lay
To millions yet to be,
Till far its echoes roll away
Into eternity."

The above is merely given as the substance of the President's remarks.

The chairman of the delegation briefly replied, that "they would hold a consultation, and in a short time give an answer." The President said, "Take your full time—no hurry at all."

The delegation then withdrew.

In pursuance of his plans of Colonization, an agreement was entered into, by the President, September 12, 1862, with A. W. Thompson, for the settlement, by free colored emigrants from the United States, of a tract of country within the republic of New Grenada—the region referred to by the

President in his remarks quoted above; and the Hon. S. E. Pomeroy, a senator from Kansas, proposed to accompany and superintend the expedition. The sum of $25,000 was advanced to him from the colonization fund, but it was soon after discovered that the Government of New Grenada objected to the landing of these emigrants upon its territory, and the project was abandoned.

In April, 1863, an agreement was made with responsible and highly respectable parties in New York for the colonization of Ile à Vache, within the Republic of Hayti, of which a favorable grant had been made by the Government—and which was represented in the published report of the Commissioner of Emigration in the Department of the Interior, as being in every way adapted to the culture of cotton and other tropical products, and as eminently favorable for such an experiment. The Government agreed to pay fifty dollars each for the removal of the consenting emigrants thither—payment to be made on official certificate of their arrival. The contractors fulfilled their portion of the agreement with fidelity, and to the utmost extent of their ability; but after an expenditure of about eighty thousand dollars, it was discovered that the representations of the fertility of the island had been utterly unfounded, and that the enterprise was hopeless. The agent of the Company, moreover, through whom the Government had made the original contract, proved to be utterly untrustworthy and incapable, and was removed. The Government at last brought the negroes back to the United States, but incurred no additional expense, as it declined to pay the contractors the stipulated sum for the removal of the emigrants, or to reimburse them any portion of the moneys expended in the enterprise.

No further experiments have been made in the matter of colonization; but the disposition and employment of the negroes has engaged a good deal of the attention and solicitude of the Government. When the rebellion first broke out there were many persons who insisted upon the instant emancipation of the slaves, and their employment in arms against the rebels of the Southern States. Public sentiment, however, was by no means prepared for the adoption of such a measure. The Administration, upon its advent to power, was compelled to encounter a wide-spread distrust of its general purposes in regard to slavery, and special pains were taken by the agents and allies of the rebellion to alarm the sensitive apprehensions of the Border States upon this subject. The President, therefore, deemed it necessary, in order to secure that unity of sentiment without which united and effective action against the rebellion was felt to be impossible, to exclude from the contest all issues of a secondary nature, and to fasten the attention and thought of the whole country upon the paramount end and aim of the war—the restoration of the Union and the authority of the Constitution of the United States. How steadily and carefully this policy was pursued, the preceding pages of this record will show.

But as the war went on, and the desperate tenacity of the rebel resistance became more manifest—as the field of operations, both military and political, became enlarged, and the elements of the rebel strength were better understood, the necessity of dealing with the question of Slavery forced itself upon the people and the Government. The legislation of Congress, from time to time, represented and embodied these advancing phases of public opinion. At the extra session of 1861 a law was passed, discharging from slavery every slave who should be required or permitted by his master to take up arms against the United States, or to be employed in any military capacity in the rebel service. At the next session the President was authorized to employ persons of African descent in the suppression of the rebellion, "in such manner as he should judge best for the public welfare," and also to issue a proclamation commanding all persons in rebellion against the United States to lay down their arms and return to their allegiance; and if any persons so warned should be found in rebellion thirty days after the date of such proclamation, the President was authorized to set free their slaves. Under these comprehensive acts the President took such steps on the subject as he believed the necessities of the country required, and as the public sentiment of the country would sustain. The Emancipation proclamation was issued on the 1st of January, 1863, and measures were adopted soon afterwards to provide for the changes which it made inevitable. On the 20th of January, the Secretary of War authorized Governor Andrew, of Massachusetts, to enlist volunteers for three years, and to include persons of African descent, organized into a separate corps. In April negro troops were enlisted by Adjutant-General Thomas for service in Arkansas, and on the 15th of that month he issued an order appointing commissioners to superintend the execution of a policy which the Government had adopted for committing the protection of the banks of the Mississippi to a negro force. On the 22d of May, orders were issued by the Secretary of War creating a Bureau of the War Department for all matters relating to the organization of colored troops, and establishing rules for their enlistment, and for the appointment of officers to command them. And, on the 20th of August, Hon. J. Holt, Judge-Advocate General, sent to the President an official opinion, to the effect that, under the laws of Congress on the subject, he had full authority to enlist slaves for service in the army precisely as he might enlist any other persons—providing for compensation to loyal owners whose property might thus be taken for the public service.

These were the initial steps of a movement for the employment of negro troops, which has gone forward steadily ever since, until, as has been seen from the President's Message, over 100,000 negro soldiers are now in the army of the United States, contributing largely, by their courage and good conduct, to the suppression of the rebellion which seeks the perpetual enslavement of their race. The popular prejudice against their employment in the army, which was so potent at the beginning, has gradually given way, even in the slaveholding States, to a more just estimate of the necessities of the emergency and the capacities of the negro race. And what is of still more importance to the welfare of the country, the people of the slaveholding States have taken up the question of slavery for discussion and practical action, as one in which their own well-being, present and prospective, is deeply involved. The Union party in every Southern State favors the abolition of slavery, and in Missouri, Maryland, Louisiana, and Arkansas, measures are already far advanced which will inevitably lead to the speedy overthrow of an institution which has proved so detrimental to their interests, and so menacing to the unity of the nation and the stability of republican institutions.

It formed no part of the object of this work to deal in eulogy or in criticism of President LINCOLN and his administration. Its purpose will have been attained if it places his acts and words in such a form that those who read them may judge for themselves of the merits and defects of the policy he has pursued. It has been his destiny to guide the nation through the stormiest period of its existence. No one of his predecessors, not even Washington, encountered difficulties of equal magnitude, or was called to perform duties of equal responsibility. He was elected by a minority of the popular vote, and his election was regarded by a majority of the people as the immediate occasion, if not the cause, of civil war; yet upon him devolved the necessity of carrying on that war, and of combining and wielding the energies of the nation for its successful prosecution. The task, under all the circumstances of the case, was one of the most gigantic that ever fell to the lot of the head of any nation.

From the outset, Mr. LINCOLN's reliance was upon the spirit and patriotism of the people. He had no overweening estimate of his own sagacity; he was quite sensible of his lack of that practical knowledge of men and affairs which experience of both alone can give; but he had faith in the devotion of the people to the principles of Republican government, in their attachment to the Constitution and the Union, and in that intuitive sagacity of a great community which always transcends the most cunning devices of individual men, and, in a great and perilous crisis, more resembles inspiration than the mere deductions of the human intellect. At the very outset of his administration, President LINCOLN cast himself without reserve and without fear, upon this reliance. It has ever been urged against him as a reproach that he has not assumed to lead and control public sentiment, but has been content to be the exponent and the executor of its will. Possibly an opposite course might have succeeded, but possibly, also, it might have ended in disastrous and fatal failure. One thing is certain: the policy which he did pursue has not failed. The rebellion has not succeeded; the authority of the Government has not been overthrown; no new government, resting on slavery as its corner-stone, has yet been established upon this continent, nor has any foreign nation been provoked or permitted to throw its sword into the scale against us. A different policy might have done better, but it might also have done worse. A wise and intelligent people will hesitate long before they condemn an administration which has done well, on the mere hypothesis that another might have done better.

In one respect President LINCOLN has achieved a wonderful

success. He has maintained, through the terrible trials of his administration, a reputation, with the great body of the people, for unsullied integrity, of purpose and of conduct, which even Washington did not surpass, and which no President since Washington has equalled. He has had command of an army greater than that of any living monarch; he has wielded authority less restricted than that conferred by any other constitutional government; he has disbursed sums of money equal to the exchequer of any nation in the world; yet no man, of any party, believes him in any instance to have aimed at his own aggrandizement, to have been actuated by personal ambition, or to have consulted any other interest than the welfare of his country, and the perpetuity of its Republican form of government. This of itself is a success which may well challenge universal admiration, for it is one which is the indispensable condition of all other forms of success. No man whose public integrity was open to suspicion, no matter what might have been his abilities or his experience, could possibly have retained enough of public confidence to carry the country through such a contest as that in which we are now involved. No President suspected of seeking his own aggrandizement at the expense of his country's liberties, could ever have received such enormous grants of power as were essential to the successful prosecution of this war. They were lavishly and eagerly conferred upon Mr. Lincoln, because it was known and felt everywhere that he would not abuse them. Faction has had in him no mark for its assaults. The weapons of party spirit have recoiled harmlessly from the shield of his unspotted character.

It was this unanimous confidence in the disinterested purity of his character, and in the perfect integrity of his public purposes, far more than any commanding intellectual ability, that enabled Washington to hold the faith and confidence of the American people steadfast for seven years, while they waged the unequal war required to achieve their independence. And it certainly is something more than a casual coincidence that this same element, as rare in experience as it is transcendent in importance, should have characterized the President upon whom devolves the duty of carrying the country through this second and far more important and sanguinary struggle.

No one can read Mr. LINCOLN's state papers without perceiving in them a most remarkable faculty of "putting things" so as to command the attention and assent of the common people. His style of thought as well as of expression is thoroughly in harmony with their habitual modes of thinking and of speaking. His intellect is keen, emphatically logical in its action, and capable of the closest and most subtle analysis: and he uses language for the sole purpose of stating, in the clearest and simplest possible form, the precise idea he wishes to convey. He has no pride of intellect—not the slightest desire for display—no thought or purpose but that of making everybody understand precisely what he believes and means to utter. And while this sacrifices the graces of style, it gains immeasurably in practical force and effect. It gives to his public papers a weight and influence with the mass of the people, which no public man of this country has ever before attained. And this is heightened by the atmosphere of honor which seems to pervade his mind, and which is just as natural to it and as attractive and softening a portion of it, as the smoky hues of Indian summer are of the charming season to which they belong. His nature is eminently genial, and he seems to be incapable of cherishing an envenomed resentment. And although he is easily touched by whatever is painful, the elasticity of his temper and his ready sense of the humorous break the force of anxieties and responsibilities under which a man of harder though perhaps a higher nature would sink and fail.

One of the most perplexing questions with which Mr. LINCOLN has had to deal in carrying on the war, has been that of slavery. There are two classes of persons who cannot, even now, see that there was any thing perplexing about it, or that he ought to have had a moment's hesitation how to treat it. One, is made up of those who regard the law of slavery as paramount to the Constitution, and the rights of slavery as the most sacred of all the rights which are guaranteed by that instrument: the other, of those who regard the abolition of slavery as the one thing to be secured, whatever else may be lost. The former denounce Mr. LINCOLN for having interfered with slavery in any way, for any purpose, or at any time: the latter denounce him, with equal bitterness, for not having swept it out of existence the moment Fort Sumter was attacked. In this matter, as in all others, Mr. LINCOLN has acted upon a fixed principle of his own, which he has applied to the practical conduct of affairs just as fast as the necessities of the case required and as the public sentiment would sustain him in doing. His policy has been from the outset a tentative one—as, indeed, all policies of government to be successful must always be. On the outbreak of the rebellion the first endeavor of the rebels was to secure the active co-operation of all the slaveholding States. Mr. LINCOLN's first action, therefore, was to withhold as many of these States from joining the rebel confederacy as possible. Every one can see now that this policy, denounced at the time by his more zealous anti-slavery supporters as temporizing and inadequate, prevented Kentucky, Tennessee, Maryland, Missouri, and part of Virginia from throwing their weight into the rebel scale; and although it is very easy and very common to undervalue services to a cause after its triumph seems secure, there are few who will not concede that if these States had been driven or permitted to drift into the rebel confederacy, a successful termination of the war would have been much farther off than it seems at present. Mr. LINCOLN did every thing in his power, consistent with fidelity to the Constitution, to retain the Border Slave States within the Union; and the degree of success which attended his efforts is the best proof of their substantial wisdom.

His treatment of the slavery question has been marked by the same experimental policy. The various letters by which from time to time he has explained the principles on which he was acting, in any particular emergency, show very clearly that he has been far more anxious to take action which should be sanctioned and sustained by the country, and thus be permanently valuable, than to put forth any theory of his own or carry into effect the dogmas and opinions of any party, The whole case is stated with great clearness and force in a letter written by him on the 4th of April to Mr. Hodges, who, with Governor Bramlette and some other gentlemen of Kentucky, had called upon him on business relating to the draft, and with whom he had some conversation in regard to the misconceptions of his policy that seemed to be current in their State. That letter is as follows:

EXECUTIVE MANSION, WASHINGTON, *April* 4th, 1864.

A. G. HODGES, Esq., Frankfort, Ky: My dear Sir:—You ask me to put in writing the substance of what I verbally said the other day, in your presence, to Governor Bramlette and Senator Dixon. It was about as follows:

"I am naturally anti-slavery. If slavery is not wrong, nothing is wrong. I cannot remember when I did not so think and feel, and yet I have never understood that the Presidency conferred upon me an unrestricted right to act officially upon this judgment and feeling. It was in the oath I took that I would to the best of my ability preserve, protect, and defend the Constitution of the United States. I could not take the office without taking the oath. Nor was it my view that I might take an oath to get power, and break the oath in using the power. I understood, too, that in ordinary civil administration this oath even forbade me to practically indulge my primary abstract judgment on the moral question of slavery. I had publicly declared this many times, and in many ways. And I aver that, to this day, I have done no official act in mere deference to my abstract judgment and feeling on slavery. I did understand, however, that my oath to preserve the Constitution to the best of my ability, imposed upon me the duty of preserving, by every indispensable means, that government—that nation, of which that Constitution was the organic law. Was it possible to lose the nation and yet preserve the Constitution? By general law, life *and* limb must be protected; yet often a limb must be amputated to save a life; but a life is never wisely given to save a limb. I felt that measures, otherwise unconstitutional, might become lawful, by becoming indispensable to the preservation of the Constitution, through the preservation of the nation. Right or wrong, I assumed this ground, and now avow it. I could not feel that, to the best of my ability I had even tried to preserve the Constitution, if, to save slavery, or any minor matter, I should permit the wreck of government, country, and constitution, altogether. When, early in the war, General Fremont attempted military emancipation, I forbade it, because I did not then think it an indispensable necessity. When a little later, General Cameron, then Secretary of War, suggested the arming of the blacks, I objected, because I did not yet think it an indispensable necessity. When, still later, General Hunter attempted military emancipation, I again forbade it, because I did not yet think the indispensable necessity had come. When in March and May, and July, 1862, I made earnest and successive appeals to the border States to favor compensated emancipation, I believed the indispensable necessity for military emancipation and arming the blacks would come, unless averted by that measure. They declined the proposition, and I was, in my best judgment, driven to the alternative of either surrendering the Union, and with it, the Constitution, or of laying strong hand upon the colored element. I chose the latter. In choosing it, I hoped for greater gain than loss, but of this I was not entirely confident. More than a year of trial now shows no loss by it in our foreign relations, none in our home popular sentiment, none in our white military force, no loss by it any how, or anywhere. On the contrary, it shows a gain of quite a hundred and thirty thousand soldiers, seamen and laborers. These are palpable facts, about which, as facts, there can be no cavilling. We have the men; and we could not have had them without the measure.

"And now let any Union man who complains of the measure, test himself by writing down in one line, that he is for subduing the rebellion by force of arms; and in the next, that he is for taking three hundred and thirty thousand men from the Union side, and placing them where they would be best for the measure he condemns. If he cannot face his case so stated, it is only because he cannot face the truth."

I add a word which was not in the verbal conversation. In telling this tale, I attempt no compliment to my own sagacity. I claim not to have controlled events, but confess plainly that events have controlled me. Now at the end of three years' struggle, the nation's condition is not what either party, or any man devised, or expected. God alone can claim it. Whither it is tending seems plain. If God now wills the removal of a great wrong, and wills also that we of the North, as well as you of the South, shall pay fairly for our complicity in that wrong, impartial history will find therein new causes to attest and revere the ustice and goodness of God. Yours, truly,

(Signed.) A. LINCOLN.

An impression is quite common that great men, who make their mark upon the progress of events and the world's history, do it by impressing their own opinions upon nations and communities, in disregard of their sentiments and prejudices. History does not sustain this view of the case. No man ever moulded the destiny of a nation except by making the sentiment of that nation his ally—by working with it, by shaping his measures and his policy to its successive developments. But little more than a year before the Declaration of Independence was issued, Washington wrote to a friend in England that the idea of separation from Great Britain was not entertained by any considerable number of the inhabitants of the colonies. If independence had then been proclaimed, it would not have been supported by public sentiment; and its proclamation would have excited hostilities and promoted divisions which might have proved fatal to the cause. Time, the development of events,—the ripening conviction of the necessity of such a measure, were indispensable as preliminary conditions of its success. And one of the greatest elements of Washington's strength was the patient sagacity with which he could watch and wait until these conditions were fulfilled. The position and duty of President LINCOLN in regard to Slavery have been very similar. If he had taken counsel only of his own abstract opinions and sympathies, and had proclaimed emancipation at the outset of the war, or had sanctioned the action of those department commanders who assumed to do it themselves, the first effect would have been to throw all the Border Slave States into the bosom of the slaveholding confederacy, and add their formidable force to the armies of the rebellion: the next result would have been to arouse the political opposition of the loyal States to fresh activity by giving them a rallying cry: and the third would have been to divide the great body of those who agreed in defending the Union, but who did not then agree in regard to the abolition of slavery. Candid men, who pay more regard to facts than to theory, and who can estimate with fairness the results of public action, will have no difficulty in seeing that the probable result of these combined influences would have been such a strengthening of the forces of the Confederacy, and such a weakening of our own, as might have overwhelmed the Administration, and given the rebellion a final and a fatal triumph By awaiting the development of public sentiment, President Lincoln secured a support absolutely essential to success; and there are few persons now, whatever may be their private opinions on slavery, who will not concede that his measures in regard to that subject have been adopted with sagacity and crowned with substantial success.

It is too soon, we are aware, to pronounce definitively on the merits of President LINCOLN's administration. Its policy is still in process of development. If it is allowed to go on without interruption,—if the measures which President LINCOLN has inaugurated for quelling the rebellion and restoring the Union, are permitted to work out their natural results, unchecked by popular impatience and sustained by public confidence, we believe they will end in re-establishing the authority of the Constitution, in restoring the integrity of the Union, in abolishing every vestige of slavery, and in perpetuating the principles of democratic government upon this continent and throughout the world.

APPENDIX.

LIEUT.-GEN. SCOTT AND MAJ.-GEN. McCLELLAN.

Allusion is made on a previous page to a letter of advice and suggestions addressed by General McClellan to General Scott, which he afterwards withdrew.

The following correspondence relates to that letter and grew out of it:

GEN. SCOTT TO THE SECRETARY OF WAR.

WASHINGTON, *Aug.* 9, 1861.

SIR:—I received yesterday from Major-General McClellan a letter of that date, to which I design this as my only reply.

Had Major-General McClellan presented the same views in person, they would have been fully entertained and discussed. All my military views and opinions had been so presented to him, without eliciting much remark in our few meetings which I have in vain sought to multiply. He has stood on his guard and now places himself on record. Let him make the most of his unenvied advantages.

Major-General McClellan has propagated in high quarters the idea expressed in the letter before me, that Washington was not only "insecure," but in "imminent danger."

Relying on our numbers, our forts, and the Potomac river, I am confident in the opposite opinion; and considering the stream of new regiments that is pouring in upon us (before the alarm could have reached their homes), I have not the slightest apprehension for the safety of the Government here.

Having now been unable to mount a horse, or to walk more than a few paces at a time, and consequently being unable to review troops—much less to direct them in battle: in short, broken down by many particular hurts, besides the general infirmities of age—I feel that I have become an incumbrance to the army as well as to myself, and that I ought, gvinig way to a younger commander, to seek the palliatives of physical pain and exhaustion.

Accordingly I must beg the President, at the earliest moment, to allow me to be placed on the *officers' retired list*, and then quietly to lay myself up—probably for ever—somewhere in or about New York. But wherever I may spend my little remainder of life, my frequent and latest prayer will be—"God save the Union!" I have the honor to be, Sir, with high respect,

Your obedient servant,

WINFIELD SCOTT.

GEN. M'CLELLAN TO THE PRESIDENT.

WASHINGTON, *Aug.* 10, 1861.

The letter addressed by me under date of the 8th inst. to Lieutenant-General Scott, commanding the United States Army, was designed to be a plain and respectful expression of my views of the measures demanded for the safety of the Government in the imminent peril that besets it at the present hour. Every moment's reflection and every fact transpiring, convinced me of the urgent necessity of the measures there indicated, and I felt it my duty to him and to the country to communicate them frankly. It is therefore with great pain that I have learned from you this morning, that my views do not meet with the approbation of the Lieutenant-General, and that my letter is unfavorably regarded by him. The command with which I am intrusted was not sought by me, and has only been accepted from an earnest and humble desire to serve my country in the moment of the most extreme peril. With these views I am willing to do and suffer whatever may be required for that service. Nothing could be farther from my wishes than to seek any command or urge any measures not required for the exigency of the occasion, and above all, I would abstain from any conduct that could give offence to General Scott or embarrass the President or any Department of the Government.

Influenced by these considerations, I yield to your request and withdraw the letter referred to. The Government and my superior officer being apprised of what I consider to be necessary and proper for the defence of the National Capital, I shall strive faithfully and zealously to employ the means that may be placed in my power for that purpose, dismissing every personal feeling or consideration, and praying only the blessing of Divine Providence on my efforts. I will only add that, as you requested my authority to withdraw the letter, that authority is hereby given, with the most profound assurance for General Scott and yourself.

Very respectfully,

Your obedient servant,

GEORGE B. MCCLELLAN.

GENERAL SCOTT TO THE PRESIDENT.

WASHINGTON, *Aug.* 12, 1861.

SIR:—On the 10th inst., I was kindly requested by the President to withdraw my letter to you, of the 9th, in reply to one I had received from Major-General McClellan of the day before—the President at the same time showing me a letter to him from Major-General McClellan, in which, at the instance of the President, he offered to withdraw the original letter on which I had animadverted.

While the President was yet with me, on that occasion, a servant handed me a letter, which proved to be an authenticated copy, under a blank cover, of the same letter from General McClellan to the President. This slight was not without its influence on my mind.

The President's visit, however, was for the patriotic purpose of healing differences, and so much did I honor his motive that I deemed it due to him to hold his proposition under consideration for some little time.

I deeply regret that, notwithstanding my respect for the opinions and wishes of the President, I cannot withdraw the letter in question, for these reasons:

1. The original offence given to me by Major-General McClellan (see his letter of 8th inst.) seems to have been the result of deliberation between him and some of the members of the Cabinet, by whom all the greater war questions are to be settled—without resort to or consultation with me, the nominal General-in-Chief of the Army. In further proof of this neglect—although it is unofficially known that in the last week (six days) many regiments have arrived and others have changed their position—some to a considerable distance—not one of these movements has been reported to me (or any thing else) by Major-General McClellan; while it is believed, and I may add known, that he is in frequent communication with portions of the Cabinet, and on matters appertaining to me. That freedom of access and consultation have, very naturally, deluded the junior General into a feeling of indifference towards his senior.

2. With such supports, on his part, it would be as idle for me, as it would be against the dignity of my years, to be filing daily complaints against an ambitious junior, who, independent of the extreme advantages alluded to, has, unquestionably, very high qualifications for military command. I trust they may achieve crowning victories in behalf of the Union.

3. I have, in my letter to you of the 9th inst., already said enough on the, to others, disgusting subject of my many physical infirmities. I will here only add that, borne down as I am by them, I should unavoidably be in the way, at head-quarters, even if my abilities for war were now greater than when I was young.

I have the honor to be, Sir, with high respect,

Your obedient servant,

WINFIELD SCOTT.

A DRAFT URGED BY GENERAL McCLELLAN.

General Scott, very soon after this correspondence, was allowed to retire from active service, in accordance with his request, and General McClellan succeeded to the command of the Army of the Potomac. His attention was first given to recovering the disaster of Bull Run, and placing the army again on a footing for the speedy resumption of hostilities. The defeat of July, and the danger with which that defeat for the moment seemed to menace the capital, had aroused the most intense enthusiasm throughout the country, and volunteers were pouring into Washington with great rapidity. Under these circumstances, General McClellan wrote to the President as follows:

WASHINGTON, *August* 20, 1861.

SIR:—I have just received the inclosed dispatch in cipher. Colonel Marcy knows what he says, and is of the coolest judgment. I recommend that the Secretary of War ascertain at once by telegram how the enrollment proceeds in New York and elsewhere, and that, if it is not proceeding with great rapidity, drafts to be made at once. We must have men without delay.

Respectfully your obedient servant,

GEORGE B. MCCLELLAN, *Maj.-Gen. U. S. A.*

DISPATCH FROM COL. R. B. MARCY TO GENERAL M'CLELLAN.

NEW YORK, *August* 20, 1861.

I urge upon you to make a *positive* and *unconditional demand* for an immediate draft of the additional troops you require. Men will not volunteer now, and drafting is the only successful plan. *The people will applaud such a course*, rely upon it. I will be in Washington to-morrow.

R. B. MARCY.

THE PRESIDENT'S SUGGESTION FOR AN ADVANCE IN DECEMBER, 1861.

The following is a copy of a memorandum marked by the President, as having been made by him about the first of December, 1861. It was while the army under McClellan was lying in front of Washington, and while the Government and the whole country were impatient for an advance upon the rebel army encamped at Manassas.

If it were determined to make a forward movement of the Army of the Potomac, without awaiting further increase of numbers, or better drill and discipline, how *long* would it require to actually get in motion?

[Answer in pencil by McClellan: "If bridge trains ready—by December 15—probably 25th."]

After leaving all that would be necessary, how many troops could join the movement from southwest of the river?

[Answer in pencil, "71,000."]

How many from northwest of it?

[Answer in pencil, "33,000."]

Suppose, then, that of those southwest of the river [supplied in pencil "50,000,"] move forward and menace the enemy at Centerville?

The remainder of the movable force on that side move rapidly to the crossing of the Occoquan by the road from Alexandria towards

Richmond; there to be joined by the whole movable force from north-east of the river, having landed from the Potomac just below the mouth of the Occoquan, move by land up the south side of that stream, to the crossing point named; then the whole move together, by the road thence to Brentville, and beyond, to the railroad just south of its crossing of Broad Run, a strong detachment of cavalry having gone rapidly ahead to destroy the railroad bridges south and north of the point.

If the crossing of the Occoquan by those from above be resisted, those landing from the Potomac below to take the resisting force of the enemy in rear; or, if landing from the Potomac be resisted, those crossing the Occoquan from above to take that resisting force in rear. Both points will probably not be successfully resisted at the same time. The force in front of Centerville, if pressed too hardly, should fight back into the intrenchments behind them. Armed vessels and transports should remain at the Potomac landing to cover a possible retreat.

The following reply is in General McClellan's handwriting—dated Washington, December 10, and marked "*confidential:*"

I inclose the paper you left with me—filled as you requested. In arriving at the numbers given I have left the minimum numbers in garrison and observation.

Information recently leads me to believe that the enemy would meet us in front with equal forces nearly—and I have now my mind actually turned towards another plan of campaign that I do not think at all anticipated by the enemy, nor by many of our own people.

George B. McClellan.

This is doubtless in allusion to his project of transferring the army to the York River, and advancing upon Richmond by that line.

THE POSITION OF KENTUCKY.

Reference is made on page 480 to the efforts of the President to prevent Kentucky and other Border Slave States from joining the Rebel Confederacy. General McClellan, while in command of the Department of the Ohio, had entered into an agreement with General Buckner by which the substantial neutrality of that State was recognized and respected. And in August, 1861, Governor Magoffin had urged the removal by the President of the Union troops which had been raised and were encamped within that State.

To this request he received the following reply:

WASHINGTON, D. C., *August* 24, 1861.

To His Excellency B. MAGOFFIN, Governor of the State of Kentucky:

SIR:—Your letter of the 19th inst., in which you "urge the removal from the limits of Kentucky of the military force now organized and in camp within that State," is received.

I may not possess full and precisely accurate knowledge upon this subject, but I believe it is true that there is a military force in camp within Kentucky, acting by authority of the United States, which force is not very large, and is not now being augmented.

I also believe that some arms have been furnished to this force by the United States.

I also believe that this force consists exclusively of Kentuckians, having their camp in the immediate vicinity of their own homes, and not assailing or menacing any of the good people of Kentucky.

In all I have done in the premises, I have acted upon the urgent solicitation of many Kentuckians, and in accordance with what I believed, and still believe, to be the wish of a majority of all the Union-loving people of Kentucky.

While I have conversed on the subject with many eminent men of Kentucky, including a large majority of her members of Congress, I do not remember that any one of them, or any other person, except your Excellency and the bearers of your Excellency's letter, has urged me to remove the military force from Kentucky or to disband it. One other very worthy citizen of Kentucky did solicit me to have the augmenting of the force suspended for a time.

Taking all the means within my reach to form a judgment, I do not believe it is the popular wish of Kentucky that the force shall be removed beyond her limits; and, with this impression, I must respectfully decline to remove it.

I most cordially sympathize with your Excellency in the wish to preserve the peace of my own native State, Kentucky, but it is with regret I search for and cannot find, in your not very short letter, any declaration or intimation that you entertain any desire for the preservation of the Federal Union.

ABRAHAM LINCOLN.

THE PRESIDENT TO GENERAL McCLELLAN.

President LINCOLN addressed the following letter to General McClellan after the latter had landed his forces on the Peninsula in the spring of 1862. It relates to several points in which the General's action had already excited a good deal of public uneasiness, and been made the subject of public comment, though the letter itself has never before been made public:

FORTRESS MONROE, *May* 9, 1862.

MY DEAR SIR:—I have just assisted the Secretary of War in forming the part of a dispatch to you, relating to army corps, which dispatch, of course, will have reached you long before this will. I wish to say a few words to you privately on this subject. I ordered the army corps organization not only on the unanimous opinion of the twelve generals of division, but also on the unanimous opinion of every *military man* I could get an opinion from, and every modern military book, yourself only excepted. Of course, I did not on my own judgment pretend to understand the subject. I now think it indispensable for you to know how your struggle against it is received in quarters which we cannot entirely disregard. It is looked upon as merely an effort to pamper one or two pets, and to persecute and degrade their supposed rivals. I have had no word from Sumner, Heintzelman or Keyes. The commanders of these corps are of course the three highest officers with you, but I am constantly told that you have no consultation or communication with them, that you consult and communicate with nobody but Fitz John Porter, and perhaps General Franklin. I do not say these complaints are true or just; but, at all events, it is proper you should know of their existence. Do the commanders of corps disobey your orders in any thing?

When you relieved General Hamilton of his command the other day, you thereby lost the confidence of at least one of your best friends in the Senate. And here let me say, not as applicable to you personally, that Senators and Representatives speak of me in their places as they please without question; and that officers of the army must cease addressing insulting letters to them for taking no greater liberty with them. But to return, are you strong enough, even with my help, to set your foot upon the neck of Sumner, Heintzelman, and Keyes, all at once? This is a practical and very serious question for you.

Yours truly, A. LINCOLN.

INDEX.

www.ingramcontent.com/pod-product-compliance
Lightning Source LLC
LaVergne TN
LVHW020918110826
845150LV00004B/707

9781425554705